Performing Commemoration

MUSIC AND SOCIAL JUSTICE

Series Editors: William Cheng and Andrew Dell'Antonio

From Plato to Public Enemy, people have debated the relationship between music and justice—rarely arriving at much consensus over the art form's ethics and aesthetics, uses and abuses, virtues and vices. So what roles can music and musicians play in agendas of justice? And what should musicians and music scholars do if—during moments of upheaval, complacency, ennui—music ends up seemingly drained of its beauty, power, and even relevance?

Created by editors William Cheng and Andrew Dell'Antonio, this endeavor welcomes projects that shine new light on familiar subjects such as protest songs, humanitarian artists, war and peace, community formation, cultural diplomacy, globalization, and political resistance. Simultaneously, the series invites authors to critique and expand on what qualifies as justice—or, for that matter, music—in the first place.

TITLES IN THE SERIES

Performing Commemoration: Musical Reenactment and the Politics of Trauma
Annegret Fauser and Michael A. Figueroa, Editors

Sounding Dissent: Rebel Songs, Resistance, and Irish Republicanism
Stephen R. Millar

Performing Commemoration

Musical Reenactment and the Politics of Trauma

Annegret Fauser and Michael A. Figueroa, Editors

University of Michigan Press • Ann Arbor

Published in the United States of America by the University of Michigan Press
Manufactured in the United States of America
Printed on acid-free paper
First published October 2020

A CIP catalog record for this book is available from the British Library.

Library of Congress Cataloging-in-Publication data has been applied for.

ISBN 978-0-472-07466-2 (hardcover: alk. paper)
ISBN 978-0-472-05466-4 (paper: alk. paper)
ISBN 978-0-472-12721-4 (e-book)

Cover Image: Rita Ezrati, *Hurler* (2015): Ink on paper 17x12 cm.

Contents

Possibilities and Impossibilities of Commemoration: Trauma's Persistence and the Politics of Reenactment

Digital materials related to this title can be found on the Fulcrum platform via the following citable URL: https://doi.org/10.3998/mpub.11560559

Acknowledgments

This project started over lunch, one spring afternoon, in the main atrium of the National Humanities Center in Research Triangle Park, North Carolina. Our conversation turned to an upcoming concert of the *Defiant Requiem* by two of the University of North Carolina at Chapel Hill's student ensembles, Carolina Choir and the UNC Symphony Orchestra. This show, brainchild of the conductor Murry Sidlin, would involve a reenactment of performances of Giuseppe Verdi's *Requiem* (the Catholic mass of the dead) by Jewish internees in Terezín for other inmates as well as for their Nazi captors between 1942 and 1944. The sponsoring organization, the Defiant Requiem Foundation, controls the mediation of these historical events through a performance of Verdi's work, framed by film clips and readings. Who framed a musical reenactment such as the *Defiant Requiem*, we asked ourselves, and how does it connect to broader issues of commemorative performance? What role does music itself play in such a context? In order to cultivate a critical conversation on the topic, we organized a meeting of scholars with a view to generating discussion between the participants prior to publishing their findings in what has become the present volume. In April 2017, many of the contributors to this volume gathered at the University of North Carolina at Chapel Hill to share their research and insights about musical reenactment of past trauma and its politics. Galvanized by the powerful individual contributions of the meeting, our contributors took an active role in shaping and framing the volume, thus creating its coherence across geographical and historical expanses. To them, first and foremost, we express our deepest respect and gratitude.

Given the crucial role of the conference in the genesis of the book, we would like to acknowledge the sponsors of the event: the Carolina

Asia Center, UNC College of Arts and Sciences, Carolina Center for Jewish Studies, UNC Department of Music, UNC Institute for Arts and Humanities, and the Sonja Haynes Stone Center for Black Culture and History. We are particularly grateful to Stefan Litwin, our co-organizer of the conference, for his invaluable intellectual and artistic engagement with the topic. As an artist whose work bears traces of his biography as the child of Holocaust survivors, he offered vital insights in the entangled nexus of memory, performance, and reenactment that shaped the configuration both of the conference and of the book.

As the book crystallized into its current form, a number of careful editors helped to sharpen its many facets into a coherent whole. We are deeply grateful for the insightful comments and vital encouragement of the editorial director of the University of Michigan Press, Mary Francis, and the two editors of the *Music and Social Justice* series who welcomed our volume, William Cheng and Andrew Dell'Antonio. As the manuscript wound its way from conception to production, our two research assistants, Christopher Campo-Bowen and Megan Ross, contributed significantly to its present quality by checking references, working through the bibliography, and adding the index. We are also very grateful to the production team at the University of Michigan Press and to our copy editor, Richard Isomaki. We further acknowledge with deep gratitude the generosity of the Canadian artist Rita Ezrati for her permission to reproduce *Hurler* (ink on paper, 2015) on the book's cover.

Finally, we thank our respective spouses, Tim Carter and Monica Figueroa, for supporting the project through the past three years so generously, both intellectually and in everyday life. We are all too aware that we would not have mustered the creative energy nor met our various deadlines if we had not been able to prioritize this volume at critical moments of its genesis.

Introduction

ANNEGRET FAUSER AND MICHAEL A. FIGUEROA

The essays in *Performing Commemoration: Musical Reenactment and the Politics of Trauma* began as responses to a deceptively straightforward question: what is it to perform commemoration? By foregrounding reenactment as a principal, though not the only, commemorative mode, the ethnomusicologists and musicologists contributing to this volume interrogate the enmeshments of performed reenactment and the politics of trauma as embodied forms of musical commemoration. Commemorative performance can reenact past trauma, seek justice, lay claim to territory, mark the passage of sacred time, and perform many other social functions around the world. Nations such as Poland and India use hymns, anthems, and folk songs to commemorate political milestones on the road to independence. Sufi Muslims from Senegal to Indonesia center their religious practice on *zikr*: a musical ritual of remembrance invoking the names of Allah. Israeli film and television, aided by musical soundtracking, serve as powerful media for reenacting and/or memorializing wars and other traumatic events. In the streets and on social media, US resistance movements such as Black Lives Matter and Say Her Name performatively place (silent) hands in the air to reenact deadly encounters with law enforcement, rendering visceral the realities of everyday violence and commemorating the last moments of victims' lives.

Performing commemoration is closely intertwined with both the fight for, and the denial of, social justice. The ritual calling of women's names in Say Her Name, for instance, forms an interconnected part of a painful and diachronic web of the high-stakes fight over memory and justice in the United States, where commemorative practices are subjected to the insidious logic of liberalism that casts justice as a commodity trafficked along economic and racial lines. As political theorist Judith N. Shklar wrote so poignantly, "When the victims of disasters refuse to resign themselves to their misfortunes and cry out in anger, we hear the voice of the sense of injustice."[1] Performing commemoration can become an expressive means through which to render those voices audible, but such performative acts can also subvert them by replacing one victim with another, erasing injustices through carefully curated memory regimes. Commemorative practices complicit in such erasures and substitutions have currency throughout the twentieth and twenty-first centuries, as the essays in this volume about the Congo, Japan, and Poland reveal. But these issues also hit closer to home. Before we turn to some of the global implications of musical reenactments of trauma and address the epistemological framework of this volume, we should first locate the complex entwinement of sound and silence in commemorative practice at events that occurred at the University of North Carolina at Chapel Hill, where both editors as well as two of our contributors are members of the faculty.

"Silent Sam," 2018

At 7:00 p.m. on Monday, August 20, 2018, the day before classes began at UNC–Chapel Hill, about 250 students, faculty, and local activists occupied McCorkle Place, one of the main quads on campus and, in effect, the "front door" of the university. They came to renew their protests against a statue erected in 1913 to commemorate the University of North Carolina students who had fought on side of the Confederacy during the US Civil War (1861–65). The statue represented an unnamed soldier with his gun facing north, though from the mid-1950s on, he was regularly called "Silent Sam." Chants, songs, clapping, and drums surrounded a monument the very name of which enshrined silence as a fitting commemorative mode to mask the sins of the past. McCorkle Place vibrated with shouts of "Tear it down!" and the rhythmic chants of students and community members alike. "No cops! No Klan! Get rid of Silent Sam!" sounded in vivid call and response, contributing to the "sonic vernacular" that had characterized the Monday-evening rallies in Chapel Hill since they began the previous year.[2] Around 9:30 p.m., the protesters settled around the monument, now covered by banners, with campus police hanging back at the margins. At that moment, a group of activists who had brought ropes to the protest so as to establish a fait accompli pulled the statue down. "I watched it groan and shiver and come asunder," recalled UNC Asian Studies faculty member Dwayne Dixon, "I mean, it feels biblical."[3] A now-iconic image of the soldier's statue—lying face down in the very soil once tilled by the slaves whose indenture he died in vain to preserve—circulated almost instantly across social media and cable-news platforms.[4] "It was all smiles and joy and dancing and jubilation," emphasized UNC alumna Jasmin Howard.[5] In this hour, the sounds of celebration replaced the deafening silence of a statue that had served, for over a century, to overwrite history in the service of white supremacy in the southern United States.

Until that evening in August 2018, this statue had been part of our professional lives: it stood barely a stone's throw away from Hill Hall, housing the Department of Music's faculty offices and concert hall. Together with buildings named after slaveholders, Klansmen, and other white supremacists—such as Saunders Hall (renamed Carolina Hall in 2015), Carr Building, and Aycock Residence Hall—Silent Sam formed part of the deceptively genteel scenery of a typical American university campus. After the violent neofascist rally in August 2017 in Charlottesville, VA, however, righteous noise began to disrupt this poisonous memory regime when, on Monday evenings through the semesters, protesters assembled in McCorkle Place to draw attention through chants, music making, and readings to the fraught relationship between commemoration, trauma, and performance in the modern world.

The monument was erected in 1913, with funding from the United Daughters of the Confederacy (UDC), a group that used commemorative statues as well as such means as the revision of grade-school textbooks to perpetuate the mythology of the "Lost Cause." According to Karen L. Cox, the UDC's sustained effort to commemorate an idealized South served the political and social goals of transforming "military defeat into a political and cultural victory, where states' rights and white supremacy remained intact."[6] Such historical revisionism in effect recast the American Civil War as the noble and heroic fight to preserve the Old South, an invented utopia where benevolent plantation aristocrats lived in ideal harmony with their "faithful and contented labor force."[7] In this quest to turn a war that was waged over the Confederate States' desire to maintain the enslavement of African-descended people into a noble cause to preserve a purportedly idyllic way of life, the UDC's memory regime relied on the figure of the young soldier slain in combat as its most poignant symbol. Where better to deploy such a monument than on the all-male flagship campus of the Old North State?

Silent Sam had been dedicated on June 2, 1913, in a ceremony in which the governor of North Carolina, Locke Craig, joined the local UDC chapter president, Mary Lyde Williams, the university president, Francis P. Venable, and the Durham industrialist and accomplished white supremacist, Julian Carr, who had footed much of the bill for the bronze statue.[8] Strains of "Dixie" opened the ceremony, which took place in the university's elegantly appointed Gerrard Hall before the assembled dignitaries processed to the monument for its solemn unveiling. There, about one thousand people who had gathered around the monument listened to an *a cappella* quartet sing, "with rare sweetness and tenderness," the Civil War song "Tenting on the Old Camp Ground."[9] Whereas Craig, Venable, and Williams kept their rhetoric to the familiar tropes associated with young men's devoted sacrifices to the Lost Cause, Carr chose a different register.[10] Within the long encomium—interspersed with poems and references to ancient Rome—praising the "courage and steadfastness" of the Confederate students who had "saved the very life of the Anglo Saxon race in the South," Carr shifted abruptly to what he described as a personal "allusion":

> One hundred yards from where we stand, less than ninety days perhaps after my return from Appomattox, I horse-whipped a negro wench until her skirts hung in shreds, because upon the streets of this quiet village she had publicly insulted and maligned a Southern lady, and then rushed for protection to these University buildings where was stationed a garrison of 100 Federal soldiers.[11]

Implied in the telling of the anecdote was the claim that—with the dedication of Silent Sam—the Confederacy took back a university tarnished by Union occupation.

The message in Carr's evocation of vigilante violence against a black woman, and the racialized rhetoric of the whole speech, would not have been lost upon the assembled audience: the statue was being erected not as a simple acknowledgment of soldiers' sacrifices but rather as a performance of white supremacy and domination. The speech itself was a commemorative performance, one of whose chief literary devices was its deployment of sound, both through sonic references—the sounds of mourning, "the sounds of the tides," "the watch-dog's bark," and "harmony with the eternal fitness of things"—and through the stylized declamation of pro-Confederate poetry interspersed throughout. After Silent Sam was revealed and the last notes of "Tenting on the Old Camp Ground" faded, the words of the dedication became embodied in the very materiality of the statue itself, as the monument transitioned from the reverberations of the commemorative performance to a performance of commemoration—a silent one, as its later name implies—that terrorized the community's black residents for the century to come. As Amanda M. Black and Andrea F. Bohlman have recently pointed out, "The notion of the 'unheard' has a particular and haunting resonance for our home campus, the University of North Carolina at Chapel Hill, which has a history steeped in racial violence, segregation, and silencing."[12]

Performing Commemoration through Musical Reenactment

Silent Sam remains in secret storage, the statue's future still a matter of significant debate in the North Carolina state legislature. Our purpose in turning to the performance of commemoration at our intellectual home, however, is to open up a discussion about commemorative practices, their sonorities, and their embodied experiences. The sonic environments characterizing the two historic moments that bookended the monument's presence on campus and their diachronic entanglements could not have been more different: a seemingly genteel Confederate ceremony, on the one hand, and the sonic vernacular of recent campus protest, on the other. Yet when such events reenact past trauma, they call attention to the capacity of sonic performance both to silence the past and to ensound it in the present.[13] The contributors to this volume bring the three dimensions of this nexus into conversation with one another: commemoration, reenactment, and musical performance are here considered as a matrix of embodied memory work wherein contemporary bodies "consort with dead bodies" through the performative act.[14] In this sense, "performative" refers to the deliberate act of performance, yet it also encompasses the understanding of performativity as the "regularized and constrained repetition of norms" proposed by Judith Butler—one that cannot be "simply equated with performance" but rather needs to be conceived "as the reiterative and citational practice by which discourse produces the effects that it names."[15]

Musicologists, ethnomusicologists, and other humanists over the past few decades have attended to the performative dimension of commemorative activity through such critical lenses as national and transnational cultures, the transfer of social memory, and the relation between individual and collective expression in music, among others.[16] Our volume indeed bears traces of this work through citation, argument, and other forms of scholarly engagement, but our task is much more specific: we ask what it is to think of commemoration as a performed and sonic mode of remembrance, and how the commemorative mode serves the ends of socialization and public power.

We aim to map a theoretical terrain for performance in the study of memory, reenactment, and commemoration. Performance, as we define it in this context, brings to the fore the intentional as well as reiterative aspects of memory work in the form of reenactments of trauma. As scholarship in performance studies has demonstrated, the word encompasses a rich kaleidoscope of meanings, referring to acts that reach from staged events such as concerts and ballets to deliberate self-representation or public spectacles.[17] According to Erika Fischer-Lichte, a performance may be cast as "inseparable from the bodily co-presence of various groups of people who come together as actors and spectators: this is linked to the medial conditions of performance."[18] When performance also commemorates a past, whether through reperformance or reenactment, the bodily copresence that Fischer-Lichte posits between performer and spectator indexes the very bodies whose absence forms the center of the performance. Through embodiment in performance, the absent body becomes a spectral presence, yet, as Mark Franko proposes with respect to danced reenactments, these performances assert "the non-correspondence of two times, two histories, two mentalities."[19] Such a performance thus renders perceptible the distance between the two—"the imaginary manifestation of a set of intersecting temporalities that converge"—in the act of commemoration.[20]

This self-consciousness as a performed mode of commemoration distinguishes danced, musical, and theatrical reenactment from reenactment in its more familiar conceptualization as a painstakingly created reconstruction of a historic event, for such an experiential form of affective history through immersion often collapses temporalities and reduces complex social and political pasts into seemingly firsthand experiences.[21] Performance understood in this way carries—in Rebecca Schneider's terms—an element of "explicit theatricality" that can also mark reenactments more broadly conceived when their participants and spectators are cognizant of the historicity of their acts of repetition.[22] This cognizance of difference, an awareness that the performance "restores" that which was stored away in memories through the very act of embodiment, also carries the possibilities of turning the performed commemoration into a form of archive, as Chérie Rivers Ndaliko points out in her contribution to this volume.[23]

Performing commemoration through musical reenactment depends on the transnational circulation of commemorative modes that enable the legibility of the performance itself and on locally specific engagements with the past and the present, blending and contrasting sonic vernaculars with a collective repertoire of commemorative tropes. Yet each iteration of reenacted trauma also faces the politics of memory regimes: control over form, content, and space can lead to the overwriting of traces from the past with new data, recoding memory and the historical record in the performance of commemoration. Such transformations and reconfigurations of past trauma in the service of official memory regimes reveal the contingencies of performative reenactments where social justice is concerned. If Say Her Name speaks truth to power, as Imani Danielle Mosley discusses in her contribution to this volume, recent commemorations of World War II uprisings against German occupation in Warsaw instrumentalized the events concerned to fit the ideological purposes of the current Polish government, as Andrea F. Bohlman reveals. To deconstruct performed reenactment as a commemorative mode opens a space for recognizing music, sound, and silence as technologies for altering the meanings of commemorative events, turning past traumas into sites of contestation in which contemporary memory regimes manipulate history for their own purposes. Yet by breaking familiar forms of commemoration through the use of laughter, irony, and alienation, such performed reenactment can also draw attention to the forgotten, and to forms of trauma that challenge prevailing or "official" narratives. In musical reenactments, however, the voices silenced through violence and trauma are sometimes ventriloquized through sound created by others, with their own agendas, contributing to the asymmetry inherent in the politicization of trauma via commemoration and reenactment. What is it, then, to perform commemoration musically?

The contributors to *Performing Commemoration* examine this question through forms of musical reenactment in different global contexts, providing a much-needed, culturally comparative perspective on commemorative musical practice. Bringing together scholars who draw on interdisciplinary frameworks of performance, film, and sound studies, (auto) ethnographies, archival and historical research, and musical analysis, the volume offers a diversity of approaches to this field while simultaneously presenting important new research on specific case studies. By interrogating the role of music in the performance of commemoration, the authors analyze how nations, states, governments, organizations, communities, and individuals across the globe deploy the specter of trauma for public, private, and political ends.

Focusing on the commemoration of traumatic events and experiences in the twentieth and twenty-first centuries, the contributors to *Performing Commemoration* ask how musical reenactments might serve to reconfigure history, and they explore the ways in which music and sound shape performed reenactments in the service of memory regimes. The authors of this volume thereby make a place in the scholarly discourse for public representations of, and responses to, trauma—not as analyzed and typologized, and not as contained only in works and texts, but as processual, active, and ensounded. Trauma refers thus simultaneously to the actual violence in the past and to its reembodied, sonic, or spectral presence in commemorative performance. As in literature, in musical reenactment "narrative itself embodies the traumatic problem, in that it represents through its narration of past events a ceaseless and obsessive return to the site of trauma at the same time that it offers an expressive mechanism that might potentially offer a solution to the problem"—so J. Roger Kurtz writes in the introduction to *Trauma and Literature.*[24] But *Performing Commemoration* also seeks to move beyond a Freudian analytic paradigm, pioneered by Cathy Caruth and others, toward more explicitly politicized frames of analysis, drawing out the disruptions and disjunctures represented by performed reenactment and its narrativizing functions.[25] Music, within this formulation, is not only or always a coping mechanism or a surrogate for that which language cannot represent when trauma creates a "breach in the mind's experience of time, self, and the world."[26] Instead, music represents a process through which performance can shape—for better or worse—people's memories and interpretations of trauma. Such public engagement with trauma molds, in turn, their understandings of performance and performativity. Approaching reenactment in this way therefore moves beyond what Stef Craps has called trauma theory's "event-based model."[27] And yet things are not quite so simple. Some of the case studies contained in this volume take on commemorations as social moments wherein historical events are reenacted in performance, while others uncover the embodiment, embeddedness, or adumbration of trauma in performative contexts that cast traumatic pasts in other terms; some angle in on past violence through a focus on victim or perpetrator, while others focus on the desperate attempt to recover lost memories or else force outright fictions on others. It is this complexity, we argue, that is borne out in trauma's echoes, its transhistorical impacts, and its political repercussions as mediated through the performance of commemoration.

This book's topical breadth covers political and social conflict of the last hundred years and presents a global perspective on the question of music and politics. Geographically, the essays concern musical commemorations across five continents, from Europe and Africa to Asia and the Americas. In historical terms, they encompass performative responses to violence and trauma since the Armenian genocide (1915) and World War I (1914–18), all the way to ongoing violence in the twenty-first-century United States, Israel/Palestine, the Syrian refugee route, and the Democratic Republic of the Congo. We embrace comparative methodologies across borders, wars, generations, and governments, and expand the conversation in trauma studies: we do not position performance as the hopeful means didactically to instruct and choreograph the end of trauma, but rather emphasize that performance—with its ability to be singular and repeated, individual and collective—can offer manifold strategies and possibilities for people to live with trauma. We also acknowledge that in performed reenactment, many ongoing traumas are left out of sight, exploited, or repressed.

Themes and Issues

Trauma, Survival, and Musical Commemoration

The essays in the opening section of this volume aim to disentangle history, memory, and trauma by examining musical practice itself in the context of commemorative reenactment. Annegret Fauser develops the concept of audible historicity in her analysis of the musical ensounding of trauma and the performance of commemoration in Europe and the United States during two world wars, including Edward Elgar's *The Spirit of England* (1917), the 1927 Beethoven Centenary, and Bohuslav Martinů's *Memorial to Lidice* (1943). Building on a comprehensive survey of Western composers mobilizing sound and silence in commemorative composition from the sixteenth century on, she demonstrates to what extent such practices in the twentieth century rely on the transnational legibility of compositional conventions and intertexts.

Philip V. Bohlman asks why, in the twenty-first century, we have endowed performance with the right to commemorate, reflecting on his own role as artistic director for the New Budapest Orpheum Society. He theorizes the "cabaretesque" by examining how the cabaret stage becomes a site for inversion, in which commemoration mirrors commemoration as performance becomes about performance, and he suggests ways of destabilizing assumed practices of commemoration in order to enhance its meaning and power in the present.

Noriko Manabe explores how differences in the local cultures of Hiroshima and Nagasaki shaped their responses to the trauma of the dropping of atomic bombs on August 6 and 9, 1945, and how the musics of commemoration ceremonies, concerts, and popular songs continue to reflect differences in the two cities' characters. Drawing attention to the silencing of the direct victims of the bombing (the *hibakusha*) in the official memory regimes after the war ended, she shows how commemorative song could be used both to cover up actual experience and to give voice to those who suffered.

Mediation, Memory, and Musical Reenactment

The politics of memory form the focus of the second section of this volume, revealing how artistic production shapes memory in the performance of commemoration through the media of concert, video, and film. As Aleida Assmann points out elsewhere, the arts themselves become actors in such creation of a commemorative archive by providing "a continuous discourse on the potentials and problems of cultural memory."[28] Memory regimes created through such artistic reenactment, however, serve a number of functions.

Lillian M. Wohl shows in her discussion of the *Memoria AMIA* (2016) music video—commemorating the 1994 bombing of the AMIA Jewish community center in Buenos Aires, Argentina—that this kind of reconfiguration of memory can serve as a prosthetic device replacing the lived experience of trauma through a digitally mediated simulacrum. Yet the video's memory work carries political authority by its very recording of remembered trauma. As the chorus in the video intones, "Todo está escondido en la memoria" (Everything is hidden in our memory). Justice, the video concludes, is only possible when the hidden trauma is laid bare and embraced in response to the mediated memory.

Michael A. Figueroa's analysis of the Israeli film *Waltz with Bashir* (2008) engages with the sonically mediated retrievals of suppressed memories through the reenactment of the filmmaker Ari Folman's own role in the 1982 massacre at Sabra and Shatila, in which the Israeli army allowed the Lebanese Christian Phalangist militia to enter two Palestinian refugee camps, slaughtering hundreds of unarmed men, women, and children. In the film's soundtrack, musical sound serves both as an archive and as a trigger in the unfolding narrative, in which the deliberately performed aspect of recovery disappears in the face of the recorded sound of grief as the victims—to return to Shklar's comment cited earlier—cry out for justice in their own voices.

Imani Danielle Mosley discusses the ways in which sound, rather than visual spectacle, forms the focus of commemorating black female death in an era of increasingly visible and audible extrajudicial police executions of black men and women in the current decade. She draws attention to a pronounced gender divide in techniques of commemoration by protest music inspired by the Black Lives Matter and Say Her Name movements. By centering their acts of remembrance on "naming" the victims, Say Her Name combines the aurality of naming with the musicality of the protest songs in order to invoke, and give life to, previously unheard voices. Moreover, the music about these black women, often made by black women, fits into a narrative of gendered trauma and collective remembrance by way of invocation.

Possibilities and Impossibilities of Commemoration: Trauma's Persistence and the Politics of Reenactment

In the scope of its horror and its claims to totality, genocide would seem to be, if not beyond representation, then at least beyond reenactment. In her essay, Vanessa Agnew shows, however, that filmmakers, composers, performance artists, historians, exhibition designers, and living-history practitioners increasingly turn to genocide as their subject, using reenactment to restage acts of mass violence perpetrated in various historical contexts, including the Ottoman Empire, Indonesia, and Rwanda. This would suggest either a loosening of historiographical conventions surrounding genocide representation, or a new respectability for reenactment as an investigative and commemorative genre. Focusing on sonic reenactments dealing with the Holocaust—Josef Bor's *The Theresienstadt Requiem* (*Terezínské rekviem*, 1963), Claude Lanzmann's *Shoah* (1985), Hotel Modern's *Kamp* (2010), Doug Schulz's *Defiant Requiem* (2012), and the use of sound in museum exhibits at Auschwitz, the Warsaw Uprising Museum, and the Jewish Museum in Berlin—Agnew examines the possibilities and limitations of sonic reenactment as a historiographical mode. She argues against sonic reenactment as a useful tool for contributing to historical knowledge, but in favor, specifically, of nonrealist, nonrepresentational forms of reenactment as a means of effectively interrogating the traumatic past in relation to a postwitness present.

Andrea F. Bohlman unpacks the work that sound does for three prominent memory projects in contemporary Poland, with an ear to their aural histories. Recently, the anniversaries of the Warsaw Ghetto Uprising (1943), the Warsaw Uprising (1944), and the first democratic elections (1989) were each orchestrated with an emphasis on the importance of participation by individual citizens. Singing out loud, making noise, lamenting in silence, and amplifying historical sounds: these practices played a part at each of these annual public commemorations. Musical repertories and commemorative performances, along with transmedia storytelling, hosted and promoted the ethics of this memory work. At the same time, as sing-along concerts, collective marches of silence, and open-access listening stations filled the streets of the Polish capital, the city also accrued an agency that at times overwhelmed the particular and subjective experiences of participants. Bohlman considers the role that aural history has in effecting this emotional and data overload. These anniversaries are both in concert and in competition with each other, and a study of their media history illuminates the mechanisms by which narratives can become overwrought, and sound and song can be overwritten.

Sylvia Angelique Alajaji continues the discourse on commemorative reenactment as a political act of contested ownership in her examination of the concerts for the centennial (2015) of the Armenian genocide, commemorating the killing of approximately one million Armenians living within the boundaries of the Ottoman Empire. Across the global Armenian diaspora, concerts and other events served to evoke the memory of trauma to underscore the demand for justice encapsulated in the centennial's slogan: "Hishum Em ev Pahanjum" (I remember and demand). Alajaji argues that the concerts—as sonic acts of remembrance—gave form to the unrepresentability of the genocide and to the ambiguities of diasporic belonging: thus remembered trauma becomes embedded in the lives and memories of generations increasingly removed from the genocide.

If the preceding essays have shown the diverse ways in which commemoration can masquerade as a congealing of metanarrative into something that passes for history and is marked by plural, if not unanimous, ingestion, Chérie Rivers Ndaliko argues that this is not the case in the east of the Democratic Republic of the Congo (and in many other tumultuous regions laboring under the label of "developing" or the like). She demonstrates how the withholding of commemoration has served as a strategy of political domination by various factions involved in the DRC's history. Yet the urge to remember persists in the face of such erasure; indeed, some would say that it is amplified. Remembrance in the provincial capital, Goma, is reflexive, strategic if at times chaotic, and relentless. It is also infinitely fragmented and subjective, and harbored in mediums—story, gesture, implication, mirth—that at least in principle remain unassailable despite their fragility.

The essays in *Performing Commemoration* cannot present an all-encompassing intervention in the current debates on performed reenactment and the politics of trauma as embodied forms of musical commemoration. Nor should they seek to do so. Rather, the authors' fractal scrutiny of commemorative performance over the past century and across five continents emphasizes the regional and historical specificities of the different case studies. But by setting out with a shared question—what is it to perform commemoration?—the contributors to this volume offer a kaleidoscope of possible answers to this question through deeply interconnected discussions of how performed reenactment might be understood as mediated sonic memory regimes.

It is clear that the discussion and engagement prompted in, and by, this volume are sorely needed in what remain difficult times. At the University of North Carolina at Chapel Hill, the area where Silent Sam once stood is now an empty space, covered with a lawn. There is, however, a monument that has become significantly more visible since the fateful events of August 2018. A few hundred feet away, the Unsung Founders Memorial—previously overshadowed by the Confederate monument—honors, as the inscription makes clear, "The People Of Color, Bond And Free—Who Helped Build The Carolina That We Cherish Today."[29] Yet McCorkle Place remains a contested space. Confederate sympathizers recently defaced the Unsung Founder Memorial, and sonic vernaculars of protest and counterprotest periodically fill the area in continued clashes over the politics of trauma.[30] As the authors of this volume make clear, music, sound, and silence emerge as central elements in the performance of commemoration, as people ensound, embody, and performatively reiterate the violence of the past.

Notes

1. Judith N. Shklar, *The Faces of Injustice* (New Haven: Yale University Press, 1990), 83, cited in David Scott, *Omens of Adversity: Tragedy, Time, Memory, Justice* (Durham, NC: Duke University Press, 2014), 127. Earlier in the book, Shklar makes it clear that "as long as we have a sense of injustice, we will want not only understand the forces that cause us pain but also to hold them responsible for it—if we can identify them" (5).

2. Benjamin Tausig, "Sound and Movement: Vernaculars of Sonic Dissent," *Social Text* 36, no. 3 (2018): 25–45. He defines (p. 26) "sonic vernaculars" as being "composed of locally trenchant sonic and aural practices and the symbolic meanings that they transduce and mediate."

3. Myah Ward and Charlie McGee, "Silent Sam Toppled in Protest the Night before Classes Begin," *Daily Tar Heel*, August 20, 2018; https://www.dailytarheel.com/article/2018/08/silent-sam-down

4. On the role of slaves and slavery in the history of UNC Chapel Hill, see the digital exhibition of the UNC Library, "Slavery and the Making of the University," https://exhibits.lib.unc.edu/exhibits/show/slavery

5. Jesse James Deconto and Alan Blinder, "'Silent Sam' Confederate Statue Is Toppled at University of North Carolina," *New York Times*, August 21, 2018.

6. Karen L. Cox, *Dixie's Daughters: The United Daughters of the Confederacy and the Preservation of Confederate Culture* (Gainesville: University Press of Florida, 2003), 1.

7. Cox, *Dixie's Daughters*, 2.

8. William Sturkey, "Carr Was Indeed Much More Than Silent Sam," *Herald Sun*, October 31, 2017, https://www.heraldsun.com/opinion/article181567401.html. The program of the ceremony is digitized at https://exhibits.lib.unc.edu/items/show/3687

9. The procession is described in "The Soldiers Monument Unveiled," *Alumni Review* 1, no. 6 (June 1913): 184–85; digitized at https://archive.org/details/alumnireviewseriv1i6chap/page/184. Quotation p. 184.

10. The speeches and the program are digitized by the university library of UNC at https://exhibits.lib.unc.edu/exhibits/show/silent-sam/archives

11. Julian Carr, "Unveiling of Confederate Monument at University," typescript, June 2, 1913, p. 9B–9C; Julian Shakespeare Carr Papers, University of North Carolina, Southern Historical Collection #00141, Box 4, Folder 26, digitized as https://exhibits.lib.unc.edu/files/original/c1160e4341b86794b7e842cb042fb414.pdf. A transcription of the entire speech may be consulted on a site run by the historian Hillary N. Green at http://hgreen.people.ua.edu/transcription-carr-speech.html

12. Amanda M. Black and Andrea F. Bohlman, "Resounding the Campus: Pedagogy, Race, and the Environment," *Journal of Music History Pedagogy* 8, no. 1 (2017): 6.

13. The concept of historiographic injustice through the case study of the Haitian Revolution is addressed in Michel-Rolph Trouillot, *Silencing the Past: Power and the Production of History* (Boston: Beacon Press, 1995), 95–107.

14. This formulation draws on Susan Leigh Foster's discussion of the intersection of dance and historiography in her "Manifesto for Dead and Moving Bodies," formulated in her introduction to *Choreographing History*, ed. Susan Leigh Foster (Bloomington: Indiana University Press, 1995), 6.

15. Judith Butler, *Bodies That Matter* (New York: Routledge, 2011), xii and 59–60.

16. See, for example, Alexander Rehding, *Music and Monumentality: Commemoration and Wonderment in the Nineteenth Century* (New York: Oxford University Press, 2009); Maria Cizmic, *Performing Pain: Music and Trauma in Eastern Europe* (New York: Oxford University Press, 2012); and *Entangled Memories: Remembering the Holocaust in a Global Age*, ed. Marius Henderson and Julia Lange (Heidelberg: Universitätsverlag Winter, 2017).

17. For example, the chapters included in *Performance Studies*, ed. Erin Striff (New York: Palgrave Macmillan, 2003), range in their topics from striptease and plastic surgery to conversion spectacles and dance choreography. See also *Performance Studies: Key Words, Concepts and Theories*, ed. Bryan Reynolds (New York: Palgrave, 2014).

18. Erika Fischer-Lichte, *The Routledge Introduction to Theatre and Performance Studies*, ed. Ramona Thomasius and Minou Arjomand, trans. Minou Arjomand (New York: Routledge, 2014), 18.

19. Mark Franko, "Epilogue to an Epilogue: Historicizing the Re- in Danced Reenactment," in *The Oxford Handbook of Dance and Reenactment*, ed. Mark Franko (New York: Oxford University Press, 2018), 497.

20. Franko, "Epilogue to an Epilogue," 500.

21. The critical discussion of reenactment and its historiographic impacts has generated a significant literature in the past two decades. See, for example, Vanessa Agnew, "History's Affective Turn: Historical Reenactment and Its Work in the Present," *Rethinking History* 11, no. 3 (2007): 299–312; and Katherine M. Johnson, "Rethinking (Re)doing: Historical Re-enactment and/as Historiography," *Rethinking History* 19, no. 2 (2015): 193–206.

22. Rebecca Schneider, *Performing Remains: Art and War in Times of Theatrical Reenactment* (New York: Routledge, 2011), 50.

23. Franko, "Epilogue to an Epilogue," 501. Recent dance scholarship has addressed the archive as (re)performance. See, for example, Gabriele Brandstetter, *Poetics of Dance*, trans. Elena Polzer with Mark Franko (New York: Oxford University Press, 2015), 30–88; and Samuel N. Dorf, *Performing Antiquity: Ancient Greek Music and Dance from Paris to Delphi, 1890–1930* (New York: Oxford University Press, 2019), 1–18.

24. J. Roger Kurtz, "Introduction," in *Trauma and Literature*, ed. J. Roger Kurtz (Philadelphia: Drexel University Press, 2016), 4; see also Andrew Barnaby, "The Psychoanalytic Origins of Literary Trauma Studies," in same volume, 21–35.

25. Cathy Caruth, *Unclaimed Experience: Trauma, Narrative, History* (Baltimore: Johns Hopkins University Press, 1996).

26. Caruth, *Unclaimed Experience*, 4.

27. Stef Craps, *Postcolonial Witnessing: Trauma Out of Bounds* (London: Palgrave Macmillan, 2012).

28. Aleida Assmann, *Cultural Memory and Western Civilization: Functions, Media, Archives* (Cambridge: Cambridge University Press, 2011), xii.

29. The *Unsung Founders Memorial* was dedicated in 2005.

30. Jordan Green, "Neo-Confederates Found Guilty of Vandalizing Statue Honoring Enslaved People Who Built UNC," *Indy Week*, September 6, 2019, https://indyweek.com/news/orange/neo-confederates-found-guilty-of-vandalizing-statue-honoring

Trauma, Survival, and Musical Commemoration

ONE | Ensounding Trauma, Performing Commemoration

Western Music in Time of War and Tumults

ANNEGRET FAUSER

Mimetic musical representations of warfare have a long tradition in Western music. Such well-known pieces as Clément Janequin's sixteenth-century *La Bataille de Marignan* and Ludwig van Beethoven's *Wellingtons Sieg oder Die Schlacht bei Vittoria* (1813) were part of an extensive corpus of compositions that memorialized pivotal battles through music. Musical commemorations have deep roots in the past, not least as a practice of the French Revolution with such works as François-Joseph Gossec's *Marche lugubre* from 1790, which honors the victims of the so-called Nancy Affair, a bloody standoff between the government and mutinous soldiers on August 31 of that year, that ended in over five hundred casualties, many of whom were civilians. Witnesses who heard Gossec's march reported that its "notes, separate and detached, broke the heart and tore out one's entrails."[1] By sonically reenacting the soundscape of battle, and by ensounding the trauma associated with war, over the past centuries these compositions contributed to the development of a transnational repertoire of musical signifiers that Western composers deployed to evoke both emotional and representational responses to war and trauma. Such works also started to form an intrinsic part of a set of practices that adopted specific compositions and such martial sounds as rifle and cannon salutes to commemorate military conflicts and their outcomes. Yet commemorative music also created convenient political tools, in particular by fostering and promoting hegemonic narratives—often aligned with the state apparatus—about suffering and its meanings both during and after war.[2] In this chapter I trace the ways in which music, sound, and silence have been configured through Western music, especially in the time of world wars, to offer rituals of sonic remembrance by developing, and relying on, the transnational legibility of compositional convention and intertexts as well as their audible historicity.

War and Commemorative Music

While I focus in this chapter on the ensounding of trauma and the performance of commemoration in musical composition and practice in Europe and the United States in the age of world wars, I start my discussion back in the eighteenth century, with a piece that might be cited as paradigmatic for the entanglements of the mimetic and the commemorative in Western musical responses to war.[3] James Hewitt's *The Battle of Trenton* (1792) commemorated a pivotal encounter in the American Revolutionary War in December 1776, after George Washington crossed the Delaware River. Published some fifteen years after the battle took place, Hewitt's work sonically reenacted the events for its salon audience, drawing on familiar battle topoi from fanfares to noisy cannon fire, while the accompanying verbal commentary clarified the meaning of each musical episode (Figure 1.1).

Yet Hewitt's piece also enacted the characteristic turn to mourning and commemoration that would become a trope in such works, including the shift toward the minor mode and a slower tempo. The composer chose for that particular moment in the work a Scottish folk song called "Roslin Castle" that was often associated with eighteenth-century funerals. Just like the mimetic rendering of cannons and bombs in the battle scene, so the use of actual funeral music signaled an element of authenticity in the musical reenactment of the battle and its aftermath (Figure 1.2). Both these topoi and the genre were a transnational phenomenon in the late eighteenth century, with better-known battle pieces such a Frantisek Kotzwara's *Battle of Prague* (1778) circulating through the salons of Europe and North America well into the nineteenth century. In Mark Twain's *Adventures of Huckleberry Finn* (1884), Emmeline Grangerford's parlor contained a "little old piano," and "nothing was ever so lovely as to hear the young ladies sing 'The Last Link is Broken' and play 'The Battle of Prague' on it."[4] Musical reenactments of battles could thus serve as trivial nineteenth-century parlor games, prized for their sonic effects

Figure 1.1. James Hewitt, *The Battle of Trenton*. New York: James Hewitt, [1797], mm. 21–33. Library of Congress.

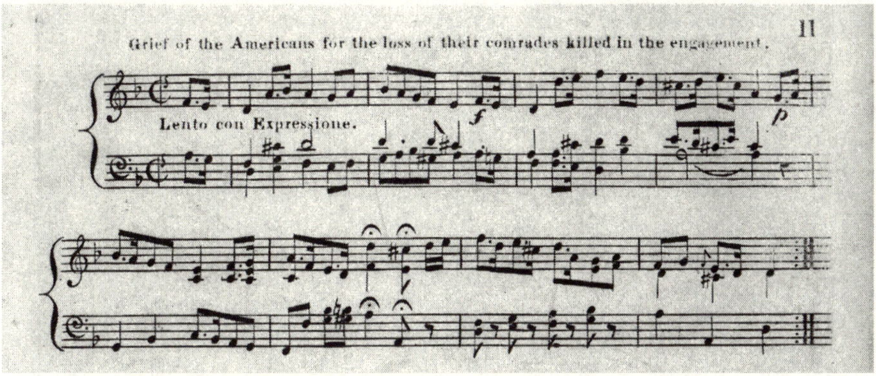

Figure 1.2. James Hewitt, *The Battle of Trenton*. New York: James Hewitt, [1797], mm. 254–62. Library of Congress.

and dramatic turns, just as Pyotr Ilich Tchaikovsky's *The Year 1812: Solemn Overture* (1880) has become a concert favorite on modern programs over the intervening century, not least as a well-worn chestnut in popular July 4 Independence Day concerts in the United States, and in England—in a particularly anti-European twist—as an ode to Brexit.[5]

According to Jonathan Kregor, sonic emblems of battle remained a feature in compositions throughout the long nineteenth century, yet changed into malleable musical signifiers in "a prolonged move from the characteristic to the poetic/ethical, and finally the ideological."[6] Recent research, moreover, has traced the presence of such belligerent tropes in Western art music well into the twentieth century, not least in such wartime symphonies as Vincent d'Indy's *De bello gallico* (1918) and Marc Blitzstein's *Airborne Symphony* (1946).[7] To take World War I compositions as an example, it is clear that mimetic topoi retained their presence in music across the political spectrum, as in Igor Stravinsky's *Trois pièces faciles* (1915), Lili Boulanger's setting of Psalm 24, "La terre appartient à l'Eternel" (1916), and Arnold Schoenberg's *Die eiserne Brigade* (1916). However—and here is where I position the intervention of this essay—it is also clear that Western art music's response to war increasingly emphasized the commemorative over the characteristic, given the shift in the terms not only of military engagement in the late nineteenth century to mechanized warfare but also of the media representation of war—first, in newspapers and, later, in radio and newsreels. In addition, given the growing "centenary fever" of the nineteenth century, commemoration as a performative mode of engaging the past pervaded not only the political sphere—in the centenary of the French revolution in 1889, for example—but also the arts, as when the 1859 centenary of Robert Burns engendered almost one thousand commemorative events across the English-speaking world.[8]

A significant work that encapsulated this modern shift from the characteristic to the commemorative was Edward Elgar's *The Spirit of England* (1915–17), based on three poems by the English poet Laurence Binyon as a symphonic cantata for soprano (or tenor), chorus, and orchestra. Dedicated "to the memory of our glorious men," the work culminated with a setting of what is perhaps Binyon's most famous poem, "For the Fallen."[9] As Rachel Cowgill has pointed out, this particular work straddled wartime mourning and postwar commemoration in Great Britain, as the BBC turned to broadcasting it annually on Armistice Day.[10] But I also want to focus on the transnational enmeshment of *The Spirit of England* as a musical reenactment of communal trauma in war. Elgar's work is about England, her heroism, and her sacrifice, as well as the construction of community in a commemorative piece of art. The composition conjures community through musical means: the combination of a single solo voice with chorus and orchestra was well established by that point transnationally as a symbolic representation of the individualized voice of a mourning community, in turn stepping out of, and blending in with, the communal musical expression. Among the best-known and most performed examples was Johannes Brahms's *Ein deutsches Requiem* (1868), with its fifth movement for soprano, chorus, and orchestra, "Ihr habt nun Traurigkeit."[11] Yet Elgar's work—like numerous others on both sides of the conflict—also drew in its musical texture, genre, and form on musical signifiers that carried national overtones. This becomes particularly obvious in the third movement, "For the Fallen." The first two stanzas set the tone:

> With proud thanksgiving, a mother for her children,
> England mourns for her dead across the sea.
> Flesh of her flesh they were, spirit of her spirit,
> Fallen in the cause of the free.
>
> Solemn the drums thrill; Death august and royal
> Sings sorrow up into immortal spheres,
> There is music in the midst of desolation
> And a glory that shines upon our tears.[12]

It is no coincidence that Elgar here combines a vocal fugue reminiscent of George Frideric Handel, who was considered a resolutely "British" composer despite being born in Germany, with a soaring melody carried by the soprano soloist, all over a symphonic orchestral texture. Elgar shifts kaleidoscopically through other musical signifiers as well, from the musical pastoralism so strongly associated with England to the universalist and religious overtones of the fugue before reaching a first dramatic climax on the words "Solemn the drums thrill." At this moment, Elgar turns to the characteristic mode of battle music by literally sounding the snare drums, integrating a mimetic reference to battle noise, before the soloist breaks out to lead the chorus with the words "Death august and royal / Sings sorrow up into immortal spheres." The poet then continues, "There is music in the midst of desolation," and Elgar allows the listener—for a fleeting moment—to focus on music's consolation through nostalgic reminiscence. As Frances Colvin wrote in a letter to Elgar after hearing "For the Fallen" for the first time, the movement would "always be the one great inspiration of the War. My heart is full of warm gratitude to you—but my eyes are sore with *tears* and I can't write."[13]

That Elgar's work was so effective a piece of musical commemoration lies precisely in its exploitation and indexing of seemingly universal musical tropes, from symphonic monumentality to the spiritual associations of its grave fugal textures.[14] Their transnational value and legibility were contingent on a long process that, throughout the nineteenth century, replaced the national signification of works such as Brahms's *Ein deutsches Requiem* or Beethoven's Third Symphony with a universalist construction of transnational artistic greatness. And while new commemorative compositions from World War I, such as *The Spirit of England* and (in Germany) Max Reger's *Requiem* on a text by Friedrich Hebbel, inscribed themselves into this transnational musical language, older works—first by Bach, Handel, and Beethoven, but soon also by Brahms—could similarly cross borders to serve national expressions of mourning and commemoration throughout the Western world.[15]

Despite the shifts in both the composition and the reception of commemorative music, these works remained thoroughly embedded in a tradition of deploying music to make an ennobled history audible to citizens of whom their respective nations demanded sacrifice, whether of their own lives or of their loved ones. But the musical reenactment of battles in the manner of Hewitt's *Battle of Trenton* in the parlor was no longer a viable option for evoking warfare sonically in the face of the death, injury, and devastation of World War I that laid waste to much of Europe and implicated the rest of the world from Australia to Egypt. More often, the home became a place of commemoration and mourning centered on remembered and reenacted music-making. When her son fell on the battlefield in Egypt in 1917, Lady Alda Hoare turned to their shared love of music to mourn his death.[16] She assembled her scores in four large volumes and annotated them with reminiscences of their joint musical endeavors. As she wrote in her diary three weeks after learning of his death, her son Harry "loved Schubert songs," although when it came to piano music, "he preferred Beethoven." To her mind this was not German music, but Harry's music. "Hands in pockets he would walk to & fro, never sit, sometimes close to two hours, while I played—coming occasionally to sing, in that beautiful, deep, rich Baryton."[17] For Lady Hoare, the music she had shared with her son served as a memorial to the soldier whose body was interred far away, in North Africa. The sonic dimension of this private memorial retained an aura of spectral presence.

Silence, Trauma, and Disability

When the modes both of reenactment and of commemoration transformed in the wake of World War I, a new dimension entered the global rituals of remembrance: silence. Just as the soundscapes of war had changed, so did the perception of their absence.[18] Indeed, the transition itself from war to armistice was marked by this shift when, on November 11, 1918, at 11:00 a.m. on the western front, the weapons fell silent (Figure

1.3). The cease-fire, so witnesses reported later, created an extraordinary experience of silence when all arms stopped almost at once, ending the relentless, mechanized noise of war with its guns, bombs, and airplanes.[19] That war could be an acoustic hell had long been reflected in letters and reports, poems and music. Written shortly before Theodor Körner perished in the battle of Leipzig in 1813, the dashing soldier-poet's famous verse, "Gebet während der Schlacht" ("Prayer during Battle"), evoked the "Schlachtendonnerwetter"—the thunderstorm of battle—with its roaring and booming of death; its imagery became part of the vocabulary through which European soldiers and civilians referred to the overpowering din of battle.[20] Yet the soundscape of World War I was different: years of incessant noise along the trenches—with the physical pain generated by its sheer loudness to the point that "your head wants to explode"—created a violent and inescapable soundscape never before heard.[21] When it was over, on that November morning, the silence that descended over the battlefields seemed alien and downright eerie. As Richard Foot, a British artilleryman stationed in Maubeuge, wrote about his experience:

> It was quite strange to ride back to the battery in the quiet that followed 11 o'clock. One had got used to the background noise of shellfire, which could often be heard as far away as the south coast of England. Near the front, it seemed a continuous orchestration of deep and echoing sound, punctuated by the sharper rat-tat-tat of rifle or machine-gun fire. . . . Peace seemed a very strange and new experience.[22]

Other soldiers, too, marveled at the acoustic shift from war to peace. Aubrey Smith recalled his disbelief: "It must be only a dream! Surely we should hear the distant sound of guns in a minute or so, which would prove that we had been deluded! We strained our ears for distant gunfire . . . Silence! Only the sound of church bells in other villages proclaiming the event."[23] Indeed, the mindful perception of silence would become the marker both of the end of World War I and of its commemoration when—for the first anniversary of Armistice Day—King George V instigated the ritual of observing a two-minute silence at 11:00 a.m., a ritual that spread quickly across the Western world.

Bounded by the viscerally experienced extremes of noise and silence at the end of global combat, that dramatic sonic shift became one of the markers of understanding sound and music after the cataclysm of World

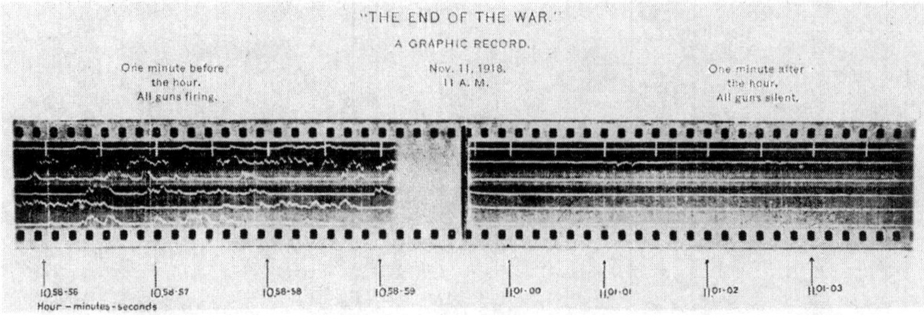

Figure 1.3. This image represents the moment of armistice, recording artillery activity with a "sound ranger" (an apparatus invented in World War I to measure enemy artillery positions). It shows the cessation of fire in the flattening of white lines, which, before 11:00 a.m., oscillated with the noise. Imperial War Museum, London, American Embassy Collection, Q 47886.

War I. The transition from war to peace was difficult. It is hard to grasp the daily struggle for physical survival between 1918 and 1920 in most of continental Europe and even Great Britain, when hunger, rubble, and infections—not least the terrible influenza pandemic that killed more people than enemy fire—dominated daily life. Music's roles were manifold at this point in time, helping to mourn the dead and a lost way of life, continuing to boost morale, affirming national identities across the western hemisphere, and—increasingly—commemorating the war as its presence began to recede in everyday life. Yet, as Deniz Ertan and William Brooks have recently pointed out, these events brought on not only the expected musical performance of commemoration in the aftermath of war but also a marked silence in the face of what was constructed as the inaudible and unheroic devastation of influenza.[24] There were no models to commemorate an epidemic musically or otherwise. This expansive sense of deathly silence differed from, and yet merged with, the sonic configuration of the end of this global war as a shift from noise to silence. In the 1920s, silence thus became both a marker of peace and a signifier of civilian postwar suffering. Silence also served to keep trauma unspoken: veterans of devastatingly brutal battles such as the 1915 battle of Gallipoli often refused to give words to their experiences.[25] "Wasn't it noticeable at the end of the war," Walter Benjamin wrote in 1936, "that men who returned from the battle-field had grown silent—not richer, but poorer in communicable experience?"[26]

But silence might also be heard in musical performance as representing absence. One such form of silence, for instance, was revealed by the display of war-generated trauma in the concert hall. Historian Jay Winter's interpretation of Maurice Ravel's Piano Concerto for the Left Hand in D major (1929–30; first performed in 1932) as composed silence is jarring, when he writes that we hear "the silence of the right hand, or the harmony of the disabled" in this work.[27] Yet this comment leads to two forms of rethinking absence: the compensatory narrative of heroic overcoming, such as when the pianist Paul Wittgenstein returned to the concert stage, and the absence of disabled veterans in musical commemorations after the end of World War I. In his review of Wittgenstein's first concert in 1916 after the amputation of his right arm following a battle injury, Julius Korngold not only praised the pianist for his one-handed achievements but also implied a redemptive pathway for musicians still in combat should they be injured: "Let us, after his debut, crowned with success, clasp the courageous hand, which he has learned to use so skillfully. The sounds produced by his left hand do not betray the artist's melancholy at no longer possessing a right hand, rather they express his triumph at being able to bear his loss so well."[28] Bearing loss well was part of the ethos associated with military honor, and Wittgenstein—by negating weakness in performance—reenacted not the trauma of battle injury but the socially sanctioned silence about veterans' disability after World War I. Indeed, where the modern historian Winter heard absence in Ravel's score, Wittgenstein's contemporaries relished in the illusion of a single-handed recreation of bodily wholeness. One of the tropes that critics returned to repeatedly was the disassociation of sight and sound: Wittgenstein's performances "sounded two-handed in their power and bravura."[29]

Yet Winter's comment about hearing absence also draws attention to the disabled survivors who were omitted from the performance of commemoration after World War I. Although veterans were in the audiences of commemorative events, their suffering—just like the deaths of the influenza epidemic—remained unheard in the official gesture of performed commemoration. Even when veteran associations sponsored or put on commemorative performances—such as the British Legion's "Festivals of Remembrance" that began in 1923—those who were remembered were the fallen, not the living disabled.[30] Avant-garde artists—from Otto Dix and George Grosz to Bertolt Brecht and Kurt Weill—might have put veterans with disabilities in the center of their paintings and stage works, but their artworks were not so much commemorative as they were anchored in the present experience, calling for social justice of those silenced by the commemorations for the dead.[31]

One musical commemoration intersected unexpectedly, however, with the sense of silence as a marker of torment: the Beethoven centenary of 1927, which took place nine years after the end of World War I. In contrast to the 150th birthday of the composer in 1920—a milestone rendered unremarkable by the exigencies of the immediate postwar period—the centenary of Beethoven's death fell into a more auspicious moment not only politically after the Treaties of Locarno (signed in 1925, which confirmed the postwar status quo) but also in economic terms, as the worst of the war's financial aftermath started to ease. The reach of this commemoration encompassed much of the world, from Moscow to Tokyo and from Buenos Aires to Sydney. Moreover, this recognition of Beethoven and his music was intertwined with pervasive postwar discourses about nationalism and internationalism. Numerous speeches and articles evoked the League of Nations while they claimed Beethoven simultaneously for national validation and international exchange. Local responses, for their part, fashioned Beethoven for their specific cultural contexts. In the Soviet Union, the centenary coincided with the tenth anniversary of the October Revolution, and Beethoven, the revolutionary educator of humanity, was easily recast as a proto-Soviet hero.[32] In the recently established Republic of China, Beethoven was similarly lauded as the heroic defender of democratic revolution, and the Shanghai Municipal Orchestra put on several concerts of his works in the spring of 1927.[33] In Germany, Beethoven's national credentials were fêted across the nation; in Belgium it was his Flemish origins; in France, the celebration was conducted in the vein of Third Republic routine, including the solemn dedication of a monument in the Parc de Vincennes. Beethoven—as Esteban Buch has shown—was infinitely malleable in the transnational field of interwar Western music and its politics, given how each nation could reinterpret the composer's significance according to particular circumstance.[34]

Yet despite the different political appropriations of the composer's memory from China to Argentina, the surviving documents from these commemorations point to a common theme across borders given the sustained emphasis on Beethoven's heroic suffering. As the French minister of public education and fine arts, Edouard Herriot, voiced during the state ceremony at Beethoven's grave in Vienna on March 27, 1927: "Today, as then, aware of our duties to humanity, we cherish in this creature of genius the poet who made music a means of persuasion and action more effective than the word; the man who, despite all, crucified by life, retained only tenderness and pity in his work."[35] The physical handicap that writers discussed was, of course, the composer's loss of hearing, and the "Heiligenstadt Testament" counted among the most reproduced Beethoven documents in the 1927 press, both in various translations and in facsimile. Implicitly as well as explicitly, Beethoven's suffering and death were connected to that of the recent world war, and the silencing of his musical world was cast as the ultimate artistic and human sacrifice.[36]

Given this connection, the official Viennese events drew on familiar rituals of commemoration for fallen soldiers rather than celebrated artists, and two compositions in particular played a key role in the official events, both there and all over the world: the *Missa solemnis* and the *Cantata for the Death of Joseph II*, WoO 87. Although the latter was written in 1790, it only became known in 1884, but in the aftermath of World War I, Beethoven's *Trauerkantate* (cantata of mourning)—so the press consistently styled it—quickly became one of the Beethoven staples in rituals of commemoration. Thus it was only fitting that Felix Weingartner should program it in the opening ceremony of the commemoration in Vienna on March 26, 1927.

Whereas the *Trauerkantate* fit familiar modes of commemoration for the dead—both in its text and in its idiom—Beethoven's *Missa solemnis* became a signifier of the heroic overcoming of disability through sheer grit and determination, yet one in need of decoding and mediation for interwar audiences. One particularly striking performance took place in Paris, in the cathedral of Notre-Dame on March 17, 1927, by "special authorization and under the effective presidency" of the archbishop of Paris. It was billed as the first of the work in a Catholic church.[37] As the critic Louis Schneider pointed out: "Yesterday was the first time that the *Missa solemnis*, that giant summit dominating over all of Beethoven's masterworks, was given in a church, and what a church it was!"[38] With French officials and much of the diplomatic corps present, the archbishop presided over the event. In his speech after the "Gloria," Father Pierre Lhande offered a view of Beethoven both humanist and catholic, truly French and universally significant. The *Missa solemnis*, he explained,

> first and foremost paid homage to Beauty, a grand thing recognized by the French; it honors the country that knew to discern in it one of the jewels of the world's shared heritage. But it also evokes the great life, the great soul of Beethoven, the pain and the tragedy of a broken life whose genius was only understood when it was extinguished, and whose heart only when it was frozen. . . . On that day, when the

musician felt himself sealed, like a corpse into the tomb of silence, the great interior Beethoven was born inside of him, and all the harmonies assembled in his heart began to sing in it; until that moment, all he wrote was "music"; now, in his relentless and gigantic works, he created "life."[39]

The 1927 Beethoven centenary consolidated the composer's reputation as the stoic hero whose traumatic disability became the crucible wherein the greatest music with the most universal impact was forged. But the paratexts surrounding Beethoven's loss of hearing performed an enactment of overcoming adversity in face of trauma—especially when coupled with rituals of commemoration—that served to overwrite the actual plight of disabled veterans who survived battle. Like the critics who celebrated Wittgenstein's polished performances on the concert stage, the transnational mediators during the Beethoven commemorations made it a point to emphasize that disability was, in the end, to be silenced. For Western society of the interwar years, those worthy of commemoration were the dead; the living had models such as Beethoven or Wittgenstein to follow, with the responsibility placed on wounded veterans to pass as able, or at least to compensate for their mental or physical disabilities.[40]

Musical Commemoration, Social Justice, and Political Causes

From poetry readings to radio broadcasts, the interwar years brought numerous commemorative rituals to honor the war dead. Memorials of the Great War in Europe, the United States, and elsewhere enshrined the myth of the fallen as the heroic embodiment of sacrifice, and they often represented the soldiers as "sleeping dead," resting in peace.[41] Yet the long-term impact of battle-inflicted trauma also led to the deployment of art in calling for social justice, including forms of reenactment of trauma. So many disabled veterans had returned without support and were forced to beg in the streets for survival—often in uniform—that the German press, for instance, spoke of a "plague of beggars." The display of disfigurement by the war wounded, moreover, was considered offensive in the postwar world. In November 1919, the *Deutsche Tageszeitung* criticized wounded veterans "who take to begging while insistently emphasizing their suffering and present an ugly sight in the streets and squares of the big cities."[42] The figure of the begging, disabled veteran became one of the most central characters in left-wing political art, embodying everything that was wrong with postwar society. As Carol Poore points out, works such as a Brecht and Weill's *Die Dreigroschenoper* (1928) showed "how ludicrous it was to expect human sympathy in a capitalist society based solely on profit."[43] Yet even here, the truly betrayed figure was the soldier who died as cannon fodder in the "Kanonensong."

Film, with its ability to offer flashbacks, became a key medium through which to present reenactments of trauma.[44] One poignant example comes from commercial Hollywood, the Warner Brothers' blockbuster *Gold Diggers of 1933*, which tackles a number of social issues connected to the Depression, from soup kitchens and unemployment to fat-cat profiteering. The call for social justice related to war-inflicted trauma is explicit in the number "Remember My Forgotten Man," sung by Joan Blondell and Etta Moten. Whereas Blondell's rendering of the verse draws on Lotte Lenya's sonic and gestural repertoire in the 1931 film version of *Die Dreigroschenoper*, Moten's blues-inflected performance brings the tradition of the black woman's lament into play.[45] Layering the dance number with cinematic flashbacks, Busby Berkeley showed columns of able-bodied men marching into battle, followed by a sequence of bedraggled men with combat wounds returning from war (Figure 1.4), only to end up standing in a line in a soup kitchen or begging in the street.

Such activist commemorations and reenactments of trauma during the interwar years had a powerful influence on the way in which musicians configured commemorative works in World War II. As in the previous war, those killed in battle were at the center of commemoration, and a work such as Bernard Herrmann's *For the Fallen* (1943) drew on now familiar modes of remembrance. This was one of seventeen short orchestral works commissioned in 1943 by the League of Composers to be "commemorative of the present war."[46] Herrmann's contribution—the title of which evoked Binyon's famous poem—was, in the composer's words, "a tribute to the war's dead. It is a berceuse for those who lie asleep on the many alien battlefields of this war."[47] Written in a highly chromatic, post-Mahlerian idiom, the work ends with a quotation of the well-known melody from Handel's *Messiah*: "He shall feed His flock like a shepherd," cast as a flute duo in parallel thirds. The quotation stands out both harmonically and instrumentally, a deliberate anachronism within the chromatic dissonance of the work. By integrating this marked reference to the well-known alto aria—often used in funeral services because of its promise that "ye shall find rest unto your souls"—Hermann brought the ritual of commemoration into the concert hall.

Figure 1.4. The Marching Wounded. Film still from the sequence accompanying "Remember My Forgotten Man," in *Gold Diggers of 1933*. Warner Brothers.

The same set of commissions yielded two commemorative works that powerfully connected the remembrance of the dead with political causes: William Grant Still's *In Memoriam* (1943) and Bohuslav Martinů's *Memorial to Lidice* (1943). Still's *In Memoriam* certainly paid tribute to the figure of the "fallen soldier," yet he cast his musical memorial as ensounding the greater struggle between good and evil in an archetypal construct of heroic sacrifice. His hero was not the symbolic unknown soldier, but the first American serviceman killed in action, who, as the composer pointed out, "was a Negro soldier."[48] Written to commemorate "The Colored Soldiers Who Died for Democracy" (the work's subtitle), Still's *In Memoriam* was, indeed, a political work. It combined the heroic gesture of a military fanfare with a lyrical theme drawing deliberately on the idiom of a spiritual. Developing its themes both contrapuntally and in several call-and-response sequences, the score culminates in an orchestral apotheosis, based on the fanfare motive and pushing to the dynamic level to *fortissississimo*, supported by timpani, snare drums, and cymbal. The masculinist, monumental affirmation leaves no doubt: the fallen African American soldier was a true hero.[49]

In his commentary on the purpose of the composition, Still emphasized the point:

> Our civilization has known no greater patriotism, no greater loyalty than that shown by the colored men who fight and die for democracy. Those who return will, I hope, come back to a better world. I also hope that our tribute to those who died will be to make the democracy for which they fought greater and broader than it has ever been before.[50]

Still was all too aware of the bitter irony of African Americans fighting for freedom and equality abroad while such basic rights eluded them in their segregated home.[51] By expressing the hope that African Americans returning from the battlefield might find better conditions, Still aligned himself with the rhetoric of the Double V Campaign, started by the *Pittsburgh Courier* in 1942, which linked the battle against fascism abroad to the internal struggle for emancipation.[52] At the same time, by celebrating African American contributions to World War II, Still joined other leading intellectuals tied to the Harlem Renaissance in encouraging black enlistment as an emancipation strategy.

Langston Hughes, for example, addressed head on the Jim Crow laws in *Brothers*, a radio play "written in an attempt to face and resolve some of the problems troubling the minds of some American Negro citizens today in regard to our war effort and their own unresolved problems of democracy at home."[53] Here an enlisted seaman confronts his younger sibling who refuses to enlist "as long as old Jim Crow's a captain in the army." Fighting Hitler in Europe, the older brother points out, meant fighting the "little Hitlers" and fifth columnists in the United States, for Hitler would support them, making "a double-barreled padlocked ghetto out of Harlem" should he win the war and bringing over "the Gestapo to back up the Ku Klux Klan."[54] Service in the armed forces, in the eyes of Hughes and other African American leaders such as the union boss Philip Randolph, combined patriotic duty with commitment to civil rights. In this context, Still's *In Memoriam* needed the final, triumphant apotheosis as a musical expression of African American pride. Nora Holt, whose highly informed criticism appeared regularly in the columns of the *New York Amsterdam News*, discussed the work in great detail. For Holt, the final apotheosis was "a resplendent closing . . . presaging undying hope for the future."[55] A lullaby in the manner of Herrmann would not do as a memorial when so much was at stake.

Martinů's *Memorial to Lidice* focused on commemorating the massacre of Czech civilians in Lidice, a Nazi atrocity that, in June 1942, had shaken the Western world.[56] In this musical cenotaph for civilian war victims, Martinů merged familiar topoi of musical commemoration with intertexts tailored to its agenda of drawing attention to Czech suffering under German occupation. The work incorporated a density of musical signifiers that embodied a powerful response to the tragic events.[57] From its opening C minor chord—the somber tone of which is colored by the use of the tam-tam, an instrument associated with the expression of traumatic pain since Gossec's *Marche lugubre*—Martinů drew on well-known and semantically overlaid musical configurations, including the "Dies irae," the Bohemian chorale *Svatý Václav,* and, toward the end of the piece, the so-called "Victory motive," the opening notes of Beethoven's Fifth Symphony, rendered in a distorted but recognizable manner. Allied victory might be coming eventually, but—the music suggests—at a high price. "According to the composer," Robert Bagar wrote in the program note for the premiere, "the work is in the nature of a religious chant, constructed along the lines of a prayer and response based on a theme which resembles in style the ancient Czech church melodies."[58] The quotation especially of the twelfth-century *Svatý Václav* carried heavy significance. It was one of the most ardently nationalist Bohemian melodies that had served as an expression of Czech protest since the Hussite Wars and regained important, transnationally legible currency in the late nineteenth century.[59] For Martinů—as for Still—musical commemoration needed to embrace more than simply remembrance of the dead: it also carried to duty to make audible the cause for which they died. Their works remained ideologically and musically closely linked to the transnational repertoire of musical commemoration, the roots of which reached back to eighteenth century and the shape of which was forged in the crucible of World War I. But they also added a new layer of political activism in the hope of a better postwar future.

In the transnational repertoire of Western commemorative music, the compositions of World War II crystallized an enmeshment of remembrance with advocacy. Like Still and Martinů, composers from Darius Milhaud to Michael Tippett reached for this intersection when they commemorated those who perished in battle or in massacres perpetrated on civilians. At the same time, older compositions—especially by Bach, Beethoven, Brahms, and Handel—continued to be used for musical commemorations both during and after the war. Although the characteristic and mimetic had retreated into the background, it did not disappear altogether, especially when musical signifiers could conjure up political or social agency. Despite Krzysztof Penderecki's disavowal of any programmatic intent behind his *Tren Ofiarom Hiroszimy* (*Threnody for the Victims of Hiroshima*, 1960), its evocative character fueled the work's reception as sonically reenacting the trauma of the American bombing of Hiroshima on August 6, 1945. Yet the silence that covered the trauma of the survivors in the interwar years continued after World War II as well. Even a work such as Arnold Schoenberg's *A Survivor from Warsaw* (1947)—though ensounding the survivor's experience of trauma—was, in the end, a musical memorial to those who perished in the Warsaw ghetto at German hands.[60] Performing commemoration musically also engenders silence, for such performances decide whose and what form of trauma is worthy to be remembered and whose suffering and death is excluded from any reckoning.

Notes

1. "Les notes, détachées l'une de l'autre, brisaient le cœur, arrachaient les entrailles." Commentary on Gossec's *Marche lugubre* in the *Révolutions de Paris*, April 1791, given in Frédéric Hellouin, *Gossec et la musique française à la fin du XVIIIe siècle* (Paris: Librarie A. Charles, 1903), 150. The public commemoration of the dead, with the dual intent to provide solace and forge national consensus, has a long history in the post-Enlightenment West. The cult of the revolutionary martyrs in France after 1789 translated monarchic and religious rites into civic ritual that could be either performative or frozen in time and space by way of monuments. See Joseph Clarke, *Commemorating the Dead in Revolutionary France: Revolution and Remembrance, 1789–1799* (Cambridge: Cambridge University Press, 2007).

2. For a discussion of ideological appropriation of battle commemoration and its musical reflections in the case of the battle of Marengo, see Stephanie Klauk, "Italienische Schlachtenmusiken zu Napoleon Bonaparte: Die Schlacht von Marengo," in *Music and War in Europe from French Revolution to WWI*, ed. Etienne Jardin (Turnhout: Brepols, 2016), 89–104. John Morgan O'Connell explores the issue in a thick description of musical and ceremonial commemorations of Gallipoli in *Commemorating Gallipoli through Music: Remembering and Forgetting* (Lanham, MD: Lexington Books, 2018).

3. For an extensive overview of musical works depicting battles, see Karin Schulin, *Musikalische Schlachtengemälde in der Zeit von 1756 bis 1815*, Eichstätter Abhandlungen zur Musikwissenschaft, vol. 3 (Tutzing: Schneider, 1986).

4. Mark Twain, *The Adventures of Huckleberry Finn*, chapter 17, http://www.gutenberg.org/files/76/old/orig76-h/p4.htm#c17. "The Last Link Is Broken" was a favorite parlor song by William Clifton (1859). Schulin makes the point that piano compositions depicting battles were part of the "Hausmusik" reper-

toire of the late eighteenth and nineteenth centuries. See Schulin, *Musikalische Schlachtengemälde,* 250–51.

5. Tim Dowling, "1812 Overture v The Lark Ascending—which best represents Brexit Britain?," *The Guardian,* April 3, 2018, https://www.theguardian.com/music/shortcuts/2018/apr/03/1812-overture-v-the-lark-ascending-which-best-represents-brexit-britain

6. Jonathan Kregor, "Disavowing the Instrumental Battle Piece," *Journal of Musicological Research* 34 (2015): 207.

7. Esteban Buch, "Vincent d'Indy et la Première Guerre mondiale: *Sinfonia Brevis de bello gallico,*" in *Vincent d'Indy et son temps,* ed. Manuela Schwartz (Sprimont: Mardaga, 2006), 21–36; Howard Pollack, *Marc Blitzstein: His Life, His Work, His World* (New York: Oxford University Press, 2012), 282–94.

8. On the musical centenary commemorations of the French Revolution, see Annegret Fauser, *Musical Encounters at the 1889 Paris World's Fair* (Rochester, NY: University of Rochester Press, 2005). On the centenary of Robert Burns, see Ann Rigney, "Burns 1859: Embodied Communities and Transnational Federation," in *Commemorating Writers in Nineteenth-Century Europe: Nation-Building and Centenary Fever,* ed. Joep Leerssen and Ann Rigney (Houndsmill, Basingstoke: Palgrave Macmillan, 2014), 40–64. For an overview of centenary celebration in the nineteenth century, see Roland Quinault, "The Cult of the Centenary, c.1784–1914," *Historical Research* 71 (1998): 303–23.

9. Edward Elgar, *The Spirit of England: Three Poems by Laurence Binyon, Set to Music for Tenor or Soprano, Chorus, and Orchestra* (London: Novello, 1917). The complete dedication reads: "My portion of this work, I dedicate to the memory of our glorious men, with a special thought for the WORCESTERS."

10. On the emergence of *The Spirit of England* as the emblematic piece for national commemoration by the BBC, see Rachel Cowgill, "Canonizing Remembrance: Music for Armistice Day at the BBC, 1922–7," *First World War Studies* 2 (2011): 75–107.

11. See Daniel M. Grimley, "'Music in the Midst of Desolation': Structures of Mourning in Elgar's *The Spirit of England,*" in *Elgar Studies,* ed. J. P. E. Harper-Scott and Julian Rushton (Cambridge: Cambridge University Press, 2007), 220–37.

12. Laurence Binyon, *Selected Poems* (New York: Macmillan, 1922), 77.

13. Frances Colvin, letter to Edward Elgar, May 8, 1916, cited in Rachel Cowgill, "Elgar's War Requiem," in *Edward Elgar and His World,* ed. Byron Adams (Princeton, NJ: Princeton University Press, 2007), 343.

14. For a discussion of these tropes, see Alexander Rehding, *Music and Monumentality: Commemoration and Wonderment in Nineteenth-Century Germany* (New York: Oxford University Press, 2009).

15. On Reger's *Requiem,* see Esteban Buch, "La Grande Guerre des musiciens: Composer pendant la guerre, composer avec la guerre," in *La Grande Guerre: Une histoire culturelle,* ed. Philippe Poirrier (Dijon: Editions Universitaires de Dijon, 2015), 133–54.

16. Michelle Meinhart, "Memory and Private Mourning in an English Country House: Lady Alda Hoare's Musical Shrine to a Lost Son," *Journal of Musicological Research* 33 (2014): 39–95. On French rituals of mourning in intimate music-

settings, see Jillian Rogers, "Ties That Bind: Mourning, and the Development of Intimacy and Alternative Kinship Networks in World War I–Era France," in Jardin, *Music and War*, 415–43.

17. Lady Alda Hoare, "Manuscript Diary, Nov. 1917–Feb. 1918," entry of January 18, 1918, cited in Meinhart, "Memory and Private Mourning," 40.

18. On the soundscapes of war and their acousmatic experience, see Martin Kaltenecker, "'What Scenes!—What Sounds!' Some Remarks on Soundscapes in War Times," in Jardin, *Music and War*, 3–27.

19. The silence after armistice and its cultural reflection form the focus of the following essay collection: *The Silent Morning: Culture and Memory after the Armistice*, ed. Trudi Tate and Kate Kennedy (Manchester: Manchester University Press, 2013). See also Esteban Buch, "Silences de la Grande Guerre," in *Entendre la Grande Guerre: Sons, musiques et silence en 14–18*, ed. Florence Grétreau (Paris: Gallimard, 2014), 128–33.

20. Theodor Körner, "Gebet während der Schlacht," in *Leyer und Schwerdt* (Berlin: Nicolaische Buchhandlung, 1814), 55–56. Körner's poem was reproduced on German postcards from World War I. A 1915 postcard showed, for instance, roaring cannons in the background with a soldier, in the foreground, deeply in prayer. See Sabine Giesbrecht, *Musik und Propaganda: Der Erste Weltkrieg im Spiegel deutscher Bildpostkarten*, Beiträge zur Medienästhetik der Musik, vol. 14 (Osnabrück: Electronic Publishing Osnabrück, 2014), 134–35. This postcard can be accessed at http://www.bildpostkarten.uos.de/displayimage.php?album=search&cat=0&pos=4

21. Walter Bloem, *Vormarsch* (1916), cited in Giesbrecht, *Musik und Propaganda*, 132: "daß dir der Schädel bersten will." On the new sonic experience of war after 1914, see also Carine Trevisan, "Le bruit de la guerre," in *La Grande Guerre des musiciens*, ed. Stéphane Audoin-Rouzeau, Esteban Buch, Myriam Chimènes, and Georgie Durosoir (Lyon: Symétrie, 2009), 5–15.

22. Cited in Nicholas Best, *The Greatest Day in History: How, on the Eleventh Hour on the Eleventh Day of the Eleventh Month, the First World War Finally Came to an End* (New York: Public Affairs, 2008), 225.

23. Aubrey Smith, *Four Years on the Western Front* (1922), cited in Best, *Greatest Day in History*, 227.

24. Deniz Ertan and William Brooks, "Modalities of Memorial: The Double Trauma of 1918 and Its Aftermaths," conference presentation, "Music, Nationalism and Transnationalism, Europe-Americas, 1918–1945: Diplomacy, Policy, Aesthetics," Royal Northern College, Manchester, November 23, 2016.

25. O'Connell, *Commemorating Gallipoli*, xxi.

26. Walter Benjamin (1936), cited in Anton Kaes, *Shell Shock Cinema: Weimar Culture and the Wounds of War* (Princeton, NJ: Princeton University Press, 2011), 1.

27. Jay Winter, "Thinking about Silence," in *Aftermath: Legacies and Memories of War in Europe, 1918—1945—1989*, ed. Nicholas Martin, Tim Houghton, and Pierre Purseigle (New York: Routledge, 2014), 187.

28. Julius Korngold (1916), quoted in translation in Blake Howe, "Paul Wittgenstein and the Performance of Disability," *Journal of Musicology* 27 (2010):

140. For a discussion of the trope of overcoming disability in performance, see Joseph N. Straus, *Extraordinary Measures: Disability in Music* (New York: Oxford University Press, 2011), 125–49.

29. Moses Smith (1934), cited in Howe, "Paul Wittgenstein," 141.

30. Cowgill, "Canonizing Remembrance," 86. George L. Mosse traces the origin of the myth of the "fallen soldier" that dominated commemorations in and after World War I back to the Revolutionary and Napoleonic Wars; see *Fallen Soldiers: Reshaping the Memory of World Wars* (New York: Oxford University Press, 1990), 9–10.

31. See, for example, Carol Poore, *Disability in Twentieth-Century German Culture* (Ann Arbor: University of Michigan Press, 2007), 1–66.

32. For an overview of various communities in the centenary celebrations, see Esteban Buch, *Beethoven's Ninth: A Political History*, trans. Richard Miller (Chicago: University of Chicago Press, 2003), 178–200.

33. Jindong Cai and Sheila Melvin, *Beethoven in China: How the Great Composer Became an Icon in the People's Republic* (Hong Kong: Penguin, 2015), 39.

34. Buch, *Beethoven's Ninth*, 178–200.

35. Buch, *Beethoven's Ninth*, 190.

36. On the complex intersection of Beethoven and disability, both in his own lifetime and in his reception, see Straus, *Extraordinary Measures*, 45–62. Blake Howe, Stephanie Jensen-Moulton, Neil Lerner, and Joseph Straus identify Beethoven as the archetypal model for the "heroic Overcomer" of disability: "Thus Beethoven is understood as a Heroic Overcomer—someone whose music and life represents a triumph over deafness." See their "Introduction: Disability Studies in Music, Music in Disability Studies," in *The Oxford Handbook of Music and Disability Studies*, ed. Blake Howe, Stephanie Jensen-Moulton, Neil Lerner, and Joseph Straus (New York: Oxford University Press, 2015), 4.

37. Adolphe Jullien, "Autour du centenaire de Beethoven," *Journal de débats*, March 27, 1927: "par 'autorisation spéciale et sous la présidence effective' de l'archevêque de Paris."

38. Louis Schneider, "La Messe solennelle de Beethoven," *Le Gaulois*, March 18, 1927: "C'était hier la première fois que la *Messe solennelle*, le sommet géant qui domine tous les chefs-d'œuvre de Beethoven, a pu être donnée dans une église, et quelle église!"

39. Charles Pichon, "Le centenaire de Beethoven and notre âme," *L'Echo de Paris*, March 18, 1927: "Elle est d'abord, dit-il, un hommage à la Beauté, une grande choses réalisée par la France ; elle fait honneur au pays qui a su discerner en elle un des joyaux du patrimoine commun de la Création. Mais aussi, elle évoque la grande existence, la grande âme de Beethoven, les douleurs et les drames d'une vie brisée, dont le génie n'a été compris que lorsqu'il s'est éteint, dont le génie n'a été compris que lorsqu'il s'est éteint, et le cœur, que lorsqu'il s'est glacé. . . . C'est du jour où le musicien se sentit scellé comme un cadavre dans le tombeau du silence, que naquit en lui le grand Beethoven intérieur et que toutes les harmonies rassemblées en son cœur se mirent à y chanter; jusque-là il n'avait écrit que de la 'musique'; dès lors, en des œuvres opiniâtres et gigantesques, il va écrire de la 'vie.'"

40. On the physical and medical repercussions of battle-sustained war injuries, see Andrew Bamji, *Faces from the Front: Harold Gillies, the Queen's Hospital, Sidcup and the Origins of Modern Plastic Surgery* (London: Helion and Company, 2017).

41. Stefan Goebel, "Re-membered and Re-mobilized: The 'Sleeping Dead' in Interwar Germany and Britain," *Journal of Contemporary History* 39 (2004): 474. In "Canonizing Remembrance," Cowgill provides an exploration of various musical programs performed and broadcast on Armistice Day in the United Kingdom.

42. Cited in Poore, *Disability*, 16.

43. Poore, *Disability*, 16.

44. Kaes, *Shell Shock Cinema*. For a discussion how shell shock affected the composition of a war veteran, see Beth Keyes, "'The Absurd Disordering of Notes': Dysfunctional Memory in the Post-traumatic Music of Ivor Gurney," in Howe et al., *Music and Disability Studies*, 447–75.

45. See Tammie Kernodle, "Having Her Say: The Blues as the Black Woman's Lament," in *Women's Voices Across Musical Worlds*, ed. Jane A. Bernstein (Boston: Northeastern University Press, 2003), 213–31.

46. Concert program, New York Philharmonic Orchestra, October 17, 1943, http://archives.nyphil.org. The discussion of the commemorative works commissioned by the League of Composers draws on and reframes the interpretation I offer in Annegret Fauser, *Sounds of War: Music in the United States during World War II* (New York: Oxford University Press, 2013), 227–39.

47. Bernard Herrmann, *For the Fallen* (New York: Broude Brothers, 1955), n.p.

48. William Grant Still, commentary in the concert program, New York Philharmonic Orchestra, January 5, 1944, http://archives.nyphil.org. For the score, see William Grant Still, *In Memoriam: The Colored Soldiers Who Died for Democracy* (Los Angeles: Delkas Music Publishing, 1943).

49. Still's turn to monumentality in commemorative compositions can be traced back to the nineteenth-century concepts discussed in Rehding, *Music and Monumentality*.

50. Still, commentary (1944).

51. For a short overview of the issues, see David M. Kennedy, *Freedom from Fear: The American People in Depression and War, 1929–1945* (New York: Oxford University Press, 2005), 760–76. On African Americans in the armed forces, see Bryan D. Booker, *African Americans in the United States Army in World War II* (Jefferson, NC. McFarland, 2008).

52. In an article for *Musical America*, Isabel Morse Jones paraphrased Still in terms that could be right out of the Double V campaign: "The present struggle for world democracy is closely bound, in Still's mind, with the struggle for democracy at home in which his race is engaged"; see Isabel Morse Jones, "Meet the Composer: (12) William Grant Still," *Musical America* 64 (December 25, 1944): 25.

53. Langston Hughes, "Brothers," typescript, September 1942, distributed by the Writers' War Board, title page, Library of Congress, Music Division,, Old Correspondence. In an article on the role of the boxer Joe Louis in promoting African American enlistment, Lauren Rebecca Sklaroff explores the vari-

ous cultural strategies employed by the Office of War Information and the War Department; see "Constructing G.I. Joe Louis: Cultural Solutions to the 'Negro Problem' during World War II," *Journal of American History* 89 (2002): 958–83.

54. Hughes, "Brothers," 6–8.

55. Nora Holt, "Still Still Impresses," *New York Amsterdam News*, January 22, 1944.

56. *Memorial to Lidice* was first performed in a concert of the New York Philharmonic Orchestra on October 28, 1943 at the occasion of the twenty-fifth anniversary of an independent Czechoslovakia. Martinů's *Memorial to Lidice* is among the composer's most frequently discussed compositions, especially in German musicology. See, among others, Peter Andraschke, "Bohuslav Martinů: Musik gegen Krieg und Zerstörung," in *Glasba in Družba v 20. Stoletju / Music and Society in the 20th Century. Ljubljana, Slovenske Konjice, 12.–15. V. 1998* (Ljubljana: Festival Ljubljana, 1999), 128–39; Stefan Hanheide, *Pace: Musik zwischen Krieg und Frieden—Vierzig Werkporträts* (Kassel: Bärenreiter, 2007), 164–68; Petra Richter, "A Music-Political Confession: Anmerkungen zu Martinů's *Memorial to Lidice*," *Czech Music* 3 (2008): 34–43; Klaus Döge, "Das entsetzliche Grauen zum Ausdruck gebracht: Anmerkungen zu Martinůs *Memorial to Lidice*," in *Bohuslav Martinů*, ed. Ulrich Tadday, *Musik-Konzepte Sonderband 2009* (Munich: Edition Text+Kritik, 2009), 78–91.

57. Döge, "Das entsetzliche Grauen." The remainder of this paragraph summarizes Döge's detailed, analytical findings.

58. Robert Bagar, "Memorial to Lidice," concert program, New York Philharmonic Orchestra, October 28, 1943, http://archives.nyphil.org. Martinů's was not the only musical work in the United States shaped by the events at Lidice. Two earlier compositions, George Antheil's Symphony no. 4, "1942," and Paul Creston's *Chant of 1942* responded to this massacre at least to some degree, though neither was shaped specifically as a musical memorial in the way Martinů's was. See Fauser, *Sounds of War*, 233.

59. Christopher Campo-Bowen, "'We Shall Remain Faithful': The Village Mode in Czech Opera, 1866–1928" (PhD dissertation, University of North Carolina at Chapel Hill, 2018), 17–19.

60. On Schoenberg's *A Survivor from Warsaw* and its complex history, see Joy H. Calico, *Arnold Schoenberg's "A Survivor from Warsaw" in Postwar Europe* (Berkeley: University of California Press, 2014).

TWO | Commemorating Performance, the Cabaretesque, and History Inside Out

PHILIP V. BOHLMAN

Prologue: Commemoration, Cornet, and Jo Cox

On June 16, 2016, the UK member of Parliament Jo Cox was assassinated upon leaving a public library in northern England, where she had been speaking with her Leeds constituency, arguing against the Brexit referendum, the vote by the United Kingdom to leave the European Union. The murder of a beloved MP—she was shot and then stabbed multiple times by fifty-three-year-old Thomas Mair, who claimed allegiance to far-right politics—traumatized the people of Leeds. On the following day, June 17, city officials responded to the public trauma by declaring a period of public commemoration in Leeds, beginning at 6:00 p.m. with a moment of citywide silence. Among the most public acts of commemoration would be a performance by two American musicians of a musical work created at another moment of trauma, Viktor Ullmann's *Die Weise von Liebe und Tod des Cornets Christoph Rilke* (*The Chronicle of Love and Death of the Flag-Bearer Christoph Rilke*; hereafter *Cornet*), a melodrama for dramatic speaker and piano, composed in the late summer of 1944 during the final months of Viktor Ullmann's life (1898–1944).

Cornet was itself a commemorative work, created in order to pursue the very possibility of commemoration: Rainer Maria Rilke's search for traces of Christoph Rilke, who fell in the European wars against the Ottoman Empire in the mid-seventeenth century, transformed by Viktor Ullmann into an allegory for love and death—for *Liebestod*—in the concentration camp at Terezín/Theresienstadt.[1] Ullmann did not live to complete the melodrama, leaving only sketches, now in the archives of the Paul Sacher Stiftung in Basel, Switzerland, before he was deported to the concentration camp at Auschwitz, where he was murdered upon his arrival, presumed to be October 18, 1944. The surviving fragments for the thirteen-scene melodrama allow multiple possibilities for performances that, in turn, augment the ways for giving renewed meaning to commemoration through performance itself. It was such renewal of meaning that the people of Leeds sought in the performance, however unexpected, yet welcomed, of Viktor Ullmann's *Cornet* on June 17, 2016 (Figure 2.1).

The Leeds commemoration of Jo Cox took place in one of the city's most public spaces, the Holy Trinity Church in the center of the city, and as a response to trauma—an immediate response to widespread, yet local trauma—Ullmann's melodrama fulfilled the shared need for mourning and commemoration. The performers on the evening of June 17, the author of this chapter as dramatic speaker and the pianist Christine Wilkie Bohlman, both of them faculty members of the University of Chicago, had not come to Leeds, however, to commemorate the life of Jo Cox, as the poster for the event makes clear, but rather to take part in a series of musical events in Leeds and York under the umbrella "Performing the Jewish Archive," a multiyear international project funded by the UK Arts and Humanities Research Council (AHRC) and based at the University of Leeds and the University of York, which is dedicated to recovering musical works lost to the Holocaust and restoring them for performances throughout the world. The concerts of this festival—the New Budapest Orpheum Society, a Jewish cabaret and ensemble-in-residence at the University of Chicago, performed the day before and the day afterward—were intensive acts of performing commemoration. None of those acts, however, could have been planned with foreknowledge of the city's trauma and its need for commemoration at that precise moment. It is as if the contexts for which they had been conceived and planned had been dislodged, moved from one instant of commemoration to another, responding critically to the immediate killing and the trauma that had brought it into being.

I begin the present chapter with the first of several reflections on moments in which one of the central themes in this book, "performing commemoration," might alternatively be transformed into a theme of "commemorating performance." Approaching the thematic threads that expand in counterpoint through the volume, I seek to turn them inside out and reconfigure them, thereby exposing their complex inter-

Figure 2.1. Poster for the performance of Viktor Ullmann, *Die Weise von Liebe und Tod des Cornets Christoph Rilke*, Leeds, June 17, 2016. Performing the Jewish Archive.

relatedness. From my personal role as a performer and scholar I also reflect on the ways in which new processes of history form around, and intersect with, the performance of commemoration. For some years now, musicians and music scholars alike have entered a period in which performance has become as much about performance as about anything else. The memory work that we bring to performance grows from explicit forms of agency—for example, those that express themselves in revival movements. As a mode of restoring repertories, historically informed performance has shifted from insisting on the authenticity of the past to striving for renewal in the present through the commemorative power of the act of performance itself. The response and responsiveness of performance to trauma, perhaps the most profound human experience necessitating commemoration, have themselves become increasingly complex.

The contrapuntal voices I follow through this chapter take several additional forms, primarily three. Subject and object are reversed, such that performance takes the place of commemoration as the product that follows from the acts that respond to trauma. Inside and outside are inverted. History and narrative, too, are turned inside out. These acts of inversion constitute what I call in my work as both scholar and performer "the cabaretesque."[2]

Second, I turn the capacity of the cabaretesque to invert my subject and object—performing and commemorating—toward the broader context that trauma provides for the themes of commemoration in this volume. In particular, I look at the different ways in which trauma stands in various relations to dream, that is, *Traum,* which I shall largely use in German, more for musical than psychoanalytical reasons. *Traum* and trauma provide me with an analytical, and reflective, pair, inside and outside in flux, mirrored, apposite and opposite. *Traum* and trauma, moreover, proffer a complementary pair for my own work as a performer, thematically linking projects I undertake as artistic director of the New Budapest Orpheum Society (NBOS).[3]

Third, uncharacteristically and somewhat uncomfortably, I take my own work as a cabaret musician as the impetus for the ways I approach the commemoration of performance. The scenes I construct, therefore, coalesce around the ways in which performance and commemoration are both codependent and destabilizing. They force my fellow cabaret players and me in the NBOS to question the limits of reality and reenactment, the ownership of past and present, response and responsibility. Accordingly, I question the ways in which commemorative agency lies both within and without the cabaretesque, even and especially at the moments of trauma when it arises unexpectedly, as on June 17, 2016, in Leeds.

Act I: Commemorating Performance

Trauma, the narratives of commemoration so often claim, strips human experience of agency. Whether responding to death, to violence and racism directed against humans because of their differences, or to the natural and unnatural acts that force human beings to flee their homes and families, those afflicted by trauma are the victims of actions beyond their control. Their response is reduced to the agentless silence of victimhood, the inability to cross the threshold of adequate expression. Silence envelops both object and subject as a totalizing condition of trauma. All that must be expressed remains inexpressible, trapped and immutable in the fear that further trauma is possible, if not immanent. Those who survive, follow, and remember must strive to unleash the voices of the silent, to enable them to be heard again, somehow transcending silence. Those who follow, not they themselves, are the only ones left to answer to the victimhood created through trauma, thereby turning commemoration into a moral imperative.

Performance and commemoration, when combined, are meant to restore some measure of the agency lost to trauma. The music of commemoration fills the void opened by trauma. Music resists trauma by insisting the voices it has silenced might be heard again, be allowed to speak again, if not for themselves, then through the commemoration of performance and performers. In different ways, those who survive and live with trauma are also able to experience the music of commemoration as a path toward expression upon which they are only tentatively able to embark. The silence of others is sounded by those left to perform commemoration. The performer seeks to recover what has been lost to trauma in its manifold forms, suturing the sonic shards of lives that are themselves irrecoverably lost in death or that survive only to live with the memory of racism, persecution, or violence enacted upon them. Music transforms silence into sound, perfectly through the illusion that performance again offers a moment of embodiment, however imperfect it must be.

Musicians and scholars dedicated to unleashing silenced voices through performance seek to resolve the imperfection at every stage of the commemorative acts they assemble. The search to resolve imperfection has been critical during the twenty-year history of the NBOS. In its earliest years, even before it had become a true ensemble with regular membership, the NBOS was largely concerned only with commemoration, offering a few works for chamber ensemble and vocalist to public libraries and synagogues as concerts of remembrance and rediscovery. The programs formed around composers—Viktor Ullmann, Pavel Haas (1899–1944), Gideon Klein (1999–1945), Hans Krása (1899–1944), among others—who had created significant works of music before incarceration and murder in the concentration camps of the Shoah. As the ensemble increasingly received invitations to perform for special occasions, conferences, or concert series in the Chicago area, it added to and diversified its repertory, plumbing the repertories of Jewish popular and political song from the end of the nineteenth century until the Shoah, expanding the languages in which it performed: two decades since its founding, the NBOS repertory regularly includes songs in eight languages—Hebrew, Yiddish, German, French, Czech, Russian, English, and Polish—as well as in their various dialects. As new languages, repertories, and contexts accrue through the concerts and recordings of the ensemble, so too does the sense that the search for commemoration through performance remains incomplete and thus must not cease.[4]

In search of the affordances of commemorating performance, the NBOS has joined with numerous partners during its twenty-year history. It has found many of its most willing collaborators in synagogues and Jewish cultural institutions. Its stages spread equally across universities and the venues more commonly associated with cabaret: concert settings enhanced by food, drink, and nostalgia. Certain performances take place annually—Reichskristallnacht on November 9, Yom HaShoah (Holocaust Remembrance Day) in April or May—for which commemoration gathers the voices of many others, solemnly woven into the chorus of performance. No less often, the NBOS imagines a new context for performance, joining forces with an academic or cultural event, perhaps a Chicago conference on the twentieth-century Romanian- and Hungarian-speaking Jewish composer György Ligeti ("Transylvania Transit—A Musical Journey through Modernism's Mirror," March 7, 2018) or a Berlin symposium on the history of documentary sound recording ("'Und sie blühen aus ihren Trümmern': Jüdische Lieder auf der Bühne des 20. Jahrhunderts," May 15, 2018). These vastly different sites for commemorating performance would at first glance seem paradoxical, as if the ensemble's raison d'être is a ceaseless search for what has passed in the present. Such paradox, however, may inevitably lie in the agency that couples commemoration and performance, an agency never lost upon my fellow musicians in the NBOS.

The restoration of agency through performance lies at the heart of the three-year project (2015–18) "Performing the Jewish Archive," generously funded by the AHRC.[5] The "Jewish archive" specified by the project's title is a space of trauma, constituted of musical works created by Jews in the twentieth century, overwhelmingly misplaced, neglected, or lost because of the Shoah. The enormity of this archive was scarcely fathomed, even by its organizers at the University of Leeds and the University of York or by participating scholars throughout the world engaged to fill the archive so that commemoration and performance might sound the voices of those previously silenced. Real libraries and archives have been opened, searched again and again for the fragments that might have slipped into an unrecognized crevice. Collections in far-flung and unexpected places were examined, revealing treasures great and small: the Yiddish songs hidden in a Helsinki attic during World War II; new songs written for Terezín operettas and stage works; cover songs, contrafacts, and cabaret forming a rich texture of music and narrative languishing in the virtual and material archives, waiting three-quarters of a century to be performed. These were among the archival works the NBOS adapted for the performances we brought to the project during June 2016 performances in the United Kingdom.

As "Performing the Jewish Archive" began to take shape and as silenced repertories from the past were sonically sutured, the NBOS was afforded agency as a sort of house band for the project. And as a house band—I deliberately use this rather crude designation of the ensemble that employed the means at its disposal to sound the recovered objects on various stages—we dedicated ourselves to performing the commemorative materials that the research team handed us. It was the ensemble's task to make the sketches, fragments, and anecdotal materials it received performable, so that they could serve the larger functions of commemoration.

There was no aspect of the materials that did not require transformation so that they could enter the archive of Jewish memory. Incomplete lyrics and melodies from oral tradition had to be reconstructed through comparison. Gaps were filled as lyrics without melodies were fitted with music implicit or explicit in eyewitness accounts or reviews of performances in a concentration camp. Harmonies were fitted to melodies and then subjected to improvisation before being transformed to arrangements that the eight-member ensemble could perform. The Yiddish dialects from Finland and Czechoslovakia were standardized according to the rules established by the YIVO Institute for Jewish Research, which provide the basis for performances from Yiddish repertories ranging from folk songs to Yiddish film music. As the NBOS artistic director, I translated lyrics in various directions—especially to the multiple languages in which we regularly perform—at each stage making the performances our own, but doing so to restore the agency necessary if commemoration were to ameliorate and resist trauma (Figure 2.2).

Figure 2.2. Poster for June 2016 UK performances of the New Budapest Orpheum Society. Performing the Jewish Archive.

Act II: The Cabaretesque

The cabaretesque forms around experimental moments, employing narrative structures that draw performance and commemoration together on the cabaret stage. As metaphor and genre, cabaret enjoys a long history. Jewish cabaret flourished on the fin de siècle stage, realizing the contact zone between Jewish migrants to the cosmopolitan culture of Europe's metropoles.[6] Jewish intellectuals, writers, and even composers turned to the cabaret stage so as to combine the old and the new in different ways, juxtaposing the popular and the political. Theodor Herzl introduced cabaret skits into his Zionist writings, and Arnold Schoenberg devoted two years to performing on Berlin cabaret stages while composing his 1902 *Brettl-Lieder*.[7] In the twenty-first century, David Grossman's novel *Sus eḥad nikhnas le-bar* (*A Horse Walks into a Bar*), a performative witnessing to trauma in modern Israel, takes place entirely on a cabaret stage.[8] In the modern history of film, it is hardly surprising that the first two sound films, *The Jazz Singer* (1927) and *Der blaue Engel* (1930), take the performance of music, extensively Jewish, on the cabaret stage as their primary subjects.

Over the course of recent years I have been drawing upon my practices as a cabaret performer to expand the theoretical dimensions and applications of the cabaretesque, and I seize the opportunity of the themes in the present volume to do so again. The first goal of my cabaretesque project has been definitional, in other words, establishing the cabaretesque as a musicological and dramatic concept that allows us to understand what it is that distinguishes cabaret and other intimate forms of performance as a genre for the stage. My second goal has been ontological, aesthetic, and political, seeking to recognize the cabaretesque for the ways it allows us to perceive cabaret in other forms and genres of expressive performance—theater, opera, film, ritual—that are not specifically or even primarily cabaret.

In order to theorize the cabaretesque, I draw upon Mikhail Bakhtin's well-known concept of the carnivalesque. The cabaretesque relates to, and distinguishes itself from, the carnivalesque in general and specific ways. I seek to relate the two concepts in textual, contextual, and historical ways. Bakhtin develops the concept of the carnivalesque by turning his concept of "heteroglossia" toward the period of carnival, in other words, the social realm created during Christian pre-Lenten festivities. The concept emerges most notably in Bakhtin's book *Rabelais and Folk Culture of the Middle Ages and Renaissance*, known usually as *Rabelais and*

His World.[9] The carnivalesque is by no means limited to carnival, with its Christian and pagan implications. Its social inversions occur no less in the musical and theatrical performance during the midwinter Jewish holiday of Purim, which commemorates the captivity of Jews in Persia. Purim draws upon the historical narrative for the book of Esther in the Hebrew Bible and generates the scenes set on the Jewish *Purimspiel* (Purim play), the medieval predecessor of what would become Jewish theater and cabaret.

The inversion that takes place during Carnival or on the stage of the *Purimspiel* depends on the performative enhancement of heteroglossia, to which I turn briefly to understand the ways it creates a theoretical connection to the cabaretesque. By heteroglossia, Bakhtin refers to two attributes in all forms of communication. First, there is the attribute of communication that is systematic, thus allowing an utterance to have a repeated and repeatable set of meanings for all who experience it. Second, the attribute of context is one that allows for extensive alteration of meaning. Heteroglossia means, then, that speech acts may mean what their fixed meanings state they mean, but in the same instance they have virtually unchecked additional and alternative meanings. I do not have to elaborate too much to make it clear that cabaret relies extensively on heteroglossia. In order for performers to bend meanings in a skit, they must have sufficient fixity to allow for malleability. The most serious of subjects, for example, may be turned inside out to trigger laughter in the audience. The interaction between fixity and malleability is crucial to the types of alteration and inversion of meaning that thrive in the carnivalesque and the cabaretesque—and in the relation between performance and commemoration.

By applying it to the performance of commemoration more broadly I extend my theoretical work on the cabaretesque to reveal specific meanings in the expressive forms and genres on the cabaret stage. In the performance contexts opened by the cabaretesque, the meanings of song multiply and their political potential grows. Cabaret song in even its most basic forms and functions possesses the repeatability of fixity in heteroglossia, for example, the traditional associations with contrafacts and cover versions of songs. Contrafacts and covers, however, must also be malleable, because fundamentally they are fitted to new texts that are able to distort meanings because of the recognition of an original melody. Again, we witness the function of the stage in distinguishing the cabaretesque from the carnivalesque. The audience has ownership of a stock of repeatable speech acts, for example, its distinctive dialect or accent. The audiences for Jewish cabaret in fin de siècle Europe generally brought some knowledge of Yiddish, as well as local dialects from immigrant neighborhoods, with them. The performers on the stage possess the skill to distort the songs, thus adapting them to constantly shifting subjectivities of their audiences. The distinction of the stage through the cabaretesque meant that the everyday world could be shifted from the world in which it took place and be recontextualized for the stage. Composers and lyricists who created works for the cabaret stage augment the potential for reframing the everyday, integrating it into the heteroglossic nature of the songs they create. When composing the songs for his *Hollywood Liederbuch* during his California exile during 1942–43, Hanns Eisler would deliberately assign new dates and local references to the lyrics he adapted from the poetry of Bertolt Brecht and others, investing the songs themselves with mobility and sharpening their immediate criticism of the conditions of war and persecution.[10] Songs that provided the stock in trade for the Jewish stage between the world wars quickly generated cover versions for the exile stage during the 1930s and 1940s.[11]

The cabaretesque as concept and theory extends beyond cabaret itself. It also extends the very concept of cabaret, creating new narrative spaces for the convergence of performance and commemoration. It is in these spaces that the audience witnessing performance recognizes itself projected by memory, the stories of pasts familiar, fragments of which they may or may not understand as their own. The cabaretesque locates music in time and place, in the worlds, both real and imaginary, that are inhabited by human beings and communities. The moment of ontology emerges when the cabaretesque provides the coordinates—the specific signs—that tell us where we are. These are the markers of the broadside ballad from northern Europe or the Spanish *romance* from the western Mediterranean and the Ladino *romance* displaced across the Sephardic diaspora. In its ontological specificity, the cabaretesque borrows much from ritual, but it also dislodges music from ritual, especially through the transformation from oral tradition to written tradition. This transformation has further ontological implications, for it creates physical forms of printed or recorded song that circulate within physical spaces, the street in early modern Europe, or across village India in the audiocassette culture of the late twentieth century. The specificity is also crucial when a song formed from cabaretesque transformation appears on the stage. Time and place are again presented in detail, and those who appear upon the stage themselves have a physical presence. The details of time and place may not themselves represent real time and place, but rather they are often metaphor and allegory. The cabaretesque, nonetheless, makes us sense them as real, as if they might well be ours.

Act III: Allegories of Self and Other

There are historical implications for the ways and moments in which the cabaretesque emerges from the carnivalesque. The cabaretesque is already incipient in medieval mystery plays from the Bakhtinian world of Rabelais, not least in the ways in which acting troupes move the stage from place to place. More specifically in Jewish tradition, it is the cabaretesque that turns the medieval *Purimspiel* into a means of reconfiguring tradition in early modern Europe. The history of the *Purimspiel* expands across the historical, sectarian, and linguistic borders of modern Jewish experience, for example, into the French Sephardic traditions that underlie Darius Milhaud's Jewish works, among them his *Esther de Carpentras* (1938).[12] The same transformation is at work in Italian commedia dell'arte in later centuries, which also relies on the mobility of the acting and singing troupes, with their heteroglossic mixture of fixed and malleable characters. Yiddish theater, which itself borders on cabaret and historically acts as a predecessor to musical theater and the film musical, relies on the mobility of theatrical and musical troupes during the renaissance of Yiddish literature and the golden age of Yiddish and Jewish film music. In my South Asian research, I find the cabaretesque in the ways Bāul singers from West Bengal and Bangladesh turn pilgrimage songs and *bhajans* on their heads, undoing the religious tensions between Hindus and Muslims.[13] In similar ways, it was the Bene Israel, a diaspora Jewish community of some two millennia in western India, that reimagined the Hindu *kirtan* as Jewish in the late nineteenth century, just as the Bene Israel were performing at increasingly intense levels as theater musicians on the Marathi-language stages of Maharashtra state in India.[14]

As the Jewish musical theater and stage spread internationally after World War I, new narrative forms of cabaretesque responded to the allegory of exile and diaspora, transforming the historical into the modern. *Der Purimshpiler* (generally glossed as *The Jester*, literally "The Purim Actor") was one among many fine Yiddish films shot during the brief but remarkable era of Yiddish film, which began in the early 1930s, flourished in Eastern Europe—especially the Yiddish film studios of Poland—until the eve of the Shoah, continued into the 1940s by relocating largely to New York, but finally declined, at least for the stage genres dependent on the Yiddish language.[15] Like many of the films that Joseph Green and other directors of this period of efflorescence created, *Der Purimshpiler* was the product of intensive triangulation and the mobility made possible by modernity. The film was shot largely in Warsaw's Yiddish studios. Many of the actors (in this case, Green, the director) came from the United States, where they had enjoyed success on the Yiddish stage in the growing metropoles, especially New York City. The majority of the orchestral musicians were engaged from orchestral and operetta ensembles in Central Europe, especially Vienna. The genres of music, theater, and film that converge in *Der Purimshpiler* almost defy reduction to one or several traditions. It is Yiddish musical theater at some levels, and it is a *Purimspiel* itself at many others.

The main characters in the musical film, Getzel and Esther, are at once biblical and modern figures. A cobbler's daughter in the film, Esther is the eponymous Queen Esther in the Purim story, while Getzel enacts the role of Ahasver, whose dual role locates him in the Purim narrative and historically follows him wandering endlessly through the diaspora. They are also contemporary figures of diaspora in Eastern Europe and the narrative of the modern journey from rural shtetl to urban ghetto. Esther ultimately escapes the shtetl to become a singing star on the stage of the big city; Getzel fails to escape the shtetl, returning instead to assume his role as a Purim actor on the stage of the past. The triangulation of the film's production is made possible because of the contextual transformation through the cabaretesque, which in turn runs parallel to the ways in which music takes different forms. *Der Purimshpiler* depends on a long tradition of juxtaposing performance—the folk tradition of the *Purimspiel*—and commemoration—remembering the trauma of Jewish exile. The audience really does see Yiddish musical theater on the screen, and it really does witness the cabaretesque as closely as possible in its indebtedness to the carnivalesque at the moment when a traveling theatrical troupe enters the shtetl and performs a *Purimspiel* on the screen.

The cabaretesque in modern Jewish music in Eastern Europe, therefore, often unfolds through narratives of individual lives or of the real-life dilemmas confronted by Jewish communities. The ballads that traveled from European Jewish villages to the metropoles of nineteenth-century empires chronicled the journeys and financial dilemmas with uncanny detail, always to make the life narratives come alive. The marketplace in Trnva, Nagyvárad/Großwardein (Oradea in modern Romania), or Iași was recognizable and even familiar because of its representation in song. In the popular songs for the cabaret stage, places have names, as do the characters who inhabit them. The familiarity of such cabaretesque specificity partially accounts for the ways in which popular songs for the Jewish stage circulated, occasionally as individual hit songs.

For the Viennese *Kleinkunstbühne* (stage for more intimate art forms), few songs illustrate the journey from the local to the global, the self to the other, better than Gustav Pick's 1885 "Wiener Fiakerlied" ("Viennese Coachman's Song"; see Figure 2.3). The life of the coachman in the most popular song of fin de siècle Europe, indeed, in much of the world at the beginning of the twentieth century, allegorically followed Gustav Pick's own life journey from the "Sheva Kehillot" (Seven Holy Cities) of the Austrian-Hungarian border through the streets of Vienna. Gustav Pick (1832–1921) was himself a symbolic composite of both the composer and the coachman in the song. The lyrics narrate the coachman's life in the city dialect of Viennese German, unfolding across the verses of the song and following his everyday labors as they accommodated the wealthy in the center of Vienna until the last journey to his final resting place at the city's periphery.

GUSTAV PICK, "WIENER FIAKERLIED" (1885)
OPENING OF VERSE 1, CLOSING OF VERSE 8

1. I fuhr' zwa harbe Rappen, Mein Zeug dös steht am Grab'n, A so wie dö zwa trappen Wer'ns net viel g'sehen hab'n.	1. I'm in command of two fine horses, My coach stands on the Graben, Two customers were riding along, But they see hardly anything at all.
8. Dös is' a "Muass," dos Umziag'n In's allerletzte Haus, Und d'Leut', do solln's mirken, An Fiaka führt ma' n'aus. Und auf mein' Grabstein da soll steh'n, Damit 's die Leut' a deutli' seh'n: Sei' Stolz war, er war halt an echt' Weanakind.	8. It's something all "must do," taking The journey to the final resting place, And all the people should take note, That it's a coach bearing me along. And on the gravestone should be written, So that all can plainly read: His pride was to be truly a child of Vienna.

Gustav Pick's Jewish life appeared in dozens of translations and hundreds of contrafacts and cover versions worldwide, making the coach-

Figure 2.3. Gustav Pick, "Wiener Fiakerlied" ("Viennese Coachman's Song"), cover of published sheet music. Source: Original sheet music. Hamburg: Verlag August Cranz, 1885.

man a universal symbol of the marginalized at the end of the long nineteenth century, even in the poetry of Hugo von Hofmannsthal, whose "Fiakerlied" contrafact appeared within seven years of Pick's popular song. Hofmannsthal, too, captured the sense of allegory afforded to Pick's song of a single coachman in Vienna. He called his anecdotally brief version a "song of life," its cynicism rich with images increasingly thriving through performance on the cabaret stage.

HUGO VON HOFMANNSTHAL, "LEBENSLIED" ("SONG OF LIFE") (1892)

Den Erben laß verschwenden	An eagle, lamb, and peacock
An Adler, Lamm und Pfau	Squander their fortune,
Das Salböl aus den Händen	The ointment from the hands
Der toten alten Frau!	Of the dying old woman!

Act IV: *Traum* and Trauma

LEO STRAUSS, "EINLADUNG" ("INVITATION")[16]

Liebe Freunde, laßt Euch sagen,	Dear friends, just for a moment tell yourself,
Geht was nicht nach Eurem Sinn,	That everything may not be as you think it is,
Wills daheim Euch nicht behagen—	If it's not as cozy at home as it might be—
Kommt hierher, wo ich jetzt bin.	Then come on in, just join me for a while.
Kränken Euch die Alltagssorgen,	If everyday worries are wearing you down,
Reicht das Wasser bis zum Kinn—	If you can barely keep your head above water—
Hier seid Ihr davor geborgen,	Here, you'll find a safe haven from all that,
Kommt hierher, wo ich jetzt bin.	So come on in, just join me for a while.
. . .	. . .
Wollt Ihr ins Kaffeehaus gehen,	If you want to visit the coffeehouse,
Ziehts zum Cabaret Euch hin,	If the cabaret might be your thing,
Wollt Ihr's Strauß-Ensemble sehen,	If you'd like to see the Strauss Ensemble performing,

Kommt hierher, wo ich jetzt bin.	Come on in, we're at your service.
Alle Sorgen sind vertrieben,	All your cares will disappear,
Hier an diesem schönen Fleck—	Here, in this beautiful little space—
Und nur eine ist geblieben,	But you need to keep one thing in mind,
Wie kommt man hier wieder weg.	Just how you can get out of here.

How remarkable—and how ironic—it is to realize that cabaret and other forms of music and theater performed on the *Kleinkunstbühne* found homes in the concentration camps and ghettos of the Shoah. At the sites of enormous suffering and tragedy, there were stages on which diverse forms of entertainment took place, some lighthearted, some profoundly serious, most a mixture from both. Cabaretesque musical performance assumed different forms in different settings and at different moments throughout the course of the Shoah, sometimes tolerated, even encouraged, at other times confined and censored. The differences between one camp or ghetto and others were enormous—as many as nine cabarets were active in Terezín, whereas the musical life of prisoners in Auschwitz at many moments only barely survived, as we know from accounts about the women's orchestra.[17] Traces from the performances on such stages do survive, even in films made during the Shoah itself, for instance *Der Führer schenkt den Juden eine Stadt* (1944).[18] Such evidence only complicates the ways in which we understand the irony of the cabaretesque as the commemoration of a moment of survival, the conclusion of which can only be forestalled through performance.

At the moment of survival, the cabaretesque strives to hold on to that which is most precious in the past, transforming it to the afterlife of memory through performance. Musically, as we witness in the traces of performance from the Shoah, the cabaretesque has neither authentic beginning nor final ending, for the performer relies on many versions and variants to weave fragments and contrafacts alike together. The musician plays in order to play again. If it is silence that lies beyond the end, singing the final verse provides no viable option. The cabaretesque contains no other option than beginning anew, where one left off. The cabaret stage becomes a metaphorical space of mirrors, the sounding and resounding of reprise and refrain. The metaphorical mirror in the cabaretesque also shapes the ways in which nothing is really what it seems to be. The cabaretesque, thus, engenders parody, and it creates the illusions that allow the audience to believe it is possible to enter alternative worlds—"so come on in, just join me for a while."

It is with the complex possibilities for return that we begin to trace the path of the cabaretesque to Jewish music and its capacity to commemorate, not least as an art and a sacred goal of survival. Among the arts, music most religiously commands that it take place in time, with return crucial to the resilient sounding of meaning. When music ceases, some measure of time is lost. Forestalling the end of time in many ways justifies the unending quality of ritual. To represent the enjoinder to survive, ritual must re-sound. So it is with the Torah, the Five Books of Moses forming the epic cycle at the beginning of the Tanach, which approaches its end in "D'varim," in the fifth book of Moses, or Deuteronomy, only to begin again, Be-Reshit (the book of Genesis, lit.: "In the Beginning"), with the holiday of Simchat Torah.

The moments of performance in the Shoah reveal that survival, too, is distorted through the mirror of the cabaretesque. Survival assumes many forms, and the cabaretesque embeds each of these in music, surely not least through the performance of Jewish music. Leo Strauss's "Invitation," which provides the performative epigraph for Act IV, inviting the audience at the Strauss Ensemble's cabaret, the "Literarisches Strauss Brettl," in Terezín to join the performers on the safe space of the stage (Figure 2.4). Leo Strauss (1897–1944), son of the distinguished operetta composer Oscar Strauss, was one of the best known of the cabaret musicians in Terezín, and his cabaret provided a venue for performance of all kinds. Entering the world of the cabaretesque, the safe space of performance becomes also a moment of survival, in which inside and outside are inverted. In that moment, self becomes other, other becomes self. The world on the stage is made to appear as if it were everyday, albeit with reflections and shadows that change the ways we perceive it. The text of "Invitation," however, does not blind those who witness the performance on the Strauss Ensemble's stage, for it too must invert inside and outside, failing to delay return to the world of death that lies beyond the stage, the concentration camp itself. The cabaret is itself an intimate space, where the self and other explore their intimacy through the interplay of darkness and light, that which is hidden, and that which is revealed. Revelation and reflection, thus, become one when the cabaretesque becomes the mirror through which the spectator and listener see themselves as others, cohabitants of worlds turned inside out.

Through performance we arrive at the cabaretesque moment that

Figure 2.4. Playbill for the "Literarisches Strauss Brettl," Terezín/Theresienstadt. Source Lisa Peschel, ed., *Performing Captivity, Performing Escape: Cabarets and Plays from the Terezín/Theresienstadt Ghetto* (Kolkata: Seagull, 2014). Original: ca. 1943.

lies beyond exile and survival, which refocuses the mirrors on commemoration and belies eschatological finality. We arrive at the cabaretesque moment that is replete with life, with the regenerative force of salvation or soteriology, the capacity to return and recover meaning after trauma. The cabaretesque invests music with the power to re-sound and live again, to shape the path of return. Salvation provides a means of theological understanding of all that lies beyond the end of things. In music, it is profoundly cabaretesque in its dimensions, for it charts the ways in which song sustains life in its many forms. At the moment of salvation, the performance of commemoration sustains the future by embodying the very processes of return that it might previously have only represented.

Act V: Afterlives of Performance—Revival, Reenactment, Remembrance

Commemoration, like all acts of memory, is selective and incomplete, all the more so when it gives life to the past through performance. Scholars of memory studies identify many reasons for the selectivity of memory: the desire to relive cherished memories from a golden past; the erasure of pain associated with a traumatic past; the varied forms of nostalgia that lead us to think time past was preferable to time present.[19] If such passive-voice selectivity shapes memory, commemoration is no less the product of active-voice encounter with the past: the acts of inventing a past that might have existed had it followed a different path; the loss of details through translation; the pure fiction that remakes the past as those in the present may prefer to remember it. For all these reasons and more, gaps appear in memory, and they become larger over time, threatening to spread until memory itself fades into more complete loss.

Commemoration provides the social and moral antidote to such loss, ensuring through performance that the gaps in memory are repeatedly filled again. The performances that fill memory's gaps, however, are themselves also selective, sometimes borrowing memory as experienced by those witnessing the past, at other times invented for those for whom witnessing the past is all but impossible. Performing commemoration, thus, is one of the most extensive forms of what Marianne Hirsch has called "postmemory," in which we witness past lives in the present so they may fulfill the narrative and moral goals we wish them to have (see also Lillian Wohl's essay in this volume). Searching for the past of Czernowitz/Chernivtsi, the previously Habsburg city and twenty-first-century Ukrainian city in which her Jewish family had lived but she herself had never known, she relied on such postmemory, allowing her to imagine the Jewish culture of a great imperial border city through its afterlife.

> My "memory" of Czernowitz, I concluded, is a "postmemory." Mediated by the stories, images, and behaviors among which I grew up, it never added up to a complete picture or linear tale. Its power to overshadow my own memories derives precisely from the layers—both positive and negative—that have been passed down to me unintegrated, conflicting, fragmented, dispersed.[20]

Postmemorial commemoration has long shaped the afterlives of Jewish life in East Central Europe and Eastern Europe, especially so during the decades since the trauma and destruction of the Shoah. Already in the nineteenth century, the afterlives of Jewish Eastern Europe spread across an identifiable geography of small, impoverished but tradition-bound villages, or shtetls. By the twentieth century, modernity brought both pogroms and economic change, mobilizing many shtetl-dwellers to leave traditional life for the city, whether the "ghettos" of Central Europe or the opportunities of the Americas.[21] Already before the Shoah, but during the era of modernization, urbanization, and emancipation for European Jews, these previous lives became the stuff of musical performance. Songbooks gathering "songs of the ghettos" provided a global soundtrack for the past (Figure 2.5).

Postmemorial performance, furthermore, takes many forms—indeed, as it does in the chapters that fill the present book—because the task of commemoration is profoundly linked to death. If commemoration becomes the response of the living, it is also they who are charged with the challenge of performance. Through performance they employ the metaphors of life and death in order to use the former to overcome the latter, at least for the moment of performance. Death haunts the ways in which commemoration takes place. It is necessary to "revive" music—to give it life again, after death—in order that it can have an afterlife. To remember through music, it is necessary to "re-member" the fragments and shards of music once belonging to those silenced through death. Postmemorial performance lives through the repetitive acts of commemoration—etymologically, sharing memories

Figure 2.5. The cover for the best-known and most widely distributed collection of Yiddish songs, Morris Rosenfeld's *Lieder des Ghetto* (1902), which was lavishly illustrated by E. M. Lilien. Source: Morris Rosenfeld, *Lieder des Ghetto*, trans. Berthold Feiwel, 6th printing (Berlin: Hermann Seemann).

that others, too, possess—in order to forestall the death to which afterlife could fall victim as well. Therein lies the paradox of commemorating performance.

Epilogue: Return Performance

Over the course of the twenty years during which the New Budapest Orpheum Society has gathered the memories of survivors and searched for traces of surviving musical material from the Shoah, my musician colleagues and I have performed commemoration throughout the world. The present chapter has itself undergone new versions, following each new performance in recent years, whether in Leeds, New York City, or Berlin. With each revision—with each search for deeper meaning—my writing turns increasingly toward my own subject position as a scholar and musician performing commemoration. For me, too, the direction in which this chapter has taken me intensifies the sense of paradox. I opened the chapter by reflecting on the ways in which Viktor Ullmann's melodrama on Rainer Maria Rilke's *Die Weise von Liebe und Tod des Cornets Christoph Rilke* moved from the history narrated by its own text and the context of its composition in a concentration camp to accommodate the immediate need for commemoration following trauma in 2016 in the city of Leeds. I close by moving in the opposite direction, from outside to inside history, by looking at the meanings of performance and commemoration we find in the melodrama itself. Questions of time and history are everywhere in *Cornet*, proliferating yet entangled in a counterpoint born of fragments signifying moments of both eschatology and soteriology, the end and the return of time.

In contrast to the way in which the performance by Christine Wilkie Bohlman and myself of *Cornet* shifted to a historical moment in Leeds that the poet and composer could not have known, the work itself still calls attention to its own time—calling forth *Traum* and trauma—from beginning to end. The very first text the narrator speaks performs an act of commemoration, locating the melodrama in history, with the opening gesture marking the final act of Christoph Rilke's love and death: "On November 24, 1663, Otto von Rilke of Langenau, Gränitz, and Ziegra of Linda was placed in charge of the estate left by his brother, Christoph, who had fallen in battle in Hungary."[22] As the Habsburg imperial army moves into Eastern Europe in the wake of the Thirty Years War and on the threshold of European battle against the Ottoman Empire, dream constantly interrupts the unfolding trauma: Part II, scene 3 begins thus: "One of the soldiers, wearing white silk, realizes that he cannot awaken, for he's already awake and confused by reality. So he flees with fear into the dream and stands in the park, alone in the black park."[23] Time returns again to close the melodrama, also to signify the very finiteness of the eschatological moment at the end of Viktor Ullmann's allegorical existence in the concentration camp. Time collapses, as does the very possibility of commemorating trauma. Concluding the sketches on September 27, 1944, noting it as his sister's birthday, Ullmann fully realized there would be no performance in the days remaining before his deportation to Auschwitz on October 18.

The utter fullness of trauma at this moment of ending and beginning is staggering. Commemoration survives, but only as afterlife, at once sustained and forestalled through performance. *Traum* and trauma become one; history and time are inverted, as are performance and commemoration. It is to commemorate the return performance of that afterlife once again that I close this chapter not with my own words, but rather with those of Victor Ullmann, who was also a poet of considerable accomplishment. It is only fitting that he be allowed to draw time and music, in the shared counterpoint of performance, commemoration, and trauma, toward the end they also share:

VIKTOR ULLMANN, "DER TIEFSTE SCHMERZ KANN ZU MUSIK NICHT WERDEN"

("THE DEEPEST PAIN CANNOT BECOME MUSIC")

Der tiefste Schmerz kann zu Musik nicht werden,	The deepest pain cannot become music,
ihn prägt kein Wort,	No word alters that pain,
er bildet Form nicht aus dem Stein der Erden—	It does not assume its shape from the rock of the earth—
er schweigt umflort.	It remains in muffled silence.
So stumme Trauer um die trauernd Stumme,	Thus, I bear silent sadness about the saddening silence
die ich versäumt,	that I missed,
trag' ich und schweige sie, daß sie nur summe,	And it is silent, that it only hums
was ich geträumt.	what I dreamed.
Der tiefste Schmerz ist nicht zurück zu können	The deepest pain cannot go back
in ferne Zeit,	into distant time,

es schlug die Wunden, die nun tödlich brennen,	It strikes the wounds, which now deadly burn:
Vergangenheit![24]	It has passed!

Notes

1. For a published piano-vocal score, see Viktor Ullmann, *Die Weise von Liebe und Tod des Cornets Christoph Rilke* (Mainz: Schott, 1995).

2. See, for example, Philip V. Bohlman, "How To Get Out of Here: Sounding Silence in the Jewish Cabaretesque," in "The Sound Issue," ed. Jonathan M. Hess and Laura S. Lieber, special issue, *AJS Perspectives,* Spring–Summer 2016, 20–21.

3. See, for example, New Budapest Orpheum Society, *Dancing on the Edge of a Volcano: Jewish Cabaret, Popular and Political Songs 1900–1945*, recorded at WFMT (Radio Station), Chicago, March 13–16, 2002, Cedille CDR 90000 065, 2002, compact disc; NBOS, Moments musicaux et modernes: *Jewish Modernism in Popular and Political Music,* accompanying compact disc for Philip V. Bohlman, ed., *Jewish Musical Modernism, Old and New* (Chicago: University of Chicago Press, 2008); NBOS, *Jewish Cabaret in Exile,* recorded at WFMT, Chicago, April 2–4, 2008, Cedille CDR 90000 110, 2008, compact disc; and NBOS, *As Dreams Fall Apart: The Golden Age of Jewish Stage and Film Music, 1925–1955*, recorded at WFMT, Chicago, March 10–14, 2014, Cedille CDR 90000 151, 2014, compact disc.

4. The ensemble has issued four recordings as of 2020, with two more planned; see New Budapest Orpheum Society, *Dancing on the Edge of a Volcano*; NBOS, Moments musicaux et modernes; NBOS, *Jewish Cabaret in Exile*; and NBOS, *As Dreams Fall Apart.*

5. See Performing the Jewish Archive (website), University of Leeds, 2018, http://ptja.leeds.ac.uk/

6. For a detailed study of Jewish cabaret in Vienna, see Philip V. Bohlman, "Auf der Bima / Auf der Bühne: Zur Emanzipation der jüdischen Popularmusik um die Jahrhundertwende in Wien," in *Vergleichend-systematische Musikwissenschaft: Beiträge zu Methode und Problematik der systematischen, ethnologischen und historischen Musikwissenschaft,* ed. Elisabeth T. Hilscher and Theophil Antonicek (Tutzing: Hans Schneider, 1994), 417–49.

7. See Theodor Herzl, "Im Speisewagen," in *Gesammelte zionistische Werke* (Berlin: Jüdischer Verlag, 1935), 5:421–35; and Arnold Schoenberg, *Brettl-Lieder* (Los Angeles: Belmont Music Publishers, 1970).

8. David Grossman, *Sus eḥad nikhnas le-bar* (Tel Aviv: Ha-Kibuts ha-me'uḥad, 2014).

9. Mikhail Bakhtin, *Rabelais and His World,* trans. Hélène Iswolsky (Bloomington: Indiana University Press, 1984).

10. Hanns Eisler, *Lieder für eine Singstimme und Klavier,* ed. Stephanie Eisler and Manfred Grabs (Leipzig: Deutscher Verlag für Musik, 1976); see also Andrea F. Bohlman and Philip V. Bohlman, "Uncovering Hanns Eisler's *Hollywood Liederbuch,*" *Danish Yearbook of Musicology* 35 (2007): 13–29.

11. For recordings of Jewish cabaret songs on the exile stage, see New Budapest Orpheum Society, *Jewish Cabaret in Exile.*

12. See Jennifer Walker, "Darius Milhaud, *Esther de Carpentras*, and the French Interwar Identity Crisis" (MA thesis, University of North Carolina at Chapel Hill, 2015).

13. See Bertie Kibreah, "Ensnare the Thief in the House of Wind: Negotiating Routes of Bāul-ness in Bangladesh," in *Resounding Transcendence: Transitions in Music, Religion, and Ritual*, ed. Jeffers Engelhardt and Philip V. Bohlman (New York: Oxford University Press, 2016), 29–42.

14. Compare Anna Schultz, "Performing Translation in Jewish India: Kirtan of the Bene Israel," in *That Thing Called Music: Essays in Honor of Bruno Nettl*, ed. Victoria Lindsay Levine and Philip V. Bohlman (Lanham, MD: Rowman and Littlefield, 2015), 56–72; and Philip V. Bohlman, "Dynamic Diasporas: 'The Song of Zion' in South Asia," in *Sounding Cities: Auditory Transformations in Berlin, Chicago, and Kolkata*, ed. Sebastian Klotz, Philip V. Bohlman, and Lars-Christian Koch (Berlin: LIT Verlag, 2018), 155–78.

15. See Joseph Green, *Der Purimshpieler* (1937; Teaneck, NJ: Ergo Media, 2002).

16. In Ulrike Migdal, *Und die Musik spielt dazu: Chansons und Satiren aus dem KZ Theresienstadt* (Munich: Piper, 1986), 61–63. The translations that appear throughout this chapter are those used in performance by Philip V. Bohlman and the New Budapest Orpheum Society in stage performances that accompany commemoration. Some translations serve as lyrics in the cover versions that express the cabaretesque, while others, such as "Invitation" and "The Deepest Pain Cannot Become Music," are used for the reading of poetry from the concentration camps.

17. Compare Fania Fénelon, *The Musicians of Auschwitz*, trans. Judith Landry (London: Sphere, 1976); and Anita Lasker-Wallfisch, *Inherit the Truth, 1939–1945: The Documented Experiences of a Survivor of Auschwitz and Belsen* (London: Giles de la Mare, 1996).

18. Compare Alain Resnais, dir., *Nuit et brouillard*, music by Hanns Eisler, production by Anatole Dauman (1955; New York: Criterion Collection, 2003).

19. Compare, for example, Aleida Assmann, *Shadows of Trauma: Memory and the Politics of Postwar Identity*, trans. Sarah Clift (New York: Fordham University Press, 2016); Marianne Hirsch and Leo Spitzer, *Ghosts of Home: The Afterlife of Czernowitz in Jewish Memory* (Berkeley: University of California Press, 2010); Eva Hoffman, *After Such Knowledge: Memory, History, and the Legacy of the Holocaust* (New York: Public Affairs, 2004); and Svetlana Boym, *The Future of Nostalgia* (New York: Basic Books, 2001).

20. Hirsch and Spitzer, *Ghosts of Home*, 9.

21. Compare Roman Vishniac, *Children of a Vanished World*, ed. Mara Vishniac Kohn and Miriam Hartman Flacks (Berkeley: University of California Press, 1999); and Philip V. Bohlman, "Jüdische Lebenswelten zwischen Utopie und Heterotopie, jüdische Musik zwischen Schtetl und Ghetto," *Lied und populäre Kultur / Song and Popular Culture: Jahrbuch des Deutschen Volksliedarchivs* 47 (2002): 25–54.

22. Rainer Maria Rilke, *Die Weise von Liebe und Tod des Cornets Christoph Rilke* (Leipzig: Insel, 1912), 3. Translation mine.

23. Rilke, *Die Weise,* 24.

24. *Viktor Ullmann—Materialien,* ed. Hans-Günter Klein (Hamburg: Von Bockel Verlag, 1992), 108.

THREE | Music Commemorating the Hiroshima and Nagasaki Bombings

NORIKO MANABE

How could music respond, let alone commemorate, an event like the atomic bombing of Hiroshima and Nagasaki—apocalyptic events that killed approximately 160,000 and 70,000 people, respectively, in the space of one year? The Committee for the Study of Music and the Hiroshima Bombing (Hiroshima to Ongaku Iinkai, hereafter "Hiroshima Music Committee") has counted about two thousand musical works that commemorate the bombing, most of which are by Japanese composers.[1] They represent a plethora of purposes: official commemoration, antiwar protest, children's education, and artistic response. They reflect a variety of styles, including Western classical, Japanese traditional, and popular music of many genres. They draw on many differing tones, from acquiescence to American power to horror and anger over nuclear destruction, sadness for the victims, or hopefulness for the future. Such a wide range of responses makes it difficult, if not impossible, to summarize this music.

Nonetheless, these pieces bear the traces of the constraints that define them. From 1945 to 1952, the Allied Occupation censored commentary that might have stirred up anti-American sentiment, and the descriptions of atomic bomb damage in particular were severely limited, curtailing any artistic output regarding these issues; only from the mid-1950s could anger about the bomb, or even detailed descriptions of it, be expressed. Furthermore, atomic bomb victims (*hibakusha*) tended to be silent about their experiences as a result of survivors' guilt and discrimination toward them; most hibakusha have never spoken about their experiences, and those who have often waited decades until they were ready to do so. Furthermore, cultural production on the atomic bomb was delegitimized in Japanese intellectual circles. Such forces discouraged the production of nuclear literature and music in Japan, which only became more abundant in the 1960s–1980s. Finally, the distinct social histories of Hiroshima and Nagasaki—the former a military city, and the latter a historical gateway to foreign influence—combined with the fact that the Nagasaki bombing disproportionately impacted the Catholic neighborhood of Urakami to prompt different responses and attitudes toward hibakusha. These conditions, which fluctuated over historical periods, have impacted prevailing political narratives, which in turn have prescribed cultural and musical responses.

A visitor to Hiroshima and Nagasaki in recent years finds a number of commemorative events around August 6 and 9. The centerpiece in both is the official ceremony that each city organizes, currently called *Hiroshima-shi genbaku shibotsusha irei shiki narabini heiwa kinen shiki* (Hiroshima Memorial Service for Atomic Bomb Victims and Ceremony Praying for Peace) and *Nagasaki genbaku gisei-sha irei heiwa kinen shikiten* (Nagasaki Atomic Bomb Victims' Memorial Peace Ceremony). Both last about an hour and include offerings of flowers, the ringing of bells, a moment of silence at the time the bomb exploded, the mayor's peace declaration, the release of doves, speeches from the prime minister and prefectural governor, and the singing of designated songs by choruses of citizens or students. Most of these practices have been in place since the cities took responsibility for organizing these ceremonies in 1947, for Hiroshima, and in 1948, for Nagasaki.[2] Despite such similarities, the Nagasaki ceremony of recent years has struck me as more political and participatory: the speakers' criticisms of the national government are sharper, the audience is more reactive, the protesters immediately outside the venue are more pointed, and the citizens sing more songs, with choruses of hibakusha and of children attending schools that had been obliterated by the bomb.[3] Most importantly, recent Nagasaki ceremonies feature testimony of firsthand experience by a hibakusha, which Hiroshima ceremonies do not have. In addition to the main ceremonies, both cities hold a multidenominational *ireisai* (memorial service to console the souls of the dead), ceremonies for various work and school groups, and a floating of lanterns in the river in the evening, all of which date back to the late 1940s. Separately, musical groups stage concerts of pieces associated with remembrance or peace; in 2019, various groups in Hiroshima held concerts featuring Ludwig van Beethoven's Ninth

Symphony, Gabriel Fauré's *Requiem*, and Gustav Mahler's *Resurrection Symphony*, while nonprofit organizations and individual musicians held free concerts and sing-alongs. Outside of the August anniversaries, concerts have been held featuring works about the bomb; to offer just two examples: a series of "No More Hiroshima" concerts were held in Hiroshima both in the 1980s and in recent years, while the Nagasaki Opera has performed its original opera *Inochi* (*Life*, 2013) in Nagasaki and Tokyo.

The vast majority of Japanese music about Hiroshima and Nagasaki consists of vocal works, many of which are meant to be sung by school or amateur choruses. This proportion seems natural, given the role of vocal music in Japanese social life before and after the war. Group singing had been an integral part of the curriculum in Japanese schools ever since songbooks were introduced by the Ministry of Education in 1881. Originally derived from American, British, and German folk songs and hymns, these school songs quickly came to be composed by the Japanese themselves; their style was adopted into songs for workplaces, railroads, colleges, and the military, so that songs in this form permeated life.[4] Group singing (minus the nationalist songs) continued to play a large part in social life after the war, contributing to the healing process; Sasamori Shigeko, who had been ostracized for her disfiguring keloid scars from the Hiroshima bomb, credited such singing for drawing her to Reverend Tanimoto's church, which reintegrated her into a community (interview with the author, New York, May 6, 2015).

How have sociopolitical circumstances of time and place colored the ways in which traumatic memory is processed and commemorated in music? This chapter explores these questions through a chronological sampling of Japanese vocal works on the Hiroshima and Nagasaki bombings. Many of these examples are songs sung in ceremonies, while the third section highlights two of the best-known Japanese classical works about the bomb. Despite the devastating impact of the bombs, as briefly described, nuclear experience and culture have been delegitimized through governmental, societal, psychological, and critical means, discouraging cultural output, particularly from hibakusha. Musical commemorations of the atomic bomb by Japanese composers reflect noticeable shifts in the way in which memory has been constructed over three time periods: in the immediate postwar period, during the Cold War, and since the fall of the Soviet Union.[5]

The Atomic Landscape, Survivors, and the Delegitimization of Hibakusha Expression

At 8:15 a.m. on August 6, 1945, the atomic bomb exploded over the center of a bustling city of three hundred thousand; it was not a "military base," as US president Truman claimed in his radio address to the American people. That morning, thousands of schoolchildren, including more than three hundred first-graders, had been mobilized to demolish buildings in downtown Hiroshima in order to create fire lanes that would minimize damage in case of firebombing, which had already leveled more than sixty Japanese cities.[6] These children, teenagers, and teachers, along with others working or living near the city center, were directly underneath the atomic blast. A sudden, blinding flash of light and a deafening boom were the only warnings they received before the nuclear blast violently flung their bodies and they lost consciousness. Thousands died on the spot, immediately carbonized. Others were badly burned, their skin peeling off, their eyeballs hanging out of their sockets, their clothes burned or blown off, their bodies covered in glass shards. The blast collapsed buildings, leaving people pinned underneath the debris of their homes, workplaces, schools, and temples. As fire blazed out of control and no one was left to help, they burned to death. Many more soon died of radiation sickness. Ninety-two percent of the buildings in Hiroshima were destroyed.[7]

Expressions about the humanitarian crisis caused by the atomic bomb were initially repressed, due both to US censorship during the Allied Occupation and to social and psychological factors experienced by the victims. While the international music audience has generally lauded non-Japanese works on the atomic bomb, Japanese works have remained in relative obscurity. The few atomic bomb-related cultural products that did come to light often met a hostile reception. These factors have led to a delegitimization of expression related to the atomic bomb, particularly the voices of its victims, the hibakusha.

Censorship by the Allied Occupation

In September 1945, scarcely a month following the devastation by the bombs, the Allied Occupation (1945–52) instituted a censorship apparatus in its General Headquarters (GHQ)—the Civil Censorship Detachment (CCD), which employed as many as six thousand people at its peak. As Yūko Shibata has argued, its aim was to control the flow of information in Japan so that the country could "be remade in the image of the Americans . . . [s]eparated from its own past, and from the developments of the world, until the transformation was accomplished."[8] In addition to censoring information, the GHQ promoted the Allied version of the war, which the Japanese media were obliged to present. Even after the dissolution of the CCD in late 1949, censorship continued in various forms until the end of the Occupation in 1952. All manner of public expression—including newspapers, magazines, books, radio, film, and plays—was subject to censorship, which controlled political content as much as information flow. Yet the existence of censorship was never publicly acknowledged, and it was taboo to talk about it.[9] As the hibakusha author Kurihara Sadako observed, authors were "not permitted even to leave traces indicating that the censors had deleted anything. All in the name of 'free speech.'"[10]

American censorship was particularly severe in the case of the atomic bomb. Silence on its devastation and consequences was imposed by press code in September 1945: indeed, no testimonies, photos, or reports related to the damage from the atomic bombs could be published in Japan. Ironically, the first widely distributed publication of hibakusha's eyewitness accounts was authored by an American—John Hersey's *Hiroshima* (1946), to which the *New Yorker* dedicated an entire issue.[11] The Americans confiscated documentary footage filmed by Japanese in Hiroshima and Nagasaki between August and December 1945. Even scientific reports about the blasts and radiation were withheld from the public, denying Japanese (and some American) scientists and physicians access to data, thus curtailing research on the bomb and hindering their ability to address the physical and emotional trauma of survivors.[12] The extent of the horror of the atomic bomb thus remained unknown to most Japanese until the end of the Occupation in 1952.

Testimonials by hibakusha rarely saw the light of day. Ubuki Satoru claims that in 1946, only three testimonies were printed, all by little-known publishers. Hersey's *Hiroshima*, published in the United States in August 1946, was not released in translation in Japan until 1949.[13] The censors warned some writers, like Kurihara Tadaichi, not to mention that the atomic bomb had long-lasting health effects.[14] As it became common knowledge that the atomic bomb was a taboo subject, rumors circulated that anyone who wrote about it would be court-martialed, sent to Okinawa, or put to death, and self-censorship became the norm.[15] Hara Tamiki's "Natsu no hana" ("Summer Flowers") had been submitted to the CCD in late 1945, but the work did not appear until June 1947 and did so in a relatively obscure journal. Ōta Yōko completed her memoir, *Shikabane no machi* (*City of Corpses*), in November 1945; it finally appeared in 1948 with one chapter eliminated not by the Occupation authorities but by the Japanese publisher, and only after an abrupt personal visit by a US intelligence officer.[16]

Impact on Hibakusha

This suppression of information on the atomic bomb served to invalidate the hibakusha's experiences and feelings. As Ran Zwigenberg points out, external censorship discouraged open expressions of grief and anger; it prevented hibakusha from sharing their experiences or feelings through writing or speech.[17] American censorship, moreover, enabled the establishment of a prescribed narrative of peace, renewal, and transformation that deliberately repressed anger toward the United States. The only way that people in Japan could speak about the destruction of the bomb was by connecting it with peace. In addition to external censorship, Hiroshima and Nagasaki society demanded that the hibakusha behave as dignified victims for the sake of peace, lest they be labeled as selfish or leftist.

Hibakusha were furthermore denied acknowledgment of any long-term medical and psychological effects from the bomb. American officials repeatedly claimed that the bomb had no aftereffects, stating in 1945, "All of those who are to die from the atomic bomb have already died," and in 1950 that survivors had "recovered completely from whatever aftereffects they experienced, and no noticeable aftereffects remain," despite ample evidence of radiation sickness and leukemia.[18] According to the psychologist Robert Lifton, the minimizing tone of such pronouncements made the hibakusha doubt that their physical suffering was real.[19] Meanwhile, hibakusha sought medical help from the Atomic Bomb Casualty Commission, which conducted medical research on them without supplying much treatment.[20]

The hibakusha were also deprived of any recognition of the effects of psychological trauma, as both the World Health Organization and Japanese psychiatry ignored their suffering from what later came to be acknowledged as post-traumatic stress disorder, and some American scholars actively minimized the long-term psychological impact of the bomb.[21] But as Lifton has explained, the hibakusha suffered psychological effects that he had also observed in Holocaust survivors, including death imprint, death guilt, psychic numbing, and the fear of contagion. The sudden saturation of death imagery that hibakusha had experienced left them with "an indelible image of the death encounter, an image more compelling than any drawn from prior or subsequent life experience."[22] Images of death persisted in their lives, their anxiety easily reactivated by any reminder of the bomb, from media reports or the anniversary to hot weather, flashes of light, or explosive noises. They suffered from survivor's guilt, often because they had survived by fleeing for their lives rather than helping trapped or injured family members or friends. The hibakusha were looked down upon as contagious due to their exposure to radiation, and they themselves felt tainted by death.[23] Many responded to these pressures by withdrawing into emotional numbness.[24]

These psychological effects left the hibakusha feeling isolated, particularly as censorship, both official and socially inflicted, prohibited them from discussing their stories in public. The feeling that only a survivor who had lived through the atomic bomb could truly understand their experience added to this sense of alienation, making it difficult for hibakusha to reach out to others.[25]

Most hibakusha retreated into silence. A Japanese psychologist specializing in hibakusha told me that only about one-tenth of them have ever told their survival stories and that many concealed their experience from their own families. Their silence was due not only to their unwillingness to recall such a horrific event but also the difficulty in finding the words to describe it, let alone the psychological recovery necessary to talk about it.[26] Furthermore, hibakusha faced discrimination from potential employers and marriage partners; the former presumed that their health was compromised, while the latter feared the taint of radiation. Many hibakusha remained silent on their status as survivors until they were retired or their youngest child was married.

If the atomic survivors themselves were tainted, so was artistic expression related to their experience. As Lifton has observed, writers and artists found it difficult to render an event so "historically sacred that recreating it in any form can be psychologically perceived as hubris by both artists and their audiences."[27] This "sacred historical truth" made it impossible for hibakusha writers like Ōta Yōko to write in a fictional mode; they felt compelled to write the truth.[28] This tendency spilled over into the other creative arts, such that artists mostly limited their output "to the memoir-novel, the documentary film, the realistic painting, and the structured musical 'accompaniment,' all of which seem[ed] relatively safe because they [sought] no alteration of the original subject matter."[29]

But their documentary style also opened these atomic-bomb works to a hostile reception, as they were not considered creative or aesthetically refined. Many Japanese critics refused to consider atomic-bomb writings as literature, which John Treat attributes partly to a shunning among literary circles of political and social themes in favor of lyrical, psychological, and individualistic ones that tended to fill the Japanese literary canon.[30] In 1953, the Hiroshima newspaper *Chūgoku shimbun* hosted a heated debate among writers and critics, among which the conservative writer Shijō Miyoko declared that atomic-bomb writing was not art, as it was created "accidentally," out of reflexive emotional responses, as opposed to naturalism, which in Japan had established the ideal of the personal novel.[31] In 1960, the hibakusha writer Kurihara Sadako accused the Hiroshima Literature Society of trying to purge Hiroshima literature of the bomb in favor of more "genuine" themes. In 1982, novelist Nakagami Kenji and critics Karatani Kōjin and Kawamura Jirō dismissed Nagasaki hibakusha author Hayashi Kyōko as an "atomic fascist" for thinking that "merely writing about atomic bombings achieves something literary."[32] To this day, many of the atomic-bomb writers remain relatively marginal in the Japanese literary canon.

While Japanese atomic culture has been relatively marginalized, some of the best-known works on the atomic bomb have been by non-Japanese. John Hersey's *Hiroshima* is better known than the works of Ōta Yōko or Nagai Takashi; *Hiroshima mon amour* is more familiar than the Japanese films whose clips it uses, uncited; and Krzysztof Penderecki's *Threnody for the Victims of Hiroshima* is more celebrated than the atomic-bomb cantatas by Hayashi Hikaru or Ōki Masao, even though Penderecki added the Hiroshima reference as an afterthought.[33]

Indeed, issues of marginalization have impacted Japanese music about the atomic bomb, as many of these works were written in conjunction with atomic-bomb literature, film, or visual art. Numerous commemorative compositions are vocal or choral, using hibakusha poetry for lyrics, and as such, the concert works tend to use musical tropes that depict fire, water, deathly silence, and other scenes that frequently occur in hibakusha poetry. Such music is likely to strike non-Japanese listeners as an extension of preexisting formulas rather than revolutionary in musical style. Hibakusha composers also faced psychological barriers to writing music about the atomic bomb. When Kawasaki Masaru, a Hiroshima hibakusha and composer, was asked to write a piece for the annual commemoration, he initially refused, saying that he did not want his music inspired by such a deadly event and that he did not want to be seen as selling his hibakusha status.[34] He eventually acquiesced, composing *Inori no kyoku dai ichi: Aitōka* (*Prayer Song No. 1: Condolence*, 1975), an instrumental piece that has been played at the annual official commemoration ceremony every year since then. Kawasaki's internal debate raises the question of how changing sociohistorical conditions have caused Japanese composers to respond differently to the bombings over time.[35]

1945–52: Music under Allied Occupation Censorship

Hiroshima

In the last four months of 1945, over sixty memorial services representing schools, associations, and companies were held in Hiroshima as survivors sought to memorialize the dead. But soon the campaign to reshape Hiroshima into a symbol of international peace was on. The city had long profited from the military industry, and with Japan's war machine at an end and the city in rubble, Hiroshima was eager to reshape its identity as a city of peace. The sacrifice of Hiroshima was now said to have ended the war. Commemoration ceremonies offered an opportunity to project this new identity.

In 1946, the city of Hiroshima organized a "peace and recovery" festival, with an assembly on August 5 and a memorial service on August 6. The following year, the first "peace festival ceremony" was held, with the mayor, Hamai Shinzō, giving the first "peace declaration." General Douglas MacArthur delivered a message that the lesson of Hiroshima was that "war's destructiveness will progress until the means are at hand to exterminate the human race." Terada Yūtaka, chairman of the Hiroshima municipal assembly, noted that the peace festival was to remember August 6 as "the day of the arrival of peace."[36] The *Chūgoku* newspaper called Hiroshima "the pride of the world" and a "mecca for world peace."[37] Already the first of the commemoration ceremonies was thus "built on a reconciliatory and forward-looking narrative" that connected survivors to the peace movement and discouraged anger at the inflicted suffering.[38]

For the 1947 peace memorial, the organizers solicited the public in a competition for the lyrics to an official song. The winning entry, by Shigezono Yoshio, a music teacher in Hiroshima prefecture, was set to music by another music teacher, Yamamoto Minoru. A chorus of students and community members from the city has been singing the "Hiroshima Song of Peace" (1947) at the annual Hiroshima commemoration ever since.

"HIROSHIMA SONG OF PEACE" (1947), FIRST VERSE

雲白く　たなびくところ	White clouds overhead,
空のはて　東に西に	To the infinite skies, East and West
おお高く　こだまひびけと	Oh way up high, resounding,
鐘は鳴る　平和の鐘に	the bell rings, the bell of peace,
いまわれら　雄々しく起て	We now rise up bravely
その栄え　ここに興さん	In the interest of regaining our glory.

Given Occupation censorship, it is not surprising that the lyrics make no mention of the suffering and inhumanity of the bomb; instead, it prays for peace. Nonetheless, both the lyrics and the music of "Hiroshima Song of Peace" harken back to the military rhetoric of the recent past. The text rhapsodizes about the infinite skies and the swelling seas that reach east and west, to the corners of the world; it encourages people to "rise up bravely" in order to "regain our glory." These are common tropes of the military marches that extolled the reaches of Japan's beautiful empire and called for its citizens to rise up to its challenges. Table 3.1 presents tropes from imperial military marches that are referenced in "Hiroshima Song of Peace."

Table 3.1. Military-March Tropes Evoked in "Hiroshima Song of Peace"

Trope in "Hiroshima Song of Peace"		Verse, line	Military march	Lyric	
空の果て	**the ends of the skies**	1, 2	"Mamore ōzora" ("Protect the Great Skies," 1933)	凱歌轟く空の果て	A triumphal song echoes in **the infinite skies.**
その栄えここに興さん	In the interest of regaining our **glory**.	1, 6	"Aikoku Kōshin Kyoku" ("Patriotic March," 1937):	皇国常に栄えあれ	May our imperial country be forever in **glory.**
海のはて	**the ends of the seas**	2, 2	"Gunkan" ("Warship," 1941)	日本の国の光を何千里、	Make the light of Japan shine for thousands of miles
				海のはてまで輝かせ。	to **the ends of the sea.**

It is not surprising that Shigezono evoked such tropes in "Hiroshima Song of Peace." Such evocations of Japan's vast and glorious empire were familiar rhetorical devices in pre-1945 Japan, and during the war, they were constantly repeated with increasing intensity, drowning out other discourse. As the war had only recently ended, this rhetoric would still have been ringing in most Japanese people's minds. Moreover, Shigezono himself had written military marches in the 1930s, served in the Japanese military in Manchuria, and only recently returned from a prisoner-of-war camp in Siberia.[39]

The music, too, bears a striking resemblance to military songs.[40] In particular, the melody has the same contour and stressed notes as "Umi yukaba" ("Across the Seas," 1937).[41] Widely regarded as the second national anthem during the Pacific War, it was frequently played to accompany news of honorable deaths—admirals, kamikazes, mass suicides of soldiers and citizens in lieu of facing defeat. The lyrics of "Across the Seas" describe the dead bodies floating in the seas and strewn across the mountains, glorified death for the emperor, and declared soldiers would not look back.[42] The opening phrase of "Hiroshima Song of Peace" sounds like an expansion of "Across the Seas," with the dominant melodic notes being ^5, ^3, and ^2, a neighbor-note motion of ^6 to ^5, and a harmony that begins and ends in the tonic (Figure 3.1). In the second period, both songs start on the harmony of IV, with the melodies arpeggiating from ^1 to ^6 before resting on the dominant. In the final phrases, both songs feature a plaintive arpeggio from ^5 to high ^3 on the climactic words.

The song may project a message of peace, yet its lyrics and music bear traces of the military past. While likely unconscious, the resemblance was understandable, as both the lyricist and composer had previously written patriotic marches, which were virtually the only music one could hear during the war. Such military traces were also present in architect Tange Kenzō's design of the Hiroshima Peace Memorial Park, where the annual commemorative ceremony now takes place.[43] It retains the lines and monumentality of his design for a wartime Shinto memorial that was never built. However buried in newly reoriented ideology, the familiar rhetorical and musical tropes helped a broad populace to accept these commemorative objects of song and monument, and the new order it represented.[44]

Figure 3.1. "Hiroshima Song of Peace" (1947), first verse

Nagasaki

The tone was somewhat different in Nagasaki. While Hiroshima was completely destroyed, Nagasaki was not: the American bombers had first diverted from the primary target, Kokura, due to cloud cover, then missed the second intended target of downtown Nagasaki. Instead, they dropped the bomb over a kilometer north in Urakami, a relatively poor district inhabited by Catholics and *burakumin,* an outcast group. The surrounding mountains contained the damage, so that about two-thirds of Nagasaki remained intact.

The unlucky victims of the bomb—the Urakami Catholics—had withstood a long history of persecution since the sixteenth century, when twenty-six Christians were hung on a cross on the outskirts of Urakami. In the fourth and last *kuzure* (mass arrest) in 1867, 3,400 Urakami Catholics were arrested, of which 662 died in detention and 808 remained missing.[45] The atomic bomb exploded near the cathedral, and the blast, fire, and radiation sickness eventually killed 80 percent of its parishioners. The other resident group in Urakami, the *burakumin,* had historically been discriminated against for working in occupations that dealt with the dead, such as gravedigging and leatherworking; a third of its population was killed by the bomb, and the survivors were turned away from refugee camps.

Since a marginalized community had borne the brunt of the catastrophe while much of the city remained unscathed, some Nagasaki residents did not see the atomic bomb as central to the city's identity in the way that Hiroshima came to see it. As echoed in the saying, "The bomb dropped on Urakami, not Nagasaki," media coverage tended to present the bomb as localized in Urakami, the photos of the destroyed Urakami Cathedral tying the tragedy to the Catholic community.[46] While Hiroshima positioned itself as the world's city of peace—a posture helped by the global publicity brought by Hersey's *Hiroshima*—Nagasaki proclaimed itself an international city of culture, aligning itself with its history as a port facing the outside world. Nagasaki had seen Portuguese traders in the sixteenth century, Dutch traders in Dejima in the seventeenth century, foreigners' enclaves recalled in *Madama Butterfly* in the late nineteenth and early twentieth centuries, and large communities of Chinese immigrants. While the city of Hiroshima sponsored a memorial service (called a "peace festival") on August 6, 1947, the city of Nagasaki did not sponsor a similar service, holding instead a "trade recovery festival" featuring *bon* dances, fireworks, and volleyball tournaments.[47] On the anniversary, four thousand mourners attended a 7:00 a.m. mass at Urakami Cathedral, while twelve hundred attended a memorial service held by the Nagasaki Sensai-sha Renmei (Nagasaki War Victim's Association).[48] After facing criticism in the *Nagasaki minyū* newspaper, the city organized a service on August 9, 1948, but it was called a "cultural festival," in keeping with its strategic vision. In 1955, the city installed an enormous "peace statue" in the Peace Park over the objections of the *hibakusha*; this statue remains the focus of the annual ceremony rather than the cenotaph at the hypocenter, unlike in Hiroshima.[49]

But not all of the marginalization was inflicted from outside of the Catholic community. One Catholic hero in the aftermath was Nagai Takashi, Nagasaki's most famous hibakusha writer. A radiologist and converted Catholic who had married into a leading family of the Christian community, he tended nonstop to the injured after the bomb fell, ignoring his own wounds. When he finally went home days later, all he could find of his wife were some bones and a melted rosary. His autobiographical account of the immediate aftermath of the bomb, *Nagasaki no kane* (*The Bells of Nagasaki*, 1949), was published three years after it had been drafted; it had been held up by disagreements among the censors at SCAP (Supreme Commander for the Allied Powers), who allowed it to be published only on the condition that it was bound with an account of the sacking of Manila by Japanese forces in 1945. However, SCAP provided large amounts of paper for printing the book, helping it to become a bestseller.

Following the atomic bomb, rumors circulated in Nagasaki that the atomic bombs were the Shintō gods' punishment of the Christians and a sign that Japan needed its own gods. Nagai turned this argument around. In a speech given at a requiem Mass in November 1945, he recounted that the bomb had originally been intended for another city and insisted that its explosion over the cathedral was an act of Divine Providence: he claimed that because Urakami had prayed for peace throughout the war, these Catholics were the sole "unblemished lambs" that could be laid at the altar of God, a "sacrifice to expiate the sins committed by humanity in the Second World War. . . . Only when Nagasaki was destroyed did God accept the sacrifice. Hearing the cry of the human family, He inspired the emperor to issue the sacred decree by which the war was brought to an end."[50] Nagai's interpretation played on the history of martyrdom in Urakami, encouraging the community to accept its victimization as a step to a peaceful world. The interpretation was embraced by the Urakami Catholics and set the tone for the memorialization that followed.

Overt criticism of Nagai's interpretation did not appear for a few decades, as he was considered too prominent a figure. In 1972, the Nagasaki poet and hibakusha Yamada Kan criticized Nagai's notion of Divine Providence as having suppressed open discussion among hibakusha, muffling their literary voice in ways that were not present in Hiroshima; he noted that Nagai "was obviously embroiled in the policies of the American occupation." Yamada was ostracized for his views.[51] Philosopher Takahashi Shinji has also noted that Nagai's ideas helped to support the American position that the bombing of Nagasaki brought an end to the war and that his words "deprived Nagasaki victims of the option to rage, pursue accountability and seek compensation."[52] To this day, Nagai's biography is prominently featured in the Nagasaki Atomic Bomb Museum, and his books fill its gift shop.

Nagai penned several poems that were set to song. In 1949, he wrote the poem "Ano ko" ("That Child"), in remembrance of the children of Yamasato Elementary School, located only five hundred meters away from the hypocenter; about thirteen hundred students, or 85 percent of those enrolled, died in the bombing.[53] He asked Kino Fumio, the head of the office of the Nagasaki city assembly and amateur composer, to set it to music. Kino's house had been only five hundred meters from the hypocenter, and he had lost his wife, two children, and home to the bomb; suffering himself from the bomb's aftereffects, he was particularly indignant about the "inhumane victimization" of women and children.[54] The song debuted on November 3, 1949, at a ceremony unveiling a stone monument to the children at the school; in 1952, the Yamasato Elementary School chorus sang it at the annual city-organized ceremony. It is now sung every other year at the annual ceremony by a children's chorus. In the verses of "That Child," the protagonist looks wistfully at reminders of a child who had died—graffiti of the child's name, the sight of a school athletic meet, summer flowers at dusk. The song alternates in the ceremony's program with another of Kino's songs, "Kora no mitama yo" ("The Souls of Children," lyrics by Shimauchi Hachirō, 1949); he wrote it for Shiroyama Elementary School, which lost fourteen hundred children to the bomb.[55] The Yamasato and Shiroyama Elementary School choruses sing their respective songs every year at the "Heiwa no Tomoshibi" ("The Light of Peace") concert, held annually on August 8 at the fountain in the Peace Park.

"THAT CHILD," FIRST VERSE

壁に残った　らくがきの	The graffiti remains on the wall,
おさない文字の　あの子の名	That child's name, scribbled in childish letters.
呼んでひそかに　耳すます	I call out privately and strain to hear.
ああ　あの子が生きていたならば	Ah, if only that child were still alive.

But perhaps the best-known song about Nagasaki is a song *about* Nagai—"Nagasaki no kane" ("Bells of Nagasaki," 1949). Inspired by Nagai's writings, Satō Hachirō, whose own brother had been killed by the Hiroshima bomb, wrote the lyrics with Nagai's life in mind. Popular songwriter Koseki Yūji wrote the music. The verses, in a minor key, describe Nagai's sorrow, particularly for the loss of his wife ("Only the keepsake of a rosary remains, evoking my tears"). In contrast, the chorus, in a major key, soars as it describes the sound of Nagasaki's church bells, comforting him and encouraging him to go on. The song inspired a hit movie of the same name (1950). Released during the Occupation, the movie could not address the bomb, the aftermath of which takes up most of Nagai's book; instead, it recounts his life, particularly his love for his wife, his conversion to Christianity, and his medical career. At the end of the film, Nagai's friends recover the cathedral's bells from the ruins and mount them on a tower, allowing them to ring. The familiar sound of the bells gives the embattled community a sense of hope. It is this hope for recovery and peace, coupled with acknowledgment of personal loss from the war (worded in a way that could apply to all of Japan), that made the song a hit in the postwar era. It continues to be a local (and national) favorite. The Himawari (Sunflower) chorus of hibakusha began singing preludes to the annual memorial ceremony in 2004; when they sing "The Bells of Nagasaki," audience members can be heard singing along.[56]

Music of Horror and Rage: Compositions Based on Hibakusha Poetry during the Cold War

The end of the Occupation in 1952 opened the floodgates to discussion of the atomic bomb. Exhibitions of eyewitness art and photographs, as well as publication of testimonials and poetry, made the true plight of Hiroshima and Nagasaki widely known in Japan for the first time.

In March 1954, the Castle Bravo hydrogen bomb test on Bikini Atoll resulted in an explosion that was twice the power expected, spreading large amounts of radiation throughout the Pacific; it contaminated the Japanese finishing boat *Lucky Dragon 5*, eventually resulting in the death of a crew member from radiation sickness. This incident triggered the rise of the antinuclear weapons movement in Japan, with petitions calling for a ban of nuclear bomb testing signed by a third of the Japanese population. At the Hiroshima Peace Ceremony of 1957, the mayor's peace declaration stated that it was a fantasy to think that keeping or experimenting with hydrogen bombs was a way to keep the peace; in 1958, the statement called for the complete abolishment of nuclear weapons. Sung at the Hiroshima Peace Ceremony in 1955, 1956, and 1958 was the antinuclear anthem "Genbaku yurusumaji" ("No More Atomic Bombs," 1954), a product of the left-wing *utagoe* (mass-singing) movement.[57] The antinuclear (or peace) movement gave atomic bomb victims moral clout as witnesses to nuclear war; it gave them a meaningful and transformative outlet as peace activists. The new atmosphere also empowered them to express their anger openly.

From the mid-1950s onward, a steady stream of music on Hiroshima and Nagasaki was produced. Many of these works are based on poetry written by eyewitnesses to the atomic bomb. As John Treat notes, these poets felt morally obligated to project the horror of the bomb directly without the adornment of metaphor.[58] The two Hiroshima poets who have attracted the most attention are Hara Tamiki and Tōge Sankichi, each of whose poetry has yielded more than twenty musical works.

Genbaku shōkei *(*Scenes from the Atomic Bomb*)*

Hara's home had collapsed from the atomic bomb blast on August 6, and he had wandered around the destroyed city without shelter for days. His observations are reflected in his poetry collection, *Genbaku shōkei* (*Scenes from the Atomic Bomb*, 1950), a pithy documentary account of what he saw. Its most famous poem is perhaps "Mizu o kudasai" ("Give Me Water"). In an experience commonly told by hibakusha, choruses of injured people, suffering from a terrible thirst due to their burns, ask desperately for water in fragmentary, grammatically incomplete language. As a delta, Hiroshima was famous for its seven rivers, which formed an important part of its landscape and imagery; in the scene depicted in the poem, badly burned people have come to the river, where they are dying. Hara wrote this collection in katakana—a syllabary usually reserved for foreign words, telegrams, and official communications—which, as Treat notes, defamiliarizes the language and estranges the reader.[59]

HARA TAMIKI, "MIZU O KUDASAI" ("GIVE ME WATER"), EXTRACT

水ヲ下サイ	Give me water
アア　水ヲ下サイ	Ah, give me water
ノマシテ下サイ	Let me drink
死ンダハウガ　マシデ	Death would be better than this
死ンダハウガ	Death would be
アア	Aah
タスケテ　タスケテ	Help help
水ヲ	Water . . .
水ヲ	Water
ドウカ	Somehow please
ドナタカ	Someone
オーオーオーオー	Ohohohoh
オーオーオーオー	Ohohohoh
天ガ裂ケ	The heavens are split asunder
街ガ無クナリ	The city has disappeared
川ガ	The river
ナガレテヰル	Is flowing . . .

(Translation by Treat, *Writing Ground Zero*, 170–71)

Tokyo composer Hayashi Hikaru was inspired to set Hara's *Scenes from the Atomic Bomb* to music in 1952, when he participated in a festival for an exhibition of husband-and-wife artists Maruki Iri and Toshi's *Genbaku no zu* (*Hiroshima Panels*). These paintings were based on the artists' own eyewitness memories of Hiroshima, where they had rushed shortly after the bomb to check on family; one of the first works to address the bomb, the panels had a strong impact on viewers. Hayashi composed *Mizu o kudasai* (*Give Me Water*) in 1958; it became the first of four movements in the suite *Scenes from the Atomic Bomb,* which he completed in 2001. In *Give Me Water,* the composer simulates the ubiquitous and omnidirectional voices asking for water.[60] The voice parts repeat atonal melodic fragments in canonic fashion from multiple starting pitches, mirroring the fragmentary nature of Hara's text. Groan-like chords in the lower voices act as accompaniment. At the end, the sopranos repeat, "The river is flowing," in fragments as their voices fade out; the music is thus mimetic of the way in which many victims came to the river and died. After debuting the first movement with the Philharmonic Chorus of Tokyo in 1958, the chorus has performed the suite every year since 1980 in its concert, "Hachigatsu no matsuri" ("August Festival").

Genbaku shishū (*Poems of the Atomic Bomb*) and *Ningen o kaese* (*Give Me Back Mankind*) Truman's announcement that he was considering the deployment of atomic bombs in the Korean War was said to have pushed Hara to his suicide. This same announcement served as impetus for the poet Tōge Sankichi to publish his collection, *Genbaku shishū* (*Poems of the Atomic Bomb*, 1951). At the time of the bomb, Tōge was three kilometers from the hypocenter and was relatively unhurt. However, he spent days looking for friends and family in the bombed-out zone, causing him to contract radiation sickness. Tōge was a leader of Warera no Shi no Kai (Our Poetry Association), which suffered under the Occupation's Red Purge of 1950, causing Tōge to feel more anger toward the United States.

Tōge's rage is clearly felt in *Poems of the Atomic Bomb*, which he published in mimeographs through Our Poetry Association in 1951 and through the publisher Aoki Shoten in 1952. His writing is graphic, documentary, and angry, reflecting many hibakusha poets' preference for direct expression. His most famous lyric, which is the prologue to the collection, has become a rallying cry for antiwar protests and is inscribed on a monument in the Hiroshima Peace Memorial Park. In a reversal of Hara's tactic, Tōge wrote this poem entirely in the hiragana syllabary, giving it to the simplicity of an elementary schoolchild's reading textbook and making it accessible to all.

TŌGE SANKICHI, PROLOGUE, *Genbaku shishū* (*Poems of the Atomic Bomb*)

ちちをかえせ　ははをかえせ	Give me back my father. Give me back my mother.
としよりをかえせ	Give me back the elderly.
こどもをかえせ	Give me back the children.
わたしをかえせ　わたしにつながる	Give me back myself, and all those people
にんげんをかえせ	Connected to me, give them back.
にんげんの	Give me back humankind
にんげんのよのあるかぎり	
くずれぬへいわを	Give me peace.

へいわをかえせ　　A peace that will not shatter
As long as humans are in the world.

(Adapted from translation in Treat, *Writing Ground Zero*, 172)

These moving and defiant statements form the rousing prologue to *Ningen o kaese* (*Give Me Back Humankind*, 1961), a cantata by composer Ōki Masao setting selections of Tōge's poems.[61] Like Hayashi, Ōki had also been inspired by the *Hiroshima Panels*, which formed the basis for his *Hiroshima Symphony* (1953); the piece had brought him to the attention of Wada Keiji of Tokyo Rō-on (the Tokyo branch of the National Workers Music Association), which commissioned the work and performed it, with laborers' choruses, for audiences of laborers.[62] The ideals espoused by the Rō-on resonated with Ōki, who embraced a leftist, antiwar, pro-peace stance after World War II and sought to "express the desires of ordinary people."[63] Having studied traditional Japanese music from a young age, he considered the cantata to be a *katari*—a narrative style found in traditional music such as *biwa* (lute) narrative, where the vocal performance is often delivered as heightened speech rather than sung. The cantata alternates soloists singing or reciting Tōge's verses with dramatic, scene-setting passages by a mixed chorus.

Ōki's cantata sets six poems from Tōge's collection, including gruesome documentary accounts ("August 6," "At the First Aid Station," "Eyes"), personal tragedy ("Death," "Little Child"), and propagandistic arguments (Prologue, "We Call to You"). Mirroring Tōge's grotesque images, the music of "August 6" and "Death" conveys the raging flames, swirling wind, and screams for loved ones in the frightful cacophony. Witnesses to Hiroshima often speak of the blinding flash, the loud boom, and sudden windblast, followed by an eerie silence; the third movement, "At the First Aid Station," seems to convey this deathly silence through a mournful hummed melody in the unsettled harmonization of open fifths. The narrator seems to be Tōge himself, searching through the wreckage of the city and the stench of dead bodies for a female friend. He has come across a group of schoolgirls who had been mobilized for demolition work, now a pile of naked flesh burned beyond recognition:

TŌGE SANKICHI, "KARIHŌTAIJO NITE"
("AT THE FIRST AID STATION"), EXCERPT

ああみんなさきほどまでは愛らしい	Ah! Who would believe
女学生だったことを	That all of you, just a short time ago,

だれがほんとうと思えよう	Were lovely schoolgirls . . .
. . .	. . .
そしてあなたたちは	You are not aware
すでに自分がどんなすがたで	What sort of form you've become,
にんげんから遠いものにされはてて	How far from human form you've
しまっているかを知らない	been taken . . .

The most haunting imagery is of a woman, a war widow with a young child. As fire and smoke whirl in "Death," she is heard screaming for her young child, "Hiro-chan! . . . Child, child, child, where are you?" The end of the movement dramatizes her death on the side of the road, lamenting her separation from her child. Her image recurs in "Little Child." The verses begin quietly as she calls out, "Little child, cute child, where on earth are you?" The melody is simple, recalling a traditional lullaby. Then the narration shifts to tell the story, accompanied by dramatic musical flourishes: the mother had left the child with neighbors as she went to work; she ran frantically back after the blast, ignoring her grave injuries, until she collapsed and died. The father, sent off to war when the mother was pregnant with the child, had been killed in the South Pacific, his body piled among those of many other soldiers. The narrator resolves to find the child and tell her the story of how a "dark power" took control of the nation and how the war destroyed families, burned Hiroshima, and took both her parents away from her. It is a powerful antiwar message, particularly when sung by a large chorus.

Post–Cold War: Songs of Hope

While Ōki's and Tōge's angry work emerged from leftist antiwar ideologies, the mainstream narrative on the bomb remains geared toward hope and renewal, especially following the fall of the Soviet Union. To commemorate the fiftieth anniversary of the bomb in 1995, the City of Nagasaki held a nationwide contest for lyrics. The winning entry, "Senbazuru" ("A Thousand Cranes") by Yokoyama Kanae, a woman from Chiba prefecture, references the often-told story of Sasaki Sadako, a twelve-year-old girl from Hiroshima who contracted leukemia because she had been exposed to black rain from the atomic bomb as a two-year-old. Following a tradition by which a person who folds one thousand origami cranes gets her wish, she folded over a thousand cranes for her health but died in 1955. Her tragedy attracted much public attention, as like Anne Frank, she was an innocent child who had been victimized by war. As her story became widely known, origami cranes became a symbol for remembering the dead and hoping for peace. Every year, schoolchildren create chains of folded cranes, which adorn fences and statues around the Hiroshima and Nagasaki peace parks.

These sentiments are reflected in the lyrics of "A Thousand Cranes." Referring to the above-mentioned chains of paper cranes, the song recounts the narrator's folding cranes for peace with great feeling. In the second verse, she mentions the dead buried in the fields and the dead at the bottom of the sea—a parallel with the war dead mentioned in "Across the Seas." But instead of the single-minded patriotism of the 1930s song, the narrator here thinks of them in sadness as she folds another crane for peace. The music, by Nagasaki composer Ōshima Michiru, adorns the lyrics with chromaticism and temporary tonicizations that reflect the multiple emotions of the narrator, but it begins and ends unambiguously in a major key, underlining the sense of hope. The song remains widely sung in Nagasaki and is performed every year at the commemoration ceremony by students of Junshin Senior Girls High School.[64] A symbol of the city, the song is broadcast on the ninth day of each month at 11:02 a.m. (the time the bomb fell) over the city's wireless network. As the penultimate item in the Nagasaki ceremony, its soaring melody uplifts the audience's mood as the listeners leave the Peace Park.

Conclusion

While both the Hiroshima and Nagasaki ceremonies follow a set pattern that has been in place for years, I find the Nagasaki one to be more participatory, as more time in the ceremony is given over to "ordinary" citizens. High school students emcee the event. Hibakusha are heard, giving personal testimony and singing songs. Officials are called out by name in Nagasaki, whereas they are often addressed only by title in Hiroshima. The more abundant singing in the Nagasaki ceremony—three songs, sung by different school and community choruses, in contrast with one song in Hiroshima—also adds to this participatory feel, as the singing inevitably invites listeners to hum along. Overall, the Nagasaki ceremony feels like a community gathering, while the Hiroshima ceremony feels like a showcase, which it is: the Hiroshima ceremony attracts a far larger crowd, which in 2019 consisted of 50,000 audience members and 89 foreign dignitaries, compared with 5,900 and 66 for Nagasaki. Officials take up most of the time in the Hiroshima ceremony, with citizen participation confined to a speech by the children's representative and the singing of the peace song.

The characteristics of both ceremonies are an outgrowth of the conditions the cities faced during the Allied Occupation. Censorship during that period enforced a narrative of peace, rather than anger, in both commemorations. Furthermore, Hiroshima purposefully positioned itself as a "mecca for world peace." Meanwhile Nagasaki staked its identity on international trade and culture; with much of the city having been spared of the bomb, and the bomb having exploded over neighborhoods of groups that had historically faced discrimination, its people did not readily accept the bomb as part of local identity. Perhaps the more abundant choruses are a compensation for this earlier neglect, a conscious attempt to involve the affected community with songs composed by a city employee. Still, the pacifist stance set by Nagai Takashi impacted commemoration in Nagasaki. In the heat of the post-Occupation antinuclear movement, Kino also set raging, graphic testimonials as songs (e.g., "Fushū no hara," 1955), but they have not found their way into the choral repertory, unlike the sad tributes to the schools still sung at the annual ceremony. And while the Hayashi and Ōki cantatas setting the poetry of Hiroshima hibakusha found a Japanese audience, they remain obscure internationally. Even today, most hibakusha remain silent.

Notes

1. As of 2004, the Hiroshima Music Committee counted 1,867 works. See Hiroshima to Ongaku Iinkai (Hiroshima Music Committee) ed., *Hiroshima to ongaku* (Tokyo: Chōbunsha, 2006), 10. However by the members' own admission, the database undercounts popular music, and this author has noticed a few pieces missing (e.g., "Hiroshima" by the Flower Travelin' Band). The database for the committee gives a partial listing of about 800 pieces. See the website at hirongaku.com

2. For the contents of the Hiroshima ceremony, see "Heiwa kinen shikiten (Hiroshima-shi genbakushibotsushairei-shiki narabini heiwa kinen-shiki) no gaiyō," City of Hiroshima, accessed August 31, 2019, http://www.city.hiroshima.lg.jp/www/contents/1347936740512/index.html

For the Nagasaki ceremony, see "Nagasaki genbakugisei-sha irei heiwa kinen shikiten," City of Nagasaki, August 23, 2018, http://www.city.nagasaki.lg.jp/heiwa/3020000/3020300/p002242.html. For the contents and organizers of early ceremonies and other events, see articles in *Chūgoku Shimbun* and *Nagasaki Nichi Nichi* for August 6 and 7, 1946–49.

3. I attended the Hiroshima and Nagasaki ceremonies and other events in

2015, 2016, and 2019, and watched videos of these ceremonies in the years I could not attend; see links in the previous note. In 2015 and 2016, the Nagasaki audience heckled Prime Minister Abe Shinzō and clapped loudly for Yamamoto Tarō, then a liberal opposition Diet member. In 2019, announcements at the Nagasaki ceremony warned that audience members holding placards or disrupting the proceedings would be asked to leave; however, protesters just outside the venue chanted loudly throughout Abe's speech, stopping immediately after his speech ended. In Hiroshima, antiwar protesters gather every year around the Atomic Bomb Dome, across the river and about five hundred meters away from the ceremony; they stage a die-in at 8:15 a.m.

4. For information on the development of school songs in Japan and their ideologies, see Noriko Manabe, "Western Music in Japan: The Evolution of Styles in Children's Songs, Hip-Hop, and Other Genres" (PhD dissertation, City University of New York, 2009).

5. Music related to the atomic bombings has not been widely studied, addressed by only two edited volumes by Hiroshima-based scholars Shibata Shingo (1982) and the Hiroshima Music Committee (2006), and a book by Notohara Yumi (2015), who heads this committee. See Shibata Shingo, Yazawa Hiroshi, and Kinoshita Sonki, eds., *Hankaku nihon no ongaku: Nō moa Hiroshima ongaku dokuhon* (Tokyo: Chōbunsha, 1982); Hiroshima to Ongaku Iinkai, *Hiroshima to ongaku*; and Notohara Yumi, *"Hiroshima" ga narihibiku toki* (Tokyo: Shunjū-sha, 2015). In this text, Japanese names are presented family name first, as per Japanese practice.

6. Hiroshima Peace Memorial Museum, *Hiroshima genbaku sensai shi*, 1971.

7. Ubuki Satoru, *Heiwa kinen shikiten no ayumi* (Hiroshima: Hiroshima Heiwa Bunka Sentā, 1992).

8. Yūko Shibata, *Producing Hiroshima and Nagasaki: Literature, Film, and Transnational Politics* (Honolulu: University of Hawai'i Press, 2018).

9. John W. Dower, *Embracing Defeat: Japan in the Wake of World War II* (New York: Norton, 1999), 406–8.

10. Quoted in John Whittier Treat, *Writing Ground Zero: Japanese Literature and the Atomic Bomb* (Chicago: University of Chicago Press, 1995), 90.

11. Hersey's article helped to raise awareness of the plight of the hibakusha and to mobilize charity efforts from the United States.

12. Dower, *Embracing Defeat*, 414.

13. Dower, *Embracing Defeat*, 414.

14. Kurihara Tadaichi was hibakusha writer Kurihara Sadako's husband.

15. Shibata et. al., *Hankaku nihon no ongaku*, 72. Okinawa is the name of both Japan's southernmost prefecture and its largest island; the chain of islands is called the Ryūkyū Islands. Previously a kingdom with its own distinct culture, language, and history, the islands were occupied by the Satsuma domain of southern Japan in the seventeenth century and annexed by Japan in the late 1870s, with much resentment among the local population. Okinawa was the site of one of the bloodiest battles in the Pacific War (April–June 1945), in which three hundred thousand civilians were killed. American forces occupied the islands until they were returned to Japan in 1972; in the immediate postwar, they were under American rule. American military bases remain a large and controver-

sial presence in Okinawa. See George H. Kerr, *Okinawa: The History of an Island People*, rev. ed. (North Clarendon, VT: Tuttle Publishing, 2011); and Masamichi S. Inoue, *Okinawa and the U.S. Military: Identity Making in the Age of Globalization* (New York: Columbia University Press, 2007).

16. Treat, *Writing Ground Zero*, 93; Shibata, *Producing Hiroshima and Nagasaki.*

17. Ran Zwigenberg, *Hiroshima: The Origins of Global Memory Culture* (Cambridge: Cambridge University Press, 2014), 70.

18. Robert Lifton, *Death in Life: Survivors of Hiroshima* (Chapel Hill: University of North Carolina Press, 1991), 343.

19. Lifton, *Death in Life*, 343.

20. Zwigenberg *Hiroshima*, 47.

21. Zwigenberg, *Hiroshima*, 147.

22. Lifton, *Death in Life*, 485.

23. Lifton, *Death in Life*, 516.

24. Lifton, *Death in Life*, 500.

25. Lifton, *Death in Life*, 524.

26. For similarities and differences between atomic bomb and Holocaust victims, see Lifton, *Death in Life*, and Zwigenberg, *Hiroshima.*

27. Lifton, *Death in Life*, 473.

28. Lifton, *Death in Life*, 403.

29. Lifton, *Death in Life*, 47.

30. Treat, *Writing Ground Zero*, 105.

31. Treat, *Writing Ground Zero*, 97–98.

32. Treat, *Writing Ground Zero*, 109–10.

33. Shibata, *Producing Hiroshima and Nagasaki*; Miekzyslaw Tomaszewski, liner notes for *Penderecki: Orchestral Works*, vol. 1 (Naxos 8.554491, 2000).

34. Jennifer Wilson, "Composer Continues to Honor Victims of Hiroshima," *Colorado Springs Gazette*, April 16, 2007, http://gazette.com/composer-continues-to-honor-victims-of-hiroshima/article/21283. See also Endō Masao, "Kawasaki Masaru," *New Composer* 9 (July 2008): 50–55.

35. Of the nearly two thousand works in the Hiroshima Music Committee's database, only five hibakusha composers are represented. See Notohara Yumi, "Ongaku ni okeru 'Hiroshima'—Taiken no katari to kioku no keishō o megutte," *Kyōto Zōkei Geijutsu Daigaku kiyō* 22 (November 2018): 118–24.

36. Anon., "M'Arthur Points Hiroshima Lesson: Says in Message to Peace Fete in Bombed City World Must Reform or Perish," *New York Times*, August 6, 1947, 13.

37. *Chūgoku Shimbun*, August 6, 1947.

38. Zwigenberg, *Hiroshima*, 66.

39. Shigezono Yoshio, *Hitori no kyōshi-zō: Shigezono Yoshio no ashiato to uta* (Tokyo: Shigezono gakkyū henshū-shitsu, 1981), 210–11.

40. The lyrics and score to "Hiroshima Song of Peace" can be found here: http://www.city.hiroshima.lg.jp/www/contents/1160023462359/index.html.

A performance from the 2016 ceremony can be found here: https://www.youtube.com/watch?v=vYsP1q4KJno

41. A recording of "Across the Seas" from 1938 can be found here: https://www.youtube.com/watch?v=pAohjCaLG6s

42. For an explanation of "Across the Seas," military songs, and their context see Noriko Manabe, "Songs of Japanese Schoolchildren during World War II," in *The Oxford Handbook of Children's Musical Cultures,* ed. Patricia Shehan Campbell and Trevor Wiggins (New York: Oxford University Press, 2012), 96–113.

43. Lisa Yoneyama points this out in her book, *Hiroshima Traces: Time, Space, and the Dialectics of Memory* (Berkeley: University of California Press, 1999).

44. Such references to familiar tropes were also seen in Germany; for example, the Dresden Kreuzkantor Rudolf Mauersberger relied on tropes regularly associated with mourning for his motet *Wie liegt die Stadt so wüst* (1945). See Martha Sprigge, "Dresden's Musical Ruins," *Journal of the Royal Musical Association* 144, no. 1 (January 2, 2019): 83–121.

45. Yuki Miyamoto, *Beyond the Mushroom Cloud: Commemoration, Religion, and Responsibility after Hiroshima* (New York: Fordham University Press, 2011), 119.

46. Chad R. Diehl, *Resurrecting Nagasaki: Reconstruction and the Formation of Atomic Narratives* (Ithaca, NY: Cornell University Press, 2018), 8–11.

47. The *bon* festival is a mid-August festival to welcome back the spirits of the dead. Group dances are held at night and have a festive nature.

48. *Nagasaki nichi nichi,* August 10, 1947.

49. The hypocenter is the ground directly below where the bomb is detonated in midair, or ground zero. As distance from the hypocenter was a key factor determining the chances of survival, hibakusha often identify themselves by stating how far they were from the hypocenter at the time of the blast.

50. Nagai Takashi, *The Bells of Nagasaki* (New York: Kōdansha International, 1984), 107–8.

51. See Diehl, *Resurrecting Nagasaki,* 138–39.

52. Tomoko Otake, "Nagasaki's 'Providential' Nightmare Shaped by Religious, Ethnic Undercurrents," *Japan Times Online,* August 7, 2015, https://www.japantimes.co.jp/news/2015/08/07/national/history/nagasakis-providential-nightmare-shaped-religious-ethnic-undercurrents/

53. The score and a recording for "That Child" can be accessed here: http://www.nagasaki-city.ed.jp/yamazato-e/05%20heiwa/03%20anoko.htm

54. His hellish testimony of his walk home and effort to find his family are in his book of songs, *Genshiya no utagoe* (Nagasaki: Nagasaki Kokusai Bunka Kyōkai, 1956).

55. A performance of "The Souls of Children" at the 2015 ceremony can be seen here: https://www.youtube.com/watch?v=ZIZH7F0qJMk

56. The Himawari chorus's performance in the 2015 ceremony (as well as the participation of an audience member) can be heard at https://www.youtube.com/watch?v=ihTTKQRh4-g, beginning around 6:50.

57. A version of "No More Atomic Bombs" by Pete Seeger can be seen at https://www.youtube.com/watch?v=AxH4FWjHdMM

58. Treat, *Writing Ground Zero,* 164–65.

59. Treat, *Writing Ground Zero,* 170.

60. A recording of "Mizu o kudasai" and the rest of the suite can be heard here: https://www.youtube.com/watch?v=HMOtIbdPiBY

61. A performance of the cantata with the Tokyo Symphony Orchestra and the Tokyo Rō-on chorus can be heard here: https://www.youtube.com/watch?v=v7DelZAPVd8

62. Ōki had also written the soundtrack to the documentary film *Genbaku no zu* (*Hiroshima Panels,* 1952), directed by Imai Tadashi, about these paintings, as well as another atomic bomb-related film that had been censored by the Occupation. He was therefore familiar with information about the atomic bomb. See Notahara Yumi, "Ōki Masao to eiga *Hiroshima no zu*: Kōkyōkyoku dai 5 ban 'Hiroshima' e no kiseki," *Hiroshima Daigaku daigakuin kyōikugaku kenkyūka, Ongaku bunka kyōikugaku kenkyū kiyō* 15 (March 22, 2013): 61–68.

63. See liner notes in Ōki Masao et al., *Cantata: Take Back the Human I,* 26847111, 1961, compact disc.

64. A performance of "A Thousand Cranes" in the 2015 ceremony can be seen here: https://www.youtube.com/watch?v=p2AHC3b8AV8. Before being replaced by "A Thousand Cranes," the Junshin student chorus sang "Heiwa wa Nagasaki kara" ("Peace Began with Nagasaki," 1949). The song was composed by Kino Fumio, with lyrics by Shimauchi Hachirō, to commemorate the passing of the Nagasaki International Cultural City Reconstruction Law in 1949 and debuted that year at the annual ceremony. The Junshin chorus sang it at the ceremony every year from 1956 to 1994.

Mediation, Memory, and Musical Reenactment

FOUR | An Anthem for the AMIA Cause

León Gieco's "La Memoria" and Public Assembly in the Benefit Music Video from Argentina

LILLIAN M. WOHL

Pobre la canción que llega tarde,
que aparece cuando todo pasó
viene atrás corriendo, como el paisaje
que dejamos cuando nos estamos yendo

It's a poor song that comes along late,
that shows up when everything's over.
It brings up the rear, like the landscape
We leave behind when we're on our way

—León Gieco, translation by Gustavo Santoloalla

More than two decades after the 1994 bombing of the Asociación Mutual Israelita Argentina (AMIA) Jewish community center in Buenos Aires, the creation of the 2016 "Memoria AMIA" ("AMIA Memory") benefit music video provided a new anthem for the AMIA cause. The video was based on Argentine musician León Gieco's rock ballad "La Memoria" ("Memory"), a song originally released on the commercial album *Bandidos Rurales* (EMI) in 2001. Exalting the political and social power of memory to resist the collective forgetting of twentieth-century human rights atrocities throughout Latin America, Gieco's lyrics commemorate the AMIA bombing, Argentina's worst foreign terror attack, as well as the 1992 bombing of the Israeli Embassy in Buenos Aires. During my fieldwork in the early 2010s, Gieco's song had already circulated within the Jewish community as an expression of commemoration for these tragic events. However, with the emergence of the "AMIA Memory" video project in 2016, and its circulation through social media, the arrival of new forms of remediation and overwriting of AMIA memory more broadly represent important shifts in the sound worlds of commemorative practices involving spectatorship and performative assembly in Buenos Aires in the 2010s.[1]

As I argue in this chapter, the "AMIA Memory" music video strategically repositions the AMIA cause as a national human rights concern by rearranging it to showcase one hundred Argentine singers and musicians. By producing a mobile media unit intended to amplify the AMIA cause without fundraising for it, this hybrid media that I refer to as a "benefit music video" privileges the aestheticization of national solidarity rather than Jewish particularity or musical essentialism. The "AMIA Memory" benefit music video thereby does the important work of expanding awareness of the AMIA cause among broad audiences, drawing its viewers and listeners into the act of AMIA commemoration beyond the physical spaces and places of commemorative time. While showcasing how practices of hearing and listening are central to the processes of remembering Argentina's deadliest foreign terror attack—which killed eighty-five people and injured hundreds of others—AMIA video commemoration projects produced for the annual commemoration of the AMIA bombing every July 18 signal efforts to cement Jewish Argentine belonging through mediated expressions of national solidarity. In this case study, I discuss how the "AMIA Memory" benefit music video links repertories of Argentine popular song to Jewish Argentine political concerns in response to the attack amid the persistence of impunity in the troubled case.[2]

With an ear to the historical conditions of experiencing commemorations after the AMIA bombing, I begin with a discussion of the presence of anthems on the *tarde de las paraguas* (afternoon of the umbrellas), a mass public *acto* (protest/memorial) held in the Plaza de Congreso on July 21, 1994, just three days after the attack.[3] As a means to unite social bodies through the melodic and lyrical affects attached to these musical symbols of personhood and collectivity, the inclusion of both the Argentine national anthem and "Hatikvah"—a Zionist anthem that became the Israeli national anthem in 2004—highlights key contradictions in discourses and practices of Jewish belonging in Argentina since the mid-1990s. In my brief discussion of the initial uses of anthemic musical forms in physical and imagined spaces of commemoration in 1994, I consider how anthems rearrange disparate publics in the streets and plazas of Buenos Aires before addressing how onscreen representations of national solidarity are enacted aesthetically in the "AMIA Memory" benefit music video. Following Judith Butler's analysis of the performative politics of public assembly, I assess the performative meanings of the benefit music video as a tool of public arts projects that are expressly designed to draw attention to a particular cause or concern after a collective trauma.[4] As a mixed-media format that incorporates the aesthetic component parts of benefit concerts, charity singles, and music videos, the "AMIA Memory" benefit music video enables listeners to participate in the politics of memory and solidarity for the AMIA cause, reinforcing yet simultaneously calling into question the social bonds and senses of belonging fomenting ethnic and religious difference within the democratic Argentine state.

In the "AMIA Memory" benefit music video, sound is distinctly unmarked as "Jewish" and, instead, resonates from the sonic markers of Argentine national and commercial musics such as tango, folklore, *cumbia*, and *rock nacional*. By incorporating the participation of fans attached to popular-music scenes in Argentina and the transnational Latin American music industry, the "AMIA Memory" benefit music video affirms the role of music and sound in the fight against impunity in the aftermath of AMIA bombing. While making audible the contradictions of Jewish belonging in Argentina amid the notable absence of identifiably Jewish sonic markers, the "AMIA Memory" benefit music video models political engagement in the fight for justice twenty-two years after the AMIA tragedy through spectacles of pluralism and solidarity.

This aestheticization of Jewish belonging thus signals a shift into what Marianne Hirsch has called the "postmemorial" stage for the transmission of memory and a sonic correlative to predominantly visual and literary cultures of memory for the AMIA bombing.[5] By musically reembodying, rearticulating, and performing what Annette H. Levine has called the "boundless spaces of grief," projects such as the AMIA Memory video attempt to fill a void through the performative arts of memory work. As the 2015 renovation of the Pasteur-AMIA subway stop demonstrates, AMIA memory has moved into a shared city space, with Gieco's song lyrics prominently featured in this public memorial (Figure 4.1).[6] These projects underscore the postmemorial dimensions of AMIA memory in the 2010s. In the following essay, I discuss two modalities for hearing practices of commemoration and listening to shifting debates and narratives in the multidecade fight for justice for the AMIA bombing. I begin by turning our ears toward the uses of anthems in the first public AMIA

Figure 4.1. Lyrics to "La Memoria" in the Pasteur Amia subway station, Buenos Aires 2017. Photograph by author.

commemoration on July 21, 1994, in the Plaza del Congreso in Buenos Aires. Then I describe the collaboration between singer-songwriter León Gieco and AMIA curator Elio Kapszuck in the development, production, and distribution of the "AMIA Memory" benefit music video. Finally, I conclude by problematizing the role of the arts of memory in the absence of justice for the AMIA bombing.

July 21, 1994: Hearing Two Anthems in the Search for Justice on the "Afternoon of the Umbrellas"

Huddled under a shield of umbrellas to protect themselves against a steady flow of rain on a cold Thursday afternoon on July 21, 1994, approximately 150,000 mourners and protesters gathered in front of the Plaza del Congreso to protest terrorism and to demand justice after the bombing of the AMIA Jewish community center that shook the Once neighborhood on July 18, 1994, at 9:53 a.m. While civic commemorations and public assemblies are often noted for the sounds and noises generated during these public gatherings, Argentine newspapers instead reported widely on the pronounced silence of the event. With only a handful of very particular sounds emitted into the air in the central plaza, derogatory whistles and boos aimed at then-president Carlos Menem marked a tense quietude, as Menem continued to stand unflinchingly alongside government officials and Jewish leaders.[7] Referred to as *la tarde de las paraguas* (the afternoon of the umbrellas), the mass protest and memorial were considered "one of the most important ones remembered in Argentina in the last decade."[8]

This quiet was not a "passive or idle silence," as journalist Luis Bruchstein for the newspaper *Página/12* observed; it was "emotional and tense," occasionally interrupted by shouts of "justicia" (justice)—pleas that also echoed the failure to detain suspects in the 1992 bombing of the Israeli Embassy in Buenos Aires. Furthermore, these calls for justice resonated with protests against the human rights abuses of the last dictatorship government (1976–83). After the return to democracy in 1983, as Silvia Tandeciarz has observed, the subsequent decade "was dominated by *políticas de olvido* 'politics of forgetting'—including the amnesty granted those military officials who had been sentenced before 1986—which the state pursued in the name of national security, economic stability, and progress."[9] The impunity laws, including the Law of Due Obedience (1986) and Final Point Law (1987), were enacted into legislation by President Raúl Alfonsin allegedly to reunite the fractured nation in the wake of deep civil discord. This legislation "effectively ended the process of bringing those responsible to justice." It also made silences surrounding the disappearances of approximately thirty thousand people during the last military dictatorship a state-sanctioned policy to move the nation beyond the dictatorship.[10] Gabriela Cerruti has referred to the decade between 1985 and 1995 as a historical period of attempted "national reconciliation," during which the imposition of political silencing and hegemonic forms of national forgetting suppressed alternative responses in the postdictatorship years. Bursting into words, sounds, and embodied performative expressions since 1995, however, the "memory boom" in Argentina began a period of public confrontation with the nation's occluded, traumatic past.[11]

In the wake of the AMIA bombing, on the "afternoon of the umbrellas," a conspicuous silence was maintained in the plaza by the conveners through periodic verbal reminders to respect the atmosphere of mourning as a means to honor the victims and their families. The imposition of silence by administrative bodies also served to contain numerous outcries of political dissent against the Menem government.[12] As Ana

María Ochoa Gautier has noted, silence is symbolic in political life, often denoting power imbalances between states and groups, which "imply an active politics of domination and nonparticipation."[13] As she argues, "Voice is rendered as a sign of identity and presence of the subject and is contrasted with types of dialogism that have historically been seen in Western modernity as a key dimension of political participation and the constitution of the public sphere."[14] The imposition of silence on the "afternoon of the umbrellas" established a physical and emotional atmosphere that made outrage over the attack deeply felt through sounds of omission, rendering the presence of particular sounds and musical anthems played during the event that much more audible as forms of recognition and misrecognition of subjectivity. They became markers of corporeal presences experienced through public assembly as well as acute bodily absences determined by violence. As Vered Vinitzky-Seroussi and Chana Teeger argue, "Silence can be understood as a complex and rich social space that can operate as a vehicle for either memory or of forgetting and thus can be used by various groups for different ends."[15] Poised to promote memory, such intentional displays of silence in practices of commemoration can produce "overt" forms of silences that result in deep bodily discomforts that limit gestural expressions—phenomena that are, in fact, supportive of the collective intent to facilitate remembrance through restriction.[16] That day, both imposed and overt forms of silence shaped mourners' experiences, and archival video footage from the gathering on July 21, 1994, shows a somber and attentive crowd.

To accommodate the large number of people streaming into the plaza, the gathering began late, with two anthems played from loudspeakers to announce the start of the *acto*: the symphonic, militaristic "Himno Nacional Argentino," the Argentine national anthem written by Vicente López y Planes and Blas Parera, and "Hatikvah" ("The Hope"), the Zionist anthem accompanying a version of Naftali Herz Imber's poem "Tikvatenu" ("Our Hope") that became Israel's official national anthem in 2004.[17] Positioning "Hatikvah" as sonically representative of the Jewish collective body in diaspora in Buenos Aires on July 21, 1994, this performance also served to recognize Israeli foreign aid to Argentina, consisting of rescue equipment and personnel for the recovery effort.[18] The embodied experience of hearing two anthems was intended to bring together mourners as active listeners in the Plaza del Congreso.[19] Furthermore, speeches by key Jewish leaders and government officials condemned the attack and demanded a full investigation, as rescue crews continued their search for the missing in the ruins of the building at 633 Pasteur Street.[20]

Página/12

el país a diario

150 mil personas llenaron Congreso en repudio al atentado y exigiendo justicia

LA DERROTA DEL MIEDO

HABLAR

32 Remover escombros, por Estela de Carlotto

Figure 4.2. "150,000 People Fill Congreso Plaza in Repudiation of the AMIA Attack and to Demand Justice." Cover page of *Página/12*, July 22, 1994. Courtesy of the Centro de Documentación e Información sobre Judaísmo Argentino Marc Turkow at the AMIA.

In retrospect, the playing of two anthems—one representing the state and the other representing the Jews—alluded to the complex history of political relations between the Jews, Argentina, and Israel.[21] In the immediate wake of the bombing and as the "afternoon of the umbrellas" progressed, the two anthems issued over loudspeakers to the crowd revealed the instability of a collective "we" in the nation, resounding cultural dissonance rather than collective coherence. Jewish Argentines became the subject of public discourse echoing anti-Semitic sentiments of the past, in which Jews were positioned as foreigners rather than citizens of the Argentine nation. The separate anthems thus served as sonic reminders of past accusations of "dual loyalty." They also foreshadowed future renewals and intensifications of public forms of discrimination and "othering" that called into question Jewish Argentine citizenship, even as calls for justice appealed to the nation as a collective body. As a result of fears of repeated attacks on synagogues, schools, community centers, and sports clubs, public calls by non-Jewish neighborhood associations to move Jewish institutions to peripheral areas of the city raised the issue of safety and belonging to the level of national debate.[22] Within the Jewish Argentine community, concerns about repeated attacks can still be seen in the presence of *pilotes*, or short barriers in front of Jewish institutions to prohibit trucks or cars from parking too close to buildings. Argentine television personality Mario Tonelli's famous reference to "Jews and 'innocent' victims" and President Carlos Menem's misplaced public condolences to then Israeli president Yitzhak Rabin put a fine point on the troubled discourse of Jewish citizenship in Argentina.[23]

As musicologist Edwin Seroussi argues, "Hatikvah" is a symbol of the "daily and unsettled contradictions of contemporary Israeli existence."[24] Moreover, this anthem also serves as an emblem of the complex contradictions of Jewish life outside of Israel. As such, "Hatikvah" brings forward the contractions of Jewish belonging and exclusion because of the multiplicity of possible readings through situated listening practices. In reference to black anthems, Shana L. Redmond argues: "The attachment of these songs, performers and performances to political struggle differently configured the acts and actors through a process of meaning making that centered the stakes involved in musical production and performance."[25] Similarly, in the context of commemorations pertaining to Jewish history, anthems reconfigure Jewish social bodies through sound, drawing attention to Jewish difference and sameness as a collective body within or in reference to a nation-state at a particular historical moment.

Musically and poetically then, anthems related to the Jewish diasporic experience can vary dramatically in their stylistic features, but each song highlights different negotiations of social, religious, and cultural meanings through musical production and listening practices as they have become attached to ideas of Jewishness. In Buenos Aires, one anthem for the AMIA cause has emerged from the repertory of Latin American popular song, originally intended for mass commercial audiences. This song, "La Memoria," generally lacks the typical markers of a Jewish anthem, such as lyrics in a Jewish language (e.g., Hebrew, Yiddish, or Ladino), allusions to religious symbolism, the evocation of a liturgical text, musical modes associated with prayer and popular song, the expression of Zionist longings, or ties to the Holocaust. The absence of conspicuously "Jewish" musical characteristics therefore raises important questions about the existence of a Jewish anthem that fails to sound Jewish at all, calling into question not only the possible affective registers of this song, but also the need to hear certain qualities of sound and musical structures in reference to Jewish culture and history. As I discuss in the following sections of this essay, León Gieco's "La Memoria" provides, in effect, a suitable anthem for the AMIA cause because of its ability to carve out a sonic space to reflect on Argentine collective identity more broadly, leveraging the political discourses of memory in order to rearrange and reassert social relations and Jewish subjectivity within the nation in an imagined space of musical solidarity. While physical bodies are no longer congregating in the plaza each time Gieco's anthem is heard, the personal act of listening to, and watching, the "AMIA Memory" benefit music video provides a new context for public engagement with the AMIA cause.

May 31, 2016: Planning and Recording an Anthem for the AMIA. León Gieco's "La Memoria" as "Memoria AMIA"

To mark the twenty-second anniversary of the AMIA attack in 2016, Elio Kapszuk, curator of AMIA's art gallery, and musician León Gieco realized a long-standing desire to elevate AMIA memory through music, an idea originally initiated in October 1997, when Kapszuk asked Gieco to write a song on the subject of the AMIA attack.[26] By 2000, Gieco had composed the lyrics and melody for the song, "Memory," which he would later release in 2001 on the album *Bandidos Rurales* (EMI). Since the late 1990s, Gieco's participation in concerts and *actos* for justice for the AMIA attack, among other human rights causes and political issues, spotlights his commitments to social justice, which are also present in his folk-inflected song repertory since his arrival on the Argentine national rock scene in the early 1970s. Playing a central role in the national rock boom in 1982, following the censorship of songs in English at the end of the last military dictatorship, Gieco's performances on guitar and harmonica (among other instruments) has led to him being frequently characterized as embodying a "Bob Dylan style together with the folklore."[27] Born Raúl Alberto Antonio Gieco in Cañada Rosquín in the Santa Fe Province on November 20, 1951, Gieco has toured throughout the world and is well known for songs that address social issues and human rights topics, for which he is generally considered to be one of the most influential Argentine rock musicians.

As early as April 2015, soon after the transformation of the AMIA-Pasteur subway stop into a space of memory, Kapszuk and Gieco began exchanging ideas about the creation of a version of the song that could be used in the twenty-second AMIA bombing commemoration in 2016.[28] A little over one year later, the resulting benefit video was recorded on May 30, 2016, in the Auditorio de la Paz (the Peace Auditorium) of the Soka Gakkai International de la Argentina, a Buddhist organization that "promotes peace, culture, and education on the basis of the principle of respect and dignity for life." This space was intentionally chosen for its potential to signal the producers' deep commitment to "diversity" in the project emblematically.[29] Earlier that year, in January 2016, Kapszuk and Gieco, along with Gieco's manager, Virginia Machuca Taranto, and the AMIA's director of communications, Gabriel Scherman, had already decided to give shape to "a declaration of principles by AMIA to demand justice, not just for its own cause, but for all."[30] Turning toward universality rather than particularity, the video organizers, along with Hector Facundo "Lito" Vitale (who served as music director and arranger), shaped a musical project around the resignification of AMIA memory as memory for all; that is, to transform "them" into "we."[31]

Opening with a simple visual declaration, "Por los muertos en la AMIA" / "For the dead in the AMIA [bombing]," the "Memoria AMIA" benefit music video is organized around seven sections. It begins with an instrumental intro, which features a trio of piano, electric guitar, and bass players together onstage and filmed in a wide shot with backlit visual glares blurring the edges of the frame (table 4.1).[32] Each line of the next three verses of the song is sung by a single musician, a duo, or an ensemble, and the doubling of voices tends to occur in the B section of the stanzas of each verse, which contain a rhyming couplet. With percussion and instrumental accompaniment gradually added as the song progresses through the narrative provided by the lyrics, so too does the tempo generally increase and the key modulate upward. The third section opens to a thirty-second instrumental interlude presenting Lito Vitale on piano and Chango Spasiuk on *bandoneón* to facilitate a transition into a unison choral recitation of "todos los muertos de la AMIA" (all those who died in the AMIA). After featured solos by Marcelo Corvalán and Elena Roger, rock musician Juan Carlos Baglietto intently intones, "y los de la Embajada de Israel" (and those killed in the Israel Embassy), acknowledging the deaths of twenty-nine people killed in the bombing of the Israeli Embassy in Buenos Aires in 1992. Returning as a unison chorale, the choir sings the final verses of the middle section, "the secret power of weapons / justice that looks but does not see," before lifting into a major key with the collective voices swelling louder to confirm: "Everything is kept safe in our memory / A dream of life and history."

Traversing additional layers of the past through the incantation of accusations against the Catholic Church for complicity in the crimes of the last dictatorship government, Gieco's lyrics acknowledge particular disappearances and deaths, including those of Enrique Ángel Angelelli Carletti, bishop of the Catholic Church, murdered on August 4, 1976;

Chico Mendes, a Brazilian environmentalist and human rights activist, murdered on December 22, 1988; Carlos Mugica, an Argentine Catholic priest who worked in Buenos Aires's slum neighborhoods, murdered on May 11, 1974; and Rodolfo Walsh, an Argentine writer and journalist murdered by members of the ESMA (Escuela Superior de la Mecánica de la Armada, or the Navy School of Engineers). The video outro concludes with the repetition of the word *justicia,* with clarinet, string, and piano arpeggios fluttering between each syllable of the word as close-ups of musicians also appear on screen. The silent credits then shift into a statement that provides a summary of the attack and the legacy of impunity. Ending at over eight and a half minutes, the final statement reads: "No queremos nada menos que la verdad, / No exigimos nada más que la justicia" (We want nothing more than the truth / We demand nothing less than justice).

In total, one hundred Argentine musicians and singers representing multiple generations of musicians from different areas of Argentine popular music participated in the project and volunteered their time and distinctive voices. Produced by K&S Films under the general direction of Sebastián Orgambide, the project was recorded on May 31, 2016, in Buenos Aires and circulated on the internet following wide news coverage that launched the AMIA cause into new digital spaces of commemoration. As I discuss in the final section of this essay, the circulation of AMIA memory in digital space establishes this song as an anthem for the AMIA cause within and beyond Argentina. At the same time, I theorize the emergence of a music video format that I call the "benefit music video." Unlike a benefit concert or charity single, the benefit music video functions not only as a tool of transmission of knowledge and remembrance, it also accrues publicity—rather than monetary funds—to the cause it champions.

July 6, 2016: From the Streets to the Screen. The "AMIA Memory" Anthem in Digital Space

What is an anthem? What functions do anthems serve as forms of commemoration? Redmond defines an anthem as a song or a hymn that is performed on particular occasions, unsettling the boundaries between art and politics, listener, and actor. It demands the attention of the listener, commands belief, and provides a new constellation of possibilities for a better future, as she argues.[33] In the aftermath of violence, an anthem can acknowledge difference or repress it, uphold values or petition for a new transformative ethics of recognition and belonging. The entry on anthems in *Grove Music Online* underlines the religious underpinnings of anthems as a genre originating in the choral repertory of the Protestant church in Britain in the sixteenth century.[34] Absent from the authors' discussion, however, is the anthem's transition from the church to the nation-state in the form of national anthems that socially embody felt experiences of "unisonance," which Benedict Anderson famously details in *Imagined Communities.* As Anderson suggests, an anthem is an entry point into a discussion and a performance of self and collectivity, sometimes serving as a shibboleth for belonging—the words and melodies used to demonstrate membership or to perform alliance with a particular cause, collectivity, or nationality.[35]

Already before the "AMIA Memory" benefit music video was recorded on May 31, 2016, Gieco's song "Memory" had more or less served as one of the unofficial anthems for the cause. During my fieldwork primarily conducted between 2010 and 2014, I was introduced to the song in a rehearsal while participating in the activities of the Mordeje Guebirtig Choir in 2012. We were preparing for a concert commemorating the eightieth anniversary of the Teatro IFT, Argentina's oldest and still active Yiddish theater. In Buenos Aires, I heard other songs commemorating the AMIA attack circulating within the Jewish Argentine collectivity as well, including Ignacio Copani's "Memoria Activa" ("Active Memory"), which shares its name with the independent grassroots advocacy organizations representing families and friends of the victims of the attack. Pop singer Kevin Johannsen's "Candombito del Recuerdo" ("A Dear *Candómbe* of Remembrance"), which he sang in a commemorative video in 2010 to mark the sixteenth anniversary of the attack, emerged in the same year that I first arrived to Argentina to conduct research. Through the years, however, Gieco's song has recalled my attention for the content of its lyrics, which places the 1992 Israeli Embassy and 1994 AMIA bombings into a longer narrative of human rights atrocities and social justice issues in Latin America, casting Jewish Argentine history squarely within the history of the Argentine nation. Featuring a narrow vocal range and easily accompanied on guitar or piano by a nonprofessional musician, the lyrical melody and sweeping suspensions of the rock ballad's refrain provide a melodic and harmonic framework to support a variety of vocal skills.

The project organizers of the "AMIA Memory" benefit music video thus leveraged the anthemic qualities of Gieco's song of memory and the emotional ties between listening publics and their favorite musicians to bring attention to the AMIA cause. The broad commercial appeal of singers such as León Gieco, the 2016 Latin Grammy nominees Diego Torres and Kevin Johanssen, and others facilitated multiple access points for audiences to connect to the video. At eight and a half minutes long, the "AMIA Memory" benefit music video is approximately two minutes longer than León Gieco's original song, "La Memoria," providing an extended reflection on the meaning of memory and allowing for the inclusion of a wider array of voices. Moreover, the video provides a comparative point of reference between AMIA memory and the collective memory of other human rights abuses in Latin America. Commemoration is a competitive space as organizations struggle for resources, recognition and finances.[36] As Kapszuk states:

> For years, it has been difficult for organisms or institutions of memory to include other tragedies in their call for justice. There was an underlying feeling that doing so would make the central axis disappear, that comparisons might trivialize a terribly painful event. But León's song and the demo captured an overarching theme: the corrosive effect of forgetting and impunity.[37]

Between song and recording session, organizers presented the project as a unique collaborative event, a special occasion in which competitions in the music industry space and personal loyalties to particular human rights causes were subordinated to national protest against oblivion and impunity. Utilizing classic elements of charity singles such as the close cropping of singers' faces delivering a line of the song, the inclusion of shots of recording equipment, such as microphones and headphones, implied a particular sense of intimacy in the experience of the recording session. The video combines several different aesthetic elements: the benefit-concert model draws together a variety of musicians and performers with an audience (for instance, George Harrison's 1971 Concert for Bangladesh); the charity single is used to raise funds for a cause (such as the 1984 UK Band Aid project, "Do They Know It's Christmas," featuring Boy George, and the 1985 "We Are the World" USA for Africa project by Michael Jackson and Lionel Ritchie, produced by Quincy Jones); and the mobile-media format of the music video can be uploaded to, and circulated on, the internet.

Reaching more than four million people in just over two weeks, the "AMIA Memory" benefit music video was widely regarded as a success. In the days before the twenty-second anniversary of the AMIA attack, it engendered thousands of positive responses and comments on YouTube, Facebook, and Twitter and served as an important conversation piece for AMIA representatives to engage in-depth conversations about the cause with journalists.[38] Feeding the national buzz prior to the video's media release, Gieco was awarded the Premio Gardel Solidario (Gardel Award for Solidarity) at Argentina's major music-industry awards in June 2017.[39] Coinciding with nationwide celebrations of Argentina's bicentennial commemoration of its independence from Spain on July 9, 1816, the "AMIA Memory" benefit music video circulated widely within the nation during a time of historical awareness of the collective past. In October 2017, moreover, the Latin Academy of Recording Arts & Sciences (the "Latin Grammys") aired the video at the meeting of the Circle of Producers and Engineers during Latin Grammy week held in Las Vegas, Nevada, an honor celebrated by the project organizers.[40]

In this multidimensional music project, memory shifts from the body of personal experience—of personal witnessing of the attack, of the embodiment of Jewishness, of active forms of listening at live commemorative events—to the screen. The moving image of celebrity musicians assembling as a sonic force of political and social change represents a musically embodied nation where "the people" are diverse but ultimately connected through memory work as a collective "we." The performance of public assembly in the "AMIA Memory" video thus attempts to account for the body of victims it means to honor, while "asserting a plural and performative right to appear" to acknowledge victims' absences through the presence of celebrities to showcase the cause.[41]

Accordingly, the "Memoria AMIA" benefit music video brings into relief a set of tensions foregrounding exchanges of power in the struggle to represent the AMIA cause. This contested postmemorial construction of memory becomes crucial in the video's omission of musical aesthetics more commonly associated with Jewish identities and the absence of Jewish Argentine musicians actively performing contemporary Jewish musics in Buenos Aires. Some questions arise: Does the absence of musicians known to perform Jewish musical repertories somehow also "gloss over" the legacy of ethnic violence and the intentional targeting of a key Jewish institution in Argentina? Does the memory of the particularity of the event suffer at the expense of the elevation of the universality of nationality? In discussing the impetus and concept of the project, AMIA administrators stated that their intent was to ask for justice not only for its own cause but also for all tragedies—a claim placing the AMIA bombing within a larger nexus of national and international human rights work.

When posed a similar question in an interview, Kapszuk's response to my question about the representation of Jewishness in the arts of memory for the AMIA cause reflects another layer of complexity in addressing Jewishness in relation to this AMIA memory project:

> There is nothing that I do that is not 100 percent Jewish. I am 100 percent Argentine, 100 percent Jewish. My conception of memory and my preoccupation with memory comes from my passionate love for the seder at Passover. All of the things I do have to do with the form of transmission that I learned at the Passover seder. What is it? You have to feel—you—as if you were going out of Egypt. And what I do with this Jewish knowledge, I am making it so that a person confronting the issue of the AMIA bombing does not feel alien to it as an "other," but rather, that you feel as if it were your own.[42]

Foregrounding his own Jewish upbringing as fundamental to the way he curates and produces public memory projects as an arts administrator, Kapszuk provides an important link between memory and Jewish identity. Through this understanding, he locates performative and embodied notions of Jewishness at the core of his artistic vision, providing an alternative to authoritative memorial modes of witness and personal experience in commemorative practices. Following Kapszuk's comments, through other commemorative modalities involving technological mediation, memory shifts from the body of personal experience to the screen, and AMIA memory is then undergirded by an artistic performance strategy rooted in Jewish religious ritual and Jewish cultures of memory. Through the use of mediated images disrupting the connection between personal experience, media, and affect, the "AMIA Memory" benefit music video brings the memory of the attack to those who never experienced it firsthand as a "prosthetic memory." As Landsberg argues, "The idea of prosthetic memory, then, rejects the notion that all memories—and, by extension, the identities that those memories sustain—are necessarily and substantively shaped by lived social context."[43] Drawing attention to the sonic elements of commemoration and practices of remembrance in their relation to the visual, the postmemorial stage of memory of the AMIA bombing "makes ideas and images available to people who reside in different places and have different backgrounds." In the "AMIA Memory" benefit music video, this transpires through the commodification of Argentine musical symbols.[44]

Conclusion: We Want Nothing Less Than the Truth, We Demand Nothing More Than Justice

Subsuming the musical fabric of the nation in the cause for the AMIA, Gieco's song "Memory" and the "AMIA Memory" benefit music video succeed at opening up the spaces of the bombing's commemorated pasts by tying together performances of memory in different temporal domains. Memories of prior eighteenths of July unfold diachronically and sometimes anachronistically to the listener at the center of the experience of commemoration through sound and song. For some listeners, the "AMIA Memory" benefit music video might be a first point of access into a much longer history of commemorations for the terrorist bombing. For others, it marks the arrival of yet another year of absences: of friends, family members, and justice. Interfacing between political bodies and social bodies, the benefit music video stages solidarity, bringing to light a complex set of relations that call into question the place of the Jewish Argentine body in the nation and Jewish corporeality in advocacy for the AMIA cause. By weaving the histories of violence targeting the Jewish collectivity of Buenos Aires into the lyrics of his ode to human rights atrocities throughout Latin America, Gieco's unlikely Spanish-language ballad serves the important role of representing the AMIA cause as an anthem to Jewish history in Argentina and the tragic paradoxes of Latin American modernity.

The "AMIA Memory" benefit music video project thus recalls the optimism of an effort to achieve justice in Argentina, yet it also enfolds the haunting resonances of other regional tragedies acknowledged in the lyrics. In late modernity, at the turn of the twenty-first century, Latin America's troubled political and social realities were often more concrete than the possibility of attaining truth and justice amid the lived experience of corporeal absences, persistent structural inequalities, and a lack of clear facts about the nation's violent pasts. In this case study of the emergence of an anthem for the AMIA cause and the "AMIA Memory" benefit music video, I showcase the entanglement of music and the violence of impunity to address through the work of musical actors rearranging sound to imagine new aesthetic forms of solidarity for political change.

The ruins of the AMIA demanded reconstruction, both physical and ideological. In this context, cultural labor and memory work provided the space and the means for debate—a way to reflect on, as well as to reengage Jewishness and Jewish Argentine identity within the political frameworks of discourses of the nation pushed to their limits. As Philip V. Bohlman and Brian Currid argue with respect to the Holocaust: "The national landscape of death forms the genealogy of human monuments, and in this sense the lives that have constituted the nation's histories also become the monuments that serve as sites for remembering it while healing its pasts."[45] Does a new ethic of artistic representation need to be reconsidered, as commemorative expressions and "modes of repair" sway toward the realms of commodification and prosthetic memory, producing audible forms of memorialization and commemoration that embrace the historical realities of the past, but may silence certain internal debates?[46]

Problematizing an anthem's multitemporal foundations may ground various performances of a song as a commemorative act in a moment of historical specificity to combat the "excesses" of memory.[47] However, as I wonder about the future of the arts of AMIA memory, does the political efficacy and widespread social practice of performing public assembly, a social practice deeply rooted in the Argentine society, fundamentally shift as well when memory work moves people from the streets and the plazas to their screens and electronic devices? If not to change political futures, can the arts of AMIA memory provide collective healing through solidarity after trauma? In the absence of truth and justice, is that enough?

Notes

A version of this chapter was presented at the Latin American Jewish Studies Association Conference held at the Universidad Iberoamericana in Mexico City in July 2017 and at the Latin American and Iberian Studies Association of the Pacific Northwest Conference at Lewis and Clark College in April 2018. This essay was completed as the Lowell Milken Fund for American Jewish Music Postdoctoral Scholar at the University of California, Los Angeles.

1. As Julie Buckler and Emily D. Johnson demonstrate, the reenactment of public ritual in commemorative sites of collective memory overwrites past historical narratives of place and belonging. In these key locations, the performance of the past is reasserted to produce symbols of solidarity and nationality in the present amid traces of rejected pasts discarded by new political regimes. See *Rites of Place: Public Commemoration in Russia and Eastern Europe* (Evanston, IL: Northwestern University Press, 2013), 6.

2. In the initial investigation into the AMIA attack, Carlos Telleldín, a car-parts dealer linked to the car that exploded in front of the AMIA, and police officers from the Buenos Aires Province were brought to trial from 2001 to 2004. During this trial, officials discovered irregularities in the investigation suggest-

Table 4.1. The Lyrics of “Memoria AMIA—Homenaje a las víctimas del atentado”

“Memoria AMIA”	Music and Lyrics by León Gieco Arrangement by Facundo “Lito” Vitale	Dedication: “Por los Muertos de AMIA”
1) Intro: Luis Salinas, electric guitar Luis Gurevich, piano Javier Malosetti, electric guitar		
2) León Gieco Valeria Lynch Abel Pintos Andrés Ciro	Los viejos amores que no están la ilusión de los que perdieron Todas las promesas que se van y los que en cualquier guerra se cayeron	Those we once loved now gone The illusion of those who lost All of the promises that are gone and those who fell victim to any war
Miss Bolivia and Palo Pandolfo Julia Zenko and Raúl Lavie	Todo está guardado en la memoria Sueño de la vida y de la historia	Everything is kept safe in our memory A dream of life and history
Pedro Aznar Horacio Fontova Patricia Sosa Peteco Carabajal	El engaño y la complicidad de los genocidas que están sueltos el indulto y el Punto Final a las bestias de aquel infierno	The deceit and the complicity of the murderers who walk the streets those military monsters who got off scot free
Verónica Condomi and Liliana Vitale Hilda Lizarazu and Lisandro Aristimuño	Todo está guardado en la memoria Sueño de la vida y de la historia	It’s all kept safe in our memory A dream of life and history
Charo Bogarín and Bahiano César Pueyerredón Celeste Carballo Paz Martínez	La memoria despierta para herir a los pueblos dormidos que no la dejan vivir libre como el viento	Memory can shake people awake If they try to curb it It will make them ache Not let it loose like the wind
Rodolfo Mederos, bandoneón		

3) Victor Heredia	Los desaparecidos que se buscan	The disappeared that are searched
Diego Torres	con el color de sus nacimientos	In the color of their births
Maxi Trusso	el hambre y la abundancia que se juntan	Hunger and abundance come together
Karina, La Princesita	el maltrato con su mal recuerdo	Abuse with its bad memory
Max Urtizberea and Luis Pecetti	Todo está clavado en la memoria	It's all etched in our memory
Ligia Piro and Kevin Johansen	Espina de la vida y de la historia	A thorn of life and history
Teresa Parodi	Dos mil comerían por un año	Two thousand could eat for a year
Rolo Sartorio	con lo que cuenta un minuto militar	With what the military spends in a minute
Axel	cuántos dejarían de ser esclavos	how many slaves would be freed
Liliana Herrero	por el precio de una bomba al mar	for the price of a bomb exploded in the sea
Lucía and Joaquín Galán	Todo está clavado en la memoria	Everything is etched in our memory
Tom Taranto and Lula Bertoldi	Espina de la vida y de la historia	A thorn of life and history
Los Tipitos	La memoria pincha hasta sangrar	Memory punctures until it makes
Leo García & Gladys (La Bomba Tucumana)	a los pueblos que la amarran	Bleed the people that don't let it run free
Raúl Porchetto	y no la dejan andar	and not let loose
Adriana Varela	libre como el viento	free like the wind
4) Instrumental Interlude		
Lito Vitale, piano		
Chango Spasiuk, accordion		
5) Choir:	Todos los muertos de la AMIA	All those who died at the AMIA
	Todos los muertos de la AMIA	All those who died at the AMIA
Marcelo Corvalán	Todos los muertos de la AMIA	All those who died at the AMIA
Elena Roger	Todos los muertos de la AMIA	All those who died at the AMIA
Juan Carlos Baglietto	y los de la Embajada de Israel	and those who died at the Israeli Embassy
Choir	el poder secreto de las armas	the secret power of weapons
	la justicia que mira y no ve	justice that looks but does not see

Table 4.1.—*Continued*"

6) Raly Barrionuevo	Todo está escondido en la memoria	Everything is hidden in our memory
Luciano Pereyra	Refugio de la vida y de la historia	A shelter of life and history
Alejandro Lerner		
Lali Espósito	Fue cuando se callaron las iglesias	When the churches fell silent
	fue cuando el fútbol se lo comió todo	And soccer consumed it all
Marcela Morelo and David Lebón	que los padres palotinos y Angelelli	the Pallottine priests and Bishop Angelelli
Dani Suarez and Cóndor Sbarbati	dejaron su sangre en el lodo	were left bleeding on the earth
Marián Farias Gómez and Mavi Díaz	Todo está escondido en la memoria	It's all loaded in our memory
Guillermo Fernández and Nahuel Pennisi	Refugio de la vida y de la historia	A shelter of life and history
Amelita Baltar		
Iván Noble	La memoria estalla hasta vencer	Memory swells and then breaks free
	a los pueblos que la aplastan	Defeating peoples who try to keep it down
Arbolito	y no la dejan ser	And who won't let it run
	libre como el viento	free like the wind
	libre como el viento	free like the wind
7) Ricardo Mollo	La bala a Chico Mendez en Brasil	The bullet for Chico Mendez in Brazil
Litto Nebbia	150 mil guatemaltecos	150,000 Guatemalans
Gustavo Santaloalla	los mineros que enfrentan al fusil	the miners who face the firing squad
Soledad Pastorutti	represión estudiantil en México	student repression in Mexico
Marilina Ross and Miguel Cantilo	Todo está cargado en la memoria	It's all loaded in our memory
Emilio Del Guercio and Bruno Arias	Arma de la vida y de la historia	A weapon of life and history
Sandra Mihanovich	América con almas destruidas	America with their ravaged souls
Cucho Parisi	Los chicos que mata el escuadrón	The children killed by police
Nacha Guevara	Suplicio de Mugica por las villas	Mugica prays for the slums
Jairo	Dignidad de Rodolfo Walsh	Rodolfo Walsh and his dignity

Los Nocheros	Todo es escondido en la memoria	It's all hidden in our memory
Adrián Barilari and Javier Calamaro	Arma de la vida y de la historia	A weapon of life and history
Natalia Oreiro	La memoria apunta hasta matar	Memory takes aim and shoots
Benito Cerati and Emme	a los pueblos que la callan	A people who try to keep it quiet
Nito Mestre	y no la dejan volar	And those who won't let it fly
Piero	libre como el viento	Free like the wind
Andrees Giménez	y no la dejan volar	And those who won't let it run
León Gieco	libre como el viento	Free like the wind
8) León Gieco	Justicia...	Justice…
And choir		

ing a cover-up carried out by Judge Juan José Galeano, prosecutors, police, and other investigating agents. In 2004, the case was officially nullified, and Galeano was removed from his position. An investigation into the cover-up was ordered, naming Galeano, prosecutors, police, various intelligence agents, ex-president of the Delegación de Asociaciones Israelitas Argentinas (DAIA) Rubén Beraja, and former president Carlos Menem of involvement in a bribery scheme to have Telleldín testify against the provincial police. The trial for the cover-up of the AMIA bombing began in 2015. Earlier that year, prosecutor Alberto Nisman was found dead of apparent suicide in his apartment—a case ruled a homicide based on a reevaluation of forensic evidence in 2018. Nisman's body was found the day before he was set to bring an accusation of conspiracy to the Argentine Congress against former president Cristina Fernández de Kirchner and former foreign minister Hectór Timmerman for their involvement signing the 2013 Memorandum of Understanding with Iran—an agreement to form an Iranian-Argentine joint commission to allow for the questioning of Iranian officials in Iran accused of planning and financing the 1994 attack. The memorandum was widely criticized globally and eventually revoked by President Mauricio Macri in 2015. References to the AMIA cause in this essay, in fact, refer to the original investigation as well as the more recent investigation into the cover-up. For more information, see the valiant work of Memoria Activa at http://memoriaactiva.com/

3. Karen Ann Faulk translates *acto* as "memorial/protest" to highlight the political and commemorative dimensions of these public assemblies. See *In the Wake of Neoliberalism: Citizenship and Human Rights in Argentina* (Stanford, CA: Stanford University Press, 2012), 50–69.

4. Judith Butler, *Notes toward a Performative Theory of Assembly* (Cambridge, MA: Harvard University Press, 2015).

5. Marianne Hirsch, *The Generation of Postmemory: Writing and Visual Culture after the Holocaust* (New York: Columbia University Press, 2012).

6. "La estación Pasteur de subte, convertida en espacio de memoria," *La Nación*, July 9, 2015, https://www.lanacion.com.ar/1808869-la-estacion-pasteur-de-subte-convertida-en-espacio-de-memoria

7. Archival materials consulted in this essay were provided by the Centro de Documentación e Información sobre Judaísmo Argentino Marc Turkow at the AMIA. I would like to extend a note of gratitude to Gabriel Feldman for all of his assistance sending newspaper articles and links to video footage. Amílcar Antognoni and Rubén Correa, "Multitudinaria condena frente al Congreso," *La Nación*, July 22, 1994; Jorge A. Elías, "Bronca y memoria guardaron silencio," *La Nación*, July 22, 1994.

8. Walter Curia, "Hubo silbados para el presidente Menem al una multitude," *Clarin*, July 22, 1994; Raúl Kollmann, "Tensión en el palco por los silbidos a Menem," *Página/12*, July 22, 1994.

9. Silvia Tandeciarz, "Citizens of Memory: Reconfiguring the Past in Postdictatorship Argentina," *PMLA* 122, no. 1 (2007): 152.

10. Tandeciarz, "Citizens of Memory."

11. Gabriela Cerutti, "La historia de la memoria," *Puentes*, March 2001, 14–25. See also Diana Taylor, *Disappearing Acts: Spectacles of Gender and Nationalism*

in Argentina's Dirty War (Durham, NC: Duke University Press, 1997). A vocal and active political call for justice against impunity expressed through discourses and performances of memory in Argentina arose in the wake of Adolfo Scilingo's 1995 confession of his participation in the death flights. The impunity laws of 1986 and 1987 were later repealed by the Argentine Congress in 2003.

12. Raúl Kollmann, "Tensión en el palco por los silbidos a Menem," *Página/12*, July 22, 1994.

13. Ana María Ochoa Gautier, "Silence," in *Keywords in Sound*, ed. David Novak and Matt Sakakeeny (Durham, NC: Duke University Press, 2015), 183.

14. Gautier, "Silence," 186.

15. Vered Vinitzky-Seroussi and Chana Teeger, "Unpacking the Unspoken: Silence in Collective Memory and Forgetting," *Social Forces* 88, no. 3 (2010): 1104.

16. Vinitzky-Seroussi and Teeger, "Unpacking the Unspoken," 1108–9.

17. James Brook, "Argentines Protest Bombing as Death Toll Reaches 44," *New York Times*, July 22, 1994; Pedro Brieger, "Argentina's Jews after the Bomb: From Scapegoats to Pariahs," *Moment*, December 1994, 88–89. See also Carlos Vega, *El himno nacional Argentina* (Buenos Aires: Eudeba, 1962); Ana María Mondolo, "El libro 'El himno nacional argentino' de Carlos Vega," *Revista del Instituto de Investigación Musicológica "Carlos Vega"* 26, no. 26 (2012): 271–95; Edwin Seroussi, "'Hatikvah': Conceptions, Receptions and Reflections," *Yuval Online* 9 (2015).

18. Ricardo Feierstein, *Historia de los Judíos argentinos* (Buenos Aires: Editorial Galerna, 2006), 428.

19. Video links provided by the Centro de Documentación e Información sobre Judaísmo Argentino Marc Turkow. Television coverage by Televisión Pública Argentina (ATC) on YouTube by the Archivo Histórico de Radio Televisión Argentina, "Atentado a la AMIA: Inicio del acto oficial de repudio, 1994" [July 1994], YouTube video, 101:49, posted January 14, 2016, https://www.youtube.com/watch?v=adoJhyVb77Q; "Atentado a la AMIA: Inicio del acto oficial de repudio, 1994 (fragmento I)" [July 1994], YouTube video, 101:49, posted January 14, 2016, https://www.youtube.com/watch?v=6DNUul_PnKk; "Atentado a la AMIA: Inicio del acto oficial de repudio, 1994 (fragmento II)" [July 1994], YouTube video, 101:49, posted January 14, 2016, https://www.youtube.com/watch?v=AWezQ5TgG0k

20. Walter Curia, "Hubo silbidos para el presidente Menem a una multitud," *Clarin*, July 22, 1994; "Ya no buscan sobrevivientes," *La Nación*, July 22, 1994.

21. Raanan Rein, *Argentina, Israel, and the Jews: Perón, the Eichmann Capture and After*, trans. Martha Grenzeback (Bethesda: University of Maryland Press, 2003).

22. Susana Wappenstein, "The Nation's Bodies: Justice and Belonging in the Aftermath of the AMIA Bombing," in *Landscapes of Memory and Impunity: The Aftermath of the AMIA Bombing in Jewish Argentina*, ed Annette Levine and Natasha Zaretsky (Boston: Brill, 2015), 8–43.

23. Wappenstein, "The Nation's Bodies," 8.

24. Seroussi, "Hatikvah."

25. Shana L. Redmond, *Anthem: Social Movements and the Sound of Solidarity in the African Diaspora* (New York: New York University Press, 2014), 9.

26. Elio Kapszuk, *Memoria AMIA* (Buenos Aires: AMIA Comunidad Judía, 2017).

27. Gerard Béhague and Irma Ruiz, "Argentina," *Grove Music Online*, published January 20, 2001.

28. Kapszuk, *Memoria AMIA*, 5.

29. Interview with Elio Kapszuk in Buenos Aires, July 21, 2017. See also the Soka Gakkai International website, http://www.sgi.org/es/sgi-en-resumen/

30. Kapszuk, interview.

31. Kapszuk, interview.

32. This analysis is based on the video "Memoria AMIA—Homenaje a las víctimas del atentado" published to the amiatv YouTube channel on July 4, 2016, https://www.youtube.com/watch?v=SuSUAElqjvc

33. Redmond, *Anthem*, 2–3.

34. Ralph T. Daniel, Elwyn A. Wienandt, and Laurie J. Sampsel, "Anthem," *Grove Music Online*, published October 16, 2003.

35. Benedict Anderson, *Imagined Communities: Reflection on the Origin and Spread of*
Nationalism, rev. ed. (New York: Verso, 2006), 145.

36. Michael Rothberg, *Multidirectional Memory: Remembering the Holocaust in the Age of Decolonization* (Stanford, CA: Stanford University Press, 2009).

37. Kapszuk, *Memoria AMIA*, 5. Translation mine.

38. Claudia Lorenzón, "A 22 años del atentado a la AMIA, cien artistas unidos reclaman Memoria y Justicia," *Telám*, July 17, 2016, http://www.telam.com.ar/notas/201607/155590-atentado-amia-artistas-reclamo-memoria-justicia-aniversario-22-anos-video.html. In an interview with Kapszuk in July 2017, he stated that the video had been viewed over ten million times worldwide.

39. "El video Memoria AMIA ya fue visto más de 3 millones de veces," July 11, 2016, http://www.lanacion.com.ar/1917363-el-video-memoria-amia-ya-fue-visto-por-mas-de-3-millones-de-personas-en-las-redes

40. Kapszuk, *Memoria AMIA*, 104–5.

41. Butler, *Notes toward Performative Theory*.

42. Translation by author. Interview with Elio Kapszuk in Buenos Aires, July 21, 2017.

43. Alison Landsberg, *Prosthetic Memory: The Transformation of American Remembrance in the Age of Mass Culture* (New York: Columbia University Press, 2004), 19.

44. Hirsch, *The Generation of Postmemory*, 18.

45. Philip V. Bohlman and Brian Currid, "Suturing History, Healing Europe: German National Temporality in Wolokalamsk Highway," *Musical Quarterly* 85, no. 4 (2001): 711.

46. Eric Santner, "History beyond the Pleasure Principle: Some Thoughts about the Representation of Trauma," in *Probing the Limits of Representation: Nazism and the "Final Solution"*, ed. Saul Friedländer (Cambridge, MA: Harvard University Press, 1992), 143–54.

47. David Berliner, "The Abuses of Memory: Reflections on the Memory Boom in Anthropology," *Anthropological Quarterly* 78, no. 1 (2005): 197–211.

FIVE | Musical Memory, Animated Amnesia

The Soundtrack of Exoneration in Waltz with Bashir

MICHAEL A. FIGUEROA

In early June 1982, seven years into the Lebanese Civil War (1975–90), the Israel Defense Forces (IDF) involved itself in Lebanon's protracted conflict in order to wage war on the Palestine Liberation Organization (PLO), which was then based in southern Lebanon. The PLO resistance fighters had been launching periodic attacks along Israel's northern border for several years until the signing of a US-brokered cease-fire in July 1981. But on June 3, 1982, the PLO broke the terms of that deal through an attempted assassination of Shlomo Argov, who was at the time the Israeli ambassador to Britain. Over the next three days, the IDF bombed PLO targets in Lebanon and launched a full-scale invasion of the country's southern territory, which it would not fully evacuate until 2000, ten years after the Lebanese Civil War officially came to a close. The war beginning in 1982 has become colloquially known in Israel as "our Vietnam," in reference to a perceived breakdown in national consensus with regard to the war's morality, similar to popular disapproval of the US–Vietnam War of 1955–75, the protest of which became an American countercultural cause célèbre during that war's second decade. The Israeli army's actions in Lebanon drew protests in Tel Aviv involving 350,000–400,000 people, roughly 10 percent of the Israeli population at that time across traditional demographic divides, and has since continued to be a controversial subject in conversations about the morality of war and occupation in the region.[1]

On September 14, 1982, three months into the fighting, a then-unknown assassin murdered Lebanese president-elect Bashir Gemayel with a bomb planted at his party's headquarters in Beirut's Ashrafiyeh district. Gemayel had been a charismatic leader of the Maronite Christian right-wing political party Phalange and a fierce commander of its militia during the civil war; his death was devastating to his multitude of followers.[2] Seeking revenge, and working on the false assumption that the PLO was responsible for Gemayel's death, Phalange militiamen entered the Sabra and Shatila refugee camp in southern Beirut on the evening of September 16 and butchered every Palestinian man, woman, and child they could find.[3] The Israeli army aided the Phalange's efforts by blockading the camps and shooting flares to light their way during the night. The massacre lasted forty hours, until the morning of September 18.[4] The event has since joined the Nakba of 1948 and the Naksa of 1967 as one of the Palestinian people's fundamental traumas.[5]

The animated film *Waltz with Bashir* (2008) depicts the moments that immediately follow the Sabra and Shatila massacre during its closing scene. Throngs of howling Palestinian women tread through the streets, as they mourn over the piles of lifeless and mutilated bodies in the camps. Musical sound, a constant presence over the preceding eighty minutes of the film, fades into a periodic rumble, mimicking the sound of the beating hearts of two Israeli soldiers whose chests heave as they gaze in horrified disbelief on what has just transpired. The pregnant silence breaks only for the screams of mourning Palestinian women processing through the streets, as they navigate around the bodies of the dead. This is also the moment when Israeli director Ari Folman's animated world subsides and archival footage of trauma washes over the viewer. The film breaks the mold of animation, ending Folman's stylized sonic and visual presentation of the preceding memory quest in a photo-realistic reveal of a memory that the filmmaker had previously forgotten. Once the suppressed memory is shown as recovered, the screen cuts to black, the credits roll, and the movie's soundtrack returns to reinforce the viewer's sense of having borne witness to Folman's reenactment of trauma and its resolution.

Written, directed, and narrated by Ari Folman, *Waltz with Bashir* is an investigation into the nature of memory and forgetting in the context of the individual and national traumas of the violence of 1982. At the film's beginning, a nighttime encounter forces Folman to confront the fact that he has no concrete memory of the Israeli invasion of Lebanon or of the Sabra and Shatila massacre specifically. Using a distinctly twenty-first-century register of Hebrew, he coolly remarks, "Lo be sistem sheli" (It's not in my system). With some initial trepidation, he sets out on a journey, using the medium of documentary film (here, rendered in animation) to recover his repressed memories. The film alternates between this diegetic narrative of Folman's "autobiographical self-examination" and metadiegetic episodes that pair the testimonies of his interview subjects with surreal renderings of the historical events that they recount.[6] Composer Max Richter's stylistically eclectic soundtrack provides aesthetic and narrative continuity to the kaleidoscopic reenactment of memory recovery and trauma. By the end of the film, and just prior to the closing scene, Folman reaches the point of remembering that he was complicit in the mass murder at Sabra and Shatila, as part of the Israeli regiment that blocked the exits and shot the flares that allowed Phalange fighters to carry out the carnage.

Waltz with Bashir is characterized by its creator and film critics alike as an "animated documentary" of the filmmaker's determination to uncover his forgotten memories; the film's central question focuses on Folman's—and, by extension, Israel's—role in the Sabra and Shatila massacre. In order to answer this question, Folman conducts interviews with surviving army friends who, as the film progresses, gradually reveal details about their memories of serving in the war, all presented in documentary style. Each interview initiates a shift in narrative frame to flashback reenactments of the war—including battle scenes—and more banal reenactments that showcase the combat fraternity that still binds Folman and his interview subjects together. Untangling the narrative agency of the film's multiple components is a complex task. *Waltz with Bashir* is a meta-reenactment, in the sense that it is a reenactment of remembering itself, and the memories that Folman, the film's diegetic narrator, eventually recovers are further reenacted as metadiegetic episodes. Nested plots give the film a compelling narrative shape, and the animated medium allows the complexities of memory to be stylized by the film's visual editors in a manner that is rarely (if ever) possible in live documentaries.

In the following essay, I argue that the film's aesthetic and moral power derives not only from its celebrated visuals but also from the memory work performed by its musical soundtrack. I analyze how the soundtrack for *Waltz with Bashir* works in tandem with its visual elements (*a*) to aestheticize the reenactment of Folman's recovery of traumatic memory and (*b*) to subordinate the trauma of Palestinian victims of the events reenacted. In so doing, I further argue that Richter's soundtrack is effective because of how the composer exploits broad cultural associations accrued to musical register and probes the very possibilities of music's narrative functions in film.

Mutual Constitutions: Music/Film, Trauma/Reenactment

Focusing on the roles and registers of music in *Waltz with Bashir* is warranted by music's pride of place in how both Folman and Richter cast the genesis of the film. In a 2009 interview published on the popular film criticism website ScreenAnarchy.com, Folman credited Richter's music as having shaped the film from the beginning:

> I wrote the script for *Waltz with Bashir* in six days, listening only to Max Richter's albums. I didn't mean for that to happen like that, but it just happened. When I finished the script, I thought, "This guy has, in effect, written the soundtrack for the script." Because scripts have soundtracks. Think about it. If you listen to Bach for a month while writing, Bach will emotionally influence the writing. Nothing influences emotions more than music.[7]

Richter, too, connected his music with the story: "Ari Folman had written it listening to *The Blue Notebooks* [Richter's second album] on loop as he wrote, so I was, in a way, embedded in the material before I started [working on the film]."[8] He claimed that Folman gave him "enormous freedom to pursue whatever direction I wanted to take with the project—and very little changed from that initial delivery. There wasn't a temp score apart from a few pieces from my albums, and the music was finished way before the film, so Ari could mold the picture edit around it."[9] In other words, the director and film scorer operated in reverse of the customary working order, with musical inspiration predating both the script (in the form of Richter's previous work) and the visuals (in the form of the soundtrack, written between the completion of the script and the animation).

Waltz with Bashir is therefore a music-oriented film to its core; however, in reception it has been recognized almost solely for its visual casting of memory, forgetting, and trauma. The film forms part of a trio of contemporary films concerning Israel's role in the Lebanon War that were released around the same time, including Josef Cedar's *Beaufort* (2008) and Samuel Moaz's *Lebanon* (2009). *Waltz with Bashir* is perhaps the best known of the three, at least internationally, and earned for its creators a Golden Globe in 2009 for Best Foreign-Language Film and nominations at the Oscars, BAFTA Awards, Annie Awards, Cannes, and other international ceremonies, along with six wins at the Israeli Academy Awards.[10] Folman won international critical acclaim, especially in the American press, much of it for the novelty of having created an *animated* reenactment of wartime trauma. In the *New York Times*, A. O. Scott characterized *Waltz with Bashir* as "a work of astonishing aesthetic integrity and searing moral power," as the film's DVD jacket boasts in quotation.[11] "It has taken an animated film to go where live-action dramas and even documentaries haven't—to tickle our synapses and slip into our bloodstream," wrote David Edelstein of *New York Magazine*.[12] In the *Christian Science Monitor*, Peter Rainer praised the film for being "a supremely courageous act, not only as a piece of filmmaking, but much more so as a moral testament."[13]

Several critics have suggested that, in spite of its visual beauty, the film advances a form of "perpetrator trauma" that claims Sabra and Shatila for Israeli history while obscuring Palestinian victimhood. In response to all of the praise in the United States and on the eve of the Oscars, Gideon Levy of the Israeli daily newspaper *Haaretz* called the film's antiwar ethos "nothing but a charade": "It deserves an Oscar for the illustrations and animation—but a badge of shame for its message. . . . The truth is it is propaganda."[14] This propaganda, the reader is meant to infer, disseminates a lie—that the Israeli military is morally irreproachable. Near the end of the film, Folman discusses his memory quest with his friend, Ori Sivan, who helps him to realize that his "interest in the massacre stems from another massacre," meaning the Holocaust of World War II and specifically the Auschwitz concentration camp, where Folman's parents had been prisoners. And in another conversation between the two, Sivan returns to the Holocaust, casting Folman as a collaborator pressed into the role of perpetrator by circumstance rather than by choice, claiming, "Unwillingly, you took on the role of the Nazi. You were there firing flares, but you didn't carry out the massacre." He therefore absolved Folman of moral responsibility for Sabra and Shatila, and Folman's expressions of emotional guilt thematized throughout the film—and which are, in fact, commemorated by the film—emerge as the only atonement necessary for his complicity in the Sabra and Shatila massacre.

The conflict between the filmmaker's moral courage in confronting his traumatic memory, on the one hand, and his myopia with regard to the trauma of others, on the other, has been the central problem driving interest in the film among Israeli cinema scholars. In her analysis of the film, Raya Morag identifies *Waltz with Bashir* as an example of "perpetrator trauma," in which "the complex subject position of the posttraumatic perpetrator is structured through a series of (mostly somatic) tensions, including total facial exposure vs. concealment behind digital masks, corporealization vs. phantomization, archival footage vs. documentary animation, simulacric aura vs. desire for referentiality, and realist vs. Brechtian reenactment."[15] While Morag and other critics carefully connect the film's visual elements to the filmmaker's moral aims, what is missing from these analyses is an accounting for the crucial role of music and sound in creating a narrative cohesion across the film's shifting narrative frames.

Max Richter's electronic soundtrack provides nondiegetic sensory continuity and, crucially, enables the slick and frequent transitions between diegetic and metadiegetic reenactment. It casts a sonic glow of dread upon contemporary Tel Aviv; period songs and their violent parodies locate the viewer in distorted memories of the 1980s; diegetic voices of screaming victims powerfully break the surreal haze. The film's sonic elements thus create the very tensions described by Morag; without sound, terms such as "exposure" and "concealment" would merely exist as bifurcations, and the film's various reenactments, with their fluctuating aspirations to realism and distancing surrealism, would not hold together as a coherent whole. Richter himself claimed that the specter of the real influenced the very conception of the soundtrack: "I decided to treat it from a score perspective as though it were not animated. In other words 'everything we are seeing is completely real' was the guiding principle for me." When the interviewer Daniel Schweiger asked him, "Is the point that reality and hallucination are one in the same?" Richter replied, "Yes exactly! Our biography is a fiction we tell ourselves."[16] Richter's music, to put a finer point on it, helps to cinch together a tidy, albeit complex, documentary narrative that ultimately creates the momentum needed for the film's motion toward Folman's moral exoneration.

As Raz Yosef points out, *Waltz with Bashir* "mostly describe[s] the Israeli soldier's psychological deliberations and pangs of conscience." She writes, "This soldier is represented as an 'enlightened' occupier who 'shoots and weeps,' sensitive to and identifying with the Palestinians' suffering, and feeling and seeing himself as persecuted."[17] Gil Hochberg puts it another way, asking "what it means to render visible one's own trauma, understood as a failure to see; and what, if any, ethical position of spectatorship can be modelled on the witnessing of such failed vision."[18]

This line of questioning raises a further question of what "spectatorship" means in the context of the film medium. In her study of the American films *Argo* (2012) and *Zero Dark Thirty* (2013), Michelle Pautz argues that a film's ability to influence audience perceptions of its subject lies in part in the film medium's facilitation of a "pseudo-experience" that comes from "the all-encompassing [sensory] experience of watching it." She further suggests that film offers the potential "to engross the audience and to comprehensively capture the senses of sight and sound."[19] In the case of *Waltz with Bashir*, the pseudo-experiential dimension of spectatorship is intensified through the use of reenactment, a form of representation that places the spectator in an immersive position of witnessing historical events. I argue, moreover, that not only sight—the sensory domain privileged in the film's reception by critics and scholars alike—but also, and especially, *sound* plays a critical role in shaping this pseudo-experience, tying together as it does the aesthetic and moral concerns of Folman and his audiences via metadiegesis.[20]

Without the deployment of strategic musical signifiers, the film would lose its ability to make the quest for memory viscerally accessible to its audience. Any analysis of *Waltz with Bashir*'s pseudo-experiential power would therefore demand, as Hilary Lapedis has posited elsewhere, "an approach which foregrounds the importance of the musical soundtrack: one that positions it as parallel to the visual and as having a discrete and intrinsic meaning in addition to its function within or beyond the diegesis."[21] Pushing things further, Berthold Hoeckner and Howard Nusbaum argue that there is a "measurable asymmetry tilted toward music in cross-modal memory" in what they term the "*Casablanca* effect."[22] Of particular usefulness here is how Hoeckner and Nusbaum, drawing on a wealth of literature on the psychology of memory, distinguish between two main types of memory triggered or facilitated by music in film: "episodic memory" and "semantic memory." They define episodic memory as "long-term memory that involves the recollection of specific events and experiences," or what Ari Folman seeks to uncover in the film's diegesis.[23] Semantic memory is "a memory of meanings, concepts, and world knowledge not directly related to such events and experiences," such as the guilt that hangs in the balance for Folman and is ultimately assuaged at the moment when he is finally able to recall the traumatic episodic memory: his help in facilitating the Sabra and Shatila massacre.[24]

In moving between reenactments of these memory forms, I argue that the soundtrack of *Waltz with Bashir* operates on three stylistic registers: an "instrumental voice" that consists of Richter's electronic soundtrack; a "classical surreal" that draws on music by Johann Sebastian Bach and Frédéric Chopin; and a "pop absurd," which plays on 1980s popular music, represented by both actual and invented songs. In addition to their distinct narrative functions, each of these musical registers commemorates different aspects and actors within the trauma reenacted in the film. Table 5.1 indicates how narrative function (split between visual and aural domains), memory type, and musical style align in the soundtrack of *Waltz with Bashir.*

Instrumental Voice

The film's composed instrumental soundtrack serves as a parallel, nondiegetic narrator to Ari Folman's nondiegetic spoken track. If the soundtrack is one of the film's main narrators, then, what is the nature of its voice? The main nondiegetic music that unites the film from start to finish is "Haunted Ocean," a five-part multimovement suite that recurs at, and develops across, five different key moments in the film. In each of these moments, Folman confronts a distorted memory that—it turns out—refers to events taking place in the immediate aftermath of the Sabra and Shatila massacre. One such moment has Folman and his fellow soldiers bathing nude in the Mediterranean Sea, just off the Beirut coast, at night. We first hear "Haunted Ocean" just after the inciting incident, in which Folman's friend Boaz Rein-Buskila confesses a recurring nightmare related to the Lebanon War. Folman claims to have no memories from the time: "It's not in my system." As the two friends part ways, suddenly Folman has his first flashback to the war. While he drives in his car, the black-and-beige image of a contemplative Folman, still against the backdrop of a street scene moving behind him, is disrupted in regular intervals by shadows that eclipse his face (one of the somatic tensions described by Morag).[25] His voice declares, "The meeting with Boaz took place in winter of 2006. That night, for the first time in twenty years, I had a flashback of the war in Lebanon. Not just Lebanon, West

Table 5.1. Narrative and Memory Function of Musical Styles in *Waltz with Bashir*

Visual	Aural	Memory type	Musical style
diegetic	nondiegetic ambient music	semantic	instrumental voice
metadiegetic	nondiegetic song	episodic	classical surreal
	diegetic song	semantic-episodic hybrid	pop absurdity

Beirut. Not just Beirut, but the massacre at the Sabra and Shatila refugee camps." While he finishes this statement, we see Folman standing on the beach in Tel Aviv looking out at the Mediterranean Sea. The scene transforms to a moment twenty years earlier in the same sea, but now off the coast of Beirut. The diegesis smoothly moves into metadiegesis, as it does at several points in the film. All the while, the swelling string pads and mournful violin of "Haunted Ocean," along with sparse diegetic sounds such as the repetitive cadence of the car's wiper blades, create a sonic palette for the semantic memory of guilt.

Richter's piece is built around a simple descending B♭-A-G melody, harmonized with chords of Gm-D-C, the latter two in inversions that keep the bass line, like the top melody, within a tight range ($\text{i-V}^6\text{-IV}^6_4$).[26] The simplicity of the melodic and harmonic material allows Richter to focus on and play with other parameters, such as dynamics and timbre, to assist the listener in wallowing in the somber murk of Folman's psyche. Richter declared that he had actively searched for a haunted quality in this instrumental voice: "I felt like the entire film should have this 'haunted' quality, so the music is like a hallucination—actually this is pretty natural territory for me. The main 'haunted ocean' music is all about that—a sort of unresolved, weightless, lost melancholia is the general tone I was looking for."[27]

Here and throughout the entire film, an instrumental sound-layer provides musical continuity between diegetic scenes and their individual transitions into metadiegetic narration. Nearly all of the film's diegetic narrative includes spoken text voiced by sources on screen or voiced by characters, ostensibly recorded in documentary fashion, over intense visuals, such as bruised yellow-brown colors and showering rain. Stylistically, most of the ambient instrumental tracks are consistent with Richter's signature electro-acoustic compositional practice, featuring some or all of the following elements: incessant sequenced drums and broad synth pads mixed with violins, piano, and other standard chamber instrumentation; tonal language that is stark—even brutal—at times signifying intimacy, grandiosity, terror, or foreboding; and contrasts that conform to deeply enculturated audience expectations for nondiegetic film music: contrasts between silence and extreme loudness (dynamics), between high and low registers, between slow and fast tempi, and between pieces occurring in sequence.

In her classic study on narrative film music, Claudia Gorbman argues that "non-diegetic film music . . . is not consciously attended to, or [is] at least perceived at a lower level of attention than the pictures or other elements of filmic narration."[28] While this may be a general principle of film music, the soundtrack for *Waltz with Bashir* explicitly departs from the norm in its deployment of *contrasts* in the musical language of the instrumental voice. In other words, the instrumental voice acknowledges what Robynn J. Stilwell has called the "fantastical gap" between diegetic and nondiegetic sound in the very process of bridging that gap.[29] It is through contrasts that the nondiegetic soundtrack announces its nondiegetic status, drawing attention to itself as a narrative device that heralds the audience's encounter with episodic memory. For all these contrasts, however, much of the diegetic narrative's nondiegetic soundtrack is conceptually and even stylistically coherent. In the flashback episode of Folman's initial army deployment, for example, a track titled "Taxi and APC" involves punishingly loud drums creating rhythmic contrast with the constant machine guns—a rhythmic counterpoint, in fact, between diegetic and nondiegetic sound. Throughout the composed instrumental soundtrack, Richter exploits several types of half-step relationships (some tonal, some not quite tonal) to create ambiguities, such as modal mixture and cyclical harmonic progressions that seem to indicate a meandering form, in which chords search in vain for a permanent, stable resolution, thus creating a musical parallel to the ostensible narrator Ari Folman, who never quite reaches catharsis even though he resolves his ethical crisis. This is precisely the function of the simple theme of the "Haunted Ocean" suite described above.

Richter's composed instrumental soundtrack thus facilitates the transitions between diegetic narration and metadiegetic flashbacks by providing aural continuity across radically shifting visual frames, and it does so through a particular stylistic coherence built around the element of contrast. This is one level where we start to see traditional narrative frameworks break down as Folman, the former soldier, gropes around for lost memories.

Classical Surreal

In analyzing how *Waltz with Bashir* exploits previously composed music from the Western canon in its soundtrack, I take a cue from Michael Long's *Beautiful Monsters*, in which Long theorizes "the classical" through a register-theory framework to explain how classical music carries meaning in the postclassical, perhaps postmodern, contexts in which it is frequently estranged from the concert hall, even appearing in fragmented or remixed forms.[30] Moving beyond Long's unit of "the classical" to a finer level of characterization, in *Waltz with Bashir*, the classical register serves a very specific purpose: it initiates a move into surrealist aesthetics that allow the filmmaker to shift not between diegetic and metadiegetic frames, as in the case of the instrumental voice discussed above, but rather between episodic and semantic memories themselves. Reenactments of events thus become representations of emotion, dispensing with any pretense of photorealistic documentation "in this animated documentary." Richter hints at the classical surreal's function in musical "Easter eggs"—fragments of Schubert's Piano Sonata No. 20 (D. 959) and Chopin's "Funeral March" (Piano Sonata no. 2, op. 35)—that he interpolated in the score, in order to place the viewer sonically within Folman's psyche: "I used these fragments in the film after discussing with Ari [Folman] his reasons for including the Schubert in the original trailer—turns out his mother was a pianist and that these pieces meant something to him personally. So it made perfect sense to refer to this material in a couple of scenes."[31]

The most prominent example of Richter's appropriation of the Western canon is a track entitled "JSB/RPG." The music undergirds a difficult scene, in which Israeli troops move stealthily through a vineyard searching for enemy combatants. The physical movement of the soldiers indicates an extremely tense mood, in which they are forced to creep under the brush for fear of being detected. This is sonically reinforced through sparse ambient diegetic sounds, such as quiet footsteps and the occasional buzzing of insects. Nondiegetic sounds dominate the scene, as the audience hears the Largo movement of Johann Sebastian Bach's Harpsichord Concerto in F minor (BWV 1056), performed by Max Richter on the piano with string accompaniment. BMW 1056 is a favorite in the modern piano repertoire—evidenced in part by Vanessa Agnew's recognition of the piece during her travel along the refugee route, as described in this volume—but it has rarely been chosen among Bach's works for film soundtracks, save for prominent appearances in the soundtracks for *Lara Croft: Tomb Raider* (Simon West, 2001) and *Tomb Raider* (Roar Uthaug, 2018). Similar to its use in *Lara Croft*, in which the Bach accompanies the acrobatic movements of Angelina Jolie's titular character (only soon to be interrupted by a fight scene), the performance made for *Waltz with Bashir* is given in an atypically rubato style. The striking departure from normative performance practice in both soundtracks, which appeared only seven years apart, forms a musical intertext that synthesizes what Anahid Kassabian calls "a logic of endless iteration," in which "even within the stories themselves, moving back and forth through time is thematized."[32] Such thematization here results in a sense of the surreal occurring through two juxtapositions: of the slow-moving largo tempo with the intensity of the battlefield, and of the noble register of the baroque with the ignobility of modern violence.

After multiple viewings of *Waltz with Bashir,* I came to understand this as a kind of foreshadowing within the soundtrack's parallel narration—by drawing on the pianistic conventions used to perform Chopin, Richter's playing with metrical time in the Bach creates a continuity with the waltz scene that gives the film its title (discussed below). The music also sits much higher in the mix than the diegetic sound I describe above, until the scene's end is heralded by a child who fires a rocket-propelled grenade (an "RPG," as in the track's title), which explodes upon impact against the Israeli jeep and sends the troops scattering. Both the RPG and the flying troops move in slow motion, while the musical performance continues toward its conclusion, indifferent to the violence that has just taken place. This is a pattern in the soundtrack, where music facilitates episodic memory that is abruptly pierced by death, or by a bringer of death such as a bullet or missile. We might perhaps understand such violent signifiers as agents of semantic memory that ensound the limits of faithful reenactment.

In the waltz scene for which the film is named, Folman's friend Shmuel Frenkel teeters on the line between heroism and insanity—a common theme for war films—as he demands and eventually steals a machine gun from his fellow soldier, then enters the open street while surrounded by enemy soldiers and begins firing in all directions. Much of the scene is focused on Frenkel's feet, which dance in time to a performance of one of Chopin's most famous waltzes, op. 64 no. 2, as empty bullet casings drop to the street around him.[33] This is clearly a hostile environment, visually signified by the torn posters of Bashir Gemayel that line the cement walls around him, but Folman and Richter manage to find beauty in the madness and bodily gestures of Frenkel and set these to music for solo piano that is associated with the intimacy of interior spaces. Frenkel somehow manages to live to tell the tale, which he does in the interview setting that introduces the metadiegetic flashback.

In her work on surrealism, Elizabeth Deeds Ermarth argues that the "estrangement of objects from their 'normal' order calls attention *to* that order *and* to its arbitrariness"—an idea that Jonathan D. Kramer extends to account for the listening effects of moments when familiar music is heard in unfamiliar, postmodern contexts.[34] In *Waltz with Bashir,* it is the classical, and in particular this chamber and solo repertory, that is estranged from its "normal" settings—not only from the concert hall, as Long has shown in his work, but also from its now-customary aesthetic register in conventional film soundtracks. Here the music is juxtaposed dissonantly with the piercing sounds of wartime violence. The sonic domain is estranged from the visual; listening is estranged from seeing. These tensions are actually in keeping with the entire production ethos of the film, for such estrangement, I argue, is a fundamental feature of both animation and reenactment themselves. If film invites spectatorial experience, in the animated reenactment of *Waltz with Bashir,* that spectatorial experience is always-already surreal, simultaneously accessible and distant. This observation will figure into the ethical conclusions that Folman reaches by the end of the film.

Pop Absurd

In addition to new instrumental compositions and appropriations from the Western canon, Richter includes three actual songs from the episodic memory worlds narrated by the film's characters: "Enola Gay" (1980) by the British electronic music group Orchestral Manoeuvers in the Dark (OMD); "(This Is Not a) Love Song" (1983) by Public Image Ltd., a British postpunk band helmed by John Lydon of Sex Pistols fame; and the Israeli postpunk band HaClique's "Incubator" (1981). These "period pieces" help locate the flashback narratives in the historical past while also highlighting Folman's youth and alienation from the cultural and political forces of the era. They also represent a uniquely 1980s play on the paradigm established by American war films, and in particular Ari Folman's professed favorite, Francis Coppola's 1979 *Apocalypse Now,* which was among the first major films in which, as Lapedis claims, "pre-existing pop music is used non-diegetically and meta-diegetically to complement the visual text" in addition to playing with distinctions between popular and classical music registers.[35] In other words, through the soundtrack, viewers connect their own personal and socially transferred memories of the historical setting to that of the characters in the film.

It bears mention that with its release in late 2008, *Waltz with Bashir* was made at a time when the 1980s were getting their due in the postmodern retromania permeating globalized popular culture. But Richter's handling of popular music is very different from the use of late 1960s rock music in the films that inspired Folman. Rather than serving as a signifier of youth revolt, the period evoked by these songs is characterized by youth escaping doom, despair, and excess, while coping with a hangover from several, now formless and conflated, political and economic crises of the 1960s and 1970s. Framing the cultural context of this film is the fact that Lebanon was the first war that Israelis protested in large numbers, breaking with decades of consensus-building in times of military conflict. As mentioned above, Israelis often referred to Lebanon as *their* "Vietnam." If Vietnam was for Americans the "rock 'n' roll war," then the soundtrack for *Waltz with Bashir* suggests that Lebanon was the "New Wave war" for Israelis.[36] Folman and Richter chose their songs well, as both music and lyrics added further layers to the webs of metadiegetic narration.

In *Waltz with Bashir*, OMD's song "Enola Gay," written to commemorate the bombing of Hiroshima, plays during a flashback narration by Folman's friend Carmi C'naan. The song's light texture of drum machine and upper-register synth melodies is juxtaposed with the midnight-blue hues of a darkened Mediterranean; the young soldiers are drinking and dancing, making the most of their boat transport from Israel to Lebanon before they join the battle. This playful moment is an allusion to an iconic scene from *Apocalypse Now*, in which Laurence Fishburne's character Mr. Clean (aka Tyrone Miller) and fellow soldiers dance around a speeding patrol boat, carefree water skier in tow, while the Rolling Stones' "(I Can't Get No) Satisfaction" blares over a handheld radio before gradually fading into a higher-fidelity, nondiegetic source for the recording. Such musical choices, I want to suggest, connect episodic and semantic memory in powerful ways: in this case, the preposterousness of finding pleasure in spite of the violent circumstances that brought the characters together (and which they themselves are perpetrating). However, as with Martin Sheen's antihero character Captain Willard in *Apocalypse Now*, whose introspection is caught in close-up shots and casts a foreboding glow over the absurd ludic behavior of his platoon, in *Waltz with Bashir* the viewer is meant to empathize with a vomiting, terrified C'naan. Narratively speaking, he is inside the metadiegetic war episode while placing his diegetic, retrospective self outside of it in moral terms. He depicts himself as the antithesis to the carefree amoral mass of troops for whom OMD's electronic pop is more than a sign of the times—it is a sign of unexamined complicity.

In the episode when Public Image Ltd.'s "(This Is Not a) Love Song" blares, the song's original music video appears in the animated world on screen—on television sets in the window of an electronics shop. Folman, on leave, walks alone as the camera homes in on his vacant state, as identifiably 1980s scenery—video game arcades and period-correct fashions and hairstyles—flashes through the background. Much like the song's lyrics, which present a flippant and sardonic image of emergent late capitalism in the late 1970s and early 1980s, he is alienated from the world that created the possibility for Israel's intervention in the Lebanon War. Through his metadiegetic narration, we learn that Folman's central concern was youthful and emotional: he simply wanted to return to his girlfriend, Yaeli, who had broken up with him just before his deployment. He broods alone in a club, holding a beer, while the youths around him carry on dancing as if there were not a war raging less than 300 kilometers away in Beirut; Folman considers this dissonance in his narration. The version of Ari Folman presented in the episodic memory stands in not only for Folman's autobiographical memory but also for his moral orientation toward the memory itself. As with Caplan's episode above, a pattern begins to emerge of narrators distancing themselves from the historical events of 1982. Alienation serves the ends of exoneration.

HaClique's "Incubator" appears following a sardonic joke, in which a diegetic Folman, sitting again with Boaz Rein-Buskila in a Tel Aviv bar, jokes about car bombs, "They're a blast!" and both men snicker at the irreverence of the joke and at their shared experience of past violence. The song's grating tritone, repeated on a distorted guitar, plays as the scene transitions to a wartime flashback. An Israeli brigade has taken over a Lebanese villa, replete with golden sinks, marble, and other gaudy decor (this is a subtly racist dig at the aesthetic sensibilities of Arabs), and the soldiers enjoy their spoils. Some lounge in hot tubs and in luxurious beds and sofas, and others pillage valuables left in the house. If the juxtaposition of a machine gun and crumpled IDF uniform next to a bubble bath weren't strange enough, the majority of the scene is focused on an Israeli officer who spends his time in the salon watching a German pornographic video, entitled *Hier kommt der Klempner 2* (*Here Comes the Plumber 2*), as one of his subordinates is charged with fast-forwarding the cassette to the preferred moment. While the ostensible male plumber and female client engage in sex on a kitchen table (the sex is animated graphically), a second woman, a parking officer, enters the room on the pretense of instructing the plumber to move his car, a red Mercedes, before she joins the copulating pair for a threesome; a dog also enters the scene, and it is implied that the dog also will be involved in the sex, thereby pushing the conceit into a broad joke about the stereotypically bizarre sexual tastes of German porn consumers. The line in the porn film about the red Mercedes reminds the IDF officer that he had received a tip that a red Mercedes, carrying a car bomb, will target Israeli soldiers (this never actually transpires). The scene and its soundtrack blur the line between fantasy and reality, creating a narrative tension that is heightened by the musical tensions in "Incubator." The tritone guitar (D♭-G) sounds like a siren, a signification that is reinforced rhythmically by its syncopated articulation over a very consistent basic beat on drums and jagged eighth-note, down-strummed guitar chords; in other words, it sounds like a siren blaring over the bustle of everyday life, thus creating a sense of emergency and dread laid over the scene of luxuriating soldiers. As it turns out, Bashir Gemayel is assassinated later that very night, and the officer instructs the soldiers to ready themselves for deployment into the city of Beirut and, as we now know, to the Sabra and Shatila refugee camps.

The pop surreal is also a site for the polystylistic play that characterizes the soundtrack as a whole, and this is apparent in the use of two *synthetic* period songs—that is, songs written specifically for the film and used to evoke the historical moment of the early 1980s. "Good Morning, Lebanon" is a simulation of a generic pop song that might have been popular among Israeli soldiers serving in the Lebanon War. Some of the intended meaning is evident in the songwriting and production itself: It features an acoustic guitar banging out alternating I and V chords, or G and D (with occasional move to the IV, or C), in open-position rudimentary voicings played in novicelike strumming reminiscent of sing-alongs held around campfires, at parties, or in bunkers. The unison singing and unpolished harmonica playing crystallize this feeling of amateur collectivity, a feeling that is performed on screen when the song moves from nondiegetic to diegetic fields of sound production and the soldiers begin to sing along with the soundtrack as if it were playing on a portable radio inside the tank.

The performance invokes a semantic memory of the Hebrew concept *re'ut*, a term I will define as "combat fraternity"—that is, homosocial (male) friendship arising from military service. The evocation of this concept in the film allows the episodic memory from 1982 to recall other Israeli wars and other musical treatments of *re'ut*, such as the eponymous 1949 song set to a poem by the poet and former soldier Haim Gouri and regularly programmed at times of commemoration, such as Memorial Day (Yom HaZikaron), where it becomes collectively performed and performatively collective. Implied in the term's contemporary usage is the idea that military service, which is compulsory for most Israeli citizens, is a core site of nation building in Israel.[37] It is the highest form of friendship and a model for national social relations; a soldier's death is a national death, and an ex-soldier's trauma is a national trauma. The audiovisual evocation of *re'ut* in these scenes thus preemptively distributes guilt, insofar as it is adumbrated in trauma, among the nation and away from individuals. Folman and his friends become, in Morag's words, "complicit indirect perpetrator[s]."[38]

In his analysis of *re'ut* in Israeli society, Danny Kaplan argues that "some of these emotions [associated with male friendship] can only be experienced through a sense of loss, and that by entering the public discourse they transform into rituals of passionate commemoration, suggesting a dynamics of collective necrophilia."[39] There can be no *re'ut*, therefore, without both death and its commemoration. At the beginning of the "Good Morning, Lebanon" scene, the audience is almost certain that at least some of the soldiers will soon die. This inevitability is also highlighted by the young Roni Dayag's carefree munching on a bag of crisps as the tank moves through the Lebanese countryside—an indication that the soldiers are sitting ducks, about to be attacked. The musical setting itself precludes the possibility of anything but trauma and so sets up expectations to be fulfilled, which they are, suddenly, as a sniper's bullet enters the neck of the soldier riding next to Dayag, and the instrumental voice interrupts the pop song to introduce a new battle scene.

Another synthetic period song, "I Bombed Beirut," represents a striking departure from the prior example and yet one where the absurdity of war is most fully articulated. Based on the song "I Bombed Korea" by the American band Cake, "I Bombed Beirut" plays with the idea of moral culpability by fully acknowledging Israeli perpetration of violence while absurdly depicting the deaths of Israeli soldiers—and what amount to war crimes, such as the accidental murder of bystanders—in a manner that renders these actions and their commemoration meaningless and irrational. While an overdriven guitar and muted drums bang away in a classic-rock style, the singer gutturally chants lyrics such as "I bombed Beirut today! / I bombed Beirut every day! / If I came close to death, I couldn't say! / I bombed Beirut every day!" All the while, Israeli soldiers shoot at, and are shot by, a variety of Arab (likely both Lebanese and Palestinian) people in and around the city of Beirut. Such an absurd representation relieves the viewer from any responsibility to empathize with victims. In this way, it evinces the central ethical problem with this film's musical reenactment of trauma: it forecloses the possibility of acknowledging the trauma of others.

What kind of reenactment is *Waltz with Bashir*? The film is not fundamentally a reenactment of the Lebanon War or of the Sabra and Shatila massacre but rather a documentary on memory, and on memory discourse that uses reenactment as a vehicle for commenting on the subject's moral culpability. The diegetic narrative is solely about Folman's journey to recover repressed memories of these past traumatic events. At the same time, the film's metadiegesis—the episodes remembered and recounted by Folman and his interview subjects—constitute reenactments of trauma, the cohesion of which is secured not only by visual elements but also by a musical soundtrack. Music mediates all of the episodic memories, hallucinations, and flashbacks to which the viewer is exposed—in other words, it mediates the primary sites of memory work in the film. As Michael Long writes, "Film music—particularly for mass-market studio productions—is a mass-media discursive arena in which shorthand communication is key."[40] Max Richter, the soundtrack's composer, has mastered this shorthand communication by playing with how audiences negotiate genre and form, thus providing the "pseudo-experience" required for a film reenactment of trauma to achieve its moral aims successfully.

In his book *Surviving Images*, Kamran Rastegar asks, "What happens when the claim of trauma is adduced by those who acted as instruments of the same violence that produced this social trauma? Does trauma's potential toward presenting an ethical framework, or articulating a cause . . . counteract the collapsing of the perpetrator and victim into *mirroring molds* as casualties of trauma?"[41] I have shown how audiences might understand the soundtrack of *Waltz with Bashir* as operating in parallel to the film's extensively studied visuals and as serving to exteriorize, and therefore dissipate, the ex-soldier Ari Folman's guilt over the traumatic memories he gradually recovers throughout the film. Music connects diegesis and metadiegesis (instrumental voice), uses ironic juxtaposition (classical surreal), and deploys forms of iconicity that distance the traumatized perpetrator from responsibility (pop absurd). In particular, the pop absurd serves to conflate episodic and semantic memory in a way that does not simply place the perpetrator into a "mirroring mold" with his victim, but rather sublates the victim's trauma within his own sublimation of trauma. This calculus, by which Folman the Israeli soldier is the real victim of the Sabra and Shatila massacre—thereby exonerating him from moral responsibility for a mass murder for which he and his fellow IDF soldiers were "complicit indirect perpetrators"—wholly depends upon the filmmakers' careful exploitation of music's multidimensional narrative function.[42]

I shall conclude by returning to the film's ending, with which I opened the essay and where both musical memory and animated amnesia fail, giving way to silence and photorealistic documentary footage. The filmmaker chooses to show us something "real," and highlights this realness (another contrast) by breaking the visual and sonic molds of the film. Ironically, both the visual and sonic domains render the victims as inhuman. The cries of these Arab women are the only utterances in the entire film without subtitles, in any language. One of them screams, "Sawaru, sawaru! Wayn al-'arab?!" In her own language, audible but inscrutable by the logic of the film, she implores the camera operator to "film! film!" and then asks, "Where are the Arabs?!"

Notes

1. William E. Farrell, "Israelis, at Huge Rally in Tel Aviv, Demand Begin and Sharon Resign," *New York Times*, September 26, 1982.

2. The party, founded by Bashir Gemayel's father Pierre Gemayel, is also known in Arabic as Kataeb, short for Ḥizb al-Katā'ib al-Lubnāniyyeh.

3. Habib Shartouni, a member of the Syrian Social Nationalist Party, was later arrested and confessed to Gemayel's murder. Although he did not face a trial, he was imprisoned for the remainder of the civil war until escaping during the chaos of 1990 and vanishing. He was tried in absentia and sentenced to death in October 2017, twenty-five years after the fact.

4. Casualty estimates range from hundreds to over three thousand, due to the paucity of official records kept of refugees at the time, to the chaotic nature of the scene—in which bodies were piled by the tens and hundreds in different places while others were placed in mass graves—and also to the politicized nature of the event, wherein Israeli, Palestinian, and Lebanese authorities all have ulterior motives to their inflation or reduction of the figure. For an overview of body-count discrepancies, see Bayan Nuwayhed Al-Hout, *Sabra and Shatila: September 1982* (Ann Arbor, MI: Pluto Press, 2004), 275–96.

5. "An-Nakba," Arabic for "the Catastrophe," refers to the forced expulsion of Palestinians during the 1948 Arab-Israeli War, known in Israel as the War of Independence. "An-Naksa," Arabic for "the Setback," refers to Six-Day War of 1967, when Israel defeated the armies of Egypt, Syria, and Jordan and occupied the Palestinian Territories.

6. Shira Stav, "Nakba and Holocaust: Mechanisms of Comparison and Denial in the Israeli Literary Imagination," *Jewish Social Studies* 18, no. 3 (2012): 92.

7. Michael Guillén, "Waltz with Bashir—Interview with Ari Folkman," ScreenAnarchy.com, January 10, 2009, https://screenanarchy.com/2009/01/waltz-with-bashirinterview-with-ari-folmon.html

8. Patrick Pittman, "Max Richter Is a Composer," Dumbo Feather, July 1, 2012, https://www.dumbofeather.com/conversations/max-richter-is-a-composer/

9. Daniel Schweiger, "Interview with Max Richter," *Film Music Magazine*, August 13, 2014, http://www.filmmusicmag.com/?p=13378

10. At the 2008 Awards of the Israeli Film Academy, the film, Folman, and his collaborators won Best Film, Best Director, Best Screenplay, Best Editing, Best Art Direction, and Best Sound, and the was further nominated for (but did not win) Best Cinematography.

11. A. O. Scott, "Inside a Veteran's Nightmare," *New York Times*, December 25, 2018, https://www.nytimes.com/2008/12/26/movies/26bash.html

12. David Edelstein, "Graphic Violence," *New York Magazine*, December 28, 2008, http://nymag.com/movies/reviews/53143/

13. Peter Rainer, "Review: 'Waltz with Bashir,'" *Christian Science Monitor*, January 10, 2009, https://www.csmonitor.com/The-Culture/Movies/2009/0110/p25s01-almo.html

14. Gideon Levy, "'Antiwar' Film Waltz with Bashir Is Nothing but Charade," *Haaretz*, February 19, 2009, https://www.haaretz.com/1.5077872

15. Raya Morag, *Waltzing with Bashir: Perpetrator Trauma and Cinema* (New York: I.B. Taurus, 2013), 131.

16. Schweiger, "Interview with Max Richter."

17. Raz Yosef, *The Politics of Loss and Trauma in Contemporary Israeli Cinema* (New York: Routledge, 2011), 67. See also Kamran Rastegar, *Surviving Images: Cinema, War, and Cultural Memory in the Middle East* (New York: Oxford University Press, 2015), 192.

18. Gil Hochberg, "Soldiers as Filmmakers: On the Prospect of 'Shooting War' and the Question of Ethical Spectatorship," *Screen* 54, no. 1 (2013): 44.

19. Michelle C. Pautz, "*Argo* and *Zero Dark Thirty*: Film, Government, and Audiences," *PS: Political Science & Politics* 48, no. 1 (2015): 121.

20. See Claudia Gorbman, *Unheard Melodies: Narrative Film Music* (Bloomington: Indiana University Press, 1987).

21. Hilary Lapedis, "Popping the Question: The Function and Effect of Popular Music in Cinema," *Popular Music* 18, no. 3 (1999): 368.

22. Berthold Hoeckner and Howard C. Nusbaum, "Music and Memory in Film and Other Multimedia: The Casablanca Effect," in *The Psychology of Music in Multimedia*, ed. Siu-Lan Tan, Annabel J. Cohen, Scott D. Lipscomb, and Roger A. Kendall (New York: Oxford University Press, 2013), 237.

23. Hoeckner and Nusbaum, "Music and Memory," 242–43.

24. Hoeckner and Nusbaum, "Music and Memory," 243.

25. Morag, *Waltzing with Bashir*, 131.

26. On the officially released soundtrack recording, everything is shifted up a half step to A♭ minor.

27. Rodrigo Perez, "Composer Max Richter Talks the 'Haunted' Music of 'Waltz with Bashir,'" The Playlist, February 20, 2009, https://theplaylist.net/composer-max-richter-talks-haunted-20090220/

28. Gorbman, *Unheard Melodies*; summarized here by Hoeckner and Nusbaum, "Music and Memory," 252.

29. Robynn J. Stilwell, "The Fantastical Gap between Diegetic and Nondiegetic," in *Beyond the Soundtrack: Representing Music in Cinema*, ed. Daniel Ira Goldmark, Lawrence Kramer, and Richard Leppert (Berkeley: University of California Press, 2007), 184–202.

30. Michael Long, *Beautiful Monsters: Imagining the Classic in Musical Media* (Berkeley: University of California Press, 2008).

31. Perez, "Composer Max Richter."

32. Anahid Kassabian, "The Sound of a New Film Form," in *Popular Music and Film*, ed. Ian Inglis (London: Wallflower Press, 2003), 95. Here Kassabian is referring to the narrative structuring of *Lara Croft* and *The Matrix* (Wachowski Brothers, 1999).

33. Although Chopin's op. 64 no. 2 is among his best-known works, it is not typically used in film soundtracks. The sole exception predating *Waltz with Bashir* was *The Avengers* (Jeremiah Chechik, 1998).

34. Elizabeth Deeds Ermarth, *Sequel to History: Postmodernism and the Crisis of Representational Time* (Princeton, NJ: Princeton University Press, 1992), 94. Quoted in Jonathan D. Kramer, *Postmodern Music, Postmodern Listening* (New York: Bloomsbury, 2016), 178. Kramer insists that surrealism is not simply a style or even period but rather something that can be heard in various musical genres and historical epochs. This is instructive for my argument, which places Bach and Chopin as familiar, nonsurrealist source materials to be estranged from their original context. Although one might listen for surrealism as "an attitude, a context, a way of seeing the world, [or] a state of mind," as he puts it, within these original compositions, I contend that their function in *Waltz with Bashir* is for the purpose of aesthetic defamiliarization that allows the filmmaker to explore the episodic memories for which Bach and Chopin provide a nondiegetic but extraordinarily conspicuous soundtrack.

35. Lapedis, "Popping the Question," 367 Here Lapedis characterizes what she calls the "contemporary *status quo*" of film music in general, although she mobilizes this insight in her analysis of popular music used in the soundtrack of *Forrest Gump* (1994) and its depictions of the Vietnam War.

36. Jonathan Romney and Adrian Wootton, *Celluloid Jukebox: Popular Music and the Movies since the 50s* (London: British Film Institute, 1995), 5; quoted in Lapedis, "Popping the Question," 371.

37. Military service is compulsory for all Israeli citizens except for ultra-Orthodox Jews and Palestinian citizens of Israel. Other minority groups, such as the Druze, also serve in the army.

38. Morag, *Waltzing with Bashir*, 131–40.

39. Danny Kaplan, *The Men We Loved: Male Friendship and Nationalism in Israeli Culture* (New York: Berghahn Books, 2006), xi.

40. Long, *Beautiful Monsters*, 23.

41. Rastegar, *Surviving Images*, 188. Emphasis mine.

42. Morag, *Waltzing with Bashir*.

SIX | Say Her Name

Invocation, Remembrance, and Gendered Trauma in Black Lives Matter

IMANI DANIELLE MOSLEY

In his essay "Necropolitics," Achille Mbembe cites Palestine as an example of late-modern colonial occupation, a "concatenation of multiple powers: disciplinary, biopolitical, and necropolitical."[1] The description that follows, however, comes disturbingly close to home:

> The *state of siege* is a military institution . . . the besieged villages and towns are sealed off and cut off from the world. Daily life is militarized. Freedom is given to local military commanders to use their discretion as to when and whom to shoot. Local civil institutions are systematically destroyed. The besieged population is deprived of their means of income. Invisible killing is added to outright executions.[2]

This account could easily be mapped onto the plight of many black communities in the United States, stretching back to the earliest days of American slavery and forward into the twenty-first century. To be black in America is to live in a *state of siege*. This siege-ness has become ever more palpable following the protests in Ferguson, Missouri, in response to the murder of Mike Brown in 2014. For decades, there have been examples of the militarization of police forces with a heightened presence solely in minority communities. But with the advances in technology and the influx of federal money into local police departments, this militarization has become ever more widespread, especially in regard to how it is deployed against nonwhite communities and spaces.

The 2010s saw the beginning of an uptick in public acts of state violence against black bodies, specifically bodies of young black men. Social media made those acts immediately visible, with videos of beatings and killings at the hands of police viewable by anyone on Facebook, YouTube, or Twitter. The Black Lives Matter (BLM) movement arose from the legal system's failure to hold accountable those involved in the deaths of Trayvon Martin (2012), Mike Brown (2014), and Eric Garner (2014).[3] Out of this breakdown arose a vocal protest movement, one that utilized several elements of media culture to raise awareness. At the same time, another movement emerged alongside Black Lives Matter. The Say Her Name (SHN) movement, organized by activist and scholar Kimberlé Crenshaw, focused on the other victims of state violence that were not as visible as those for whom BLM appeared to advocate: black women (and subsequently, black trans women) who were killed by the police but whose deaths were going unnoticed and unacknowledged both by the public and by the media.[4] The two movements have points of overlap (as noted by Crenshaw and others) but are fundamentally different in their aims and modes of protest.[5] BLM is, perhaps unconsciously, focused on the embodiment of black maleness and the spectacle of black male death. Police brutality and violence is often understood as a (black) men's issue rather than an issue for all people of color.

The BLM movement has, in one form or another, always centered around the concept of reenactment due to the emphasis on the body and the bodily. This performance of reenactment spans a wide gamut. Such types of performance include the straightforward act of raising one's hands while shouting "Hands up, don't shoot" during a protest. More artistic renderings include the reclaiming of the popular #MannequinChallenge trend by Simone Shepard in order to depict examples of police violence against black people and the photographic essay by Dru Donovan entitled *Positions Taken*, where he stages encounters between young black men and the police on the streets of New York City.[6] As a result of BLM's positioning around black male embodiment, reenactment figures largely into how its message is presented, perhaps far more than the idea of commemoration. There has been a slight shift in this dynamic as the BLM movement ages and looks back upon both its progress and what has not changed. But just as BLM's dependence upon black male bodies furthers performances of reenactment, the absence of bodies in the SHN movement necessitates a focus on commemoration. Kimberlé Crenshaw clarifies this by using language that evokes vocality, re-presentation, amplification, and remembrance: "We have to exercise agency, we have to actually look for the stories of Black women and girls. Once we see them, we cannot unsee them. If you say the name, you're prompted to learn the story."[7] The African American Policy Forum's 2017 "Say Her Name: An Evening of Arts and Action" emphasizes this need to tell and celebrate the stories of the lives of those women whose names are unknown to so many, namely through the absence of the visual and reenacted.[8] The night begins with a cacophony of voices filling a darkened room, telling the audience about themselves, pleading with the police, voicing their struggle. It then moves on to video confessionals from those who knew the women who lost their lives at the hands of the American police state, stories not about the end of their lives and the brutalization of their bodies but how they are remembered by those who loved and cared for them. This perhaps may be a by-product of not always knowing what happened to those women in their last hours, but it seems more rooted in the desire of SHN to tell and provide stories that compel others to take action and to remember. As BLM uses the story of gruesome physical violence located within the body as an impetus to spur activity and protest, SHN uses commemoration, the call to remember, and sonic and narrative storytelling to inspire others toward action.

Black female death is often hidden, unseen, and unfilmed by the technological eyes of police body cameras and smartphone videos. Because SHN cannot rely on a preponderance of visual material in order to advance its movement, it places a focus on the *sonic*. As a result, SHN locates itself around *naming* as an act of remembrance and bringing unknown victims to the fore. The aurality of naming combined with the musicality of the protest songs invokes and gives life to previously unheard voices. This process is part of a long history of recognizing and acknowledging the pain of black women and thereby taps into a network of female trauma, just as BLM's focus on the black male body connects with a history of black male death as spectacle.[9] This division of trauma separates the two movements in key ways, and the artistic productions connected to these movements mirror this division. In this essay, I explore how the protest music inspired by Black Lives Matter and Say Her Name reflect the differences between the two movements and show how the music about those black women, often made by black women, fits into a narrative of gendered trauma and collective remembrance by way of invocation.

American Death-Worlds

> The louder she screamed, the harder he whipped. . . . It was a most terrible spectacle.[10]
>
> —Frederick Douglass

Mbembe provides a helpful framework through which one can understand the emergence of both the BLM and SHN movements. The concept of necropolitics builds on the Foucauldian notion of biopower, a theory that maps out the relations between the sovereign state and its citizens.[11] Crucial to this theory is the understanding that the state has the sanctioned right to decide life or death for its citizens, a right that has evolved as the state itself has evolved. The legally inscribed right to kill is fundamental to such modern-day states as the United States of America, as it is a way of enacting sovereignty when other forms of sociopolitical control are no longer possible. What is also crucial in this context is the relationship of race to biopower and, therein, necropolitics. Hannah Arendt locates race at the end of humanity, "not the natural birth of man but his unnatural death."[12] Race—seen by Foucault as a division, separating one from an/the other—provides a seemingly "natural" demarcation by which some states enforce life and death. Class and political ideology also provide demarcations in other states to a similar effect, with one group (the bourgeoisie) wielding the tools of the state to enact death sentences against the other.[13] In practice, this racial enforcement is best viewed through the examples of the Holocaust and—in the United States—the history of American slavery and its enduring effects.[14]

The plantation, as a quasi-sovereign territory ruled by the white men who had nearly absolute control over the land and people they owned, was an exercise in biopower (control of and subjugation over bodies) and necropower (control over life and death). Mbembe calls the plantation "one of the first instances of biopolitical experimentation."[15] Unsurprisingly, the plantation gave birth both to the idea of black death as spectacle and to the gendered, sublimated trauma that would be passed down through generations. The plantation and subsequent violence of Reconstruction and the Jim Crow era created, enacted, and solidified a gendered binary of violence regarding black men and black women that is still in practice today. This historically grounded binary of male visibility and female hiddenness forged a structural framework for the violation, oppression, and silencing of black men and women in ways that produce differing types of trauma. Joy DeGruy coined the term *post-*

traumatic slave syndrome to denote the way in which the traumas of slavery were retained and passed down through generations, feeding into the ongoing oppressions of black Americans.[16]

In the body politic of the plantation, the black male body was made a site of unrestrained, animalistic lust, marked by a need to rape white women. With African Americans able to enter white public space post-slavery, the sociopolitical overwriting of black men as rapists made public lynchings justifiable—a claim that Ida B. Wells problematized in her pamphlet *Southern Horrors*.[17] She posited that rape was the only crime that could be inscribed onto the black male body eo ipso in a way to warrant death by mob, a public death that served both as a warning and as a display of (necro)power.[18] This labeling of the black male body and the killing that inexorably followed has remained in the American consciousness to this day, with only subtle changes in terminology. The most recent murders of black men regularly involved some kind of mislabeling, a need to affix a racialized marker that makes killing palatable: thug, thief, drug dealer, and so on. Moreover, such a label reduces the victims of these killings to empty, corporeal vessels unworthy of sympathy or engagement. This form of labeling is borne out in the American press and media as well, in a further phase of public lynching that not only satisfies its audience but also satiates the desire for the spectacle of black male death.[19]

The focus on visible punishment and destruction of the black male body as a form of oppression represents one side of a trauma binary imposed on black people since slavery. The black female body has been conceived of, and oppressed, in a way that centers on hiddenness, a body that internalizes the crimes and pain inflicted against it and that responds with silence. Shatema Threadcraft identifies the inability to see black women as victims of state violence as being a problem located within American constructions of the black female body itself,

> Female embodiment itself appears to work against activists recognizing one's body as a body with which necropower has intersected. Female embodiment (as well as gender-nonconforming embodiment and trans embodiment) heightens the risk that any given subject's dead body will not be counted, will go unrecognized.[20]

In an interview with Radio Boston, Andrea Ritchie discusses the case of Charnesia Corley, who was raped by two officers in Texas at a traffic stop. She lays out how the conception of the black female body can lead to biopolitical crimes that center around invisibility and silence:

> What happened to her [Corley] is how the war on drugs is waged on the bodies of black women, whether it's at the airport, on the side of the road, or in their homes which is that officers have these deep-seeded perceptions of black women's bodies as inherently consuming, concealing, or conveying drugs in some kind of way, and act on those perceptions whether it's doing what they did to her, which is publicly strip search her and submit her to a vaginal search by the side of the road, at a gas station, in full public view, for eleven minutes.[21]

Ritchie connects this erasure of, and ownership over, the black female body to both the war on drugs and the prison-industrial complex, wherein black women are the fastest-growing population.

The state's ability to commit acts of *hidden* violence against unseen bodies and then forcibly remove them from the population through a form of state-sanctioned neoslavery silences and hides black women internally and externally. Rape can be understood as a hidden crime, an act that is invisible and the repercussions of which often remain obscured from view, even when the act takes place in plain sight. Rape and other acts of sexual violence—first by the slave master and later by agents of the American state—are also a form of (necro)power that essentializes and then eradicates the black female body. The connection of silence to rape is not one that is limited to the black female experience, but occupies an intersecting, albeit separate, space in how it perpetuates and internalizes trauma. Melissa Wright acknowledges that trauma as well as the destruction of women's bodies is integral to current-day necropolitics: "As the proliferation of gendered violence around the world indicates, this type of violence is constitutive of necropolitics: the politics of death and the politics of gender go hand in hand."[22] Silencing as a tool that enforces the products of state violence is experienced by various bodies; bodies of color, trans bodies, and women's bodies. The black woman, as receptacle for both race- and gender-based necropower, has over time received the full force of the American state.

During and after slavery, silence after rape was believed to be a form of protection as well as a necessity due to the precariousness of the situation. The silence of black women—what Patricia Broussard calls a "practiced silence"—presumably protected not only themselves but their community.[23] That community would face the repercussions of an outcry because "when Black women spoke of the abuse visited upon them, not only was there no justice, but many times there were dire consequences to pay for having revealed the abuse."[24] Silence here reinforced a death-in-life, a reminder of the *state of injury* in which black women lived at the same time silence offered a protection from it.[25] Beyond slavery, Reconstruction, and Jim Crow, silence has evolved into an active state of being for black women in America. Broussard identifies this as a "third layer of silence" that comes into sharp relief as the discussion around the lynching and violence of black men begins to grow.[26]

The reclaiming of visibility and vocality from hiddenness and silence has been an aim of black female scholars, activists, and artists in the late twentieth and twenty-first centuries as a way of combating the transgenerational trauma of slavery and rape. As Stephen Dillon puts it, "Black feminist scholars have worked tirelessly to *make visible* what often goes *unseen* and *unsaid*, to reckon with the endings that are not over."[27] This language from Dillon re-presents the framework of black male death as spectacle, perhaps, because the visual referent is so pervasive. Conversely, focusing on silence and the *unspoken* couches methodology specifically in the realm of the auditory in order to demarcate the gendered difference between black male and black female death. To make those silenced heard serves to combat the continuous erasure of black women and the violence perpetuated against them. Mina Karavanta sees this reclaiming through the lens of an "affective memory" as the transformation of a body—here the black (Caribbean) female slave—from a signifier of absence and silence to one that counterwrites a history of loss through the presence of community.[28] Affective memory counters a history of slavery that centers around silence "in which the black woman is doubly expropriated . . . first as a black woman turned into a slave and then as a black woman remaining a subject-less subject, someone who bears witness to the disaster but does not speak."[29] Jaleesa Smiley takes this one step further by placing black women at the center of those communities that once demanded silence, and in "making black women the subject within the context of enslavement, the veil of silence is lifted and the experiences of black women are brought to the forefront."[30] Centering the voices and experiences of black women, bringing them from out of the shadows, acts as a form of resistance against the oppression of necropolitics. By naming women, their bodies and voices are identified. They are reembodied and removed from their status as living corpses. Susan Brison sees the use of narrative and naming as a way to reconstruct what has been disembodied and unmade by trauma, a "speech act that diffuses traumatic memory . . . helping the survivor to remake the self."[31] As many of the black women who were subject to police violence, in addition to the intergenerational trauma of slavery, did not survive their encounters with the state, the burden of telling their narratives and reembodying those women lies at the feet of the living. Black female musicians and artists act as the creators of and conduits to these narratives, providing "not only the words with which to tell . . . stories, but also an audience able and willing to hear and understand words as [they] intend them."[32]

Hearing Movements

> Sister in my joy, sister in my pain,
> the woman's burden placed upon us time and time again.[33]
>
> —Rhiannon Giddens

The rise of BLM saw with it a surge of inspired protest music by black artists. Capitalizing on the momentum of an ever-growing social movement coupled with the seemingly unending number of tragic events that fueled the movement, an increasing number of artists released music that expressed the immensity of black anguish, rage, and trauma. Magazines such as *Rolling Stone* and *Pitchfork* put together essential BLM playlists featuring songs that were written as reactions to specific events, like The Game's collaborative "Don't Shoot" and Lauryn Hill's "Black Rage," as well as a Soundcloud-era play on "My Favorite Things" and albums that captured the activist zeitgeist such as Solange's *A Seat at the Table* and D'Angelo and the Vanguard's *Black Messiah*.[34] And just as there was a gendered bifurcation of trauma and experience within the black community, so too did that split replicate itself within the subject matter and style of the music produced. While songs about black men represented the visuality of spectacle refigured through the aural, songs about black women commanded listeners to pay heed and listen to and for the voices that were once silenced. Songs reacting to the deaths of Mike Brown, Trayvon Martin, Eric Garner, and others located the material of their lyrics within the body. These songs reproduce the spectacle of black male death that Threadcraft argues is necessary to perpetuate a movement like BLM and that has "gained ground . . . in the extremely important contest over the meaning of the bodies of the black dead."[35] It is not difficult to see why this type of embodiment would be the foundation for many protest songs. BLM created protest slogans out of embodiment: "Hands up," "I can't breathe," and so on. As phrases of a galvanized movement, they were natural signposts for singers and rappers to craft music and stories.[36] By ensounding and embodying black male death, however, these songs essentialize not only the victims but also black maleness as bloody vessels that can only be understood in and through death.

Often, the locus of these songs is at the moment just before death, when the artist-as-subject is confronted by the police. As characters come into direct contact with the police state, they are rendered powerless and reduced to what is now an almost clichéd bodily performance: freezing or standing still, putting their hands above their head (to show they are not armed), and verbal pleading. Songs with subjects of this nature show how edicts from the police like "Hands up!" and "Freeze!" become reflexive and performative actions, ingrained in the black male conscious. The recreation of this scene, on the one hand, shows what seems like an inescapable, recurring narrative. On the other, this moment is part and parcel of the death-world that black men inhabit. It also renders the subject voiceless by reducing it to a series of repeating bodily patterns. In N.E.R.D.'s song "Don't Don't Do It!" Pharrell Williams acts almost as an omniscient narrator, making available to the listener the thought process to which not even the subject has access, or at least cannot obey. The song is based on the murder of Keith Lamont Scott, who, while waiting to pick his children up from school, was shot by police as his wife looked on.[37] Pharrell as narrator tells a helpless Scott of his fate ("They're gonna do it anyway"), but Scott is unable to answer or heed Pharrell's words. Instead we hear—and through hearing, visualize—Scott's body leave the car and put up his hands. The listener is able to decipher the rest, aided by the repeated verse "They're gonna do it anyway." "Hands Up" by Vince Staples also focuses on this moment of bodily confrontation where, instead of the act of putting up one's hands as a (futile) way to save one's life, it is part of a command from the police. The chorus consists of a repeated "Yeah, put your hands in the air / nigga freeze put your hands in the air," exasperated and redundant. Instead of the chorus shifting the subject to an imaginary police officer, the words become echoes of the many times that Staples has heard them before.

The idea of death as spectacle is not solely centered around the bodily performance of death. Spectacles have to be seen, broadcast, and viewable by many. The pervasive nature of the media, specifically social media, and the visibility of black male death also serve as inspiration for protest music that places black male death at its center. And while emphasis is often placed on the visuality of black male death, the audible nature of these moments—screams, cries, and pleas—often adds credence to these events. Many songs that focus on these death moments replicate that audibility in choruses and refrains. Songs that foreground spectacle act as aural counterparts to visual protests. As calls to action, they are analogous to what Threadcraft terms "witnessing," a mobilizing tool around "the spectacle of public, violent death, where technology facilitates the multiplication of witnessing so that a nation sees the lethal violence, when before it had only heard about it, and is there motivated to act."[38] In the video for the song "This is America" by Childish Gambino, we hear the lyrics "this a celly / that's a tool" performing two functions. It refers both to the murder of Stephon Clark—who the police said was holding a gun ("tool") that was, however, an iPhone ("celly")—and to how smartphones have become instrumental in the documenting and mass-witnessing of black male death. Even the possibility of death has caused an increased vigor in the documentation of police encounters with black men. In the music video for the song, one sees several young black kids above Gambino on a scaffolding, mouths covered by masks, all filming the events below with their camera phones. To witness here means both to see and to testify, even if that testimony is technological, mediated, and nonvocal. Killer Mike of Run the Jewels alludes to this double witnessing on "Early," where, in a confrontation with an officer, he notes, "When my woman screamed, said 'shut up' / *Witness with the camera phone on* / Saw the copper pull a gun and put it on my gorgeous queen." The *New York Times* has compiled many of the dash cam footage and cellphone videos into a constantly updating article that chronicles the horror of black male death and the effect that spectacle has had on the public at large.[39] The article makes clear the power of witnessing where black male death going viral compels people to act. Yet it also enables people to fetishize (and worse) death as spectacle in the comfort of their own homes.

These songs about black male death share a common focus on the visible, a need to place the image at the forefront of the conversation around police brutality. Yet as most black female deaths go unseen and are un*witnessed*, there is no body around which one can rally. There is no spectacle. Therefore, the slogans that vitalize BLM and its protest music are not useful when trying to shine a light on the female victims of police brutality and murder. Indeed, the songs mirror the binary of visibility and hiddenness between BLM and SHN. The patterns that surrounded the fallout of the rape of a black female slave by her white master were passed down along with the trauma of those rapes. Today, that scenario is reworked and reperformed by black women and the states apparatus or, more specifically, agents of the state such as the police. The crimes themselves happen in darkness, and fear often stops women from reporting those crimes. Even when those acts are witnessed, either by dash cameras or by actual bystanders, black women and their bodies are *unseen.* As Ritchie emphasizes, it is frequently not the location of the crime that creates this invisibility but rather the tendency of the American public and media not to acknowledge the presence of black women:

> It's true that many interactions that police officers have between black women or women of color take place away from the views of cameras or cop watchers or they take place in private locations like homes or welfare offices or clinics, responses to domestic violence calls, policing of prostitution, more private locations. But what's also, I think, particularly disturbing, is that they also take place in plain view and we, in some ways, *just don't see them.*[40]

This inability to see black women and the state violence enacted upon them, coupled with the intergenerational trauma that comes with centuries of state violence against black women and their bodies, reinforces a code of silence that further obscures black women. With no body and with no voice, trauma becomes internalized and repeats itself, unendingly.

As a result, SHN and the music it inspired focus on and locate themselves around moving from the silenced to the vocalized. Music can and has played a role in the unsilencing of black women through reworking the performance of (gendered) trauma. Broussard posits a correlation between the emergence of female-driven black musics and the increased silence of black women in the twentieth century,

> Is it any wonder that the musical genre called the Blues grew into popularity at this time? Were the famous female Blues singers who emerged during that period using songs to speak truth to power and to sing what they could not say?[41]

By speaking the names of black women, the movement and the music try to restore and reclaim the presence of those women from out of the silence of trauma. The very speaking of their names could also be understood as a performative speech act in which their *naming* brings something—their presence—into existence. The process surrounding this musical naming encounters the complex issues around the silence of and around black women and the difficulty involved with making the hidden visible and audible. Often these songs are not commercially successful, or they reveal the biases of the black activist community, while in other instances they make profound statements about the pain of intergenerational trauma and abuse. The first verse of Blood Orange's "Sandra's Smile" is all about the giving and taking away of voices and seeing the invisible: "You watched her pass away / the words they weren't faint." Band member Devonté Hynes explains in his annotations of the song for the website Genius how those who continually take from black culture (and black women) are also complicit in the silencing and erasure of black women.[42] Hynes notes that even he did not *see* Sandra Bland at first—"but I think a part of me had my eyes closed, as a form of numbness"—and had to recognize both her body and her death actively.[43] But in doing so, in naming her (and Sybrina Fulton, mother to Trayvon Martin and victim of a different kind of state violence), he makes her visible and gives her the speech that was "taken away."[44]

Philadelphia rapper Leen Bean's take on Sandra Bland differs from the prosaic nature of Blood Orange, resulting in a track filled with familiar aspects of reality rap. In "Sandra Bland," Bean takes on the voice of Bland herself as well as the police officer, reenacting the confrontation between the two at the traffic stop that resulted in Bland's arrest and subsequent death, ruled a suicide. Similar to N.E.R.D.'s "Don't Don't Do It!" here we are party to a semi-imagined (there was dash cam footage of the stop) play-by-play in which Bean gives Bland an actual *voice*, one that expresses feelings such as anger, fear, and confusion. Unlike the Scott case on which "Don't Don't Do It!" was based, there are no smartphone videos, no witnesses, no pleading for Bland's life, and, most importantly, no death spectacle. Bland's death is literally and figuratively hidden, having taken place in a jail cell. Bland's death reinforces the narrative posited by Ritchie and others regarding the relationship between black women, their bodies, and the prison industrial complex. Prisons swallow women of color whole, removing them from our sight. Leen Bean tries to counter the stereotypes attached to that narrative when mentioning Bland's death, rapping, "Suicide? I love my life, I have too much pride / I wouldn't dare hurt myself / I am a child of God."

Perhaps the best-known example of musical naming in the BLM and SHN movements is Wondaland Records' "Hell You Talmbout." The song features Janelle Monaé, Jidenna, and other artists from Wondaland Records (the label formed by Monaé) and is a sparse track articulated by the percussion, chants, and gospel choir accompaniment associated with historically black colleges' and universities' marching bands. These sonic markers were born from black American culture and often exist in radical spaces of resistance: the historically black college, the black church, and so on. Performances of these sonic events carry within them that connective thread to those who are familiar with the history of those spaces—another example being Beyoncé's 2018 HBCU-inspired Coachella performance, after which Tina Knowles-Lawson wrote, "I told Beyonce that I was afraid that the predominately white audience at Coachella would be confused by all of the black culture and [b]lack college culture because it was something that they might not get."[45] In her dissertation on the Fisk Jubilee Singers, Marti Newland connects those radical spaces, that of church and university, in order to show how those sites of (black) resistance are tethered to sound:

> Black performance and black politics are inseparable through an existential argument—that violence is the evidence of existence for an oppressed black bodied-commodified-object, and the resistance of said violence constitutive of blackness. Blackness then ontologically operates as ((re)productions of) instances of resistance most profoundly enacted in sound, particularly vocal sounds.[46]

After the song's release, the cry of "hell you talmbout" became a powerful slogan of both movements. The entirety of the song is a list of names of black men and women killed by police, stretching back through Amadou Diallo (1999) all the way to the murder of Emmett Till in 1955. The refrain of the victim's name followed by "say [his/her] name" is spoken, often shouted, rather than sung and leaves singing to the mixed-voice gospel choir-style chorus. The use of African American vernacular English in the chorus, accompanied by elements from across the black musical landscape, puts forward a particular identity and agenda centered around the performance of blackness. Antonio Brown denotes this as "Black Speak," speech that acts and performs a kind of truth-telling.[47] Black Speak conveys an insider knowledge and communicates "clearly and concisely a 'truth' to an*other* or *others* who have shared the cultural history and who are conversant in the vernacular form."[48] But what is the 'truth' that is being conveyed here? In Monaé's statement on the song, posted on her Instagram account, she writes,

> This song is a vessel. It carries the unbearable anguish of millions. We recorded it to channel the pain, fear, and trauma caused by the ongoing slaughter of our brothers and sisters. We recorded it to challenge

> the indifference, disregard, and negligence of all who remain quiet about this issue. *Silence is our enemy. Sound is our weapon.* They say a question lives forever until it gets the answer it deserves. Won't you say their names?[49]

Monaé acknowledges in her comment that erasure is and has been happening and that it can only be combated through a rejection of the customary silence and through the act of naming. However, out of the eighteen names that are mentioned in the song, only four of them belong to women. Even in a song devoted to the idea of naming as a way of fighting against trauma and erasure, black women are left out. This hearkens back to Threadcraft's point that activism often fails black women, even here through a slogan created to make black women visible:

> The activists who launched the #SayHerName campaign, like those in the broader #BlackLivesMatter movement, also attempt to intervene at the level of socially accepted meanings given to the bodies of the dead, but they struggle to have names such as Sandra Bland, Rekia Boyd, Tanisha Anderson, and those of other women who have been murdered by police repeated as often, and in truth carry as much meaning as the names of Martin, Gray, Castile, Sterling, and Brown.[50]

The names of women uttered by various female artists on "Hell You Talmbout," aside from Sandra Bland's, are nowhere near as familiar as the other names chanted throughout the song. And although the rawness of the vocals, unsung and filled with cracking voices, conveys the anguish to which Monaé alludes in her statement, the choice to privilege the names of black men (whose names and bodies were made heard and visible in the moment of their deaths) over black women silences once more those who needed to be named the most.

Vita E. Cleveland's response to Wondaland, "Hell Y'all Ain't Talmbout," focuses on the erasure of names and bodies, specifically those of trans women of color, from both the original protest anthem and from the larger movement itself. Cleveland, a black trans woman, percussionist, and poet, has been a creator of activist art through "positive representation and advocacy for the experiences of marginalized peoples."[51] Co-opting the track, Cleveland inserts her own list of names after making clear that "it's all of us or none of us, flat out."[52] Instead of directing us to "say their names," as in the original, the track shouts the names of trans people of color who have been killed over a repeated, anthemic cry of “Black lives matter!” Listeners are not so much engaged in the collective action of naming as they are subjected to it, forced to confront the names of those murdered by the state. By presenting those names against the call of “Black lives matter,” the relationship cannot be misconstrued: these names represent the hidden and silenced bodies who deserve to be remembered, recognized, and counted as integral to the BLM movement. Cleveland’s track stands as reminder to those within BLM that the lives (and deaths) of black trans people are a legitimate part of the movement, something reiterated by BLM’s founders. This desire to place the names of trans women of color stems possibly from issues within black communities themselves around acknowledging abuse and violence toward black women and black trans men and women. Although BLM was founded, in part, by black queer female activists, its growth as a movement revealed the ways in which black communities can prioritize certain types of death, instances of “black men and women caring less about murdered black women, of cis blacks caring less about slain trans blacks, and so on.”[53]

Conclusion

What does music achieve when it confronts deeply complex and problematic narratives of and around violence? How does music reframe stories of trauma? Susan Fast and Kip Pegley consider the role of music as a frame for understanding or resituating violence, for speaking where words fail as inherently problematic:

> This notion of music as somehow “naturalized” means that it is figured as lying outside of the social, that the individual can interpret musical sounds broadly with respect to their own experience, with little recourse to a larger social context, or at the very least, that music is considered too abstract to signify the social very particularly.[54]

But this musical instance to which they refer implies instrumental, seemingly asocial, Western art music rather than the politically charged, socially dependent protest music of BLM and SHN. Protest music is defined by the social and cultural, and it is therein removed from the essentializing that can plague music as art, separating it from the real-world violence that music can reflect, encapsulate, and sometimes inflict. The songs described in this chapter deal with violence on an atomic level and reenact that violence in performance, at times problematically, in order to convey the profound pain and despair of the African American experience. Just as bystander videos provide a visual witnessing of *the state of siege* in which black Americans live, these songs provide an aural witnessing, a sonic reminder not to turn away.

Music as a cultural product and as a reflection of society can also mirror back that society's hidden fissures, cracks, and omissions. The protest music around BLM unintentionally reproduces the internal issues and problems within the black community around a hierarchy of social and bodily values. And just as black female activists and scholars have fought to reconfigure that hierarchy in an effort to make the lives of black women matter, so too have black (female) musicians and artists given voice to this effort. Poet Aja Monet encapsulates the invisibility of black womanhood and black female death, as well as the desire to let the silenced be heard, from the very beginning of her spoken word poem "#Say Her Name."

> I am a woman carrying other women
> in my mouth
> behold a sister
> a daughter
> a mother
> dear friend
> spirits demystify
> on my tongue. . . .
> I am not here to say look at me how I died
> so brutal a death I deserve a name to fit all the horror in
> I am here to tell you how if they mentioned me
> in their protests and rallies
> they would have to face their role in it too.[55]

She asks her audience to take heed and to listen for her voice and the names of women as they "fly toward your ear."[56] The symbolism of voicelessness appears throughout the poem, connecting threads of resistance and futility. Monet makes clear that many are complicit in the silencing of black women, including black men. It is not only through naming but also through hearing and listening that justice for black women can be achieved. She asks us to meet "in the valley of a voice," where we "lay our bodies down" to speak the names of so many who have been lost in so many ways. Monet's words recall the sound of Mahalia Jackson singing the text of Psalm 23 (to which Monet's poem alludes) in Duke Ellington's *Black, Brown, and Beige*, again revealing the connectedness of the sonic and of black female resistance. By focusing on reembodiment and vocalization, Monet and others make clear a path toward the recognition for so many black women whose bodies and voices have been stolen and hidden away. By pushing the names and stories of black women forward to the front of the narrative around black death and American necropolitics, musicians are attempting to dismantle the cycle of violence, silence, and trauma that began centuries ago. Through music, black female artists are confronting "the difficulty of regaining one's voice, one's subjectivity, after one has been reduced to silence."[57] These artists and musicians are telling us to remember, specifically, that black women's lives matter.

Notes

1. Achille Mbembe, "Necropolitics," *Public Culture* 15 (2003): 29.
2. Mbembe, "Necropolitics," 30.
3. I will refer to Black Lives Matter as BLM throughout the rest of the chapter.
4. I will refer to Say Her Name as SHN throughout the rest of the chapter.
5. Lily Workneh, "#SayHerName: Why We Should Declare That Black Women and Girls Matter, Too," *Huffington Post*, May 21, 2015, https://www.huffingtonpost.com/2015/05/21/black-women-matter_n_7363064.html
6. Cady Lang, "How This Vine Star Is Using the Mannequin Challenge to Spotlight Black Lives Matter," *Time Magazine*, November 10, 2016, https://time.com/4566455/black-lives-matter-mannequin-challenge/; Priscilla Frank, "Staged Photographs Reenact Real, Hostile Encounters with NYPD," *Huffington Post*, August 3, 2015, https://www.huffpost.com/entry/staged-photographs-reenact-hostile-encounters-with-nypd_n_55bbea21e4b0b23e3ce2e68c
7. Kimberlé Crenshaw, quoted in "Statement: Say Her Name | The Mothers behind the Movement," *African American Policy Forum*, December 3, 2018, http://aapf.org/2018/2018/12/statement-say-her-name-the-mothers-behind-the-movement
8. "#SAYHERNAME: An Evening of Arts and Action," *African American Policy Forum*, March 28, 2017, https://livestream.com/accounts/5045103/events/6767114/videos/152886258/
9. Amy Louise Wood, *Lynching and Spectacle: Witnessing Racial Violence in America, 1890–1940* (Chapel Hill: University of North Carolina Press, 2009); James Allen, *Without Sanctuary: Lynching Photography in America* (Santa Fe, NM: Twin Palms, 2000).
10. Frederick Douglass, *Narrative of the Life of Frederick Douglass, an American Slave: Written by Himself* (Cambridge, MA: Harvard University Press, 2009), 19.
11. Mbembe, "Necropolitics," 12.
12. Hannah Arendt, *The Origins of Totalitarianism* (New York: Harvest, 1966), 157.

13. Louis Althusser, *On the Reproduction of Capitalism: Ideology and Ideological State Apparatuses*, trans. G. M. Goshgarian (New York: Verso, 2014), 110.

14. The Holocaust serves as a foundational element in the field of (intergenerational) trauma studies, and its connection to a racialized necropower connects it closely with that of American slavery. Literature on the parallels between the Holocaust and slavery include *Decolonizing Trauma Studies: Trauma and Postcolonialism*, ed. Sonya Andermahr, special issue of *Humanities* (Basel: MDPI, 2016); and Robert Stam and Ella Shohat, "Critical Ethnic Studies, Identity Politics, and the Right-Left Convergence," in *Critical Ethnic Studies: A Reader*, ed. Nada Elia, David M. Hernández, Jodi Kim, Shana L. Redmond, Dylan Rodríguez, and Sarita Echavez See (Durham, NC: Duke University Press, 2016), 416–34.

15. Mbembe, "Necropolitics," 21.

16. Joy DeGruy, *Post-traumatic Slave Syndrome: American's Legacy of Enduring Injury and Healing* (Portland, OR: Uptone Press, 2005).

17. Ida B. Wells, "Southern Horrors," in *On Lynchings* (Mineola, NY: Dover Publications, 2014).

18. Wells, "Southern Horrors," 9.

19. The involvement of the press in affixing labels to murdered black men is also not a contemporary phenomenon. Wells discusses this very procedure in the section of "Southern Horrors" entitled "The Malicious and Untruthful White Press."

20. Shatema Threadcraft, "North American Necropolitics and Gender: On #BlackLivesMatter and Black Femicide," *South Atlantic Quarterly* 116, no. 3 (2017): 566.

21. Meghna Chakrabarti, Brian Bushard, and Jamie Bologna, "The Invisibility of Police Violence on Women of Color," *Radio Boston*, November 29, 2017, http://www.wbur.org/radioboston/2017/11/29/andrea-ritchie-invisible-no-more

22. Melissa Wright, "Necropolitics, Narcopolitics, and Femicide: Gendered Violence on the Mexico-U.S. Border," *Signs* 36, no. 3 (2011): 710.

23. Patricia Broussard, "Black Women's Post-slavery Silence Syndrome: A Twenty-First Century Remnant of Slavery, Jim Crow, and Systemic Racism—Who Will Tell Her Stories?," *Journal of Gender, Race and Justice* 16, no. 2 (2013): 386.

24. Broussard, "Black Women's Post-slavery Silence," 386.

25. Mbembe, "Necropolitics," 21. Mbembe discusses slavery as a state of injury rather than a state of siege due to slaves' value as labor), and Pamela Bridgewater expands upon the lack of protections for black female slaves in "Ain't I a Slave: Slavery, Reproductive Abuse, and Reparations," *UCLA Women's Law Journal* 89 (2005): 89–162.

26. Broussard, "Black Women's Post-Slavery Silence," 408.

27. Stephen Dillon, "Possessed by Death: The Neoliberal-Carceral State, Black Feminism, and the Afterlife of Slavery," *Radical History Review* 112 (2012): 116, emphasis added.

28. Mina Karavanta, "The Injunctions of the Spectre of Slavery: Affective Memory and the Counterwriting of Community," *Feminist Review* 104 (2013): 42–60.

29. Karavanta, "Injunctions of the Spectre," 47.

30. Jaleesa Smiley, "Breaking the Silence: The Voices of Black Women and the

Path towards Liberation," American Cultural Studies Capstone Research Papers 3, Western Washington University, 2015, 7.

31. Susan Brison, "Trauma Narratives and the Remaking of the Self," in *Acts of Memory: Cultural Recall of the Present*, ed. Mieke Bal, Jonathan Crewe, and Leo Spitzer (Hanover, NH: University Press of New England, 1999), 40.

32. Brison, "Trauma Narratives," 46.

33. Rhiannon Giddens, "We Rise," North Carolina Music Love Army Records, 2014.

34. Corey Smith-West, "The Sounds of Black Lives Matter," *Pitchfork*, October 17, 2016, https://pitchfork.com/thepitch/1327-the-sounds-of-black-lives-matter/; Brittany Spanos and Sarah Grant, "Songs of Black Lives Matter: 22 New Protest Anthems," *Rolling Stone*, July 13, 2016, https://www.rollingstone.com/music/pictures/songs-of-black-lives-matter-22-new-protest-anthems-20160713/lauryn-hill-black-rage-sketch-20160713

35. Threadcraft, "North American Necropolitics," 559.

36. An example of this would be the number of songs entitled "Hands Up" (Vince Staples; Daye Jack; Chris Brown; Boosie Badazz) or "I Can't Breathe" (Lil B; Marcus Miller; Queen Ifrica).

37. The title of the song comes from the video footage of Scott's murder in which his wife could be heard saying, "Don't do it" to the police.

38. Threadcraft, "North American Necropolitics," 566.

39. Sarah Almukhtar, Mercy Benzaquen, Damien Cave, Sahil Chinoy, Kenan Davis, Josh Keller, K.k. Rebecca Lai, Jasmine C. Lee, Rochelle Oliver, Haeyoun Park, and Destinée-Charisse Royal, "Black Lives Upended by Policing: The Raw Videos Sparking Outrage," *New York Times*, August 29, 2017, https://www.nytimes.com/interactive/2017/08/19/us/police-videos-race.html

40. Chakrabarti, Bushard, and Bologna, "Invisibility of Police Violence."

41. Broussard, "Black Women's Post-Slavery Silence," 408.

42. Evan Minsker, "Blood Orange Annotates 'Sandra's Smile' Lyrics," *Pitchfork*, October 29, 2015, https://pitchfork.com/news/61809-blood-orange-annotates-sandras-smile-lyrics/; https://genius.com/8070068

43. Blood Orange, "Sandra's Smile," *Genius*, https://genius.com/8070068

44. The first lines of "Sandra's Smile" are "Who taught you how to breathe / then took away your speech," what Hynes calls a reference to those who do not acknowledge black lives but in some way animate their bodies.

45. Tina Knowles-Lawson, *Instagram*, April 17, 2018, https://www.instagram.com/p/Bho-WDiBzpV/; Caroline Framke, "Beyoncé Knew Coachella's White Audience Wouldn't Understand Her Set. That's Why She Did It," *Vox*, April 17, 2018, https://www.vox.com/culture/2018/4/17/17247954/coachella-2018-beyonce-beychella-references

46. Marti Newland, "Sounding 'Black': An Ethnography of Racialized Vocality at Fisk University" (PhD dissertation, Columbia University, 2014).

47. Antonio Brown, "Performing 'Truth': Black Speech Acts," *African American Review* 36 (2002): 213–25.

48. Brown, "Performing 'Truth,'" 214.

49. Janelle Monaé, "Hell You Talmbout," *Instagram*, August 13, 2015, http://bit.ly/2GY5CEm, emphasis added.

50. Threadcraft, "North American Necropolitics," 569.

51. Vita E. Cleveland, "Our Story," *Facebook*, April 8, 2018, https://www.facebook.com/twocpoetry/

52. J Mase III, "Hell Y'all Ain't Talmbout: An Epic Response to Trans Erasure," *Huffington Post*, August 28, 2015, https://www.huffingtonpost.com/j-mase-iii/hell-yall-aint-talmbout-a_b_8038996.html

53. Threadcraft, "North American Necropolitics," 568.

54. Susan Fast and Kip Pegley, eds., *Music, Politics and Violence* (Middletown, CT: Wesleyan University Press, 2012), 8.

55. Aja Monet, "Aja Monet's #SayHerName Poem Asks All to Remember," *Empathy Educates*, May 21, 205, http://empathyeducates.org/Journeys-to-and-through/aja-monets-sayhername-poem-asks-all-to-remember/

56. Monet, "Aja Monet's #SayHerName Poem."

57. Brison, "Trauma Narratives," 47.

Possibilities and Impossibilities of Commemoration

Trauma's Persistence and the Politics of Reenactment

SEVEN | Songs of Flight

War and Genocide Reenactment on the Refugee Route

VANESSA AGNEW

The hills of Sarajevo rise sharply from the Baščaršija, Sarajevo's Ottoman bazaar and the heart and soul of this ancient city. It has been twenty years since mortars rained down from the hills and the alleyways were a shooting gallery for snipers. But these twenty years are as nothing. Pockmarked, gap-toothed buildings surround the square, and the city's inhabitants bear their scars still. Their eyes are not frankly dismissive like Berliners', but deep and pained. In their softness there is perhaps even a glimmer of hope for the future.

On this day, we have walked through the city barefoot, leaving a trail of red footprints to commemorate the 5,434 civilians killed during the four-year siege of Sarajevo, and we have come to settle on the steps of the Baščaršija's famous fountain. Behind us, a pianist is playing Bach on an electronic keyboard, and a crowd has gathered to listen. Some older people sway a little, close their eyes. What are they hearing, what do they remember? Is this the largo from the F minor Harpsichord Concerto BWV 1056? In my weariness, I am unsure. We have walked a long way—some of us, all the way from Berlin. Walked these thousand miles to draw attention to another war, the war in Syria, and to show solidarity with the sea of refugees who have arrived at our doors in the past few years. The pianist plays on, and we listen with relief, overwhelmed by the demands of our own undertaking, by the journey ahead, and by an imperative to realize peace.

This peace march from Germany, through the Czech Republic, Austria, the Balkan Peninsula, and Greece, via Lebanon, to Syria, loosely reenacts—in reverse—the 2016 refugee flight from the Middle East to Western Europe.[1] From destination to point of origin, every step away from Berlin and nearer to Aleppo takes the participants back in time, as it were. What we are to learn from this juxtaposition of time and space remains unclear. On the day we gather in Sarajevo, two-thirds of the journey lie ahead. We anticipate still greater hardship and face the prospect of sites of past and present trauma. But such is the perennial question for practitioners as well as scholars of reenactment: What can reenactment usefully teach us about the past? What can we learn about war, ethnic cleansing, refugee flight, and genocide by revisiting the sites of historical conflict, and by simulating past occurrences and experiences? At the very least, the undertaking seems to be a way of gathering present experiences that can be mapped to unfamiliar earlier ones. We will ask ourselves whether the gains in personal experience, along with the powerful emotions generated by following in others' footsteps, bear any relation to what people have already lived through. We will reluctantly conclude that the confluences of experience and historical palimpsest do not necessarily withstand rigorous historical scrutiny. By the same token, the reenactment will be found to raise the possibility of new questions, new modes of interpretation, and new means of communicating.

This refugee reenactment through Europe's liminal regions is simultaneously a commemoration of sorts. We tread gingerly between uncleared minefields in Bosnia-Herzegovina, reminded that we might be reversing the steps of recent refugees from Syria and Afghanistan, but we are also following in the footsteps of the NATO military units and NGOs that attempted to clear these woods and fields of ordinance. Memorials to those who died in this undertaking pepper our route. We pass through historical sites of the Holocaust—Terezín, the old Theresienstadt in the Czech Republic, and Crveni Krst, the "Red Cross" concentration camp in Niš, Serbia—places of which few marchers were hitherto aware, let alone had visited. These genocide sites lie in various states of neglect and disintegration, attracting dark tourists but often failing in their mandate to educate, reconcile, promote transitional justice, and forestall mass slaughter in the future. Taking my own dark tourism to its apogee, I leave the peace march and make a detour to Kraków and nearby Oświęcim to visit Auschwitz-Birkenau. At a mental loss to comprehend what I have known only by report and from images, I grasp for the first time what Adorno and others might have meant when they pointed to the "unspeakableness" of the Holocaust and the barbarism of writing poetry after Auschwitz.[2] But with this journey, my perception of the Holocaust—its center of gravity—also shifts to encompass Eastern and southeastern Europe. Thinking about genocide comparatively—once contentious among historians—seems newly possible, even necessary. Globally, the commemoration of mass atrocities remains strongly influenced by Holocaust discourse and, increasingly, the commemoration assumes forms that are performative, identificatory, and affective.[3] Our foot journey along the current refugee route brings home the fact that Germany's latest arrivals from the Middle East will fall under the mantel of Germany's historical legacy, with the compunction to engage in forms of memory culture and civic engagement predicated on *Vergangenheitsbewältigung* (coming to terms with the past).[4]

As we are repeatedly reminded walking these Baltic landscapes, old animosities are easily reanimated; the imposed peace in the former Yugoslavia is delicate. A group of Serbian men sitting outside a café holds up the three-fingered Orthodox sign as we pass—a latter-day fascist gesture and provocation to the Muslims in our company. Unsettling as this is, we also find new, more terrifying challenges at Europe's margins. A stone's throw from the Sarajevo fountain where the piano concert takes place, there lurks an Islamic State follower, the logo on his T-shirt a refusal of history and a disavowal of the cosmopolitanism of which this city has long been proud.

I am drawn back to the concert. It *is* the largo, I decide. The piece wanders determinedly around its tonality, exploring possibilities and outcomes. It is neither heroic nor nationalistic—a judicious choice on the part of the Sarajevan pianist. Indeed, the music seems to be doing its work, and the audience is palpably moved. Yet reenactment always poses challenges to authenticity. When it comes to historical fidelity, it ought not be a pianist playing Bach, but a cellist performing the Albinoni G minor Adagio.[5] Twenty years ago, Vedran Smijlović, a member of the Sarajevo Philharmonic Orchestra, risked snipers and mortar fire to perform the Adagio at funerals and in ruined buildings, and, in so doing, drew world attention to the devastation of the city. The discrepancy between the current choice of music and its historical referent raises the question as to whether our reenactment needs to be literal—the same music played in the same place, in the most similar possible way—for present audiences to grapple with the past and to gain insights into events of long ago (Figure 7.1).

It is a question for the peace march and, indeed, a question for all

Figure 7.1. Songs of flight, Sarajevo 2017. Photograph Janusz Ratecki.

reenactments: how much historical fidelity is sufficient for historical understanding? How much historical authenticity is needed or even possible? Conversely, we might ask whether the "excess" of fidelity—a sense of hyperrealism—deters from the commemorative enterprise, tipping it into the realm of kitsch and facile consumption. As the Bach performance draws to a close, we are prompted to ask what specific role musical and sonic reenactments can play in elucidating the past and in commemorating atrocities. It is a question complicated by the frequent misuse made of music during war.[6] Orphic-like, music's power will straddle opposing forces of resistance, succor, and hope, but also acquiescence, humiliation, and torture. Finally, we might ask whether, as a nonrepresentational form, music can be adequate to its commemorative task.

To explore these questions, the essay will look at examples of documentary film, fiction, theater performance, and museum sound design—Claude Lanzmann's *Shoah* (1985), Josef Bor's *Theresienstadt Requiem* (1963), Hotel Modern's *Kamp* (2005), the Warsaw Uprising Museum, the Hungarian exhibition at the Auschwitz Museum, and the Jewish Museum in Berlin. Their variable use of music and sound will be understood as forms of historical reenactment that are investigative, commemorative, resistant, and restorative, making claims that are epistemological, ontological, and ethical. Through comparison, I will argue against musical reenactment as a useful tool for advancing historical knowledge but in favor, specifically, of nonrealist, nonrepresentational forms of reenactment as powerful means of interrogating and commemorating the traumatic past in relation to a postwitness present.

Reenacting Genocide

In *The Past is a Foreign Country*, David Lowenthal's classic work on the ways in which societies understand and deal with history, the author argues, "The past's worst horrors are beyond the power of replication."[7] While this might once have been believed to be the case, it was only ever true in the literal sense. Today, the reenactment of mass atrocities is a common representational strategy seen in films like Joshua Oppenheimer's *The Act of Killing* (2012), which restages genocidal killings in Indonesia in the 1960s, and the twentieth-anniversary commemoration of the Rwandan genocide, which saw large numbers of participants simulating the days of slaughter from 1994.[8] Lowenthal's comment notwithstanding, such examples suggest that the understanding of genocide can possibly be served by reenactment for the very reason that reenactment puts an individual face on collective suffering. Perhaps more importantly, it enables contemporary audiences to engage affectively with historical suffering in the absence of surviving witnesses. To use Alison Landsberg's term, reenactment helps construct a "prosthetic memory" of events beyond the time of their actual remembering. Landsberg sees in prosthetic memory the possibility for "a progressive politics based on empathy for the historical experiences of others," one "that awakens the potential . . . for increased social responsibility and political alliances that transcend the essentialism and ethnic particularism of contemporary identity politics."[9] At its best, then, reenactment contributes to a new form of public history that generalizes empathy and contributes to a more capacious public sphere. Useful, too, in this context, is Marianne Hirsch's concept of "postmemory," which describes the relationship of later generations to trauma they have not experienced themselves—to experiences they "remember" only via "stories, images, and behaviors" transmitted from the past.[10] By drawing on the concepts introduced by Landsberg and Hirsch, we can ask how reenactment might use such a postmemorial aesthetic to reanimate the past without, however, misappropriating it.

Reenactment has typically been associated with the restaging of significant historical events like American Civil War and World War II battles, and with living history performances that attempt to recreate past lifeways by simulating modes of dress, recreation, work, transportation, speech, and performance practice. As is increasingly common in the field, however, reenactment can be conceived in broader cross-disciplinary terms.[11] It can be playful, taking the form of video gaming, historical toys, theater performance, and live action role-play. It can be investigative, as in experimental archaeology, which attempts to recreate past lifeways and technologies, and restorative, as in truth and reconciliation tribunals, which use the process of discovery and testimony to simulate and redress past injustices within a juridical context. It can be expository, as in historical reality television and film, which embed reenactment within a documentary framework. It can be secular, as many of these examples suggest, or have an explicitly sacred character, familiar to us from pilgrimages and neopagan rituals. And it can be musical, extending beyond the simple performance of a musically notated work from long ago. As in historically informed performance, musical reenactment can attend to the particularities of earlier performance practices and instruments with the aim of recapturing earlier modes of playing and listening. Reenactment can also entail the use of music and sound to augment the representation of the past in museum exhibits and living history displays.

Linking these diverse manifestations of reenactment is an effort to invoke the past through an emphasis on individual experience—through immersion, embodiment, heightened emotion, and empathy.[12] Decisively, reenactment attempts to collapse the distance between the past and present, such that reenactors and their audiences gain a sense of "really being there." Reenactors aim to access the past "as it really was" by experiencing "period rush"—a sense of complete immersion in the past—and by suffering emotionally and physically in order to gain what would appear to be "firsthand" historical experience. This impression of experiencing the past, up close and personal, lends reenactment a testimonial function: the reenactor, immersed in another world, bears witness to the sensory impressions, suffering and pleasure, attendant upon this experience. In an effort to further these aims, the reenactor focuses on the minutiae of their historical experience through fidelity to details of dress, food, speech, and manner. Typically occluded are questions of macrohistorical and macroeconomic processes.[13]

Claims to authenticity underscore most reenactments, whether through the use of historically accurate techniques, materials, and performance practices or through technological means like CGI, which generates a heightened sense of realism and historical "completeness." It is for this reason that practitioners as well as scholars have taken the "authenticity pretext" to be a defining feature of the practice. Reenactment has what Iain McCalman and Paul Pickering call a "realist aesthetic."[14] As we will find, however, simulative historical performances need not be constrained by claims to authenticity. The auditory examples under discussion here suggest that also nonrealist, nonrepresentational modes of reenactment can collapse temporalities and generate an affective engagement with the past. This recognition marks a departure from most scholarly work on reenactment, signaling a need for a revision in our understanding of reenactment that goes beyond its realist aesthetic. Within musicology, these debates have long centered on the question of whether it is possible for music to be performed and heard as it was in the past, or whether such efforts are merely shaped by contemporary aesthetic values—something Richard Taruskin refers to as the "pick[ing] and choos[ing] from history's wares" to satisfy a "modern(ist)" agenda.[15]

Following Taruskin and Lydia Goehr on the question of historically informed performance, I will suggest that if reenactment is to make a useful contribution to historical understanding and commemoration, then it will not do so by perfecting the historical mise-en-scène, nor by pursuing what public historian Stephen Gapps refers to as reenactment's "holy grail" of authenticity.[16] It is not by faithfully simulating period musical instruments, neglected performance techniques, and audience listening practices, nor by donning historically accurate costumes, uniforms, and weaponry; it is not, to use a reenactment term, by becoming a "stitch Nazi" that historical understanding will be furthered.[17] Rather it is the fragmentary, aleatoric, and nonrepresentational forms of reenactment that will be more likely to breach that gap in understanding identified and lamented by Holocaust survivor Elie Wiesel. "For the living and the dead," he said, "we must bear witness." Yet, he added, "It is not because I cannot explain that you won't understand, it is because you won't understand that I cannot explain."[18] Wiesel left his audience with a representational conundrum that placed the onus on the listener, not just the teller. It will be our task to determine what shape that listening might take.

Theresienstadt and the Limits of Musical Reenactment

Terezín was not on the itinerary. In fact, the Czech Republic in toto was incidental to our reenactment. Droves of refugees from Afghanistan and

Syria never made a beeline for Prague; expediently, they headed north via bus, taxi, or train from Austria to Germany. In the Czech Republic, we did not meet even one refugee. No Czech we encountered had met one either, though a few had views on the "refugee character" and the "threat" they posed to Europe's integrity. Still, the Czech Republic lay before us, the landscape flatter than routes due south, and through it we would go. Terezín was not our destination, either, but we passed within a few miles of it. "Over there," said our guide, "across the river." In the direction of his pointing was little to see—rolling hills in the distance, hops plantations, a murder of crows rising in the fields. Has it always been thus, I wondered? Marching within spitting distance of concentrated suffering but seeing and hearing nothing?

We felt compelled to visit. It was a gray day, midwinter. Hardly a visitor about, pigeons wheeling in the courtyard, swallows nesting in the delousing chamber, and water dripping through holes in the barracks' roof. Only the sign above the arched entryway, "Arbeit macht frei" (Work sets you free), seemed to have received due attention. Had it been repainted? Its contours looked crisp and its paintwork suspiciously bright. Otherwise, all was quiet. I could find no traces of what has come to be thought of as Terezín's protest to the world, its act of defiance against Nazism. Was I looking and listening in the wrong places? I skirted in and out of buildings and thick-walled tunnels. The walls did not sing out, not even whisper. No Brundibár, no cabaret songs, no Verdi *Requiem.*[19]

The musician Josef Bor (1906–1979) was not so limited in his imagining of musical life in the concentration camp. He was deported from Prague in 1942, arriving at Terezín along with his family, before being sent to Auschwitz, where he alone survived.[20] I discovered his book in the museum gift shop, where the proprietor was desultorily shuffling the merchandise, while in the background a video showed an endless loop of Nazi transports, selections, and killings. We read the book later, looking over one another's shoulders, camped out on the floor of a community house in a nearby town.

Theresienstadt Requiem, first published in 1963, provides a vivid invocation of the camp's cultural life, using an omniscient third-person narrator to tell the story of Raphael Schächter (1905–1945), a Jewish Czech composer, pianist, and conductor sent to Theresienstadt in 1941 and killed, it is thought, during the death march evacuation of Auschwitz toward the end of the war. Based on actual events, the work's genre definition is tricky. It is part novella, memoir, and creative nonfiction. For our purposes, it will be useful to think of it as a literary reenactment for the way in which it conjures the past in the present, vividly evoking not just the musical activities of the camp but the music itself. Musicologist Siglind Bruhn refers to the translation of prose into music as musical ekphrasis, a term conventionally used to describe the rendering of painting or sculpture into poetry, like Achilles's shield in the *Iliad,* with its graphic account of the fate of Troy.[21] The ekphrastic gesture in Bor's work similarly renders one artistic form as another, reanimating the music in literary terms and allowing it to be heard by the reader.

The plot of the book is spare, amounting to not more than preparations for a musical performance—the smuggling into the camp of the Verdi score, manuscript paper, and instruments, the auditioning of soloists, training of the chorus, and the loss of the performers to the transports and death camps. Though the action in the book occurs over many months, the plot is condensed and the described events provide little narrative tension. Rather, it is the tension within the music that the reader is meant to hear as he or she is transformed into a reader-listener. Together with the character of the conductor, the reader-listener is also to anticipate the musical performance that the chorus is rehearsing for fellow inmates, SS officers, and Adolf Eichmann, orchestrator of the Theresienstadt deception.

Although the author writes as a survivor, he does not foster the reader's identification with the imprisoned musicians. The reader thus gains few insights into daily life in the concentration camp, the experience of performing, or even the musicians' terrible choices to follow their families to the extermination camps. In focusing almost exclusively on the rehearsing of the Verdi *Requiem,* Bor offers the reader a window into musical process and interpretation. The specific timbre of the soloists' voices, compromises in orchestration, and the inflection of a particular word are central to the author's purpose, such that the *Requiem* itself assumes the role of a character in the work.

Theresienstadt Requiem informs the film *Defiant Requiem* (2012, dir. Doug Schulz), a documentary on the 2005 reenactment by conductor Murry Sidlin of Schächter's wartime Verdi performances. Sidlin conceived of *Defiant Requiem* to honor Schächter and his chorus, restaging the work at Terezín and incorporating into the performance a number of camp survivors and a singer from Schächter's original chorus. While a number of interpretive frameworks might have been possible, the documentary squarely interprets music making in the concentration camp as a gesture of spiritual resistance, using both the testimony of witnesses and the reenactment itself to emphasize that Schächter's Verdi undertaking was a form of "artistic uprising" against the Nazis.

This is not entirely a misrepresentation of Bor's work. Bor's *Theresienstadt Requiem* indeed construes the Verdi performance as an act of defiance. Schächter's labored choice of soloists and his scrupulous auditioning, for example, can be read as a metaphor for the selections that daily threatened the existence of the Theresienstadt inhabitants. In the counterworld of the ghetto, it is artistic adjudications that will prevail rather than the life-and-death selections on the Nazi ramps and in the *Schleusen* (sluices). Yet Bor's book also does something more complicated than attempt to use music to defy fascism. It posits music as universal and beyond religious, ethnic, or national particularity. In taking this position, Bor cleaves this prerogative from Germans as the arbiters of musical interpretation.[22] By his account, a ragtag collection of Jewish singers and musicians from Bohemia, Austria, Germany, Holland, Denmark, Poland, and Hungary will perform a Catholic Mass for the dead—a medieval Latin text set to Italian music, led by a nonbeliever.[23] At the same time, Bor offers a musical interpretation of the *Requiem* as a work concerned with justice. He posits an ideal listener in the future, a listener concerned with restorative justice, and it is within this framework that the character of Schächter makes his aesthetic choices. We see this in the Offertorium, which poses a choice between damnation and salvation that hinges on the inflection of the word *sed* (but).[24] And we see it in the final Dies Irae, with its emphasis on a sense of higher justice.

> The day of wrath is here, we have lived to see it. Your armies have been torn to shreds just like you tore and lacerated us. Streams of blood gush from your deep wounds and your land is split asunder in the din and smoke of thousands of falling bombs. And rightfully so: not out of vengeance or hatred, simply for the sake of human justice.[25]

Stressing the juridical interpretive frame of *Theresienstadt Requiem* follows historian Shirli Gilbert's insights into music and Holocaust memory. Gilbert objects expressly to the way in which scholars investigating the relationship between music and Holocaust memory frequently adopt an interpretive umbrella of spiritual resistance. This, Gilbert argues, associates music "overwhelmingly with affirmative frameworks such as defiance, faith and heroism."[26] She goes on to add that music in the transit camps, ghettos, and extermination camps served a plethora of functions. In keeping with these observations, the challenge is to capture the diversity of that musical experience—from solace, parody, and defiance, to capitulation, flattery, sadism, and torture. In stark contrast to the uplifting musical performances at Terezín, for example, was the use of enforced singing, music for humiliation and the reeducation of political prisoners, music used for guard entertainment, for sadistic pleasure, and as an augmentation to Nazi megalomania.[27] Such historiographic insights are worth keeping in mind. Reenactment has a tendency toward reductionism, and its messages do not always enjoy close interrogation. To use musical reenactment to commemorate genocide begs the question of which music needs to be reanimated, what is to be commemorated, and whether it is to serve individual, national, or ethnoreligious identities.

Museum Soundscapes

With the peace march heading inexorably south on its journey to besieged Aleppo, I veer north to Poland to investigate war and genocide commemoration there. Specifically, it will be to Warsaw that I go to visit the Warsaw Uprising Museum, popular with tourists and with "preppers," survivalists actively preparing for a postapocalyptic breakdown of society. Opened in 1994 to commemorate the 1944 uprising, the museum is as well known for its jingoism as for its visitor experience and its commercial success.

The Warsaw Uprising Museum stands in marked contrast to the traditional configuration of museums as a quiet, contemplative, even reverent space, in which the museumgoer's attention was visually directed to the objects on display, and where proper behavior—silent appreciation and decorous, restrained physical movement—is expected. Recently, exhibition designers have come to appreciate not just that sound can convey historical content, but also that soundscapes affect visitors' emotional responses and behavior. As Michael Stocker points out, more noise is made in environments that reverberate, while people are quieter in "acoustically dampened environments."[28] This in turn impacts the flow rate of visitor traffic, with visitors pausing to reflect and absorb information in quieter areas or passing rapidly through noisy ones.

The Warsaw Uprising Museum makes significant use of psychoacoustics to generate a visitor experience that is meant to invoke the impression of "really being there." A simulated urban environment, with cobbled streets, rubble, and sandbags, is augmented by sounds of bombing raids, shouts and cries, patriotic singing, and other acoustic effects. Visitors duck and recoil at the sudden sound of gunfire and mortars exploding; they lean in to hear the whispered voices emanating from a "listening wall." Elsewhere, they linger to hear recordings of piano playing and oral interviews. In its design, the museum coheres with what Valerie Casey describes as a "performing museum," a form that has arisen within the context of the proliferation of war and genocide memorialization.[29] Marked by a growing acceptance of theatrical display, performing museums like the Warsaw Uprising Museum make use of reconstructions, stage-like sets, and oral testimony that couple the visitor with the survivor to create a powerful sense of identification, albeit at the expense of a contemplative, critical subject.[30]

Increasingly, a large segment of the museumgoing public takes such experiential modes of historical representation as a given. Moreover, the nature of the experience at Holocaust remembrance sites, it is argued, is not to be dictated by specialist interpreters, professional historians, and cultural "elites," nor by cultural producers themselves. Embracing a polyvocality that scholars themselves have long called for, such visitors, and many reenactors, regard historical experience more and more as the purview of the layperson. Some cultural institutions are actively contributing to this shift in order to expand visitor numbers and to promote more visceral public engagement with historical subject matter. Until recently, the Jewish Museum in Berlin, for example, invited museumgoers via its audio guide—and apparently at the instigation of artist Menashe Kadishman himself—to walk over *Shalekhet* (*Fallen Leaves*), an installation comprising more than ten thousand steel faces representing the victims of war and violence, arrayed on the floor of one of the museum's "voids," or hollow chambers (Figure 7.2). Museumgoers could be observed varying their walking pace, running and jumping, picking up and dropping the Munch-like faces, and reveling in the brittle sound of the steel plates clanking together. That museumgoers understood Kadishman's intention to have the faces walked upon as an attenuated form of reenactment is evident from visitor comments that likened the experience to "walking on the bones of dead Jews."[31] For some visitors, it seems, the sound produced by their engagement with the installation invoked something akin to recuperating a "historical" experience. As Barbara Kirshenblatt-Gimblett reminds us, such an experience could be visceral, kinesthetic, and haptic, and an intimate bodily experience.[32] Yet it remains an open question as to whether the emotion associated with

Figure 7.2. The Sound of "Walking on the Bones of the Dead." Menashe Kadishman, *Shalechet*, Jewish Museum, Berlin (Wikimedia Commons).

"walking on the bones" in *Shalekhet* was one of unanimous "unease," as critics like Arturo Schwartz have assumed when claiming that uneasiness is a "metaphor for the emotional turmoil that seizes a concerned person when reminded of the tragedy of the Shoah."[33] Rather, it would seem that such performative installations, like reenactments generally, harbor a range of interpretive possibilities. Some visitors found the corporeal engagement with the metal plates pleasurable, while for others it was both sonically and psychically jarring. Many museum guards, in turn, regarded the visitors' behavior as unseemly and transgressive.[34] The Holocaust Museum has since prohibited visitors from walking across the installation, which is now cordoned off and viewable—without sonic and haptic engagement—only from viewing areas outside the "void." Whether this change in museum policy was motivated by unruly visitor behavior or for reasons of conservation is unclear. It can be seen, however, as indicative of a wider shift within public engagement with Holocaust representation, one that advances transgressive modes of consumption and which signals that the Holocaust has become part of what Sophia Komor and Susanne Rohr in *The Holocaust, Art, and Taboo* refer to as "a semiotic universe of images circulating the globe, a kind of iconography of horror that art can avail itself of"—an "aesthetic event."[35]

It is a truism in heritage studies that place matters—art historian Annie Coombes calls it "a metonymic representation of traumatic memory"—and, consequently, it is thought that the museum exhibition space itself may do part of the commemorative work.[36] Such is the claim in the Hungarian exhibition, *The Citizen Betrayed: A Remembrance of Holocaust Victims from Hungary*, at the Auschwitz Museum, opened in 2004. As one of several national exhibitions, the Hungarian exhibition, designed by László Rajk, set designer for the film *Son of Saul* (2015), is intended to depict the plight of Jews in Hungary after the Nazi occupation, with themes that include ghetto life and deportation, resistance, incarceration, and extermination (Figure 7.3).[37]

In contradistinction to some of other national exhibitions at the Auschwitz Museum, the Hungarian design is dimly illuminated with a postindustrial feel, in which sound design plays a distinctive role. Visitors enter a subterranean space and move through the exhibition on glass floors and clattering metal gantries. Photographs projected onto the walls are augmented by looped soundtracks from directional speakers. These are intended to create visitor disorientation but also to promote viewer identification with the subject matter, as the exhibition design plays with the tension between simulation and dissimulation. Making

Figure 7.3. The permanent exhibition *The Citizen Betrayed—The Memory of Holocaust Victims from Hungary*, Block 18, Auschwitz I, uses projections and sound effects, such that visitors "become part of the past themselves, for a moment," according to its designer, László Rajk. Photograph László Rajk.

use of photographs and reverberant ambient sound generated by visitors interacting with the space, the exhibition de-emphasizes objects. Rajk explicitly distances himself from the accumulation of depersonalized personal effects—glasses, brushes, pots, suitcases, and human hair—that are on display elsewhere in the museum: "Can individual objects be displayed without any attempt at personalization? Can a dish, a toothbrush or a shoe be exhibited without our knowing whom they belonged to?"[38] The past, not the present, Rajk adds, is virtual. Instead, the designer stresses that the space itself constitutes the "objective reality," one that "bears testimony to all the horrors that happened there and everything that followed."[39] Consequently, the only objects displayed are replica ones—plastic identification cards and other simulacra. And yet the exhibition building, and the Auschwitz site generally, do not appear to be adequate to the task the designer assigned to them, that of bearing witness. Visitors' affective response is not the prerogative of visitors themselves. Instead, it is carefully manipulated through the use of sound, with video projections of the selections at Birkenau accompanied by the sound of trains and a pounding heartbeat. Visitors' senses are further mobilized by smell, as they enter the dank and dark space of the exhibition. According to Jani Scandura, odor is the "hidden element of the design," achieved through the use of linseed and bitumen in a special wall preparation intended to invoke the sense of aging.[40]

Filmic and Theatrical Reenactment

Claude Lanzmann's nine-and-a-half-hour documentary *Shoah* (1985) opens with an elegiac boatman, a latter-day Charon conveying the souls of the dead across the river Styx to Hades.[41] In opening the film thus, Lanzmann draws on classical imagery of the boatman as an intermediary between the past and present and on the river as a conduit between the here and now and the everlasting. But the scene also taps into Enlightenment tropes of the singing boatman as the embodiment of simplicity and authenticity—during his Italian journey, Goethe, influenced by Rousseau, sought out the Venetian gondoliers who sang barcaroles to Tasso and Ariosto.[42] The singing boatman was, Goethe suggested, a musical truth-teller and an authentic purveyor of culture. In light of this tradition, it seems fitting that Lanzmann draws on a trope that establishes the witness's reliability on the basis of his honesty and simplicity. He is, in an invocation of Montaigne, an untutored witness whose account is unmediated by artifice. The singing boatman, the conduit from the past to the present, will act as a guarantor of truth for the whole film.

"The story begins," according to the opening script-over in *Shoah*, in present day at Chełmno in Poland, fifty miles northwest of Lodz, where once lived a sizable Jewish population. It was here beginning in December 1941, in the province annexed to the German Reich and renamed Wartheland, that gas was first used as a means of extermination. Of the four hundred thousand Jews transported to Chełmno to be killed, reports the film, only two survived.

The viewer sees one of these survivors, Simon Srebnik, in the opening scene, by now a middle-aged man, being punted in a flat-bottomed boat down the Narew River (Figure 7.4). The scene, with its slow panning shots is, we learn, a reenactment of Srebnik's own experiences as a thirteen-year-old Jewish boy during his incarceration in Kulmhof concentration camp. A few times per week, the boy was punted down the river to the alfalfa fields outside the village in order to replenish the fodder for the Nazis' rabbits. On account of his fine voice, Srebnik was entreated to sing. His singing was also a form of musical exchange, for in return for the Polish folk songs, the German guard taught him Prussian army songs. This musical exchange provided only a temporary reprieve for the young Srebnik. In January 1945, with the imminent arrival of Soviet troops, the remaining Jews of the so-called work details were shot individually, Srebnik included. Srebnik survived being shot in the head, took refuge in a farmer's pigsty, and, nursed back to health, was eventually able to leave Poland for Israel.[43]

What work, we might ask, does this musical reenactment do in the film? The song sung by the boy-now-man is a poignant one: "A little white house lingers in my memory / Of that little white house, I dream each night." For the reenactor, Srebnik, the song gives expression to incalculable loss, viscerally conjuring decades of personal suffering in his face. Yet within the film the reenactment serves an additional purpose. As the camera pans along the river, a silent figure is seen sitting on the banks of the river. Similarly impassive is Srebnik's boat companion: both appear not to hear. It is as if, in the marked absence of a soundtrack, the singing in the film were merely a nondiegetic device. The subsequent scene reveals, however, that Srebnik's singing is indeed diegetic, for it acts powerfully on one of Lanzmann's Chełmno interviewees. In a largely silent portrayal of the countryside where mass exterminations took place, Srebnik's singing breaks the stillness. Srebnik, we learn, was

Figure 7.4. Screenshot of Simon Srebnik returning to sing in Chełmno from *Shoah* (dir. Claude Lanzmann)

known in the village and had, at the time, often been heard singing by the SS, German colonists, and local Poles. To hear him again, says Lanzmann's Polish interviewee forty years later, is to reinstate that time: "When I heard him again my heart beat faster because what happened here . . . was a murder. I really relived what happened."[44]

This statement by the Chełmno resident makes a strong claim for the work that reenactment can do: rehearing the song collapses present and past, transporting the listener to that earlier time of horror. The man's beating heart—a somatosensory effect induced by listening—rekindles suppressed memories. Yet, while the music functions as a mnemonic, its referent is not the singing boy but murder, "*a* murder." What the interviewee in fact "relives" remains occult—whether his role as witness to atrocities perpetrated by others, a specific act of murder, or heart-thumping anxiety about his complicity. In contrast to many of Lanzmann's other interviewees, the peasant's response to the singing signals a power for reenacted music that other forms of oral testimony seem to lack. In marked contrast to the interviewees who unequivocally refuse culpability, this man's body produces a sign. The reenacted singing elicits a physiological response in the listener, a response that hints at agency and a tentative acknowledgment of historical injustice.

The poignancy of the song elegizes the evacuated landscape, seeming to provide what Walter Benjamin in "Über den Begriff der Geschichte" ("On the Concept of History") referred to as "ein Echo von nun verstummten [Stimmen]" (an echo of now silenced [voices]).[45] If music functions here as a way of collapsing time, a survivor testimony that recuperates something of what has been lost, it does not have, as some suggest, an Orphic effect.[46] Srebnik's singing was not the pacifying force that, according to classical mythology, charmed wild beasts and caused rocks and trees to move. It had no civilizing or ameliorative effect on his Nazi guards: singing did not exempt the boy from his duties—emptying bags of crushed bone into the Nagew River to remove even the traces of exterminated Jews—and he was, as we now know, targeted for execution along with the other Jews of Chełmno.

Reenactment in *Shoah* jogs the memory of reluctant witnesses, who as victims, perpetrators, or bystanders cannot or would prefer not to recall—witnesses who misremember, obfuscate, and feign ignorance. There is an affective response that arises through repetition, whether driving a train into Treblinka, cutting hair, or singing a song. Repetition, with its recounting of technical expertise and procedural detail, forms a scaffold for memories and affective response to those memories. Entreated and cajoled into reenacting their own specific fields of expertise and experience, Lanzmann's interviewees were all privy to the events to which they testify. What remains to be investigated is the question of whether reenactment serves as a form of prosthetic memory. Can it provide insights into events for which there are no living witnesses and no firsthand experience?

Whereas *Shoah* eschews historical footage of Nazi guards and concentration camp inmates, the 2005 performance piece *Kamp*, by the Dutch theater collective Hotel Modern, draws explicitly on this visual corpus (Figure 7.5). The set for *Kamp* comprises a 36-foot by 33-foot scale model of Auschwitz populated by three thousand three-inch-tall figures made of wire and modeling clay.[47] Surrounded by an audience, the three performers use puppetry and restrained, stylized movement, as well as video, music, and sound effects to animate the scene in what the director Pauline Kalker refers to as a form of "live animation film onstage."[48] In the work, the audience observes a model train delivering deportees to the camp, figures assembling, eating, sleeping, sweeping, and shoveling rocks, being beaten, hanged, gassed, and cremated. The action is simul-

Figure 7.5. Reenacting genocide: Hotel Modern's *Kamp*. Photograph: Leo van Velzen (www.hotelmodern.nl).

taneously filmed with a handheld camera and projected onto a screen above the model concentration camp.

The force of the performance comes from its intimate familiarity. The piece draws on stock World War II images to catalog and interrogate atrocities. Scenes of a train arriving at the extermination camp are familiar to viewers not only from historical footage but also from their recycling in popular filmic representations like Spielberg's *Schindler's List* (1993), documentaries like *The World at War* (1973–74), and the more recent *Auschwitz: The Nazis and the Final Solution* (2005). Images of prisoners entering the gas chambers, of abandoned belongings, of cremations, and of piles of bodies all belong to a corpus of iconographic Holocaust imagery. And yet in *Kamp*, this referencing only unsettles. It does so partly because of its doubling on stage and screen—a proliferation of images and actions that destabilize the authority of the original. The action also has uncomfortable proximity to play; the toy train and the tiny figures are a perverse and sinister reconfiguration of innocent dollhouses and toy soldiers. By recalling audience members' own toys and play practices, the miniature figures become in and of themselves a marker of an individualized sense of historical time. The viewer is thus brought into proximity with the genocidal past not by any insistence on historical verisimilitude, but through an involuntary act of the imagination.

At the same time, the performance piece recalls Benjamin's insights into the function of play. Children, says Benjamin, long for repetition not only because it is a way of "mastering frightening experiences—by deadening one's own response, by arbitrarily conjuring up experiences, or through parody." Repetition, he continues, also means

> enjoying one's victories and triumphs over and over again, with total intensity. An adult relieves his heart from its terrors and doubles happiness by turning it into a story. A child creates the entire event anew and starts again right from the beginning. . . . Not a "doing as if" but a "doing the same thing over and over again," the transformation of a shattering experience into habit—that is the essence of play.[49]

Such repetition in play, argues film scholar Miriam Hansen, is what makes the original event productive for the future.[50]

The productivity of Hotel Modern's performance piece lies, then, in its use of reenactment's repetitions to unsettle familiar narratives. In contrast to Jake and Dinos Chapman's installation *Fucking Hell* (2008), which incorporates Nazi imagery into a silent Boschian dystopia, *Kamp* resists a sensational or gratuitous handling of violence. The medial complexity of *Kamp* places competing demands on the viewer, whose attention vacillates between the screen and the performers, and between the micro and the macro. Identification is, in the Brechtian sense, forestalled through alienation effects that preclude a facile consumption of the aesthetic work. Fascination with the miniature world gives way to recognition of the perversity of the undertaking: the vulgarity of manipulating puppets in acts of genocide—the banality of the performative act itself—prompts historical awareness. The miniaturization of the concentration camp also allows an appreciation of the scale of the undertaking, obviating the need for a representative victim with whom the viewer is to identify. At the same time, the use of close-ups gives a particularity to the figures. Each puppet has its own face, a distinct victim among an incalculably vast number of victims.

Whereas reenactment typically protests its authenticity, *Kamp* brackets the authenticity problem. The use of puppets means that reenacting the mistreatment of camp prisoners is never constrained by concerns over the welfare of participants, nor by the kinds of ethical considerations that govern the use of survivor testimony and its potential misappropriation. Puppetry allows the *Kamp* performers to suspend the use of the conditional as the dominant mode of reenactment and to substitute that Benjaminian "doing as if" with a "doing over and over." The Auschwitz puppet can, in fact, be beaten to death.[51]

As in Lanzmann's use of Srebnik's singing, in *Kamp*, the music exerts a powerful effect. An Auschwitz band is heard playing Strauss's "Radetzky March" (op. 228) as prisoners in a work commando are shown shuffling out of the camp gates. This, we know, was common practice in camps like Auschwitz, where music was used daily to regulate marching and maintain discipline, with a repertoire that included popular German tunes, marches by Strauss and Sousa, as well as pieces like "Arbeitslager-Marsch" and "Arbeit macht frei-Marsch" composed by camp inmates.[52] As Shirli Gilbert points out, the discrepancy between the cheery and familiar marching tunes and the desperate circumstances of the camp meant that the music exacerbated the prisoners' suffering. Unable to keep time, prisoners were beaten and killed. But the music itself was also an instrument of torture. Primo Levi describes the torment of hearing "the same [tunes] every day, morning and evening: marching and popular songs dear to every German." These, he says, "lie engraven on our minds and will be the last thing in the Lager that we shall forget: they are the voice of the Lager, the perceptible expression of its geometrical madness, of the resolution of others to annihilate us first as men in order to kill us more slowly afterwards."[53]

Using a device we recall from *Shoah* in *Kamp*, the music shifts from a diegetic usage to a nondiegetic one, as the scene transitions from the camp puppet-musicians to the theater performers rearranging the set and themselves dancing to the music. The continuation of the "Radetzky March" forces a repurposing of our role as listeners. *Kamp* and *Shoah* are clearly different yet related enterprises. Both set out to investigate genocide through processes of reenactment. Whereas Lanzmann's film has a revelatory character, however, Hotel Modern's performance piece returns the viewer to a familiar narrative to unsettle the viewer's relationship to history. *Kamp*'s very open-endedness forestalls any tidy resolution. Lanzmann's *Shoah,* in contrast, holds out the possibility of a transformative moment within the film—the possibility that perpetrators and bystanders might acknowledge their own guilt or complicity and empathize with the victims. For Lanzmann, music is a medium that can facilitate this process: it is both a guarantor of historical authenticity and a direct conduit into the past, but it also mounts an appeal to human dignity and the necessity for justice. *Kamp* offers no such redemptory potential. We listen first historically, with interest and dispassion, to the use of music in the camp; then we listen as aesthetic consumers, with enjoyment as the music becomes the backdrop for a dance-like scene change. This shift in the role of the listener points to the multifarious uses of music in the Holocaust: it did not only exert a civilizing force, as Juliane Brauer emphasizes in her work on music as torture in the Nazi concentration and extermination camps.[54] The shifting role of the listener exemplified by the *Kamp* reenactment also highlights our uneasy relationship with the past and how we hear it—whether we listen empathetically, reflectively, inquiringly, or demandingly; whether we listen at all.

Coda

We return to the reenacted refugee peace march, and there is, of course, singing. The singing is that of the participants' Polish protest songs, German folk songs, arias, nursery rhymes, 1960s American peace songs, and rock classics. And there is the *darbuka* and *baglama* playing of the Syrian refugees who accompany us, reversing their own journey and following in their selfsame footsteps. In Sarajevo, Ahmad sings a song of Aleppo. We do not know its meaning, nor its meaning to him. But it functions as a marker of authenticity—a sonic warrant for the integrity of the undertaking—as if a voice from the past had come to sing in the present and attest to its probity.

Did the Syrian and Afghan refugees have the time or energy to sing on their flight to Europe? Footsore and hungry, I have wondered this often. The question, though, is easily enough answered. The mid-Aegean sound recordings made on cell phones tell no tales of seafarers' derring-do. With the children drugged to keep them quiet on the journey, our informant tells us, we hear only the adults crying and screaming. Besides the desperate calls to coast guards in Greece, there is over and over and ever again, the keening "Ya Allah." If there is more to be heard, then it needs a determined listener to recover what Philip V. Bohlman calls "music dislodged from time and place."[55] We will need to inquire hard as to whether their songs of flight are, as Kay Kaufman Shelemay said of the Syrian Jews before the current conflagration, "shot through with remembrance and . . . explicitly perceived as commemorative when performed."[56] This raises questions for us. In years hence, when we look to commemorate the recent mass deaths in the Aegean and the Mediterranean, what will we find beyond the washed-up life jackets, inflatable boats, and bodies on beaches? What will be the sonic legacy of these journeys? The songs of flight, resistance, and mourning? How, I ask, will we re-sing, reenact, and rewrite their loss? And how will we re-sing our own?

Notes

1. The peace march, Civil March for Aleppo, was started by Berlin-based blogger, Anna Alboth, in December 2016, to draw attention to the ongoing war in Syria and to the siege of Aleppo. Participants walked southeast from Berlin for a total of 232 days, crossing eleven countries, to reach the Lebanon-Syria border in August 2017. Departing from the actual route taken by Syrian and Afghan refugees in 2015–16, the peace march was routed through Lebanon, when, for political reasons, official permission to cross Turkey was denied by the Turkish government. On the peace march, see "Civil March for Aleppo," http://civil march.org; and "Civil March for Aleppo seen by Janusz Ratecki," https://www.civilmarchphotos.art

2. Theodor W. Adorno, "Cultural Criticism and Society," *Prisms* (Cambridge, MA: MIT Press, 1981), 34.

3. See, for example, Rebecca Jinks, *Representing Genocide: The Holocaust as Paradigm?* (London: Bloomsbury, 2016).

4. This argument was made in relation to Germany's so-called guest workers. See Leslie Adelson, "Touching Tales of Turks, Germans, and Jews: Cultural Alterity, Historical Narrative, and Literary Riddles for the 1990s," *New German Critique* 80, "Special Issue on the Holocaust" (2000): 93–124.

5. John F. Burns, "The Death of a City: Elegy for Sarajevo—a Special Report; a People under Artillery Fire Manage to Retain Humanity," *New York Times,* June 8, 1992, https://www.nytimes.com/1992/06/08/world/death-city-elegy-for-sarajevo-special-report-people-under-artillery-fire-manage.html. The Adagio in G minor, attributed to Tomaso Albinoni, was composed by musicologist Remo Giazotto and published in 1958. Used in Peter Weir's 1981 film *Gallipoli,* the Adagio is juxtaposed against scenes of extreme violence. The ensuing sonic-cognitive dissonance has become a familiar device in filmic depictions of war. Similar juxtapositions are seen in Oliver Stone's 1986 Vietnam war film, *Platoon,* which uses the second movement from Samuel Barber's 1936 String Quartet, op. 11.

6. See J. Martin Daughtry, *Listening to War: Sound, Music, Trauma, and Survival in Wartime Iraq* (New York: Oxford University Press, 2015).

7. David Lowenthal, *The Past Is a Foreign Country* (Cambridge: Cambridge University Press, 1985), 194.

8. For examples of scholarly literature that treats genocide reenactment, see Deirdre Boyle, "Shattering Silence: Traumatic Memory and Re-enactment in Rithy Panh's *S-21: The Khmer Rouge Killing Machine,*" *Framework* 50, nos. 1–2 (2009): 95–106; Bill Nichols, "Irony, Cruelty, Evil (and a Wink) in *The Act of Killing,*" *Film Quarterly* 67, no. 2 (2013): 25–29; Elke Heckner, "Screening the

Armenian Genocide: Atom Egoyan's *Ararat* between Erasure and Suture," *Shofar* 28, no. 4, "Holocaust and Genocide Cinema" (2010): 133–45.

9. Alison Landsberg, *Prosthetic Memory: The Transformation of American Remembrance in the Age of Mass Culture* (New York: Columbia University Press, 2004), 154.

10. Marianne Hirsch, *The Generation of Postmemory: Writing and Visual Culture after the Holocaust* (New York: Columbia University Press, 2012), 5.

11. See Vanessa Agnew, "What Is Reenactment?" *Criticism* 46, no. 3 (2004): 327; see also Rebecca Schneider, *Performing Remains: Art and War in Times of Theatrical Reenactment* (New York: Routledge, 2011), 2; Bill Nichols, "Documentary Reenactment and the Fantasmatic Subject," *Critical Inquiry* 35, no. 1 (2008): 72–89; and *The Routledge Handbook of Reenactment Studies: Key Terms in the Field,* ed. Vanessa Agnew, Jonathan Lamb, and Juliane Tomann (London: Routledge, 2020).

12. Vanessa Agnew, "History's Affective Turn: Historical Reenactment and Its Work in the Present," *Rethinking History* 11, no. 3 (2007): 299–312; see also Inke Arns, "History Will Repeat Itself: Strategies of Reenactment in Contemporary (Media) Art and Performance," in *History Will Repeat Itself,* ed. Inke Arns and Gabriele Horn (Frankfurt am Main: Revolver Press, 2007), 37–63.

13. Agnew, "History's Affective Turn," 301.

14. Ian McCalman and Paul Pickering, "From Realism to the Affective Turn: An Agenda," in *Historical Reenactment: From Realism to the Affective Turn,* edited by Ian McCalman and Paul Pickering (London: Palgrave Macmillan, 2010), 1.

15. Richard Taruskin, "The Modern Sound of Early Music," *Text and Act* (New York: Oxford University Press, 1995), 164.

16. Stephen Gapps, "On Being a Mobile Monument: Historical Reenactments and Commemorations," in McCalman and Pickering, *Historical Reenactment,* 52, cited in Kate Bowan, "Historically Informed Performance," in Agnew, Lamb, and Tomann, *Routledge Reenactment Studies.* See also Kate Bowan, "R. G. Collingwood, Historical Reenactment and the Early Music Revival," in McCalman and Pickering, *Historical Reenactment,* 134–58; and Bowan, "Historically Informed Performance."

17. The term "stitch Nazi," in widespread use among English-speaking reenactors, derives possibly from the 1990s US NBC sitcom *Seinfeld,* in which the "Soup Nazi" was a character that rigidly adhered to the rules. Among reenactors, the term "stitch Nazi" has less negative connotations. It stands in opposition to the term "farb," a reenactor who remains indifferent to historical fidelity and whose costume is haphazardly and amateurishly put together. See Anna Brædder, "Expertise and Amateurism," in Agnew, Lamb, and Tomann, *Routledge Reenactment Studies Handbook.*

18. "Elie Wiesel's Remarks at the Dedication Ceremonies for the United States Holocaust Memorial Museum, April 22, 1993," https://www.ushmm.org/research/ask-a-research-question/frequently-asked-questions/wiesel

19. *Brundibár* is a children's opera by Jewish Czech composer Hans Krása with a libretto by Adolf Hoffmeister. The *Brundibár* footage from the film is included in the documentary *Voices of the Children,* directed by Zuzana Justman, a Terezín survivor, who sang in the chorus. The Verdi *Requiem* was performed a number

of times at Terezín, including for Nazi officers and an International Red Cross delegation on June 23, 1944. See https://www.defiantrequiem.org/about/more-about-theresienstadt-rafael-schachter-and-the-requiem

20. *Theresienstadt Lexikon,* http://www.ghetto-theresienstadt.info/pages/b/borj.htm

21. See Siglind Bruhn, *Musical Ekphrasis: Composers Responding to Poetry and Painting* (Hillsdale, NY: Pendragon, 2000); see also Lydia Goehr, "How to Do More with Words: Two Views of (Musical) Ekphrasis," *British Journal of Aesthetics* 50, no. 4 (2010): 389–410.

22. See Celia Applegate and Pamela Potter, "Germans as the People of Music: Genealogy of an Identity," in *Music and German National Identity,* ed. Celia Applegate and Pamela Potter (Chicago: University of Chicago Press, 2002), 1–35.

23. Josef Bor, *Theresienstadt Requiem,* trans. Gerald Turner (Göttingen: Wallstein, 2010), 10.

24. Bor, *Theresienstadt Requiem,* 30–31.

25. Bor, *Theresienstadt Requiem,* 109.

26. Shirli Gilbert, "Buried Monuments: Yiddish Songs and Holocaust Memory," *History Workshop Journal* 66, no. 1 (2008): 109.

27. Katarzyna Naliwajek-Mazurek, "Music and Torture in Nazi Sites of Persecution and Genocide in Occupied Poland, 1939–1945," *World of Music,* n.s. 2, no. 1 (2013): 45–46.

28. Michael Stocker, "Exhibit Sound Design," *Museum International* 47, no. 1 (1995): 181.

29. Valerie Casey, "The Museum Effect: Gazing from Object to Performance in the Contemporary Cultural-History Museum," *Archives and Museum Informatics, Europe: Cultural Institutions and Digital Technology* (Paris: École du Louvre, 2003), cited in Paul Williams, *Memorial Museums: The Global Rush to Commemorate Atrocities* (New York: Berg, 2007), 96.

30. Ladislav Kesner, "The Role of Cognitive Competence in the Art Museum Experience," *Museum Management and Curatorship* 21 (2006): 5. See also Nikos Bubaris, "Sound in Museums—Museums in Sound," *Museum Management and Curatorship* 29, no. 4 (2014): 391–402.

31. Museum visitor comments; personal observation, February 17, 2017.

32. Barbara Kirshenblatt-Gimblett, *Destination Culture: Tourism, Museums, and Heritage* (Berkeley: University of California Press, 1998), 194.

33. Arturo Schwartz, "Shalechet," http://new.menashekadishman.com/articles/shalechet-by-arturo-schwartz/#more-438

34. Personal conversation with Jewish Museum docent, February 17, 2017.

35. Sophia Komor and Susanne Rohr, eds., *The Holocaust, Art and Taboo: Transatlantic Exchanges on the Ethics and Aesthetics of Representation* (Heidelberg: Winter, 2010), 10.

36. Annie E. Coombes, "The Art of Memory," *Third Text* 52 (2000): 50.

37. *Son of Saul,* directed by László Nemes (New York: Sony Pictures Classics, 2015).

38. Lásló Rajk, "The Betrayed Citizen: On the Design of the Exhibition," in *The Citizen Betrayed: In Memory of the Victims of the Hungarian Holocaust* (Budapest:

Hungarian National Museum, 2006), 186–88; quoted in *Entangled Histories of the Balkans,* vol. 4: *Concepts, Approaches, and (Self-)Representations,* ed. Roumen Dontchev Daskalov, Diana Mishkova, Tchavdar Marinov, and Alexander Vezenkov (Leiden: Brill, 2017), 625.

39. Daskalov et al., *Entangled Histories,* 625.

40. Jani Scandura, "Sweat: A Memory of Waste," *M/C Journal* 13, no. 4 (2010): 2.

41. "Kharon," http://www.theoi.com/Khthonios/Kharon.html

42. These songs were already widely known in the eighteenth century: in *The Present State of Music in France and Italy* (1771), Charles Burney reported that they were 'so celebrated that every musical collector of taste in Europe is well furnished with them." Maurice J. E. Brown and Kenneth L. Hamilton, "Barcarolle," *Grove Music Online. Oxford Music Online,* Oxford University Press, http://www.oxfordmusiconline.com.libezproxy.open.ac.uk/subscriber/article/grove/music/02021

43. Srebnik died in 2006. "We will never hear his song outside of this film." Timothy Snyder, "The Holocaust We Don't See: Lanzmann's 'Shoah' Revisited," *New York Review of Books,* December 15, 2010, http://www.nybooks.com/daily/2010/12/15/holocaust-we-dont-see-lanzmanns-shoah-revisited/

44. Interviewee, *Shoah,* directed by Claude Lanzmann (1985; New York: Criterion Collection, 2013).

45. Walter Benjamin, *Gesammelte Schriften,* with Theodor W. Adorno and Gershom Scholem, ed. Rolf Tiedemann and Hermann Schweppenhäuser (Frankfurt am Main: Suhrkamp, 1974), 2:693.

46. Etty Mulder, "Orpheus on His Way to the Gas Chambers," http://www.ettymulder.nl/m/images/noodzaak.pdf.

47. Available at http://www.hotelmodern.nl/flash_en/p_kamp/kamp.html

48. See Rachel E. Bennet, "Staging Auschwitz, Making Witnesses: Performances between History, Memory, and Myth," in *History, Memory, Performance,* ed. David M. Dean, Yana Meerzon, and Kathryn Prince (New York: Palgrave Macmillan, 2015), 153–68. See also Patricia Cohen, "Miniatures Amplify a Story of Horror," *New York Times,* May 31, 2010, http://www.nytimes.com/2010/06/01/theater/01kamp.html?_r=0

49. Walter Benjamin, "Toys and Play," in *Selected Writings,* trans. Rodney Livingstone, ed. Michael W. Jennings, Howard Eiland, and Gary Smith (Cambridge, MA: Belknap Press, 2005), 2:120–21; first published in *Die literarische Welt,* June 1928. Quoted in Martin Harries, "Shadow Puppets," http://www.hotreview.org/articles/shadowpuppets.htm

50. Miriam Bratu Hansen, *Cinema and Experience: Siegfried Kracauer, Walter Benjamin, and Theodor W. Adorno* (Berkeley: University of California Press, 2012), 195.

51. Stephen L. Esquith, "Re-enacting Mass Violence," *Polity* 35, no. 4 (July 2003): 513–34.

52. Shirli Gilbert, *Music in the Holocaust: Confronting Life in the Nazi Ghettos and Camps* (Oxford: Oxford University Press, 2005), 182–84.

53. Primo Levi, *If This Is a Man / The Truce* (London: Penguin, 1979), 57; quoted in Gilbert, *Music in the Holocaust,* 184–85. See also Juliane Brauer, "How Can Music Be Torturous? Music in Nazi Concentration and Extermination Camps," *Music & Politics* 10, no. 1 (2016): 1.

54. Brauer, "How Can Music Be Torturous," 2.

55. Philip V. Bohlman, "'Das Lied ist aus': The Final Resting Place along Music's Endless Journey," in *Music and Displacement: Diasporas, Mobilities, and Dislocations in Europe and Beyond*, ed. Erik Levi and Florian Scheding (Lanham, MD: Scarecrow Press, 2010), 15. Here Bohlman uses the term "aesthetics of displacement" to describe "music dislodged from time and place." He goes on to say, "We witness the experience of a Terezín concert from a distance, drawing closer because of what was sounded but now reaches us only as traces of rhythm and echoes of history." Insisting on the challenges and imperatives of musical reenactment, Bohlman cautions that "translating Theresienstadt through performance in the twenty-first century demands of me that I bring more rather than less to the experiences that may be unknowable but must not be left to an eschatology of loss" (18–19). At the same time, quoting Viktor Ullmann ("Der tiefste Schmerz kann zu Musik nicht werden"), he reminds us of the limits of such a reenactment (28)

56. Kay Kaufman Shelemay, *Let Jasmine Rain Down: Song and Remembrance among Syrian Jews* (Chicago: University of Chicago Press, 1998), 6; quoted in Gilbert, "Buried Monuments," 109.

EIGHT | Overwriting Sound

Polish Commemoration in Concert

ANDREA F. BOHLMAN

I could hardly hear the beginning of *Freedom* (*Wolność*), a four-movement jazz symphony composed by Grammy-winning pianist Włodek Pawlik on the occasion of the twenty-fifth anniversary of the first democratic elections in Poland, June 4, 2014. The performance was situated to bring the official public ceremonies, which had included an address by then US president Barack Obama, to a close. Tentative string swells and exploratory motivic play on the piano floated above the moderate crowd assembled around Warsaw's Castle Square.[1] Yet Pawlik's brand of barcarolle-inflected smooth jazz could not penetrate the open-air space of the ceremony, despite an elaborate installation of speakers and jumbotrons. Few heads were strained in attention, few hips swayed with the syncopated beat. At the piano, Pawlik's light touch comfortably evoked impressionistic harmonies as he fiddled with melodies in the upper register of the instrument. A choir and symphonic orchestra filled out the muted and comfortable sonic palette. I still strained my ears during the bossa nova climax of the final movement, with its ebullient title: "Let Us Rejoice in Song" ("Radujmy się pieśniami"). The only fragment of the work's text I could decipher was its title—*wolność*—a phrase emblazoned on banners through the square and trumpeted throughout the addresses of the hour-long event, the "Festival of Freedom" (Figure 8.1).

In addition to the world leaders and diplomats—who enjoyed a first-row seat to the performance by Pawlik's trio, the Polish Chamber Choir, "Schola Cantorum Gedanensis," the Sinfonia Varsovia, and a

Figure 8.1. "Festival of Freedom," Warsaw, Castle Square, June 4, 2014. Photographs by the author.

group of teenaged dancers (who reenacted the "victory" over the Polish Communist Party)—a heterogenous mixture of spectators had assembled around the square's perimeter for this midday ceremony. These elements worked together to generate a "sense of occasion," as Elihu Katz would describe it, grounded in the live-witnessing of a momentous event.[2] But something was amiss. Some of the European and American tourists intrigued by the pomp and circumstance left as the final act began. Government and embassy workers lurked at the fringes and exclaimed their boredom to me. I watched teachers lead Polish school groups toward the stage, only to urge them away from the aggressive banners of right-wing protesters that expressed disillusionment from post-socialist transformation ("God, save us from *this* freedom!"). Activists waving Ukrainian flags to advocate for intercession in the ongoing Russian military intervention pressed closer to the dignitaries, which included then Ukrainian president-elect Petro Poroshenko, as employees of a nearby historical museum tried to redirect the audience to their week-long festival in a nearby park.

Had I not listened in Warsaw on June 4, I would still find support for a reading of Pawlik's *Freedom* as enacting understatement, its *largo cantabile* opening as a kind of music-historical tale of the incremental processes that characterized the dissolution of the People's Republic of Poland. Over the course of 1989, the spring "Round Table Talks" reestablished the senate and negotiated open elections—effectively side-lining the Communist Party. By December 1989, this new senate, driven by members of the Solidarity Party, had approved plans to effect a free market economy.[3] *Freedom*'s modesty expresses a counterpoint to the strain toward the sublime of, for example, the fireworks and Beethovenian reaches for brotherhood requisite to the major anniversaries of November 9, 1989, the climactic moment of the Berlin Wall's fall, in Germany.[4]

Freedom disengages from the sonic projects of extreme scale—both monumental volume and antimonumental silence—now canonic for performing commemoration in Central Europe.[5] Pawlik himself speaks of the project in terms of its bounds and not its ambitions:

> There was a time limit: the piece could not last more than twenty minutes. We thought about the form, together with representatives from the President's Chancellery, so that the composition would have the substance and prestige associated with such a grand [*wielki*] event. This was a consequence of a certain fascination of the two presidents [Barack Obama and Bronisław Komorowski] with my album *Night in Calisia*. They wanted to celebrate this anniversary of freedom without unnecessary pathos, but with jazz and symphonic elements.[6]

The description suits Pawlik's composition: this is no nineteenth-century choral fantasy, nor, with a substantial orchestra and choir, is it visibly pathetic. Yet at the same time, *Freedom* resists categorization within Andreas Huyssen's concept of "antimonumentality," which refers to (predominantly German) attempts to draw attention to the ephemeral in order to eschew the physical permanence and weighted rhetoric of memorials such as, in Warsaw, that of the Warsaw Ghetto Uprising or, musically speaking, Krzysztof Penderecki's *Polish Requiem*, which was performed at the unveiling of the Monument to the Fallen Shipyard Workers of 1970 in Gdańsk in 1980 (Figure 8.2).[7] *Freedom* further avoids specific reference, whether via musical quotation, textual allusion, or orchestration, to the many repertories that have crystallized, and continue to shape, cultural memorial practices in Poland.

For Pawlik, it is jazz that provides an escape from historical repetition

Figure 8.2. The unveiling of the Monument to the Fallen Workers, Gdańsk, December 16, 1980. Source: Ośrodek KARTA, photographer unknown.

and musical monumentality: a twenty-first-century sonic relief for musical memory work. As a celebrity, he embraced the alterity of his style—as an imported music and explicitly not "classical"—precisely because of its ethos of freedom.[8] "As music, jazz is very fresh when compared, for example, to classical music," he explained when asked about his understanding of musical freedom at another 1989 event. "It has dynamic potential and a very interesting origin . . . an origin in the emancipation—maybe this is a platitude—of the black citizens of North America from oppression. For this reason, the music has rational and concrete purpose . . . to serve as protest music, as music of contestation."[9] Pithy suggestions like these—that jazz lays bare Western values, especially democratic freedom—were the stuff of the Cold War. In the words of the jazz host for Voice of America, Willis Conover, in 1959: "People in other countries can feel this element of freedom. They love jazz because they love freedom."[10] Thus we *could* understand the comfortably chill atmosphere of *Freedom* as programmed to suit the story of 1989 as a gateway to liberation—an "end" to one history—in which monumental ideology produced Hitler and Stalin and led to the lack of sovereignty in Poland.[11] Such an interpretation, however, disregards the musical work in situ—its relatively unremarkable presence within the excessive programming of the 1989 celebrations and its failure in live performance. In this essay, I connect the observations I made in person of *Freedom*'s modest cultural significance with a broader analysis of the excessive—overwritten—commemoration landscape in contemporary Warsaw.

As I listened on June 4, 2014, I expected Pawlik's commission would get lost in the range of 1989 projects. Presidential funds targeted events across Poland that were even remotely related to the quarter-century anniversary: from an informational event about forestry ("Trees of Freedom") to the Warsaw Capital Market Summit. Freedom was at once a universal value, a tired cliché, and a liberal economic goal. I counted twenty-four conferences and academic discussions, thirteen celebratory occasions, and eighteen exhibitions, concerts, competitions, and festivals (including two picnics) in Warsaw alone.[12] Amid this excess, Pawlik's piece is perhaps better understood as an occasional offering in the tradition of a different strand of musical commemoration prizing quickly composed, comfortably tonal, and deferential works like Ludwig van Beethoven's *Wellington's Victory* (1813 Battle of Victoria), Edward Elgar's *Polonia* (1915 Polish Victims' Relief Fund), and John Williams's *Air and Simple Gifts* (2009 US presidential inauguration).[13] We can see this, too, in how it has been captured for posterity: video

Figure 8.3. US president Barack Obama and Polish president Bronisław Komorowski (far right) in conversation while listening to Włodek Pawlik's *Freedom*. Screenshot from "Koncert Włodek Pawlik z okazji 25-lecia wolności," *NCKultury*, August 4, 2014 (https://www.youtube.com/watch?v=5xrQqLr1S9Q).

of the June 4 performance streamed by the Polish National Centre for Culture underscores music as marginal instead of instrumental. Rather than filming the musicians, the camera focuses on the politely attentive heads of state. Ambient microphones relegate the muted music to the far right of the capture (Figure 8.3).[14]

The tenuous grasp of Pawlik's music on the public at the 1989 celebration set this essay in motion, not because it undoes any of music's sublime power to unite a crowd, to mark traumatic loss, or to mobilize individuals against powers beyond themselves. Rather, *Freedom* calls us to remember music's ability to be ignored, to underwhelm, and to be poorly miked. It demands that we pay attention to the lived experiences of an event rather than just its design and rhetoric. The musical assemblage of anniversary, emergent from Pawlik, reveals mistakes, inconsistencies, and differences in the robust, even excessive, culture of commemoration in contemporary Poland. With this essay, I posit a fresh perspective on Eastern European cultural memory that not only is attuned to the importance of music and sound, but responds to the way commemorative space is necessarily overlapping, networking, and collecting—blurring the boundaries of experience and performance, memory and revival, nation and narrative.

Overwriting Commemoration

I take the "failures" of performing 1989 seriously as a cue to engage the work that musical performance, historical memory, and nation do to produce—while going unnoticed in—the saturated mediascapes of the twenty-first century. The apathy I witnessed on June 4, as I shall argue, had its counterpoint in the symbolically bloated and pathos-laden spirit of the celebrations of the Warsaw Uprising. The year 2014 was, in effect, saturated with commemoration in Poland: not only did that year mark the twenty-fifth anniversary of 1989, but it was also fifty years since the Warsaw Ghetto Uprising in 1943 and the Warsaw Uprising in 1944, as well as the fifty-fifth anniversary of the outbreak of World War II in 1939. Many of these commemorations hovered precariously at the limit of living memory and spoke to central traumas of the twentieth century. Over 2014, I attended over forty events funded through the official memory regime.[15] These received funding from the government, were flanked by military salutes and marches, and were broadcast on television and radio, including livestreams online. Following sociologists Michael Bernhard and Jan Kubik in their discussion of memory work during postsocialist transformation, I understand these events as a crucial aspect of the public performance of a "political process" that articulates a new Poland in conversation with post-World War II cultural memory in Europe.[16] The anniversaries produce space in the Lefebvrian sense, across the streets and squares of the nation's capital, Warsaw, in the bureaucratic pipelines of cultural programming and international diplomacy, and in the symbolic imaginary of national belonging. Beyond the boundaries of the official stage and the texts of prepared statements, each choreographed audiences—as proxies of the nation—to participate in cultural memory through embodied acts of performance. For example, the ghetto uprising ceremonies commanded both a focused moment of silence and a taciturn walk, and the Warsaw Uprising festivities concluded with a large, open-air sing-along.

It would seem, *pace* Pawlik, that sound and music have key structural roles to play in the memory regime, even when they reveal inattention. The official programs for sound and memory work build a sensorium of public history in the twenty-first century that interfaces with interactive museum exhibitions, experience-oriented reenactments, and immersive films and gaming worlds, connecting acoustic territory and virtual space.[17] These generate what Ben Anderson has called "affective atmospheres": sensory-driven environments that are instrumental to collective experiences.[18] My fieldwork follows the festivalizations from live events through the virtual spaces in which they are archived and made history.[19] They are a twenty-first-century remix, digitization, amplification, and even distortion of music's special potential "between the private and the public, between the small and the outsized, between the commemorative and the sublime" to generate affect and do memory work.[20]

"Auditory attention may be demanded by a sound," writes Tom Rice on listening.[21] If *Freedom* reveals that conditional mode ("may"), what might it mean to follow Rice's cue and focus on the sonic demands of the redundant anniversary landscape? Consider a more recent example—a brief soundbite proliferating across public demonstrations in Poland as of this writing. The renowned Polish-Jewish cultural theorist Maria Janion, speaking in October 2016, drew attention to the audibility of competing public historical narratives by paying attention to a frequently shouted slur. In her opening address at the Congress of Culture—submitted to be read in absentia—she bemoaned the polysemous nature and ubiquity of "*This* is Poland!" ("*Tu* jest Polska!"). "I am sick of these shouts and ditties!" she exclaimed, calling out performative utterances as vectors of emotional disturbance.[22] Notably, this entreaty contradicted an address she had given thirty-five years earlier at another cultural congress, this one held one year after the legalization of the Solidarity trade union in Poland—the first independent and self-governing organization of its kind in the Eastern bloc. Then she had spoken with hope about the conciliatory role of historical songs and slogans for political work: "Small, easily hidden, easily copied by hand, easily remembered, [songs and chants] reached everywhere, [they] squeezed in where the book was forced to stop."[23] The two understandings of utterance as memory work position sound as directional and dispersed: Janion underscores that the work of sound and song on collective identity is historically circumscribed *and* unstable.

Julie Buckler and Emily Johnson use the concept of "overwriting," with both its palimpsestic and spectral overtones, to describe the folding of history as memory production in the public squares of Eastern Europe since the collapse of the Soviet Union.[24] Revivals, reenactments, and anniversary ceremonies give presence to the past through *communitas,* but also by emplacing performed responses to historical trauma in city spaces. I understand the performative assemblage of official memory regimes as both enacting Poland's investment in public history for the writing of history and as underscoring the structures of text, image, and urban space to the point of obscuring sound and music's memory work. Overwriting, building on Buckler and Johnson, describes a process (over time and in place) of encoding new data to replace the old: to intervene in, distort, and delete the past.[25] Overwriting serves as a reminder that writing can be too much—too many words, too many messages. It can subsume sounds' importance in bringing a space to life. The public square is no disk drive, no scribbled-through manuscript, but always presenced through human bodies who mediate performance. Just as people hear, see, and scream, they can—to borrow media-inflected language again—fail (on ethical or political terms), reboot/rebel, and become unplugged.

Some of the anniversaries' invitations to mark and remake history are aggressive, their sounds unavoidable, such as the minute of silence at 5:00 p.m. on August 1 commemorating the outbreak of the Warsaw Uprising. Poles rearticulate the clandestine action's significance annually by ringing sirens and bells throughout the city. Traffic, work, and conversations come to a halt: the moment is frenzied and reflective at once. The moment of silence for the ghetto uprising had a different mode: over the course of half an hour, on April 19, 2014, a lone performer marked time with a drum pattern on a snare as successive wreaths were placed at the foot of the 1948 monument commemorating its heroes. Other sonic memory work provoked more private listening: for the 1989 anniversaries in 2014, consoles were installed across the city to celebrate that music banned under socialism was now available for purchase in a free market economy: scan the QR code with your smartphone, pay twenty-five zlotys by credit card or electronic bank transfer, and the music is yours to possess.

Through music and sound studies, oriented through ethnography and other witness writing, we can situate the challenging redundancy of historical accumulation and competing amplification. How do the demands of sounds and songs to attend to them put these collective assemblies *in concert* with each other? What are the limits of sound and music to make these demands and to transform public spaces by resonating outside? I take anniversaries' liveness seriously here. Standing at the borders of the public gatherings, probing the zone of diffusion, for example, keeps me attuned to the challenges of analyzing music's presence, embracing sociologist Georgina Born's challenge to focus on the "capacity of sound to reconfigure space" and ethnomusicologist J. Martin Daughtry's concern that too much mapping of terrain "eras[es] the listener."[26]

Performance Failure

The reticence of the 2014 celebrations had its origins in 1989 itself. Newly independent at the end of the twentieth century, Poland's public discourse has been steeped in the symbols and burdens of nineteenth-century nationalism.[27] The annus mirabilis, 1989, turned into an ambiguous reference point for contemporary Poland, given the uncertain legacy of the Polish opposition to state socialism, the Solidarity movement. Heralded in the early 1980s for its coalition of workers, intellectuals, and clergy, the opposition to state socialism splintered through postsocialist transformation along questions of European integration, economic policy, and the future of the Roman Catholic Church in Poland. These cleavages generated antagonisms that dictate the rules of play in contemporary political life.[28] For Bernhard and Kubik, the self-evidently ambiguous historical legacy of 1989 in Eastern Europe shaped their study of the fractured, pillarized, and unified politics of memory, which offers a window onto the continued tensions experienced around democracy.[29] 1989 is also an ambiguous reference point because no one quite knows what events from that year ought to be the primary points of reference. Poland's 1989 does not have a dramatic climax to match that of the toppled Berlin Wall, with its Hasselhoff hysteria and "Ode to Freedom," to project and perform the Brandenburg Gate as a gateway to freedom.[30] Historian James Mark has provocatively claimed that one reason for November 9's resilience as an anniversary—its normative force in memory work—is that "scenes of West and East Germans vandalizing and crossing the Berlin Wall . . . seemed to conform to what a popular anti-Communist revolution was expected to be: crowds borne along by the desire to be free and to overthrow a spent dictatorship."[31]

Faced with the monumental fall of the Berlin Wall, the anniversaries of which only become more and more spectacular as five-year plans go by, Poland's 1989 seems wholly unremarkable. The infographic released by the official celebration campaign, "Together '89," might serve as one barometer for Polish ambiguity in 2014. Its aggressive name already hints at divided publics (Figure 8.4). A circuitous timeline connects the birthday of a left-leaning opposition leader and the recognition of women in the opposition to state socialism on International Women's Day with anniversaries of political events: three from 1989, economic reforms implemented in 1990, and Poland's 2004 accession to the European Union. "Together '89" still claimed an extraordinary scope: nearly 250 events throughout Polish communities at home and abroad. From a musicologi-

Figure 8.4. "Together '89" infographic (previously hosted at http://www.razem89.pl/).

cal perspective, none of its events—least of all the June 4 elections—were associated with signature anthems that had been evergreens through the 1980s, such as Jan Pietrzak's "So That Poland Will Be Poland."[32]

Communal song's absence is conspicuous in the New Europe.[33] Recall the final movement of *Freedom*, which calls out, "Let us rejoice in song," but provides no opportunity for the public to respond to this call. Accounts of public celebration and commemoration where music fails or confuses are rare; this is particularly true of communal song. Thomas Turino, for example, paints a picture of crowd involvement and participation as ideological coercion *or* essence of dissent in his discussion of group singing and politics.[34] For Benedict Anderson, the simplicity of well-known songs gives rise to their unisonal potential. With sweeping confidence, he writes, "No matter how banal the words and mediocre the tunes, there is in this singing an experience of simultaneity."[35] The assumption that everyone sings such easily known songs—*and with gusto*—conflates text and act, configuring song as the icon of ideology. These narrative shortcuts evoke an overwhelming feeling of music in readers, leaving them to dwell in imagined sound rather than urging them to stay attuned the particularities of performance. Much writing stops at describing music's presence or by presuming the wonder and "plural-singular that is the choral voice," even if that attention is suspicious in nature.[36]

European twentieth-century history has, in fact, drawn attention to the dangers of communal singing, leading to the frequent metonymic conflation of singing together with political coercion in popular writing. Journalist Artur Domosławski sounded an alarm when describing the commemoration of the 2010 airplane crash in Smolensk, Ukraine, which had killed ninety-six Polish dignitaries. Describing the presence of the right-wing party Law and Justice at the 2011 event in Warsaw, he wrote, "A measure of its politicians' hysteria was their rendition on the anniversary of the crash of the hymn 'Return, Oh Lord, Our Free Fatherland'—as though they were stuck in the nineteenth century."[37] We would, I contend, learn more about the impact and cohesion of this event if we attend differently to the realm of affect and experience: How did this group sing? Who heard it? Was this chorus loud? Did civilians join in? Did those who listened respond to this religious hymn with applause, by crossing their chest, or by cheering/jeering?

The powerful assumptions made about singing in chorus crucially configure an eerie New Year's scene in the composer and pianist Władysław Szpilman's well-known account of his wartime experience, first in Warsaw's ghetto and then in hiding. Walking in the streets of occupied Warsaw on December 31, 1942, he and some Jewish friends are halted by a drunken SS officer. After a beating, they are commanded to return to the ghetto. "Sing! . . . Sing something cheerful! . . . And sing it good and loud!" the officer shouts after them. Szpilman comments wryly in his retrospective account, "It hardly mattered what we sang." He continues, remarking on the German's misdirected hearing: "That New Year's Eve a small group of utterly exhausted Jews walked through the streets of a city where declarations of Polish patriotism had been forbidden for years on pain of death, singing at the top of our voices and with total impunity the patriotic song, '*Hej, strzelcy wraz!*'—'Hey, marksmen, arise!'"[38] Volume lends the performance power, disguising a patriotic song's resistant nationalism. The unison effort is further immune to critique, since it sings obedience and subjugation to the SS officer.

Warsaw in Concert

Like Berlin, Belgrade, Moscow, and other European cities war-torn by the twentieth century, Warsaw is a cultural-historical palimpsest, where conflicting pasts are layered and reconfigured upon its geography.[39] Structures bear witness to their own persistent presence, as in the case of the apartment building at Walecznych Street 35, which maintains house

Figure 8.5. House numbers at Walecznych Street 35. Photograph by the author.

numbers from the interwar period, state socialism, and contemporary Warsaw side by side (Figure 8.5). Since World War II, the city streets have borne what Eugeniusz Cesary Król calls an "inflation of symbols": the use of plaques to particularize, refine, and magnify history.[40] Throughout the city center, the signs fix the stories of resistance fighters slain, institutions evacuated or demolished, and national heroes to place. State symbols mark the Polish capital; traces of clashing political powers are visible. Take the Royal Castle, the backdrop for *Freedom.* The seat of the Polish-Lithuanian Commonwealth was rebuilt in the 1970s after its destruction during World War II. The former locus of power is a stone's throw away from the Presidential Palace, the office of the president. Following the death of Lech Kaczyński in the Smolensk crash, the building has become the endpoint of contested monthly marches to honor the dead through Catholic ritual on the streets.[41]

Central Warsaw's broad avenues were designed as central stages for civic activity, and state pageantry according to stalinist ideology confounds the narrative of total destruction during World War II.[42] The layers are performed, configuring those spaces as the continued targets of mobilized action: present-day manifestations happen along the route of the official parades of communism—May Day, International Women's

Figure 8.6. May Day Parade, May 1, 1969. Source: National Digital Archive, Warsaw.

Day—and the protests of the opposition to state socialism (Figure 8.6). At Rondo Dmowskiego, the intersection of Marszałkowska Street and Jerozolimskie Boulevard, I have cheered as the London Gay Men's Chorus sang Britney Spears off of a float during Euro-Pride in June 2010. At this intersection I was confronted with my limited understanding of voice-as-heard as a Deaf Rights March signed the Polish national anthem in July 2015. Watching online coverage of Polish Independence Day in November 2017, I accessed Reuters videos and independent television stations' raw footage to see brutal sonic violence: right-wing nationalists abusing a megaphone to blast a peaceful counterdemonstration.[43]

Patrice Dabrowski has called the long nineteenth century the "age of Polish commemorations": a period in which "miniature history lessons" reached across the public living in partitioned Poland to tug at heart-strings and inspire concrete nation-building action.[44] A codified set of rituals organized the historical pageantry in open spaces, often through songs with moral imperatives to sacrifice oneself for national freedom. This past sets the tone. As Joanna Niżyńska has argued, present-day anniversaries redeem this moment, but also compensate for the losses (of human lives, of state sovereignty under communism) of the twentieth century by calling on contemporary Varsovians to identify with resistant nationalists of the past. These martyr-protagonists of nineteenth-century uprisings are summoned and choreographed to effect "the symbolic gain of a reaffirmed Polish identity."[45] Commemoration culture is in concert not only across the calendar year, but across centuries of nation formation through performance.

Consider the renewal of November 11, Polish Independence Day, as an exemplar of overwriting festivalization.[46] In the Third Republic, the holiday's very observance resolves its removal from the official calendar in 1945. The fact that it had only been celebrated twice before World War II further contributed to its mythical importance during the People's Republic of Poland, when traditions of unofficial celebration developed in homes and churches. Since then, the celebrations have also recapitulated a historical narrative, interweaving the restoration of sovereignty in 1918 with that of the postsocialist transformations of the country from 1989 onward. Historiographical tensions and contemporary political frictions have escalated each year in the public celebrations of independence as rioters and countermarches have attacked and sidled up to the official procession since 2008.

The state ceremonies unfold in an open square—named after the commander in chief on November 11, 1918, Józef Piłsudski—in front of the remnants of the Saxon Palace, destroyed by German forces after the 1944 uprising. The public gathers behind barriers to watch divisions of the military march in formation to the accompaniment of the unamplified army band. The voice of an emcee—a woman in 2009, when I was in attendance—over a loudspeaker system steers the flow of the assembled, announces each regiment's arrival and recounts historic Polish military victories. Vendors take advantage of the atmosphere of waiting to pawn flags, pins, and other memorabilia on the crowd. Without the constant punctuation of fanfares, marches, and an occasional virtuosic flourish—when I listened, the army band pulled from Hollywood scores by John Williams as much as it did from anthologies of its own almanac—the event would feel listless. The loudspeakers oriented the crowd, mostly children off from school and veterans with stakes in the ritual, to the official observance of the holiday: a military salute at the Tomb of the Unknown Soldier and a commendation by the president.

From the corner of the square where I stood in the first row behind a barrier, the cavernous architecture ricocheted echoes of the fanfare and gunshots through the misting rain off the buildings. It left then president Lech Kaczyński's *laudatio* of the military as protector and defender of the nation distorted and unmemorable. A group of six senior citizens near me, representing a Roman Catholic parish from the city's northeastern districts, began singing as he finished speaking. Their hymnody—hard to hear but recognizable as the ubiquitous and malleable "God Save Poland"—told a story of Poland "occupied" by the European Union. I stood and listened without company, first as they protracted the hymn with at least fifteen new stanzas, then as they cycled through other patriotic hymns associated with insurrectionary units from 1830, 1848, and 1861. Military units clomped by them, children tossed small change in the coffin the seniors had brought to symbolize the sacrifice and burial of the Polish spirit, and they carried on singing. In retrospect, I hear their hoarse and modest chorus as a firm presence at the margins of the square—persistent in its vulnerability and despite fatigue, asserting performance's capacity to delimit memory regimes by encroaching at the margins.

Singing Along?

If the 1989 anniversaries set audiences up to listen, the anniversary of the outbreak of the 1944 Warsaw Uprising roars. The city—and, since 2017, the whole country—sounds signals through the first minutes of the annual commemoration of the final, failed attempt to fight back against the occupying German forces from August 1, 1944, to the day of surrender on October 2. At 5:00 p.m. the bells of the city's churches are rung incessantly, warning sirens go off, and fireworks set off by individuals and scout units confound the cacophony. Traffic comes to a halt in the city center, where people mill in the streets to pay their respects. In the minutes leading up to the "W Hour" (*Godzina W*)—the historical code name for the start of the insurrection—restaurants and cafes turn on and up the radio so that their customers can "hear" this minute of silence.[47] I have frequently observed people spotted sitting, in conversation, or inattentive receive a reprimand and a reminder to stand out of respect. No matter one's politics, there is no standing on the fringes of this anniversary. It begins by calling bodies to perform.

The uprising is one of the most emotionally laden of Polish cultural memory practices, and from its second day, songs have been conveyors of its history and instrumental to collective practice. The carefully strategized but ultimately failed resistance of the Home Army against the German occupying forces symbolizes, for many, the eternal faithfulness of Poles to their fatherland and honor. During the uprising, the writers and musicians who fought in the units across the city composed song texts and poems that set the process of remembering in motion. These were sung immediately, as were other tunes from occupied Warsaw that rallied the forces, such as Krystyna Krahelska's "Hey Lads, Attach Your Bayonets!" ("Hej chłopcy, bagnet na broń!"); 1942–43, a peppy march that became known as the anthem of the Home Army after its author succumbed to battle wounds during the uprising's first night.[48] The uprising had a musical hero as well. During the fighting, crooning sensation Mieczysław Fogg created what he called a "barricade of song," using a post in Mokotów to adapt interwar popular music hits to the fighting around him.[49] After the war, he would review these tunes in concert, popularizing them and endowing with them memorial function alongside the films, books, and other projects devoted to the uprising.

Over the course of my research in Poland, the uprising has invariably been the easiest and most difficult topic of conversation with my elderly research associates, many of whom were teenagers at the time. One elderly engineer was brought to tears trying to tell me the story of "Nurse Margaret" ("Sanitariuszka Małgosia"), a song composed in September 1944 in which the protagonist croons his thanks to the nurse who saved him. When we listened to old concerts of young actors singing the songs together, a radio journalist told me that there were "no words" to describe why she thought these "flippant broadsides [were] so precious." Others were less moved to their own limits, calling the tunes "nice" or dwelling in the significance of the events for contemporary political faction. Without fail, however, they mentioned the emotional weight of the music for many Poles, guarding and owning the continued affective power of the uprising and its music.

Joanna Niżyńska writes of the uprising commemoration's valence and demands on people: "The traumatic loss is compulsively staged and repeated—in other words, 'acted out.' 'Acting out' presupposes a symptomatic relationship with the past; its mechanism is transferential and identificatory."[50] Song is a crucial component of the emphatic and reiterative tenor she highlights. From the uprising's first anniversary, there is record of singing at the center of historical reenactment.

Teodor Niewiadomski recalled, "We walked as we had the previous year and loudly sang the Mokotów Anthem [March] of the uprising: 'We are walking arm in arm . . .' Members of the Home Army ran near the soldiers of the People's Army and members of the Polish Army, flanked by members of the Farmers' Army, and joined in the 'Bravo!' cheers of the onlookers."[51] The nebulous danger, he emphasizes, of "singing patriotic song" heightened the risk and meaning of making one's body vulnerable by making music and song, just as it had in Władysław Szpilman's memories of ghetto surveillance.

In collaboration with the city of Warsaw, the Museum of the Warsaw Uprising has organized annual open-air sing-along concerts on August 1 since 2008, titled "Varsovians Sing: (Un)Forbidden Songs." The choral evening has a didactic and sentimental spirit that is emphasized across its mediation.[52] The 2012 television promo, for example, opens with panoramic views of an engaged audience, listening, waving flags, and beaming at the large festival stage. A warm male voice gently recounts: "With every year, more Varsovians come. A wonderful (*wspaniała*) tradition has taken shape: a sing-along of *un*forbidden songs. The youngest in attendance need songbooks, some took clues from the teleprompter." Strains of the Mokotów March—"Let song flow from the barricades"—drive the message home as the commentary continues. The camera pauses on a final spectator, a middle-aged woman whose face is lined with a single glistening tear: "For many, the words can be found in their memories—and hearts."

The concert updates a long-standing tradition that gained momentum during the final decade of the People's Republic of Poland when music critic Tadeusz Kaczyński founded the Traugutt Philharmonia, an ensemble of student actors and singers who performed as part of the unofficial artistic life during the martial law.[53] In the years that followed, it became quite common for churches to turn over their sanctuaries to young performers before or after Friday Mass during the month of August. Kaczyński's model of half-staged pageants continues: I counted fifteen in 2014 across official and neighborhood advertisements, but there were certainly more. As one performer reiterated from the stage on August 2, 2014, at the Church of St. Jacob the Apostle on Narutowicz Square in Warsaw, these concerts are "aimed at our community, our neighborhood. They give young performers an opportunity to tell their story their way." Guitars in hand, the singers share anecdotes about their favorite songs and acknowledge the skirmishes on nearby streets, commemorating blood shed and lives lost.

In 2014, the central concert, hosted from a temporary stage in the expansive Piłsudski Square, was broadcast on national television at top production value. Across the plaza, a crowd gathered for the evening concert, including generations of Warsaw residents, a smattering of tourists, and scout groups that had traveled to the capital from across Poland. Everyone in attendance received a songbook with the evening's texts. We were invited to sing along with the performers on stage: a small band that mimicked an ad hoc street music collective and a choir made of amateur singers from Warsaw.[54] Some tunes were arranged to rouse the crowd to join in easily. Józef Szczepański's "Michler's Little Palace" ("Pałacyk Michla"), a song written on the fourth day of battle, tells the story of fighting in the Wola district. Like many of the songs, it is uncannily playful: a march whose arpeggiated baseline has a jaunt instead of a pulse that prompts order. Its text gestures to the social camaraderie of singing together as analogous to that of fighting together as a range of resistance units are celebrated. The vowels that accompany the drawn-out outline of a dominant seventh chord to exhort voices to join in the refrain ("Czuwaj wiaro" [Guard your faith!]) sound like nonsense syllabus of a mock fanfare—something like the English "Tra la la la!" When I stood in the middle of the public chorus on August 1, 2014, we cheered the trios of amateur singers that sang each verse, but bellowed along with the refrain, overpowering the prepared performance from the stage.[55]

Like the QR code booths of the 1989 commemoration, this concert celebrated freedom from censure by disseminating music. By anthologizing the sing-along as a window onto the forbidden, the museum made not only an allusion to the allure of the taboo, but also made an explicit connection with the popular feature film *Forbidden Songs* (*Zakazane piosenki*), the first postwar production in Poland. The 1947 film, directed by Leonard Buczkowski, tells the story of life in Nazi-occupied Warsaw in the style of a jukebox musical. A playlist of popular songs, especially broadsides popular in interwar Poland, weaves together a story about families surviving the war.[56] The songs are "forbidden" because of their anti-German contrafact texts, which hold the German army responsible. On the one hand, diegetic performances reclaim the agency of resistance through music within the wartime context. On the other hand, when characters sing they are also centered as storytellers who avoid discussing historical trauma through what Eric Santner has theorized as "narrative fetishism."[57] It is this "acting out" that the museum overwrites with the concert. Building on the film's original function to promulgate a cultural memory founded in resilience, the concerts extend the truth claims of city belonging and faith demanded by heroic sacrifice. The concert also obscures the film (no longer commercially available); its cast of survivors are recast as contemporary Varsovians whose strident song is as much about a future-oriented national belonging as it is about the historical specifics of the Warsaw Uprising. The museum's loud concert not only dominates the tenor of commemoration practices in the twenty-first century, but reconfigures those of the past.

Walls

Building on Walter Benjamin, Svetlana Boym develops the notion of "porosity" as a metaphor for the city that emphasizes its fundamental theatricality as "a place of continuous improvisation," highlighting "the variety of temporal dimensions embedded in a physical space."[58] The metaphor easily extends to sound: in cities, there is sound bleed, and we (also as ethnographers) overhear. The porous nature of city spaces, too, facilitated many of the performances of commemoration I experienced. However, if the limits of musical participation and attention were patently obvious at the *Freedom* premiere, the breakdown of the sing-along and the identifactory magnetism of the uprising was, for me, at the 2014 concert's midpoint and built into its dramaturgy. Right in the heart of the evening, there was an impenetrable wall that was both historiographic and historical. The lights dimmed; a soprano and a violinist stood spotlit at the front of the stage. The lone ballad of the review emerged out of a commanded quiet that had many expectantly waiting: "My Warsaw, / oh, my Warsaw, / I always cry when I see you, / Oh, my Warsaw."

"My Warsaw" ("Warszawo ma") is a story from occupied Warsaw—another song lifted from the postwar blockbuster film after which the uprising concert is named. It tells a story of hunger and yearning. Its narrator fears that they will never see the city again. The song, though, is not a story about a Warsaw to be fought for, defended, and reclaimed in perpetuity, but a Warsaw walled off from its protagonist's life. The container of this song reroutes its memory work, too, by writing this scene from Warsaw in concert as the performance of Polish-Jewish culture. The ballad is a contrafact of the Yiddish theater song "Belz, mayn shtetele Belz," which has itself done work as an object through which memoirs of displacement and genocide in Eastern Europe have been written.[59]

The song's walls are that of the Warsaw ghetto, which is explicitly named in the second verse "There in the ghetto / There's hunger, misery, and cold. / And worse than the hunger and cold, there's longing / Oh, my Warsaw!" As Barbara Milewski has shown, this new Polish text, for *Forbidden Songs*, emerged out of lived trauma: its lyricist Ludwik Starski escaped the ghetto and survived the war in hiding; she suggests he used this new text to write a personal testimony.[60] If Starski sought to make a place for the Jewish experience of occupation—of belonging in Warsaw—in the film, this subtle message was hard to hear during its 2014 performance. As a female vocal soloist and violinist wove together the melody and countermelody, replete with augmented seconds that sound Eastern European Jewishness, my neighbors refrained from singing along. With furrowed brows, they turned to their program books for the first time. The song simultaneously overwhelms—unplugs—the audience from a role as performers of commemoration with its soaring lament. It also draws attention to the disconnect between the reserved and contained culture of commemorating the ghetto uprising and the "*This* is Poland!" rhetoric of the uprising concert. As I watch the sentimental performance produced for television to write this text about peering in ("*There* in the ghetto"), I hear again the witness poetry of Czesław Miłosz, who, watching burning behind the ghetto's walls from the outside, wrote in "Campo di Fiori": "The bright melody drowned / the salvos from the ghetto wall."[61]

Musical performance binds memory work to time, buttressing events that unfold in time and space. Marching bands add a sonic component to the flow of processions, symphonic works can amplify pomp and circumstance, and sing-alongs transform the pace of ritual participation. Many modes of musical commemoration exist within particular events and are, of course, compounded by other sonic cues and disjunctures that heighten our awareness of the passing of time: clapping, call-and-response, broken microphones, helicopters beating overhead, and more. As I hope to have shown, these do not merely have a structural function—organizing or interrupting. They are moments in which audience members are called upon to configure and reconfigure attention, formulate and reformulate the history that they are honoring and the memory they are weaving. In the excessive memory regime of contemporary Poland, sound reveals power structures, but it also paves possibilities for individuals to knit together granular histories: an overwriting that foregrounds complexity over historical progress, awareness of the potential of recursion over a confidence in resolution. Heart-wrenching ballads like "Warszawo Ma," even if their historical context is absent and too much at once, offer moments of inward reflection in which listeners themselves can sound out what it means to listen. It is not, then, the formal elements of commemoration—like *Freedom*'s volume and musical content—that orchestrate the performance of the past in concert, but the embodied memory work and sociability of those assembled and directing their attention across the stages of history.

Notes

Many thanks to Thomas Hilder, Ana Hofman, Barbara Milewski, Joanna Niżyńska, and J. Mackenzie Pierce for their comments on earlier drafts of this article, as well as to the editors of this volume and conference participants for their lively discussion and feedback.

1. The suite was recorded and released on a noncommercial promotional CD available at events through 2014 by the Ministry of Culture and National Heritage.

2. Elihu Katz, "Media Events: The Sense of Occasion," *Studies in Visual Anthropology* 6 (1980): 84–89.

3. Andrzej Paczkowski, *Revolution and Counterrevolution in Poland, 1980–1989: Solidarity, Martial Law, and the End of Communism in Europe*, trans. Christina Manetti (Rochester: University of Rochester Press, 2015).

4. For an analysis of unification of freedom, Beethoven, and 1989 see Alexander Rehding, "'Ode to Freedom': Bernstein's Ninth at the Berlin Wall," *Beethoven Forum* 12, no. 1 (2005): 36–49.

5. Studies of the large-scale reckonings with history, memory, and erasure from music, East Central European history, and cultural studies include Alexander Rehding, *Music and Monumentality: Commemoration and Wonderment in Nineteenth-Century Germany* (New York: Oxford University Press, 2009); Michael Meng, *Shattered Spaces: Encountering Jewish Ruins in Postwar German and Poland* (Cambridge, MA: Harvard University Press, 2011); and James E. Young, *The Texture of Memory: Holocaust Memorials and Meaning* (New Haven: Yale University Press, 1993).

6. "Były ograniczenia czasowe, utwór nie mógł trwać więcej niż 20 minut. Nad formą myśleliśmy wspólnie z pracownikami Kancelarii Prezydenta, żeby kompozycja miała powagę i rangę związaną z tym wielkim wydarzeniem. To była konsekwencja pewnej fascynacji pary prezydenckiej płytą 'Night in Calisia.' Chcieli uczcić tę rocznicę wolności bez zbędnego patosu, a z elementami jazzu i symfoniki," quoted in Magdalena Jasińska, "To miłe, że Polacy odkryli mnie na nowo," *Dziennik Toruński*, July 8, 2014, http://nowosci.com.pl/313682,To-mile-ze-Polacy-odkryli-mnie-na-nowo-mowi-Wlodek-Pawlik-pianista-i-kompozytor-WYWIAD.html.

7. Andreas Huyssen, *Present Pasts: Urban Palimpsests and the Politics of Memory* (Stanford, CA: Stanford University Press, 2003), 30–48.

8. Somewhat unusually for Polish artists, Pawlik actually tends to use the word *klasyczna* (classical) rather than *poważna* (serious, from the German *ernste Musik*), a move that skirts an entrenched discourse of high versus low.

9. "Jazz jest muzyką bardzo świeżą, po równo ją na przykład do klasycznej

muzyki. Ma w sobie potencję o dynamizmu i bardzo ciekawą genezę . . . genezę właśnie wyzwolenia się—to jest może banał—ale jednak czarne obywateli Ameryki Północnej. I w związku z tym ma swoje i bardzo racjonalny i konkretny powód bycia muzyką przynajmniej u początkach, czy jako dawną muzyką protestu i muzyką kontestacji." Włodek Pawlik, interview from the "Persons of Freedom Gala," January 2015, https://www.youtube.com/watch?v=UhP4-LkqFDo.

10. Quoted in Penny Von Eschen, *Satchmo Blows Up the World: Jazz Ambassadors Play the Cold War* (Cambridge, MA: Harvard University Press, 2004), 17.

11. While I play upon Francis Fukuyama's oft-critiqued triumphalist essay "The End of History?" in the *National Interest* 16 (Summer 1989): 3–18, this suggestion offers a more ludic play with the cultural studies sensibility of Joshua Clover, *1989: Bob Dylan Didn't Have This to Sing About* (Berkeley: University of California Press, 2009).

12. The official promotional website has since been removed: http://www.prezydent.pl/swieto-wolnosci/wydarzenia/wojewodztwo-mazowieckie/ (accessed August 15, 2015).

13. See Nicholas Mathew's *Political Beethoven* (Cambridge: Cambridge University Press, 2013), 1–16, for a synthesis of the dismissal commemorative works have experienced in the Western classical tradition.

14. The video was accessible, via an embedded YouTube video on the official website, https://www.youtube.com/watch?v=5xrQqLr1S9Q (accessed June 1, 2018). As of March 2020 one can still watch the entire concert on TVP, http://www.tvn24.pl/wideo/z-anteny/wolnosc-zachwycila-baracka-obame-koncert-na-placu-zamkowym,1290445.html?playlist_id=17344.

15. On memory regimes in Eastern Europe see Jan Kubik and Michael Bernhard, "A Theory of the Politics of Memory," in *Twenty Years After Communism: The Politics of Memory and Commemoration*, ed. Michael Bernhard and Jan Kubik (New York: Oxford University Press, 2014), 14–16.

16. They write, "Remembering the past, particularly collectively, is always a political process; thus the politics of memory and commemoration needs to be studied as an integral part of the establishment of new collective identities and new principles of political legitimacy," in Jan Kubik and Michael Bernhard, "Introduction," in Bernhard and Kubik, *Twenty Years After Communism*, 3.

17. I borrow "acoustic territory" here from J. Martin Daughtry, who parses it as one analytic of soundscapes. He defines it as "the shifting environments, structures, and other absorptive and resonating elements that enclose, modify and otherwise mediate the sounds in a given timespace, *and* the distinct places whose boundaries and characters are constituted by sound and listening," in *Listening to War: Sound, Music, Trauma, and Survival in Wartime Iraq* (New York: Oxford University Press, 2015), 126. Space precludes me from a full analysis of the Warsaw Uprising Museum and, for example, the biking scavenger hunt that museum sponsored in August 2017, which targets adolescents and asks participants to use smartphones to craft storyboards on Instagram of their searches. Tom Rice, "Listening," in *Keywords in Sound*, ed. David Novak and Matt Sakakeeny (Durham, NC: Duke University Press, 2015), 100.

18. Ben Anderson, *Encountering Affect: Capacities, Apparatuses, Conditions* (London: Routledge, 2014), 137–61.

19. For a discussion of the concept of festivalization as a localization of political ideology, event, and sound see Carolyn Birdsall, *Nazi Soundscapes: Sound, Technology, and Urban Space in Germany, 1933–45* (Amsterdam: Amsterdam University Press, 2012), 65–68.

20. Rehding, *Music and Monumentality*, 15.

21. Rice, "Listening," 100.

22. "Mesjanizm to przekleństwo, List Marii Janion do Kongresu Kultury," *Gazeta Wyborcza*, October 10, 2016, http://wyborcza.pl/7,75410,20813344,mesjanizm-to-przeklenstwo-list-marii-janion-do-kongresu-kultury.html?disableRedirects=true.

23. Maria Janion, "Słowo i symbol w miesiącach przełomu," in *Kongres Kultury Polskiej, 11–13 grudnia 1981*, ed. Władysław Masiulanis (Warsaw: Oficyna Wydawnictwa Volumen Instytut Kultury, 2000), 37–44.

24. The collected chapters in their book treat anniversaries across centuries, but the work takes its cue from this orientation: "Each site is a cultural-historical palimpsest: successive political and religious power structures have claimed them, in each case substantially overwriting its predecessor's cultural-historical narrative, but also leaving traces of the rejected past that then became incorporated into the whole." Julie Buckler and Emily D. Johnson, "Introduction," in *Rites of Place: Public Commemoration in Russia and Eastern Europe*, ed. Julie Buckler and Emily D. Johnson (Evanston, IL: Northwestern University Press, 2013), 6.

25. Here I am reminded of Dominick LaCapra's discussion of processing, experiential processes, and processes of identity in *Experience in Transit: Experience, Identity, Critical Theory* (Ithaca, NY: Cornell University Press, 2004), 40. Magda Szcześniak and Łukasz Zaremba engage with a critique sympathetic to mine from a visual studies perspective. Their concept of "paranoid looking" identifies the ways that modes of seeing are ideologically complicit in postsocialist Poland. See Magda Szcześniak and Łukasz Zaremba, "Paranoid Looking: On De-Communization," *Journal of Visual Culture* 18: 2 (2019), 209–33.

26. Georgina Born, "Introduction: Music, Sound, and the Transformations of Public and Private Experience," in *Music, Sound and Space: Transformations of Public and Private Experience*, ed. Georgina Born (Cambridge: Cambridge University Press, 2013), 3; Daughtry, *Listening to War*, 122.

27. For extended and comparative discussions of commemoration in Eastern Europe see Ljiljana Šarić, Karen Gammelgaard, and Kjetil Rå Hauge, eds., *Transforming National Holidays: Identity Discourse in the West and South Slavic Countries, 1985–2010* (Amsterdam: John Benjamins, 2012); and Buckler and Johnson, *Rites of Place*.

28. David Ost, *The Defeat of Solidarity: Anger and Politics in Postcommunist Europe* (Ithaca, NY: Cornell University Press, 2005).

29. Bernhard and Kubik, *Twenty Years After Communism*.

30. Seth Brodsky offers an analysis of the stakes of history that remixes Beethoven and Hasselhoff thrice in *From 1989, or European Music and the Modern Unconscious* (Berkeley: University of California Press, 2017), 29–34, 63–68, 88–99.

31. James Mark, *The Unfinished Revolution: Making Sense of the Communist Past in Central-Eastern Europe* (New Haven: Yale University Press, 2010), 1.

32. Andrea F. Bohlman, *Musical Solidarities: Political Action and Music in Late-Twentieth Century Poland* (New York: Oxford University Press, 2020).

33. On choral singing and national stages in the context of European nationalisms see Philip V. Bohlman, *The Music of European Nationalism: Cultural Identity and Modern History* (Denver, CO: ABC-CLIO, 2004), 96–114.

34. Thomas Turino, *Music as Social Life: The Politics of Participation* (Chicago: University of Chicago Press, 2008).

35. Benedict Anderson, *Imagined Communities: Reflections on the Origin and Spread of Nationalism,* rev. ed. (New York: Verso, 2006), 149.

36. Steven Connor, "Choralities," *Twentieth-Century Music* 13, no. 1 (2016): 3.

37. Artur Domosławski, "Old Poland, New Nationalism," *New York Times,* November 13, 2013, http://www.nytimes.com/2013/11/21/opinion/old-poland-new-nationalism.html.

38. Władysław Szpilman, *The Pianist: The Extraordinary True Story of One Man's Survival in Warsaw, 1939–1945,* trans. Anthea Bell (New York: Picador, 1999), 124–25.

39. Huyssen, *Present Pasts*; Bożena Shallcross and Ryszard Nycz, eds., *The Effect of Palimpsest: Culture, Literature, History* (Frankfurt am Main: Peter Lang, 2011); Geneviève Zubrzycki, "History and the National Sensorium: Making Sense of Polish Mythology," *Qualitative Sociology* 34 (2011): 21–57.

40. Eugeniusz Cesary Król, "Perzeptionen des Aufstands in Polen," in *Der Warschauer Aufstand 1944: Ereignis und Wahrnehmung in Polen und in Deutschland,* ed. Hans-Jürgen Bömelburg, Eugeniusz C. Król, and Michael Thomae (Paderborn: Ferdinand Schöningh, 2011), 186.

41. Under election pressure, the 2018 leader of the Law and Justice Party, Jarosław Kaczyński, declared the march on April 10, 2018, to be the last.

42. David Crowley, *Warsaw* (London: Reaktion, 2003).

43. The footage was taken up by Wirtualna Polska TV, "Polska bastionem Europy," accessed June 1, 2018, https://video.wp.pl/i,polska-bastionem-europy-tak-wygladal-marsz-narodowcow-w-warszawie,mid,1992799,cid,4051,klip.html?ticaid=11b63f. See, as an example, "Marsz Niepodległości 2017 Warszawa Narodowcy," accessed June 1, 2018, https://www.youtube.com/watch?v=t_7rmb0jm8o. This repetitive violence is also thematized in filmmaker Artur Żmijewski's ongoing series *Democracies* (*Demokracje,* 2009–present).

44. Patrice M. Dabrowski, *Commemorations and the Shaping of Modern Poland* (Bloomington: Indiana University Press, 2004), 5.

45. Joanna Niżyńska, *The Kingdom of Insignificance: Miron Białoszewski and the Quotidian, the Queer, and the Traumatic* (Evanston, IL: Northwestern University Press, 2013), 61.

46. M. B. B. Biskupski, *Independence Day: Myth, Symbol, and the Creation of Modern Poland* (Oxford: Oxford University Press, 2012).

47. For a historical analysis of the institution and choreography of the minute of silence as between noise and silence, see Karsten Lichau, "'Noise' or 'Silence?': Listening to Sacred Sound in 20th-Century Europe," in *Exploring the Senses: South Asian and European Perspectives on Rituals and Performativity,* ed. Axel Michaels and Christoph Wulf (London: Taylor and Francis, 2013), 145–63.

48. Władysław Bartoszewski, *Dni walczącej stolicy* (Warsaw: Wydawnictwa ALFA, 1989), 18.

49. Mieczysław Fogg with Zbigniew K. Rogowski, *Od palanta do belcanta: Wspomnienia* (Warsaw: Iskry, 1970), 100.

50. Niżyńska, *The Kingdom of Insignificance*, 62.

51. Teodor Niewiadomski, "Kopiec miał być powstańczym pomnikiem," *Stolica* 47 (1984): 28.

52. "Warszawiacy śpiewają (nie)kazane piosenki," posted to the city's official YouTube channel on August 2, 2012, https://www.youtube.com/watch?v=3ytKeuMp-58.

53. Martial law was declared December 13, 1981, but the Philharmonia first performed in January 1983. For an overview of the Traugutt Philharmonia's commemorative practices see Cindy Bylander, "Reponses to Adversity: The Polish Composers Union and Musical Life in the 1970s and 1980s," *Musical Quarterly* 45, no. 4 (2012): 485–90.

54. In other years they have used other strategies to not-so-subtly suggest the choir as embodiment of the uprising. The performers on stage have emphasized the postwar rebuilding effort (children), the loss of the war (family members of those who perished), and the endurance of resistance (survivors).

55. One audience video of the performance captures this unison, "Pałacyk Michla," accessed June 1, 2018, https://www.youtube.com/watch?v=eMBW71XvTGU.

56. Robert A. Rothstein, *Two Words to the Wise: Reflections on Polish Language, Literature, and Folklore* (Bloomington, IN: Slavica Publishers, 2008).

57. Eric Santner, "History beyond the Pleasure Principle: Some Thoughts on the Representation of Trauma," in *Probing the Limits of Representation: Nazism and the "Final Solution"*, ed. Saul Friedländer (Cambridge, MA: Harvard University Press, 1992), 144.

58. Svetlana Boym, *The Future of Nostalgia* (New York: Basic Books, 2001), 77.

59. A representative recent example is Daniel Mendelsohn, *The Lost: A Search for Six of Six Million* (New York: Harper Perennial, 2013), 288–90. Mendelsohn recalls his own grandfather singing it and recounting the song sung—long before the song was written in 1932. To uncover his family's past in Belchów, in the Ukrainian Oblast, he also transcribes oral testimonies from Yad Vashem that recount the compulsory performance of the song by those waiting for the trains that would deport them to the Belzec concentration camp.

60. Barbara Milewski, "Hidden in Plain View: The Music of Holocaust Survival in Poland's First Post-war Feature Film," in *Music, Collective Memory and Nostalgia in European Cinema after the Second World* War, edited by Michael Baumgartner and Ewelina Boczkowska (London: Routledge, forthcoming 2020).

61. Czesław Miłosz, "Campo di Fiori," trans. David Brooks and Louis Iribane, *New York Review of Books*, October 23, 1980, http://www.nybooks.com.libproxy.lib.unc.edu/articles/1980/10/23/campo-di-fiori/.

NINE | Music and the Mediation of Remembrance

Reflections on the Commemoration of the Centennial of the Armenian Genocide

SYLVIA ANGELIQUE ALAJAJI

Presencing the Past

I am often asked how I first learned about the Armenian genocide. It is not an easy question to answer, for to be Armenian is, in some way, always to have known—somehow, improbably, to be born knowing.[1] It is to know the genocide as our ending and our beginning. To know that we are, both because of and in spite of it. And to know that even its absence is in itself a sort of presence, for it is never simply not there—it is forgotten, written out, silenced.

And yet, I wonder, how *do* we first learn about the genocide? For me, there are two moments that stick out in my memory, both encompassing different types of knowing. The first instant is the one I usually recount when others ask how I found out about it: I was in the first grade and was given an assignment to fill out a family tree. The simple, gentle explanation from my parents regarding the many branches that were to remain blank told me, then, all I needed to know, all I really could process. It was the second moment, however, that affected me most profoundly, although it is one much more difficult to explain. For whereas as a first-grader I may have learned *about* the genocide, it was during that second moment that I began to understand it—or, at least began to understand *how* I was to understand it.

I was perhaps ten or eleven years old, and the small Armenian community in my hometown of Tulsa, Oklahoma, had gathered for its annual genocide commemoration. This was the first year that I was allowed to join the adults. Yet, typical child that I was, I tuned out for much of the event, until a man around my parents' age—one of the many *amos* (uncles) in the community who liked to tease us kids and hold forth loudly on next year's reunion in the homeland—stood up to read a poem. I recognized the poem as being in Armenian, but I could hardly understand the dialect it was in. The reading began simply enough, and given that I could barely follow it, I was ready to tune out, just as I had all evening. But then I began to notice something: with every word, Amo became more and more overcome with emotion. The words, already somewhat nonsensical to my ears, became a sort of music, undulating with his quivering voice, absorbing the heaving and shaking of his body as he wept and read. His voice would dip down low, so quiet that I could barely hear, and then suddenly rise to anguished bellows I could hardly bear to listen to. I became fidgety. Too embarrassed to look at this person I knew only as a teasing *amo* directly, I looked away. I scanned the room, expecting to see similarly embarrassed faces, and instead saw tears streaming down the faces of the aunties and *amos* all around me. I wanted to escape his voice but I could not; it wrapped itself around me, filling every nook and cranny of that room. So I squeezed my eyes shut and surrendered. I listened. I absorbed the pain, the sadness, the despair, and the anger being conveyed by the melodies of his voice—oh, that voice—and I cried. Something shifted for me then. I cannot say that I learned any new facts about the genocide that day, but my understanding of it was profoundly and forever altered. The genocide was no longer just about my family, as I had thought that day in first grade when I absorbed why so many relatives were absent from the family tree—it was something more. Anything I would learn in the coming years passed, consciously or not, through the framework of that day of commemoration. Through sound, I recognized how I was to understand the genocide—how I was to know what it was to be Armenian and to be marked, in the present, by the past.

The year 2015 commemorated the centennial of the Armenian genocide. That year, public declarations of mourning and remembrance took place throughout the Armenian diaspora, each declaration affirming and insisting upon a past called into question through decades of state-sponsored denial.[2] From Moscow to Buenos Aires, Jerusalem to Tehran, Paris to Los Angeles, commemorative concerts served as a highlight of these events. In accordance with the forget-me-not flower—the official logo of the centennial—these concerts were presented as commemorations: occasions to engage in collective acts of remembrance. Works by the Ottoman Armenian Komitas Vartaped and the Soviet Armenian Aram Khachaturian intermingled with Mozart's *Requiem* and Beethoven's *Eroica*.[3] The concerts engaged in forms of musical discourse that broadened systems of cultural exchange and framed the genocide and its remembrance—and, consequently, framed the Armenian people—within the matrices of the sonic worlds evoked by the programmed works.

This chapter explores the implications of these sonic acts of remembrance by examining them through the lens of melancholia. In "Mourning and Melancholia," Sigmund Freud defines the melancholic subject as one who "cannot consciously perceive" what has been lost.[4] The melancholic subject is aware "of the loss which has given rise to his melancholia, but only in the sense that he knows *whom* he has lost but not *what he has lost in him*."[5] In these commemorations, there is indeed a grappling with a loss that cannot be ever fully known, and the manifold tributes can be seen as attempts to represent the unrepresentable: struggles to narrate something that, as Marc Nichanian writes, is "beyond the representable, beyond all possible narration."[6]

However, in these efforts to represent the unrepresentable, it is not merely the past being articulated. The melancholic fixation on the loss—the refusal to allow the past to remain in the past—brings the past fully into the present, placing it into a narrative context that speaks as much to the present and the future. As David Eng and David Kazanjian write,

> We find in Freud's conception of melancholia's persistent struggle with its lost objects not simply a "grasping" and "holding" on to a fixed notion of the past but rather a continuous engagement with loss and its remains. This engagement generates sites for memory and history, for the rewriting of the past as well as the reimagining of the future.[7]

To engage with a loss that cannot be known is to relate invariably to that which *can* be known—that which remains. The loss is read through and by what remains, what remains read through the loss, each constituting and transforming the other.

The concerts I discuss below give form to both the unrepresentability of the genocide and the ambiguities of diasporic belonging. They are sites of memory, yes, but also sites of identity construction. In their framing and positioning of the genocide, they consequently frame and position the Armenian diaspora. Though presented as acts of remembering, these are moments of sonic positioning and alignment—positionings and alignments that work against the ruptures and multiplicities of the diaspora and thus stabilize, and give meaning to, the diaspora. As Stuart Hall writes, it is a positioning that "makes meaning possible."[8] In this sense, these concerts operate as vectors: they are active, propulsive and productive, setting into motion how the genocide is to be remembered, and how, consequently, the Armenian diaspora is to be known and is to know itself.[9]

April 24, 1915

The genocide of 1915, which resulted in the deaths of approximately one million Armenians living in the Ottoman Empire, is one of the most contested events of recent history. At the heart of the controversy is the very naming of what happened in 1915. Each year, on the official Remembrance Day for the genocide (April 24), come renewed calls for the recognition of the killings, death marches, and deportations as genocide. Mourning and remembrance are thus made inseparable from the demand for recognition. The slogan for the 2015 centennial commemoration was, in fact, "I remember and demand" ("Hishum Em ev Pahanjum").

With every April 24 also comes an opportunity for Armenians both from the diaspora and in Armenia to speak as one. In the slogan "I remember and demand" there is only "I," an unequivocally singular voice that belies those many contrapuntal layers of the Armenian diaspora—a multidimensionality that dates back to at least the mid-sixteenth century, with the division of historic Armenia between east (Safavid Iran) and west (Ottoman Empire), and which became all the more complex with the diaspora that multiplied throughout the late nineteenth and twentieth centuries.[10]

The genocide took place in the waning days of the Ottoman Empire. One important yet often overlooked fact is that those massacred were the Armenians living in the *western* portion of historic Armenia (also referred to as Anatolia), which, in the early fifteenth century, had become a part of the Ottoman Empire and today remains a part of Turkey. The eastern portion, which is linguistically and otherwise distinct from the western portion, became first a part of Safavid Iran, then, in the early nineteenth century, a part of the Russian Empire, and eventually a part of the Soviet

Union.[11] In 1991, this portion became—and remains today—the independent Republic of Armenia.

Although a small Armenian diaspora existed before the genocide, the size of it increased greatly as Ottoman Armenians began to flee the empire in the late nineteenth century. By 1921, approximately five hundred thousand Ottoman Armenians had been resettled throughout the world, with the majority ending up in the Middle East, Western Europe, and the United States. Thus, until the 1990s, when greater numbers of Armenians from the country of Armenia would begin to emigrate, the Armenian diaspora was primarily made up of the survivors of the Ottoman massacres and their descendants.

As numerous scholars have noted, while the country of Armenia as it exists today is viewed as a "homeland" by many diasporic Armenians who trace their ancestry to western Armenia, it functions as such in a (largely) symbolic capacity.[12] Despite the cultural, historical, geographic, and linguistic gulfs between "eastern" and "western" Armenians, there has been great dependence on certain tropes, such as the genocide and the concept of Armenia as homeland, that discursively unite Armenians the world over. The complications inherent within these identifications are, of course, immediately apparent, as they implicitly, and at times explicitly, foreclose certain histories (such as those that do not include the genocide), homelands, and ways of being Armenian—something that became all the more apparent during the 2015 commemorations.

April 24, 2015

The scope of the 2015 centennial commemorations was on a scale never before seen. Throughout the world, massive demonstrations, conferences, concerts, film screenings, lectures, panel discussions, memorial constructions, museum exhibits, and book launches took place, accompanied by unprecedented coverage in the global media. While the annual commemorations typically garner a passing mention in the media, the centenary invited far more substantial and sustained coverage, including numerous articles exploring the historical dimensions of the genocide and the continuing controversy over the use of the word "genocide." The international press covered the numerous political delegations traveling to Armenia and analyzed the various statements made by political and religious leaders throughout the world. Moreover, the centenary brought the publication of survivor testimonials and op-eds by the descendants of those who survived. The centennial endeavors even received coverage in places as unexpected as *Us Weekly*, *Entertainment Tonight*, *People Magazine*, and *TMZ*, thanks to heavily publicized trips to Armenia made by such celebrities as Kim Kardashian, Kanye West, and George Clooney. The world was watching in a way that it had not before. The centenary year of 2015 thus presented a critical opportunity to shape the narrative of the genocide and, by extension, the narrative of the Armenian people.

As expected, remembrance was an overt theme of a number of the commemorative concerts. From the titles of the concerts alone, it was clear that their purpose was to remember, pay tribute to, and honor the lives of those who died in the genocide: in Paris, "100 Years of Remembrance"; in Detroit, "A 100 Year Journey of Remembrance and Song"; in Los Angeles, "A Concert of Remembrance"; in Fresno, "Witness and Rebirth: An Armenian Journey"; in New York, "Remembrance and Rebirth in Commemoration of the Armenian Genocide Centennial"; and for a series of concerts presented in Finland, Denmark, and Norway, "I Remember and Demand" (after the official slogan of the commemorative year). According to one review, approximately fifteen hundred people attended the Detroit concert.[13] The pieces in the first half of that concert, titled "Remembrance," were accompanied by photo montages featuring Ottoman Armenian villages, pictures of survivors, and photographic evidence of the atrocities committed during the genocide and were interspersed with readings of testimonies that recounted the horrors of what occurred.[14] Included in that part of the concert were some pieces directly evocative of those who died and the lands from which they had come—works such as "A Song of Eulogy for the Martyrs," set to the poetry of Vahan Tekeyan, a renowned Ottoman Armenian poet; "Bingyol," a folk song from an Ottoman Armenian village; and "Der Zor," a song evoking the town in the Syrian desert where 150,000 Armenians who had been sent on forced marches were massacred. Also included in this concert, and a number of others, were requiem masses. Mozart's *Requiem*, for example, was performed at concerts in London, Paris, Beirut, and Vienna, while requiems by the Armenian composers Tigran Mansurian, Petros Shoujounian, and Alexander Haroutunian were featured at concerts in Vienna, Montreal, London, Paris, Boston, Detroit, and Washington, DC.

The Fresno concert, titled "Witness and Rebirth: An Armenian Journey," featured a specially commissioned three-movement piece, *Cantata for Living Martyrs*. The first movement, ironically titled "The Dance," sets the poetry of Siamanto (né Atom Yarjanian), an Armenian poet who died in the genocide. The music attempts to evoke the bloodshed and horrors of the genocide. As the composer, Serouj Kradjian, describes it, "The text is very dark, and I wanted to go to the extremes, with violent fortissimos and soft, almost sobbing harmonies to describe the situation."[15] Between that, the sounds of cracked whips, and the manner in which the text comes through—sometimes shouted by the singers, sometimes wailed—this movement sonically evokes the horrors of the genocide.[16] The more somber and subdued second movement sets text from the memoirs of Aram Haigaz, a survivor of the genocide, whose father and siblings were killed and who became separated from his mother during the forced marches. The third movement opens with a direct confrontation of the genocide denial, with the choir repeating, in Turkish, the statement, "Ermeni soykırımı olmamıştır" ("The Armenian genocide never happened). Out of the blistering force of the setting of that phrase comes redemption in the form of the nation: the movement moves into a patriotic march while the choir sings the iconic words of the Armenian American writer William Saroyan: "I should like to see any power of the world destroy this race. . . . Send them into the desert without bread or water. Burn their homes and churches, then see if they will not laugh, sing and pray again. For when two of them meet anywhere in the world, see if they will not create a new Armenia!"[17]

In many ways, Kradjian's *Cantata for Living Martyrs* is the music of the melancholic subject that Freud had identified in 1917, only two years after the genocide. The work can be understood as sonically representing that "persistent struggle with the lost objects." In this piece, the past is not in the past; rather, it is brought fully into the present. With its title referring to "living martyrs," the living are marked by, and understood through, the narrative progression of death, resurrection, and reconstruction in that "new Armenia."

Melancholy in/of Diaspora

In their reflections on Freud's conception of melancholia, Eng and Kazanjian write, "To ask, 'What is lost?' is to invariably [slip] into the question, 'What remains?'" They continue, "Loss is inseparable from what remains, for what is lost is known only by what remains of it, by how those remains are produced, read, and sustained."[18] As I looked at Kradjian's cantata and the programs of other commemorative concerts more closely, they revealed a deeply melancholic character. Although they were ostensibly centering on past losses, they seemed to be saying as much (if not more) about what and who remains as they were about what and who was lost. *Remembrance* and *rebirth*: to remember, to witness, to demand is the work and the responsibility of those who are still here—of those who remain. The genocide denial, too, is in the hands of those who remain. In the *Cantata for Living Martyrs*, any shared cultural history between western Armenians and present-day Turkey receives a bludgeoning, when the Turkish language, which many of the survivors spoke, was made synonymous with the violence of denial. It carries a stark message to those Armenians who remain: you are not them, you are Armenia.

What remains of western Armenia both constitutes and is constituted in how the losses were mourned, the framework through which the genocide was understood and remembered, and the ways in which the Armenians in the diaspora were made to speak as one in these concerts. They produced, read, and sustained the Armenian subject by and through an articulation as well as accumulation of loss. While the positivist aims of the commemorations fixated on an accounting of the losses—an accounting of the numbers of dead, the lands lost, the reparations owed—so as to prove that what happened was indeed genocide, the concerts simultaneously produced the narrative worlds through which the present-day Armenian is to be read.

As I looked more closely at those concerts that explicitly referenced or drew upon the losses of the genocide, I began to notice something that, perhaps naively, I did not expect. While it was clear the purpose of the concerts was to commemorate the genocide and while some of the pieces did reference the genocide directly (or evoke the lands from which those who survived had come), such pieces appeared rather infrequently. Though labeled as commemorative events, references to the genocide were more often than not indirect, musically speaking. For example, one concert in London, titled "With You, Armenia: A Concert to Commemorate the Centennial of the Armenian Genocide" and presented by the Royal Philharmonic Orchestra, was advertised as recognizing "the courage and endurance of the Armenian people," yet featured only pieces by Johann Sebastian Bach (Concerto for Two Violins in D minor), Max Bruch (Violin Concerto No. 1), and Johannes Brahms (Symphony No. 1).[19] The "I Remember and Demand" concerts, which were given by the Armenian National Philharmonic Orchestra (ANPO) and held in Finland, Denmark, and Norway, featured the music of the eastern Armenian composer Aram Khachaturian (excerpts from *Spartacus*) along with pieces by Edvard Grieg (Piano Concerto in

A Minor) and Peter Tchaikovsky (Symphony No. 6).[20] A concert given by the ANPO in Beirut, home to one of the most historically important Armenian diasporic communities, also dedicated to the "Centennial of the Armenian Genocide Concert," featured Khachaturian's *Spartacus* Suite, Brahms's Violin Concerto in D Major, and Mozart's *Requiem.*[21] Over three thousand people attended this concert.[22] Another centennial Beirut concert, presented by the State Youth Orchestra of Armenia, featured compositions by the eastern Armenian composer Ghazaros Saryan along with pieces by Niccoló Paganini and Tchaikovsky.[23] The program of the Fresno concert included, in addition to the *Cantata,* two pieces by Khachaturian (both *Spartacus* and his Violin Concerto) and Antonín Dvořák's *Te Deum.* And finally, while the concert in Tehran (which was attended by the ambassadors of Armenia, Belgium, Bulgaria, Cyprus, France, India, Japan, and Uruguay) predominantly featured Armenian classical and folk music, it closed with a performance of Franz Schubert's "Ave Maria."[24]

Looking at these concerts, question after question began to run through my head. Admittedly, these are but a sampling of the concerts that took place in 2015, yet they revealed certain patterns that brought the implications of their programming to the forefront and made explicit what the programs were saying implicitly. I began to wonder, why these pieces? To put it bluntly, yet earnestly: What do these works have to do with the genocide? Where in the concerts are those who perished? Where is the genocide? Is the focus indeed the loss or is it what remains? Is the loss meant to be read through that which remains? What exactly was being articulated through the sonically intermingling worlds presented in these concerts?

Thinking about the intersecting matrices of the sonic worlds that were evoked in these concerts, it seemed that they were opening realms of political possibility that both situate and position the Armenian subject while, at the same time, foreclosing other conceptual spheres. Returning to Eng and Kazanjian's description of melancholia, this "continuing engagement with loss and its remains" generated sites from which to reimagine the future, and, I would add, the present. In these concerts, the Armenians not only are made to speak—to remember, to witness, to demand—as one, but are made to speak through the musical languages and represented in the programs. Indeed, the predominance of repertoire of Western concert music in these concerts—especially when performed by diasporic Armenian musicians—served as a sonic emblem of Armenian selfhood in the broader, transnational terms.

Sara Clarke Kaplan relates Freud's concept of melancholia to a specific form that she terms "diasporic melancholia." As she writes, diasporic melancholia "exceeds the expression of past griefs . . . to provide a historically and geographically specific militant articulation of present and future political desires that is rooted in the unending mourning of a past genocide and continuing subjugation."[25] She continues,

> [Diasporic melancholia] suggests that the work of embodied memory is to not only bear witness to long-past, historically-disavowed wounds and losses [but also] *produce new political communities*. . . . If, however, the practice of diasporic melancholia is best understood as the articulation of certain ethical impossibilities—the impossibilities of forgetting, the irremediable nature of the loss—then the spatio-temporal community which it constitutes and by which it is maintained is, at its best, a geography of political possibility.[26]

And in effect, what emerges in these concerts is a "geography of political possibility." Yet this particular geography of political possibility was bounded by the deliberate construction of communities of mourning. Taking place across numerous continents, these concerts represented an opportunity to mourn not only together with specific groups of non-Armenians, but also as Armenians eo ipso, east and west.

Over the past years, the discourse of the commemorations has become increasingly pan-Armenian, revealing a political project that conflates the needs of the present-day diaspora with the needs of present-day Armenia, consequently putting the genocide into a narrative that centers Armenia as the homeland. As can be seen in Kradjian's *Cantata for Living Martyrs*, this narrative world defined the remains through the lens of present-day Armenia, while the Ottoman Empire—which held the homes, the memories, the lands, the histories of those who died and survived in the genocide—appears as present-day Turkey. The sins of the empire have now become conflated with the denial by Turkey.[27] In the commemorations, the remains and thus consequently the loss are placed within the discourse of the nation-state. As Anahid Kassabian notes,

> While "nation" has no meaning as a description in an Armenian history, it is used unselfconsciously as the privileged concept in representations of Armenian history. The use of the name "nation" may be the necessary "mistake" which makes narratives about genocide possible. . . . In other words, "nation" covers over inconvenient history, it makes identity, it makes possible the claim to genocide.[28]

The evocation of "nation" consequently invites a narrative shift that realigns and repositions western Armenia with a discourse consistent with the historiography of Armenia. This narrative slippage shifts the construction of western Armenia away from the shared histories and connotations of the Ottoman Empire (made now synonymous with Turkey) and into a discursive domain that places the Armenian self in opposition to the Turkish Other. What they are, we are not: Turkish, Armenian; Muslim, Christian; East, West.[29]

This discursive shift becomes apparent in the sonic alignments and geographical affinities brought to bear in the concerts. While placing the Armenians into a spatiotemporal realm that is distant from the Ottoman Empire, these concerts simultaneously intervene against the fractures and multiplicities of the diasporic reality by presenting a rooted, united people with a shared past. This strategic essentializing echoes Hamid Naficy's assertion:

> Exilism is doomed to failure unless it is also rooted in some type of specificity and locality, even essentialism of some strategic sort. . . . Without such rootedness, exile discourse, like all other oppositional or alternative discourses, will be co-opted and commodified through defusion and diffusion. In the cultural domain . . . specificity, locality, and detail are all.[30]

Sounding the Lost

In many ways, the centennial commemoration was an overtly pan-Armenian effort.[31] In 2011, Serzh Sargsyan, then president of Armenia, commissioned the creation of a group—the State Commission on Coordination of the Events for the Commemoration of the 100th Anniversary of the Armenian Genocide—that, as the name implies, coordinated officially recognized commemorative events throughout Armenia and the diaspora. The commission was headed by Sargsyan himself and included a number of representative delegations from the diaspora, along with the two heads of the Armenian Apostolic Church. The commission officially kicked off the centennial year on January 29, with a gathering at the Tsitsenakaberd Memorial Complex, Armenia's official memorial to the victims of the genocide. At this event, the commission presented the "Pan-Armenian Declaration on the Centennial of the Armenian Genocide," a document that made demands upon Turkey and the international community regarding the recognition of the genocide and the current geopolitical struggles of Armenia (Figure 9.1).[32]

The State Commission on the Coordination of Events Dedicated to the 100th Anniversary of the Armenian Genocide, in consultation with its regional committees in the Diaspora...

[...]

10. Proudly notes that during the last century the Armenian people, having survived the genocide, have:
    - demonstrated an unbending will and **national self-consciousness** and **restored their sovereign statehood**, lost centuries ago;
    - **preserved and developed national values**, achieved the **renaissance of their national culture**, science, and education, bringing a unique contribution to the development of world heritage; [...]
    - **united and restored the national gene pool** that was facing extermination as a result of the genocide, through pan-Armenian cooperation and an extensive repatriation program; and made valuable contributions to international peace and security during the First and Second World Wars and won glorious victories in the heroic Battle of Sardarapat and the Artsakh War.

[...]

12. Calls upon the coming generations of Armenians to protect their sacred native heritage with patriotism, consciousness, and intellect, and resolutely struggle and serve for:
    - **a stronger Homeland, a free and democratic Republic of Armenia**;
    - the progress and strengthening of independent Artsakh;
    - the efficient unity of Armenians worldwide; and
    - the realization of the centuries-old sacrosanct goals of all Armenians.

Figure 9.1. Excerpt: Pan-Armenian Declaration on the Centennial of the Armenian Genocide

The document also served as a clear effort to bring together the diaspora and the country of Armenia. Point 10 of the document, for example, emphasizes the nationhood and national self-consciousness of the Armenians, speaking of their "national" values, their "national culture," and the restoration of the "national gene pool," while the final point of the document (point 12) calls on Armenians to "protect their sacred native heritage" through struggling for "a stronger Homeland, a free and democratic Republic of Armenia."

This centering of "Armenia" was clear in a number of the concerts. Events such as, in Toronto, "Ararat: Music of Armenia" and "Forget Me Not: A Musical Tribute to the Enduring Spirit of a Nation"; in London, "Music for Armenia" and "Together for Armenia"; and in Jerusalem, New York, Italy, London, and Vienna, a series of concerts titled "With You, Armenia," sonically aligned Armenia—both the republic and as imagined community—with the North Atlantic world. Two of the "With You, Armenia" concerts became, in essence, political events, in Jerusalem with speeches given by the Armenian foreign minister, Edward Nalbandian, and, in Vienna, through the attendance of numerous Armenian state officials.[33] Save for the London concert, which featured only the music of Bach, Bruch, and Brahms, these concerts highlighted a mixture of compositions by diasporic and eastern Armenian (i.e., from the country of Armenia) composers along with Western concert repertoire: for example, the Vienna concert presented music by two Armenian composers, Komitas and Arno Babadjanian, together with works by Johannes Brahms, Sergei Rachmaninoff, Georges Bizet, and Wolfgang Amadeus Mozart.

Of the "Armenian" works in these concerts, the music of eastern Armenian composers featured the most frequently, though none evoke the genocide directly. Only one Ottoman Armenian composer (Komitas) and two diasporic Armenian composers (Tigran Mansurian and Alan Hovhaness) were present on the programs. Moreover, the Ottoman world of those who perished and of those who survived was audible only in the work of Komitas, an Armenian priest and musicologist who was arrested during the genocide and has since become revered for his work in isolated Armenian villages where he attempted to find and notate Armenian melodic forms and folk songs that were free from what he identified as Turkish, Persian, and Arab influences. An icon among Armenians, Komitas was, in fact, not only included on the majority of the commemorative concert programs, but generally the only Ottoman Armenian composer who appeared.

These concerts certainly intervened in the pan-Armenian discourse of the centennial year, although, again, I emphasize that it was a nation-state-centered discourse, where the diaspora appears through the country of Armenia. Yet they also position this discourse strategically within a sonic framework that shifted decisively away from the world of the Ottoman Other, ostensibly eliminating non-Western elements of the self. The communities of mourning constructed through these concerts were often clearly framed, both through the choice of standard concert repertoire and through the new works by diasporic Armenians. For example, in response to a question regarding why he chose Latin for the setting of his requiem, Tigran Mansurian explained that he hoped it would make the work "accessible to non-Armenians."[34] While the use of Latin would certainly make the piece accessible to non-Armenians, the follow-up question inevitably needs to ask: to *which* non-Armenians would it be accessible? In his review of a concert held in London (titled "Together for Armenia"), the Armenian folk singer Hasmik Harutunyan offered an unequivocal answer: "Armenians through centuries have embraced the Western culture, integrated and flourished in their host countries, at the same time remaining close to their roots."[35] Harutunyan's assessment captured perfectly the alignments and positionings inherent in the intersecting sonic matrices of the programmed works. The concert's soundscape thus gave rise to alignments that constituted, for the Armenians, this particular and cherished "geography of political possibility."

And yet, as I think about these programs, I wonder about this geography of possibility. For they seem to me to be carving out a geography of impossibility as much as a geography of possibility. On the one hand, they constituted a possible world through that which was lost and that which remained, and yet, on the other hand, they also foreclosed and excluded cultural and historical geographies entangled in an Ottoman past. Perhaps the positionings and alignments brought to the forefront of these concerts are, in some way, the only way of making audible the demands for recognition of the genocide. "Through your language, through this language that we now share, I will grieve my loss. Please join with me." After all, through whose language, through what framework, must the demands be made in order to be heard, and by whom?

At the same time, I cannot stop thinking about the geographies and the worlds that have been made *im*possible in some of these programs. Even if within them lies the promise of possibility—the possibility of worlds made whole—the question remains: "Who will be excluded from that repaired whole?"[36] I think about my grandparents and I wonder: will it be them? I look through the programs for a sign of them. At times, I cannot quite see them—my grandparents who survived the marches, whose stories I will never fully know and never understand. Perhaps therein lies the irony of the melancholic subject. For in this need to recover that which can never be known, it becomes all too easy to forget who was lost.

And yet, we try. We try to somehow fill the empty spaces of our family trees, to grow those missing branches into roots and into a rootedness denied by the ravages of genocide, of denial, and of homelessness. We try to grow, in a sense, in reverse, building a past from the present, a present from that past, and back and forth again and again. For what are these commemorations if not a yearning for a wholeness denied? In these concerts that took place in the centennial year, like that poem I heard so many years ago, our lost pasts are sonically instantiated and given form, enveloping us and ensounding those losses that we can never fully know. In these moments, the sound penetrates; we cannot turn away. And so, we listen.

Select Programs[37]

Finland, Denmark, Norway, April 11–14, 2015

"I Remember and Demand"
Khachaturian: *Spartacus*
Grieg: Piano Concerto
Tchaikovsky: Symphony No. 6

Paris, April 21, 2015

"100 Years of Remembrance"
Khachaturian: *Masquerade*
Komitas: Folk songs
Petrossian: *Ciel à vif* (commission)
Mozart: *Requiem*

Toronto, April 22, 2015

"Ararat: Music of Armenia"
Komitas: Various songs
Khachaturian: Violin Concerto, *Masquerade,* and *Spartacus*
Danna: Suite from *Ararat*

Fresno, CA, April 25, 2015

"Witness and Rebirth: An Armenian Journey"
Armenian sacred choral works
Khachaturian: *Spartacus* Suite
Kradjian: *Cantata for Living Martyrs*
Dvořák: *Te Deum*

London, May 3, 2015

"Music for Armenia"
Mozart: *Requiem*
Górecki: *Symphony of Sorrowful Songs*
Komitas: *Groong*
Yekmalian: *Armenian Mass*
Khachaturian: Violin Concerto, *Spartacus, Sabre Dance*

Los Angeles, May 12, 2015

"A Concert of Remembrance"
Khachaturian: *Spartacus* Suite
Mansurian: Violin Concerto
Shostakovich: Symphony No. 5

New York, May 26, 2015

"With You, Armenia"
Komitas: Various songs
Sharafyan: *Waterfall Music*
Azizyan: *The Little Prince and the Fox*
Mansurian: *Three Portraits of Women*
Sandström: "Es ist ein Rose in entsprungen"
Britten: "Maiden in the Mor Lay"
Penderecki: Psalm 3 (world premiere; dedicated to the centennial of the Armenian genocide), Agnus Dei
Chopin: Various works

London, July 21, 2015

"With You, Armenia: A Concert to Commemorate the Centennial of the Armenian Genocide"
Bach: Concerto for Two Violins in D minor
Bruch: Violin Concerto No. 1
Brahms: Symphony No. 1

Beirut, August 8, 2015

"A Concert Dedicated to the Centennial of the Armenian Genocide"
Khachaturian: *Spartacus*
Brahms: Violin Concerto in D Major
Mozart: *Requiem*

Rome, September 5, 2015

"With You, Armenia"
Khachaturian: Waltz Suite from *Masquerade*

Beethoven: Piano Concerto No. 3 in C minor
Dvořák: Symphony No. 8 in G Major

Toronto, November 7, 2015

Forget Me Not: A Musical Tribute to the Enduring Spirit of a Nation"
Mirzoyan: "Epitaph" (in memory of Aram Khachaturian)
Arutiunian: Violin Concerto
Mansurian: *Canti Paralelli*
Sharafyan: Divertissement
Khachaturian: *Masquerade*

Vienna, November 7, 2015

"With You, Armenia"
Shostakovich: Piano Trio No. 2
Schumann: Adagio and Allegro
Babajanian: *Poem*
Komitas: Various songs
Mozart: *Requiem*

New York, November 21, 2015

"Remembrance and Rebirth in Commemoration of the Armenian Genocide Centennial"
Bach: Piano Concerto in D Minor
Komitas: Songs for Soprano and Orchestra
Babajanian: *Vocalise for Soprano and Orchestra*
Hakobyan: Adagio for String Orchestra and Timpani, Fantasia for Piano and String Orchestra
Sharafyan: Waltz from Suite for Cello and Orchestra
Arutiunian: Impromptu for Cello and Orchestra
Mirzoyan: Symphony for Timpani and Strings

Notes

My sincerest gratitude, first and foremost, to Annegret Fauser and Michael Figueroa, for their tireless work in organizing the conference that led to this book, for their patience and attentiveness as editors, and for the indispensable suggestions that greatly benefitted this chapter. My gratitude, also, to my research assistant, Ilana Hirsh, for her invaluable work and her probing questions and sharp insights. Many thanks, also, to Margaret Sarkissian, Lilit Yernjakyan, Jon McCollum, Alyssa Mathias, Badema Pitic, Beverley Diamond, Martin Daughtry, and the participants of the Performing Commemoration conference for their invaluable comments, questions, and suggestions on earlier presented versions of this article. Any shortcomings in the article are mine alone.

1. Given the multiplicities among Armenians, to discuss them in the singular is highly problematic. The genocide, for instance, did not affect all Armenians, nor did it affect all Armenians similarly. And yet it has become, discursively at least, a marker of Armenian-ness—something that became abundantly clear in 2015, the centennial year of the genocide. See, among others, Khachig Tölölyan and Taline Papazian, "Armenian Diasporas and Armenia: Issues of Identity and Mobilization. An Interview with Khachig Tölölyan," *Études arméniennes contemporaines* 3 (2014): 83–101.

2. For an analysis of the centennial year, see Sossie Kasbarian, "The Politics of Memory and Commemoration: Armenian Diasporic Reflections on 2015," *Nationalities Papers* 46, no. 1 (2018): 123–43.

3. See note 9.

4. Sigmund Freud, "Mourning and Melancholia" (1917), in *On the History of the Psycho-Analytic Movement, Papers on Metapsychology and Other Works*, vol. 14 of *The Standard Edition of the Complete Psychological Works of Sigmund Freud*, ed. and trans. James Strachey (London: Hogarth Press, 1957), 245.

5. Freud, "Mourning and Melancholia," 245.

6. Marc Nichanian, "Catastrophic Mourning," in *Loss: The Politics of Mourning*, ed. David L. Eng and David Kazanjian (Berkeley: University of California Press, 2003), 113.

7. David L. Eng and David Kazanjian, "Introduction: Mourning Remains," in *Loss*, 4.

8. Stuart Hall, "Cultural Identity and Diaspora," in *Identity: Community, Culture, Difference*, ed. Jonathan Rutherford (London: Lawrence & Wishart, 1990), 230.

9. Some notable concerts not discussed in this chapter include, among others, those given by Armenian-American heavy metal band System of a Down as part of its #WakeUpTheSouls tour (which included a free concert in Armenia's capital city, Yerevan); a concert of Armenian music from the past three thousand years given by Danny Bedrosian (multi-instrumentalist and vocalist with George Clinton and Parliament-Funkadelic), which featured several Armenian and non-Armenian musicians; a concert of folk and original music performed by the a cappella trio Zulal and oudist Ara Dinkjian at the Kennedy Center; and an unprecedented, historic concert given at the Istanbul Congress Center in Istanbul, Turkey, featuring a slate of Armenian and Turkish musicians. This concert, titled "In Memoriam, 24 April: In Memory of the Armenian Intellectuals Sent to their Deaths in 1915," was organized by Anadolu Kültür, a nonprofit arts organization, and Kalan Müzik, an independent record label. See Alyssa Mathias, "'They Were Sent to Their Deaths from Here': Sounds of Plurality and Solidarity in Istanbul at the 100th Anniversary of the Armenian Genocide," *Ethnomusicology*

Review, May 4, 2015, https://www.ethnomusicologyreview.ucla.edu/content/they-were-sent-their-deaths-here

10. The massive growth of the diaspora was largely a result of Armenians fleeing the Ottoman massacres of the late nineteenth and early twentieth centuries (culminating with the genocide) and those emigrating from Armenia after the breakup of the Soviet Union. Given the largely distinct historical and sociopolitical trajectories experienced by "eastern" and "western" Armenians, I will be distinguishing them as such throughout the chapter (unless a more specific designation is appropriate). These designations are merely to distinguish geographic points of origin and their attendant histories and relationship to the genocide. For example, Armenians who come from the present-day country of Armenia will be referred to as eastern Armenians, while those whose familial roots are in Anatolia and who were directly affected by the genocide (either having survived it or descending from someone who did) will be referred to as western Armenian. Obviously, these designations are vastly imperfect, as they imply a neat dichotomy where none exists. These designations are not meant to imply that eastern Armenians were not affected by the genocide or that all western Armenians were. However, for the purposes of the chapter, such a distinction will be necessary, and caveats will be provided where necessary.

11. There are two distinct Armenian dialects: Eastern Armenian and Western Armenian (not including various regional dialects). Eastern Armenian is predominantly spoken in present-day Armenia, among Armenians in Iran, and within eastern Armenian diasporic populations. Western Armenian is spoken by Armenians whose lineages can be traced to western Armenia and is a largely diasporic language.

12. See, for example, Sylvia Angelique Alajaji, *Music and the Armenian Diaspora: Searching for Home in Exile* (Bloomington: Indiana University Press, 2015); Anny Bakalian, *Armenian-Americans: From Being to Feeling Armenian* (New Brunswick, NJ: Transaction Publishers, 1993); Sossie Kasbarian, "The Myth and Reality of 'Return': Diaspora in the 'Homeland,'" *Diaspora* 18, no. 3 (2009): 358–81; Razmik Panossian, "Between Ambivalence and Intrusion: Politics and Identity in Armenian-Diaspora Relations," *Diaspora* 7, no. 2 (1998): 149–96; and Susan Pattie, "New Homeland for an Old Diaspora," in *Homelands and Diasporas: Holy Lands and Other Places* (Stanford, CA: Stanford University Press, 2005), 49–67.

13. Elizabeth Aprahamian, "A 100-Year Journey of Remembrance and Song Presented in Detroit," *Armenian Mirror-Spectator*, July 23, 2015, https://mirrorspectator.com/2015/07/23/a100-year-journey-of-remembrance-and-song-presented-in-detroit/

14. Aprahamian, "A 100-Year Journey."

15. Quoted in Donald Munro, "Fresno Philharmonic Takes on Ambitious Choral Piece on Armenian Genocide," *Fresno Bee*, April 23, 2015, http://www.fresnobee.com/entertainment/performing-arts/article19675455.html. See also Maddy Guekguezian, "World Premiere of Kradjian's 'Cantata for Living Martyrs,'" *California Courier*, July 23, 2015; and Mark Rudio, "'Witness and Rebirth' Explores Armenian Genocide through Music," *San Francisco Classical Voice*, April 29, 2015, https://www.sfcv.org/reviews/2015/04/29/-quot-Witness-and-Rebirth-quot-Explores-Armenian-Genocide-Through-Music

16. Munro, "Fresno Philharmonic."

17. This text originally appears in Saroyan's short story "The Armenian and the Armenian," in *Inhale and Exhale* (New York: Random House, 1936), 438. For an overview of how the text has been altered over the years, see C. K. Garabed, "Mincing Words," *Armenian Weekly*, August 8, 2009, https://armenianweekly.com/2009/08/08/ck-garabed-mincing-words/

18. Eng and Kazanjian, "Introduction," 2.

19. As advertised on the Royal Philharmonic Orchestra's website: https://www.rpo.co.uk/whats-on/eventdetail/285/85/with-you-armenia. This concert was one of a series of "With You, Armenia" concerts that took place in various cities around the world, each of which featured different programs. The series kicked off with a concert in Jerusalem, followed by New York City, London (described above), Rome, and Vienna. The complete program for each concert can be found at the end of the chapter. See also http://yerevanfestival.am/en/special-projects/with-you-armenia for the complete programs.

20. Gayane Mkrtchyan, "Genocide 100: Musicians Plan Concerts under 'I Remember and Demand' Slogan," *ArmeniaNow*, April 3, 2015, https://www.armenianow.com/genocide/62044/armenia_genocide_100_philharmonic_orchestra_concerts

21. "Concert Dedicated to Armenian Genocide Centennial Was Held in Lebanon," *Hayern Aysor*, August 9, 2015, http://hayernaysor.am/en/archives/124350

22. "Concert Dedicated to Armenian Genocide."

23. Siranush Ghazanchyan, "Concert in Lebanon Dedicated to the Centennial of the Genocide," *Public Radio of Armenia*, March 12, 2015, http://www.armradio.am/en/2015/03/12/concert-in-lebanon-dedicated-to-the-centennial-of-armenian-genocide/

24. "Foreign Diplomats Accredited to Iran Attend Concert Dedicated to the 100th Anniversary of the Armenian Genocide," *Hayern Aysor*, February 24, 2015, http://hayernaysor.am/en/archives/86275

25. Sara Clarke Kaplan, "Souls at the Crossroads, Africans on the Water: The Politics of Diasporic Melancholia," *Callaloo* 30, no. 2 (2007): 521.

26. Kaplan, "Souls at the Crossroads," 521–22; emphasis mine.

27. While it is necessary to make clear that the genocide took place in the Ottoman Empire, it is also important to note that Turkey, which succeeded the Ottoman Empire, does not officially recognize the events of 1915 as genocide. Over the years, Turkish scholars, politicians, writers, and activists (among others) who have publicly described what happened as genocide have faced varying degrees of official condemnation. See Taner Akçam, *A Shameful Act: The Armenian Genocide and the Question of Turkish Responsibility* (New York: Henry Holt, 2006); and Fatma Müge Göçek, *Denial of Violence: Ottoman Past, Turkish Present, and Collective Violence against the Armenians, 1789–2009* (Oxford: Oxford University Press, 2015).

28. David Kazanjian and Anahid Kassabian, "Naming the Armenian Genocide: The Quest for 'Truth' and a Search for Possibilities," *New Formations* 8 (1989): 83. Sebouh D. Aslanian has written at length on this issue, tying the turn toward nationalist discourses in the Armenian diaspora in part to the denial of the genocide, which results in "a conception of Armenian history that privileges the

teleological and linear unfolding of the nation-form in history towards its natural nirvana of the nation-state." Aslanian, "The Marble of Armenian History: Or Armenian History as World History," *Études arméniennes contemporaines* 4 (2014): 129–42. See also Aslanian, "From 'Autonomous' to 'Interactive' Histories: World History's Challenge to Armenian Studies," in *An Armenian Mediterranean: Words and Worlds in Motion*, ed. Kathryn Babayan and Michael Pifer (London: Palgrave Macmillan, 2018), 81–125.

29. This opposition has been shored up on numerous occasions. For example, the 1919 silent film *Ravished Armenia*—the first filmic representation of the genocide—has a scene that depicts Armenian girls and women nailed to a series of crosses. This still from the film appears often on the internet as historical artifact. The film is based on the book *Ravished Armenia: The Story of Aurora Mardiganian, the Christian Girl, Who Survived the Great Massacres* (1918).

30. Hamid Naficy, *The Making of Exile Cultures: Iranian Television in Los Angeles* (Minneapolis: University of Minnesota Press, 1993). Discussed in David Kazanjian and Anahid Kassabian, "Mass Mediating Diaspora: Iranian Exile Culture in Los Angeles," *Diaspora* 5, no. 2 (1996): 320.

31. An important counterpart to the Armenia-centered approach to the centennial can be found in the work of Project 2015, which made Turkey the site of its commemorations and events, thus asserting its historic centrality to the lives of the survivors and their descendants. See http://www.armenianproject2015.org

32. For the full document, see "Pan-Armenian Declaration on Genocide Centennial Adopted," *Armenian Weekly*, January 31, 2015, https://armenianweekly.com/2015/01/31/pan-armenian-declaration/

33. See "Armenian FM Attends Armenian Genocide Centennial Concert in Jerusalem," *Panorama*, March 6, 2015, https://www.panorama.am/en/news/2015/03/06/nalbandyan/99109; "Concert in Vienna, Dedicated to the Centennial of the Armenian Genocide," *Embassy of Armenia to Austria*, November 7, 2015, http://austria.mfa.am/en/news/item/2015/11/07/2015/; and Maxim Reider, "With You, Armenia: A Concert in Jerusalem Commemorates the Centennial of the Armenian Genocide," *Jerusalem Post*, February 25, 2015, https://www.jpost.com/Not-Just-News/With-you-Armenia-392149

34. Aram Arkun, "Mansurian Reveals the Roots of His Music and Requiem Prior to Boston Premiere," *Armenian Mirror-Spectator*, October 1, 2015, https://mirrorspectator.com/2015/10/01/mansurian-reveals-the-roots-of-his-music-and-requiem-prior-to-boston-premiere/

35. Hasmik Harutunyan, "'Together for Armenia' Genocide Remembrance Concert at London's St. John Smith Square," *Armenian Community Council of the United Kingdom*, November 15, 2015, http://www.accc.org.uk/genocide-centenary-remembrance-concert-together-for-armenia/

36. David Kazanjian, "Diasporic *Flânerie*: From *Ruinenlust* to Armenia's Walkscapes," in Babayan and Pifer, *An Armenian Mediterranean*, 224.

37. These programs were compiled based on information available in published reviews and on the websites of the venues in which the performances took place and/or the websites of the featured performing groups and artists. Any discrepancies are the author's alone.

TEN | The Accidental Archivists

Memory, Resonance, and Decay in Kivu

CHÉRIE RIVERS NDALIKO

Commemoration is, traditionally, a suturing of time and place—a congealing of metanarrative into something that passes for history and is marked by plural, if not unanimous, ingestion. But in the east of Congo, as in many other tumultuous regions laboring under labels of "developing" or "South" (whatever the prefix), that is not the case. In this region, commemoration is withheld as a politic of domination. Or eviscerated as the collateral damage of natural disaster. Either way, it is not. But the urge to remember persists, some would say is amplified. And mutated. It is reflexive, strategic if at times chaotic, and relentless. It is also infinitely fragmented and subjective, harbored in mediums—story, gesture, implication, mirth—that remain unassailable, at least in principle.

I learned this the hard way.

It started when I set out, robustly, to uncover the recent past. Despite its classification as a war zone, I followed culture to this place, Kivu, determined to tune my eyes and ears to the intimate nuances of creativity in this region that proclaimed to me, vibrantly, its "not-Kinshasa-ness," its distinct identity as a borderland in every sense of the term.[1] I understood, at least in principle, the decimation wrought by strategic erasures and interruptions—colonial, dictatorial, geopolitical, cyclical, and deadly—that lay siege to memory here. I understood, at least in principle, the collective and sequential fermentation of dismembered histories and historic dismemberments. Plural. But it is something else entirely to encounter, in the flesh, the concentrated and escalating fissures of "imperial disorganization."[2]

Much to my own retroactive chagrin, I confess I sought a metanarrative that I could ingest as synonymous with history, though I could not see that at the time. Eager to do my ethnographic due diligence, I anticipated, rather giddily, that there would be "complications," and I knew it would require unusual rigor to "parse" and "unpack," "contextualize" and "frame," but I let myself believe that with persistence I would, eventually, unveil a distinguishable polyphony that leant itself to structure.

What I found, instead, were stories that do not yield to ethnographic aspirations, stories honed against decades of unavenged brutality and unsanctioned laughter, stories that have grown sinewy and stolid in the face of human-made disaster and natural assault, yet stories that are intractably chimerical, chameleon-esque. These stories do not bend to outside aspirations, neither ethnographic nor political; more succinctly, they do not bend to anything but their own internal rhythm. This omnidirectional obstinance makes them uncontainable and, at times, unaccountable. But always real and, in some sense, always true.

Take, for instance, this story of trees:

> In 1993, an optimistic group of youth started Maïdeni, a nonprofit association that promotes nature conservation through arts in Goma.[3] Among other things, they planted trees.
>
> In 1994, the genocide in Rwanda propelled hundreds of thousands of refugees into Goma, where, among other things, they cut down the trees for makeshift shelters and cooking fires.
>
> In 1995, Maïdeni replanted the trees, as best they could in what was by then becoming a war zone.
>
> It is hard to estimate how many of those trees survived the refugee crisis. What's certain, though, is that everyone of that era cringes at the scent of green wood burning. It smells to them of war.
>
> Despite the war and despite the smell, in 1998, Maïdeni joined World Ecology Day and, among other things, planted new trees. This time they filmed themselves doing so—for posterity.

In 1998, returning from World Ecology Day, the filmmaker was arrested, and, among other things, images of Congolese youth planting trees were confiscated.[4] So much for posterity.

In 2000, an increasingly militant group of youth started making music videos about, among other things, the importance and history of planting trees in Kivu.[5] For activism, but also for the record.

In 2002, the eruption of volcano Nyiragongo buried both the trees and their celebratory videos under a bed of lava and, with them, any record they had.

From then on, this militant group of by-then-not-so-young people continued filming, on occasion planting trees, and, when possible, sending footage to safe houses in Europe. Still for posterity, but also in case they were assassinated.

But people in Europe move, and only some of them keep old tapes from Congo.

Then there were wars and more wars in Kivu, pushing the planting of trees further from the forefront of anyone's mind.

Until, in 2017, the UN awarded $97,627 to Maïdeni. To plant trees.

In 2017, founding members of Maïdeni celebrated the UNs financial contribution and, among other things, mourned the official loss of their history. For Maïdeni's story now circulates in a glossy pamphlet, with motivations modified to corroborate the UN's version of history (which is about war, not art). And who will doubt that?

So now Maïdeni is, officially, a project of reintegrating demobilized rebels, other at-risk youths, and vulnerable women. Thus, what started as art is now a carapace of war, a testament to the power of international aid.

And the ones who might prove otherwise are too busy laughing with despair.

Such stories were my initiation into the palindrome of commemoration in Congo. With time, I, too, learned to chuckle (if not yet belly laugh) at the uncanny precision of the cycle—preservation, erasure, preservation, erasure, whether human, natural, political, official, or other—to see the tragicomic heroism of memory chasers in this region. Indeed, such stories inducted me, slowly, into what De Boeck describes as the "universe," in which "various pasts implode in the present, which itself is increasingly disconnected from 'real time.'" Evoking the language of theory, De Boeck continues: "It is here that history acquires oneiric dimensions, and the postcolonial historian emerges as oneirocritic of a disparately collective social imaginary and memory."[6] In sensory terms, perhaps it is here that nebulous intangibilities—memories, remnants, and their afterlives—converge, transform, mutate, and become indistinguishable from dreams. And yet (or perhaps therefore) they remain potent ways of knowing.

Close kin to the postcolonial historian (yet distinct from the dream chaser), is, I suggest, the politically infused artist, who wrangles disparately collective social imaginary and memory into material form, however fleetingly. I encountered a handful of such artists in Kivu. They are self-appointed custodians of a volatile temporality in which the present turns more oft to ash than to memory; embodied barometers of the near-schizophrenic dissociation between cultural reverence for historic knowledge and the material, spiritual, and psychological offensive that systemically annihilates commemorative possibilities in sites of surreptitious geopolitical warfare.

They do more than plant trees. They do more than evince the perpetual washing-over of things. But it is a mighty struggle to prove it. With all due respect, I call these artists accidental archivists. Despite the odds, they have harvested from the "subjectivity of crisis" a haphazard assortment of art that persists somehow.[7] They have retained, in their muscles, the choreographies of political (d)evolution, in their lungs the soundtrack of collective response, in their writings a record of aspiration, and in their photographs and videos evanescent timestamps that stand in for proof. They are, in short, the ligature of incremental existence even if they, like the stories in their custody, are impermanent.

But they did not set out to be the historians, the memory keepers: neither record-keeping nor preservation was among their aspirations. For them, the reflex to document their present was one of survival as history disintegrated around them. For these upper-middle-class young people whose lives had theretofore unfolded in a prime destination of global tourism (think gorillas), grabbing a camera—whether to capture dance performances or police brutality—was an instinctual response to change: genocide (in Rwanda), the collapse of a decades-long dictatorship (in Zaire), and the eruption of wars (in Congo). It was quite simply an accident that their records, however incomplete, are the last ones standing.

Over time, I have lost my taste for metanarrative, but I remain seduced by the stories I have gleaned from the accidental archivists whose paths I have crossed in Kivu. More pressingly, I am compelled to share these stories in my own scriptural echo of their impulse to preserve. But I no longer set out to contain or qualify them. Rather, I decided to share them as they came to me—unbridled, indignant, and oftentimes with their own very explicit agenda; to yield, in other words, to the compound aesthetic of commemoration withheld, to bear witness, in whatever language, to ellipses, echoes, shadows, detritus.[8]

Such are the politics and priorities of this essay—to lay bare some intimacies of preservation, decay, memory, and irony in Kivu. In this undertaking I am alert to the implications of voice, my own and the artists' from whose stories I draw, and to the paradox of penning (and claiming authorship of) a commemorative essay that preserves the very stories I use as proof of systemic absence. This is an ethical quagmire that itself echoes my first lesson about commemoration in Kivu, which was presented to me with the blunt self-assurance of a ten-year-old girl mystified by the need to state the obvious:

> Hadithi zinatolewa na waeleza hadithi, mtu yeyote aliye na hadithi ya kueleza anaweza kuambia, lakini si wote walio na hadithi ni waelezaji wa hadithi, na si hadithi zote zinaundwa sawa.
>
> Stories are told by storytellers, and anyone with a story to tell may tell it, but not all with stories are storytellers, and not all stories are created equal.

With time, I have come to see her point. And I agree, in principle. But in practice, in many cases the power of the pen prevails and, in this case, I have access to the pen. I have also been implored, in no uncertain terms, to use it. Accordingly, I have written this essay, documenting stories—theirs and my own, for the sake of transparency—but I make no claims of storytelling.

Prehistoricizing

At the time of the UN announcement of funding for Maïdeni, I was immersed in my own effort to cobble together—and fund—a digital repository for a voluminous and far-flung collection of materials documenting art and culture for the last three decades in North Kivu. For the sake of mirth, I refer to it as an "archive," and the irony is not lost on my Congolese colleagues. For "archive" is, practically speaking, a synonym for improbability: archives are targets of politically motivated destruction;[9] archives are looted;[10] archives are the collateral damage of war;[11] archives share bloodlines with institutionalized celebration of imperial theft;[12] and so on. Thus, archives are suspect. They are a physical manifestation of political questions—Who preserves? Which memories? And why? And archives are curious. They are a litmus test of sanity—Who cares? About what? And why? And archives are precarious. They are, in Congo, a testament to violence and exodus, fight *and* flight. So they incite much, much laughter. Because trying to hold on to anyone's memories is a quixotic endeavor at best. And because laughter is the best armor in the face of perpetual improbability.

In deference to this subtext (and for the sake of mirth), I refer to my struggle to curate materials that document the last three decades of art and culture in North Kivu as an archival effort. It entailed, among other things, a retracing of steps that took me back through safe houses in Europe, where I uncovered many memories (and much dust) that I carried with me to the United States on the penultimate leg of what was for these material remnants a serpentine pilgrimage. But of course, they were not my memories (nor my dust), so they were malleable to me at first. Whether they became more or less so over time is a matter of opinion. The point is, I was most entranced by the holes they preserved. In these I found not only the expected echoes of politics and war, but also strains of music.

Actually, not strains—whatever it is that remains when sounds are referenced but rendered inaudible. More specifically, what I found were VHS tapes labeled "Musical Theatre Show, Goma June 1995" (but someone had erased the sound); notebooks promising scripts and lyrics (but coffee spills and moths had conspired, almost strategically); and so on. This circumstantial inaudibility, while frustrating, was proof not only of pervasive microerasures, but also of an intriguing body of work that eventually led me to the accidental archivists.

Excerpt of a Memory

"I will speak with you on condition of anonymity," s/he said. Then later, "My anonymity is my power here—I could be anyone, I should be *every-*

one. I want anyone who encounters my memories to know that I could be any Congolese, to suspect us all!

This, on condition of anonymity, is what one accidental archivist told me:

> I have the impression that our history in this region is constantly being erased, always under threat. Our story is constantly being rewritten—from without, from within—with no references.
>
> I am obsessed with the future, and I feel like our future is always in jeopardy because the past is never taken into account. There are no mechanisms to keep memories. Instead, each day the "youth" "invent" something "new." And they pride themselves on being the "first." And they find some unsuspecting do-gooder from abroad, eager to crown them so. And so it is—they are "officially" the "first." Again. But there is no footnote indicating that all of this is "according to no one who remembers." That footnote is important. Or it would be. If it existed.
>
> The absence of references, of footnotes, is not incidental. (The militant in me would add that it is also not accidental, but that is a topic for another day.) We are the products and subjects of our memories, but we are less and less the agents or authors of our history. This pains me. We are, instead, the collateral damage of a system that entices each generation to reinvent an already defunct wheel, tether ourselves to it, and collide with the inevitabilities of history even as the next generation takes up the clarion call. This cycle ends in ruins. But we don't mourn those who went before. We don't commemorate them either. In fact, we simply do not remember them and therefore cannot learn from them, build on them, honor or demonize them. This is a tragedy of a different sort than slaughter, but amounts to much the same thing in certain ways.
>
> But I'm a storyteller, not a philosopher, not that there's always much difference in Congo . . .

Before s/he could continue, the accidental archivist's mobile phone rang, and the spell was broken. I tried, simultaneously, not to eavesdrop and to hold onto the thread of conversation. I failed at both. But I was struck, viscerally, by one of two sensations I want to evoke in this essay: the constant washing-over of things. This is not a circumstance of burial or layering, of sediment compacting, of composite veins that yield to excavation, however grudgingly; it is a circumstance in which the winds and the tides are omnipotent, capable of conjuring strategic evaporations and of leaving no trace.

Prehistoricizing (Continued)

Without realizing it, in attempting to create my "archive," I stumbled, twice, upon the prehistory of Maïdeni, that is, on the stories and other detritus that have, courtesy of the UN's glossy pamphlet, been sidelined from History. My first encounter was with material scraps—notebooks and recordings containing the ghosts of plays, songs, and dance performances the collective of young artists produced in North and South Kivu in the 1990s.[13] Second, I encountered the people themselves. Or at least their disembodied voices propelled through cellular devices (when the accidental archivist's mobile phone rang, it was, quite fortuitously for me, another former member of the group whom I later interviewed). Thus began my journey into an era of undocumented political art and the resonant counterpoint it signals between memory and decay.

On this quest, I "discovered," among other things, long-dormant origin stories at risk of permanent ruination.[14] Indeed, despite the UNs acontextual references to Maïdeni in a pamphlet concerned with "disarmament, demobilization, repatriation, reintegration and resettlement," according to its founders, Maïdeni is—and has always been—a cultural organization.[15] It was among a handful of local NGOs in North Kivu supported by the Programme d'éducation Virunga Katchetche, founded in 1987 as a joint initiative of the Coopération Européenne and the World Wildlife Foundation. Maïdeni's aim was to raise awareness about ecological issues through art and culture. To that end, in addition to planting trees, members of the organization performed (and in some cases, wrote) plays and songs, choreographed pop-up dance performances, and organized community gatherings.

They did this because, in their words, art makes knowledge sexier, inspires others to care. They saw that the factual presentations delivered by agents of the Virunga Katchetche project failed to ignite the interest—much less the actions—of Congolese students, who were not in the least interested in issues of ecological degradation. But, as the popular kids in school, the founders of Maïdeni also saw that by singing and dancing, writing poems and plays, they could make anyone think planting trees was cool.[16] So they did. And it worked.

But their artistic works are now extinct. They have been evaporated courtesy of the winds and the tides. The more I search for them, the

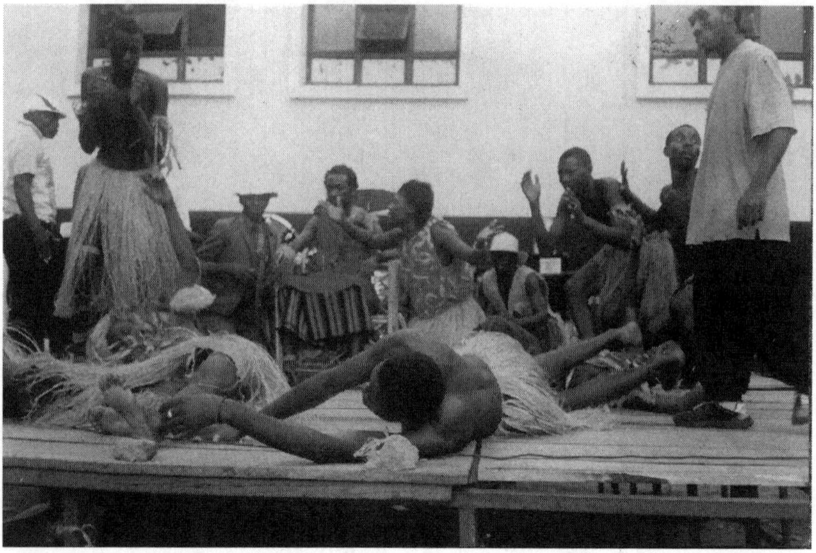

Figure 10.1. Ecological theater group Maïdeni performing in Goma, DRC on World Tree Day. Photo by Maïdeni.

more I think of them as "invisible ruins," as the cultural equivalents of the physical sites of destruction Gastón Gordillo describes as occupying liminal and contested spaces on the peripheries of empire. Indeed, Maïdeni's early oeuvre represents one of countless symbolic sites of destruction in the liminal and contested spaces on the peripheries of global conceptions of Congolese personhood. For the struggle for cultural and psychological autonomy mirrors, with alarming precision, the struggle for physical autonomy—in both, "Positive expressions of power dissolve on the imperial edge of the void: the unsettling space of friction that is internal and external to the geography of global imperial formations."[17] That the imperial edge now takes humanitarian form is, in this argument, of negligible consequence—the point is about the friction that is internal and external to geographies of dissolving power. For Maïdeni, any productive potential of this friction was engulfed by resounding silences in the now official version of its history.

Thus I return to the glossy pamphlet, in which culture is the collateral damage of politics. On the one hand, the UN's failure to reference Maïdeni's emphasis on art is logistical—words are limited, war is pressing, and after all, they set out to write about planting trees. But on the other hand, from the vantage point that culture is "constitutive of agency(ies) and politics because it provides the resources through

Figure 10.2. MONUSCO DDR/RR Bulletin, June 2017

which individuals learn how to relate to themselves, others, and the world around them," this omission is noteworthy.[18] In this context, the officious sleight of hand that substitutes facts of agency with rhetorics of conflict is an instance of washing-over more than mere detail; it is an instance of codifying desperation rather than creativity as the measure of Congolese humanity. It is, in uglier language, a systemic evisceration of personhood, for it obliterates vibrant endeavors to relate to the world with proofs of failure and inevitability. This, to borrow from David Scott, "is an experience of time standing *away*, so to speak, from its conventional embeddedness in history, its modern handmaiden, so that time and history, once barely distinguishable, seem no longer synchronized, much less synonymous, as though time had been found itself *betrayed* by history, or that history now confronted us as inauthentic time, the irreversibly lapsed time of our former anticipations of political futurity."[19] Whatever their former anticipations of political futurity may have been, Maïdeni's founders and a generation of its members have been recast from aspiring (or successful) artists to targets of disarmament, demobilization, repatriation, reintegration, and resettlement.

So why would anyone seek their old songs and plays? Or their memories for that matter? Most wouldn't. But for some these works are among the histories that, as Anne Laura Stoller suggests, "despite having been so concertedly effaced, yield new damages and renewed disparities."[20] The damage in this case is one of metanarrative, of selective silences that suture time and place into something that passes for history without raising questions of authorship. And the disparity that preoccupies me in writing this essay is the relative importance assigned to art as compared to war.

Excerpt of a Memory

This extension of my conversation with the accidental archivist was not immediately post-phone call; it was another day, weeks later. The assumption of continued anonymity was explicit, conveyed through the raising of an eyebrow, the waggle of a finger, the fleeting tension tainting an otherwise friendly smile. So I reiterated my promise. And, without prompting, s/he began:

> I got a phone call today. It was from the leader of the cultural division of an important foreign embassy. He wants to partner with my organization and support our work. I tell you this because this story is funny, and I don't want to be the only one who knows that! He certainly doesn't know. And I hope no one ever tells him.
>
> It's funny because years ago their embassy did support our work. But their employees were stealing money, so we tactfully exposed this to them [the agency] because we value transparency and would hope for the same in return. They verified the chain of corruption, verified

that we were not part of it, thanked us profusely, fired the offending employees, then blacklisted us. Through four ambassadors they have shunned us. And then the retinue changed again, perhaps in more of a hurry than usual, for it seems they forgot to gossip. Recently they hired one of our former beneficiaries as cultural attaché. Of course, they didn't make the connection—there is, after all, no record they would consider official. Because he knows what he knows (which is about our achievements, not about the "scandal"), our former beneficiary spoke highly of my organization. So the leader of the cultural division visited and was impressed and has now called me to offer support.

I said, "Thank you" and, "I'll think about it." But I didn't makc any promises. I guess he's not used to such hesitation. He said he'll call back tomorrow. Perhaps I'll answer.

But, besides making me laugh, his phone call made me think. It made me think about kinds of memory—muscle memory, institutional memory, social memory, and such; it made me wonder how many of them go both ways? How many of them are circles that repeat, and how many are one-way paths?

For some time now, I have been in search of a new strategy for responding to constant erasure. Then you came along asking about Maïdeni, digging up what now amounts to ancient history (which, as you well know, does not exist in this place until the UN, the EU, or some entity-with-the-power-to-proclaim says so). That hasn't made it easier. I wanted to have something to tell you. But I'm still thinking. I hope it's not rude, but I'm not inclined to apologize. Because it's complicated, and I'm just one person. Who am *I* to speak for a city, a region, or a country? No one, that's who!

But since you asked, I'll tell you what I do know: I have encountered two problems—the lack of references or structures that contain memories in this place, and the presence of forces that prey on that lack. I ask myself, "What is a healthy community?"—one in which history and social experiences can be passed from one generation to the next, where it is up to each generation to guard, study, and do with them what they will. But without that system, we are prey for invaders. And they are here and not afraid of their own cannibalism. (It also makes me laugh that people in the West call *us* the cannibals! But . . .)

So my puzzle is how to pass things on. And I've decided on bodies, live ones, of course, because bodies contain memories. And I want to build on the memories in the minds of people who have been witnessing from a distance. I want to build a legacy of the mind and body. I want to teach, to share skills that lead to economic autonomy, to set people free—no, more to *force* them free, to make a network that can't be blocked by the same old politics, or at least one that can be circumvented and find other living bodies on the other side, a sort of underground railroad of liberated artists. Maybe that's too much, but it seems as good a foundation for future institutions as any. And who would I be if I couldn't dream?

No, they can't eat my memories *and* my dreams.

There was a pause, a very long one. I hoped for more, but s/he said,

All this talking raises the dead. I have too much more to say to continue.

And that was that.

Resonance

I could only ever write of these accidental archivists from and through diaspora. To retrieve the melodies and lyrics of early Maïdeni songs, the synopses of plays, the reminiscence of choreographies, I had to seek out those who left. I heard from disembodied voices in Kinshasa, Belgium, Haiti, the United States. Each memory keeper I contacted was buoyed by my questions, by the notion that someone so much later wanted to know, by the fact of being found, being asked to remember. And so they laughed, for a long time, chided me on trying to scratch up "that old stuff." But the laughter and the teasing were an invitation to wait. For a very long time. To call again, and again, as connections uncannily "went bad" just in time for strategic relocations that allowed passersby to deduce that an import-person-from-America had called in need of consultation. They laughed through these negotiations of digital ethnography, affirming that the politics of position would be left unvoiced. But when the laughter finally subsided they recalled long-forgotten lyrics with remarkable speed.

It began when one of them, as a word of caution (about something entirely different), said, "Attention!" (beware) and they all erupted in laughter as, in unison, they shouted, "Kwa nyama" (of animals), then, after a beat, "kama wewe!" (like you!). I was lost. They roared with laughter then began to sing:

Le voilà venir avec machette à la main	Here he comes with a machete in his hand
Le voilà venir avec sa hache à la main	Here he comes with an ax in his hand
Pauvre bucheron ne m'abatte pas	Poor farmer, do not chop me down
Puisque demain tu vas le regretter.	Because tomorrow you'll be sorry.
Le voilà venir avec son fusil à l'épaule	Here he comes with his rifle on his shoulder
Le voilà venir avec sa lance à la main	here he comes with his spear in his hand
Pauvre braconnier ne tuez pas	Poor hunter to not kill
Puisque demain tu vas le regretter.	Because tomorrow you'll be sorry.
Ne me laissez pas, ne me quittez pas	Don't let me go, don't leave me
Puisque demain tu vas le regretter.	Because tomorrow you'll be sorry.[21]
Les parcs nationaux	The national parks
et les autres réserves forestiers	and all the other nature reserves
sont créés pour notre bien être	are created for our well-being
Protégions les forêts	Protect the forests
Ceux des montagnes	and the mountains
et surtout ceux des collines	and also the hills
qui nous protègent contre les érosions.	that spare us from erosion.
Ne fais pas semblent, je sais qui tu l'aime	Don't pretend otherwise, I know you love it [nature]
Ne fais pas semblent, je sais qui tu l'aime	Don't pretend otherwise, I know you love it
Ne fais pas semblent, je sais qui tu l'aime	Don't pretend otherwise, I know you love it
Ne fais pas semblent, je sais qui tu l'aime	Don't pretend otherwise, I know you love it
O, ne fais pas semblent	O, don't pretend otherwise[22]

Eventually they let me in on the joke. It was from one of their more popular plays, *ATASIO kwa nyama . . .* (*Animals Beware . . .*), which was one of Maïdeni's early theater pieces.[23] It is the story of a conflict between a hunter and a farmer, who accuse one another of destroying the habitats necessary for their respective survival—the hunter accuses the farmer of cutting down too many trees, thus chasing the animals away, while the farmer accuses the hunter of chasing animals into his fields, thus ruining his crops. As their conflict escalates, their families and eventually the entire region become enmeshed in mutual accusations (and much ensuing hilarity). To prevent further friction (and probable bloodshed), they are forced to seek outside council from a group of nature conservationists, who give them each instructions. The woodcutter is to be strategic when clearing new fields and to reforest treeless territories, while the hunter is only to hunt during open season, to preserve meat so he can leave animals in peace during the rest of the year, and to protect nature reserves.

Didacticism aside, what was, by their account, the most beloved part of this play was the escalating fight between farmer and hunter, which they relived boisterously, if remotely, when we spoke. The hunter, who had a reputation of never missing his target, proudly wore a jacket with the inscription, "ATASIO kwa nyama,"—prominently featuring a phonetic misspelling of the French *attention* (beware)—to warn animals of his legendary skill. When confronted by the farmer, the hunter warned his foe to read his jacket, shouting "Attention kwa nyama," simultaneously threatening and insulting the farmer. But the farmer's witty retort, "kama wewe" (like you), reversed the insult and fueled the feud. As crowds gathered around their escalating fight, the hunter threatened to shoot the farmer like prey, while the farmer threatened to chop the hunter like a tree. And the crowds, eventually including the audience, continued to chant "Attention kwa nyama . . . kama wewe!"

This refrain outlived the play. It became the tagline of an expanding network of neighborhoods, an inside joke that surreptitiously inducted the city into ecological activity.[24] It reverberated as a growing number of people planted trees—first (and then again, and again) on Mt. Goma, then later (and even still) on the city's public streets and boulevards; it reverberated through conferences organized by Maïdeni, echoed in the tree nursery they launched. It proved, to anyone listening, that art had power.

And *ATASIO kwa nyama* was not Maïdeni's only success. They had a number of popular songs, each with its own function. Their anthem, for example, was an excerpt of text published in the Virunga Katchetche's quarterly *Revue Katchetche*, set to music by founding Maïdeni member Jules Tulinabo:

Verse:	Verse:
Sachant que l'homme dépend	Remember that humans depend
des diverses éléments de la nature	on nature's diverse elements
Nous devons nous unir	We must unite
pour lutter contre ces services qui	for the fight against
détruisent . . .	destruction . . .
Cœurs:	Chorus:
cette nature . . .	The natural world . . .
Cette nature dans son état naturel	In its natural state
Cette nature dans son état naturel	In its natural state
Verse:	Verse:
O Maïdeni,	O Maïdeni,
que ta voix et la mienne	that together our voices, yours and mine
Puisse être entendu	can be heard
Par tous ces nobles gens	by noble people everywhere
Et au-delà de la terre.	and in the heavens.

In retrospect, they laugh abashedly at the lyrics (and at their adolescent enthusiasm for them, which they frame as a colonially imposed infatuation with French). But they remember the words verbatim. Indeed, the chorus of this anthem, like the punchline of *ATASIO kwa nyama*, was another refrain that entered the popular musical lexicon of the city at the time, insinuating environmentally conscious ideas into everyday conversation via music, however pedantic the text.

There was also a rap, written and performed by Petna Ndaliko Katondolo (another founding member of Maïdeni), that did much to persuade young people that ecological conservation was cool. The accidental archivists erupted into a frenzy of enthusiasm describing—but not performing—this rap, conveying (with the Kinande equivalent of scatting) the song's lyric virtuosity if, inadvertently, also conveying that, unlike the anthem, it did not have a memorable refrain. Indeed, it took weeks for the accidental archivists to piece the lyrics back together. And they're still not convinced they got it all quite right, but they did share this short excerpt:

Oko wetu tukanasata	Back home [in the village] we danced
itune mutimba oko muliro	circling the fire
itune muvuwa tuti kikumutiu.	singing in unison.[25]

These songs existed. And in a manner of speaking, they still do—if I could find them, so could others. But in another manner of speaking they are, effectively, extinct, because who would think to look for them? There is no repository for the scraps and detritus of culture that—both before and during the wars—provide the resources through which individuals learn how to relate to themselves, others, and the world around them. So performing commemoration is, in this case, a multiparty Skype call, a digitally orchestrated fleeting moment of disparate resonance that sutured time to space for those who remembered the songs. That is, until the connection, once again, "went bad."

Decay

For the record: I am not arguing that the oeuvres of aspiring adolescent artists necessarily warrant archival preservation in Congo or anywhere else. My point is not about specific works but about compound erasure. It is one thing for Maïdeni's repertoire to remain unknown; the consequences of that, while regrettable for reasons of nostalgia and mirth, are comparatively few. It is another thing entirely for the *fact* of Maïdeni's existence, and that of the many other local organizations in Kivu (then and now) that address violence through art, to go uncommemorated. That erasure has consequences. It allows the world to perceive the region as one of uninterrupted warfare, as one in which things happen to people and not vice versa, as one in which help, of any kind, is better than nothing. But that perception is the blueprint for a lethal and self-fulfilling diagnosis that leaves Congo perpetually exploited by people who choose to think they are helping.[26] The plays of Maïdeni could have taught otherwise, could have provided clever examples of local strategies that address both human and material problems. But they—and all but a few lingering memories of them—no longer exist. What is worse, they have been hermetically sealed over by the "international community's" official translation of "History."

There is more than one register of violence in such compound erasure. Like the colonial violence traced by Tansi and Mbembe, compound erasures of creativity, on whatever scale, commit "'violence in regards to the past' . . . which is 'emptied of all substance'; and violence and insult in relation to the future."[27] For, like the colonial regime, charity "offers itself as having to be eternal."[28] To wit, Maïdeni is emptied of art and instead, the perpetual demobilization of violent rebels becomes the highest imagined aspiration. And the UN graciously foots the bill.

Telling—and believing—such stories is a form of precipitated decay that erodes from without and from within. It is an act of retroactively coagulating selective facts into official truths to negate the possibility of being human in this place. This is nothing new. In so many words, every generation's liberationist intellectuals have insisted that "memory, remembrance, and forgetting are powerful systems of representation and, strictly speaking also symptomatic acts."[29] In this case, the systems of representation curated by mutually destructive versions of the past are symptomatic not only of power and domination, but also of a festering war on autonomy and creativity. Unfortunately for the artists, pity sells better than plays. And while I am not convinced that a handful of songs, poems, or theater pieces would change the pattern of compound erasure, they might at least create subtle dissonances, they might at least expose that in this context, decay, like ruin, is a "vibrantly violent" active verb.[30] Or, as one accidental archivist put it, "How many times must we fight over the same trees?"

Resonance (Reprieve)

My conversations with the accidental archivists were wrought with nostalgia, but also with a disarming resonance. It is a kind of resonance that animates memory: "an intensely bodily, spatial, political affair"; a kind of resonance that, although not synonymous, is the closest I have seen to a performance of commemoration in Kivu.[31] Of course, technically it did not happen in Kivu, but never mind. It was still tied to place, despite distance, exile, and time.

The accidental archivists' disarming resonance triggered the second sensation I want to evoke in this essay: that of concentrated dissipation, that force field of energy—amplified, but severed from source—which must stand in for home in conditions of exile. It is the pulsing, throbbing vigilance required to survive diaspora, the "ever-gathering accretion of force-relations" that erupts on contact with anyone who remembers.[32] This is the silent code of conduct animating those many lonely bodies who occupy what Paul Gilroy calls the "historical rift between the location of residence and the location of belonging."[33] It triggers tears of laughter in the face of crisis, shared lexicons of taste, and, among other things, what no one would dare voice as a lethal longing for home—concentrated dissipation. The bodies have left, so the memories have fortified, the performances of place intensified.

To my ear, these accidental archivists' disarming resonance is the residue of creativity uncommemorated. And, as it was for James Baldwin, "Music is [their] witness, and [their] ally. The beat is the confession which recognizes, changes, and conquers time. Then, history becomes a garment [they] can wear and share, and not a cloak in which to hide; and time becomes a friend."[34] I heard such a beat in my many conversations with the accidental archivists. It was the invisible conductor synchronizing their breath (and their songs) despite technology's many flaws; it is what allowed them to bellow into mobile apps on disparate continents, knowing in their bones that the others were dancing along, that being off-key is less important than being alive. It is more than a pulse or a memory. It has congealed into a way of being, of being away.

But such resonance is disorienting. It is not unique to Congo or to "postcolonies." It is, instead, both symptom and proof of Scott's assertion that

> the existential rhythms of [the] enduring relation between past, present, and future have been broken—or, at least, they somehow have been very significantly interrupted. So much so that now remains from the past stick unaccountably to the hinges of the temporality we hitherto relied on to furnish ourselves with the confidence that we are in fact going somewhere—somewhere other and maybe *better* than where we currently are. Time, in short, has become less yielding, less promising than we have grown to expect it should be. And what we are left with are *aftermaths* in which the present seems stricken with immobility and pain and ruin; a certain experience of temporal *afterness* prevails in which the trace of futures past hangs like the remnant of a voile curtain over what feels uncannily like an endlessly extending present.[35]

The accidental archivists' endlessly extending present is subsumed by cycles of choreographed decay and by the palindrome of commemoration in Congo, where time is regularly betrayed by history. Because I asked, they sutured a story with roots in Maïdeni. Perhaps it is true, but more importantly, they say it did them good to remember.

Chances are good that they will never see each other again. Some of them do not have the money to travel, others are denied visas, life expectancy is what it is for those who have lived through too many wars. And besides, they are all Black in a world of hate. One of them was attacked between interviews, put into a coma for days, hanging in the precarity of the ICU, his/her future and past equally uncertain. S/he survived. And, among other things, s/he wrote me a letter. About what it meant to be in Maïdeni. Because it was life changing. Regardless of who remembers.

Obviously, I will keep that letter.

Afterness

This essay has no conclusion. Instead it has remnants suspended somewhere between time and imagination (my own and others'), remnants harbored in mediums—story, gesture, implication, mirth—that remain displaced.

In one version of the future there is an "archive," a digital repository for a voluminous and far-flung collection of materials documenting the last three decades of art and culture in North Kivu. But archives are suspect, curious, and precarious. They are, in this case, contingent—dependent on accident or institution. And, in every case, they are contingent on political will.

Should it come to fruition, I envision my archive as a trace of futures past, a dissensual portal into pasts (temporal and geographic) that further unravel rather than suture metanarrative; I imagine it as a virtual operating theater in which the accidental archivists could, however briefly, become oneirocritics, dream catchers, politically infused artists of a disparately collective social imaginary and memory of their own making.

But time has indeed become less promising, as have accidents and institutions. So I have my doubts. And I know that, in another version of the future, there is no such thing as posterity for the accidental archivists; that what remains will shrink to the glimpses curated in this essay. So I include a page from *Homeless,* a play written, from exile, about refugees.[36] I came across this page when interviewing an accidental archivist who happened to have a keen memory for dialogue (s/he indicated it was page 17 or thereabouts). And I laughed aloud because its title strikes me as a prescient ode to the irony of displacement that riddles commemoration of people, things, and thoughts in this place. Whether or not that is accidental is, among other things, a matter of opinion.

Homeless: Page 17 (or Thereabouts)

[Midday, main office of the United Nations High Commission of Refugees (UNHCR), capital city of unidentified "war-torn" "African" country.]

UNHCR OFFICER (LOOKING DOWN, WRITING IN A CASE FILE): Name?

[CAMP REFUGEE, URBAN REFUGEE, RAPED GIRL, and others stare silently at UNCHR OFFICER until he eventually looks up and makes brief eye-contact]

UNHCR OFFICER: Name?
UNHCR OFFICER (BECOMING IMPATIENT): Name?!
CAMP REFUGEE: Me no namei
UNCHR (INCREASINGLY FRUSTRATED): Name!
URBAN REFUGEE: Refugee
UNHCR OFFICER: Name!
CAMP REFUGEE: Me don't want iti
UNHCR OFFICER: Name!
URBAN REFUGEE: UN shamba boy
UNHCR OFFICER: Name!
CAMP REFUGEE: Tent too coldi
UNHCR OFFICER: Name!
RAPED GIRL: IMF
UNHCR OFFICER: I see, economic refugee. Ok, let's do this: what made you leave your country?
URBAN REFUGEE: They did.
UNHCR OFFICER: Who "they" is?
URBAN REFUGEE: Those who did.
UNHCR OFFICER: Did what?
URBAN REFUGEE: Made me leave.
UNHCR OFFICER: It's 12 o'clock. You're eating into my lunch time. Shall we resume this at 4? Shall we?

[Officer exits, Refugees freeze]

Notes

1. This essay is specifically about the North and South Kivu provinces in the east of the Democratic Republic of the Congo. North and South Kivu are

mineral-rich, conflict-ridden regions; they are culturally distinct from Kinshasa and other part of the DRC. See Chérie Rivers Ndaliko, *Necessary Noise: Music, Film, and Charitable Imperialism in the east of Congo* (New York: Oxford University Press, 2016).

2. Achille Mbembe, *Critique of Black Reason* (Durham, NC: Duke University Press, 2017), 5.

3. Maïdeni stands for Mouvement et Actions Intellectuels pour le Développement Ecologiques des Naturalistes Intégré. Founding members include (alphabetically): Batumike Chambu, Jackie Kasana, Kanz Mangolopa, Allyn Masheke, Petna Ndaliko Katondolo, Jules Tulinabo, Touvé Wunde, and Chantalle Zabibu.

4. Ndaliko, *Necessary Noise*, 33.

5. Most of these songs and music videos have been lost; surviving examples include "Safari Africa" by Popal Isse, and "Twaomba Amani" by Mack el Sambo.

6. Filip De Boeck, "Beyond the Grave: History, Memory and Death in Postcolonial Congo/Zaïre," in *Memory and the Postcolony*, ed. Richard Werbner (London: Zed Books, 1998), 33.

7. De Boeck, "Beyond the Grave," 26.

8. A note on language: my conversations with the accidental archivists moved fluidly between Kiswahili, French, and English. At their request, the specific stories included in this essay were told in English. I have edited them minimally, to reduce redundancies of spoken dialogue. Lyrics and other details about performances were conveyed to me in French and Kiswahili, and I have provided transcriptions of the original as well as my own translations.

9. There are many examples of politically motivated destruction of archival collections in Congo, including the collection of audio recordings, musical instruments, and field notes compiled by musician and ethnomusicologist Ray Lema, which was destroyed by Mobutu's regime in the 1970s before Lema was forced into exile.

10. One example, of many, was the looting of Marc Colignon's private collection of audio and video materials documenting experimental and cross-cultural musical productions held in Kinshasa, which was looted by the president's special guard (Special Presidential Division) under Mobutu.

11. In the east of Congo, local institutions face a number of challenges that impact their ability to maintain records. They are often forced to relocate without notice, and they are targets of looting and theft as rebel armies temporarily overtake cities. Due to these and other factors, many of the records housed at the Yole!Africa cultural center, including those referred to in this essay, have been lost or destroyed.

12. In many parts of Congo, the history of colonial extraction of artworks to supply museums in Europe has strongly influenced local understandings of institutional efforts to preserve material culture.

13. In addition to many performances in Goma, Maïdeni also performed in Bukavu and Rutchuru.

14. I am referencing Ann Laura Stoler's definition of "ruination," which she argues "is more than a process that sloughs off debris as a by-product. It is also a *political project* that lays waste to certain peoples, relations, and things that accumulate in specific places." See "Introduction. 'The Rot Remains': From

Ruin to Ruination," in *Imperial Debris: On Ruins and Ruination,* ed. Ann Laura Stoler (Durham, NC: Duke University Press, 2013), 11. For more on ruination in the context of commemoration in Congo see Chérie Rivers Ndaliko, "In the Presence of Absence: Commemoration and Disavowal in Congo," *Critical Inquiry* 44, no. 4 (2018): 766–80.

15. MONUSCO DDR/RR, "La reduction des violences communautaires au Nord Kivu," *Bulletin de la RVC* 1 (July 2017): 1.

16. Part of the Virunga Katchetche project was to create clubs at middle schools and high schools. Maïdeni's activities increased the popularity of these clubs in Goma.

17. Gastón Gordillo, "The Void: Invisible Ruins on the Edges of Empire," in Stoler, *Imperial Debris,* 228.

18. Henry Giroux, "Public Pedagogy as Cultural Politics," in *Without Guarantees: In Honor of Stuart Hall,* ed. Paul Gilroy, Lawrence Grossberg, and Angela McRobbie (London: Verso, 2000), 141.

19. See David Scott, *Omens of Adversity: Tragedy, Time, Memory, Justice* (Durham, NC: Duke University Press, 2014), 2.

20. Stoler, "Introduction," 7.

21. This verse is written from the point of view of nature.

22. This verse is written from the point of view of nature.

23. *ATASIO kwa nyama* was written by Petna Ndaliko Katondolo with music by Jules Tulinabo.

24. Like all of Maïdeni's plays, *ATTASIO kwa nyama* was performed in many locations throughout Goma, including schools, popular churches and cathedrals, Cap Tureko (a VIP theater owned by a prominent Protestant group), and the Katchetche conservation institute.

25. The notion of unity conveyed in this lyric builds on its double meaning in Kinande, which includes both synchronicity and literal togetherness as well as the practice of engaging in community debate to agree (or not) on ideas.

26. See Ndaliko, *Necessary Noise.*

27. Mbembe, *Critique of Black Reason,* 106, citing Tansi.

28. Mbembe, *Critique of Black Reason,* 106.

29. Mbembe, *Critique of Black Reason,* 104.

30. Stoler, "Introduction," 9.

31. Gastón Gordillo, "Resonance and the Egyptian Revolution," *Space and Politics* (blog), 2011, accessed April 17, 2018, http://spaceandpolitics.blogspot.com/2011/02/resonance-and-egyptian-revolution.html

32. Melissa Gregg and Gregory J. Seigworth, eds., *The Affect Theory Reader* (Durham, NC: Duke University Press, 2010), 2.

33. Paul Gilroy, "Diaspora," *Paragraph* 3, no. 17 (2010): 7.

34. James Baldwin, "Of the Sorrow Songs: The Cross of Redemption," *Views of Black American Music* 2 (1984–85): 12.

35. Scott, *Omens of Adversity,* 6.

36. *Homeless* was written and directed by Petna NdalikoKatondolo in Kampala, Uganda, in 2001.

Afterword

Musical Commemoration and the Imagination of the Future

KAY KAUFMAN SHELEMAY

On Sunday, March 31, 2019, the American rapper Nipsey Hussle was murdered in front of the Marathon clothing store he owned in his South Los Angeles neighborhood. Widely known for his Grammy-nominated 2018 debut album, *Victory Lap*, Hussle, who was of Eritrean descent and whose given name was Ermias Asghedom, had devoted a great deal of time and resources during his brief musical career to caring for others and, most particularly, to revitalizing his neighborhood. At his funeral ceremony, titled a "Celebration of Life" and held at LA's Staples Center two weeks after his death, Hussle's hits were played along with a live performance of Stevie Wonder's "Rocket Love," as friends, family, and community remembered Hussle's legacy of engaged action and generosity.[1] Yet a week earlier, Hussle's life, music, and roots in the African Horn had already been commemorated in Addis Ababa, Ethiopia, by his numerous admirers there.[2] In this case, the fast-moving communication networks of the twenty-first century ensured that a ceremony of commemoration had already been held half a world away, in fact predating the late rapper's funeral.

Over the course of time and across the globe, commemorative events have been ubiquitous in human life, sparked by traumatic events such as acts of war, massacres of entire populations, and uncountable other instances of aggression and violence. As each of these events becomes part of individual and collective memory, it gives rise to a range of cultural practices. The authors of the essays in this volume perform a dual act of commemoration, remembering many violent events as well as the performances intended to revive them in memory. In response to the volume editors' query, "What is it to perform commemoration?," these essays interrogate the role of musical performance in sustaining memories of trauma, the manner in which these memories have informed concepts of history, and the myriad ways in which so many of these commemorations have been politically driven.

Commemoration must be acknowledged as a core need of human emotional life that resolves the primal anxiety that individuals, as well as the communities of which they are a part, will be forgotten over time. As a result, commemoration emerges as a theme inspiring musical expression found across most temporal and spatial borders, providing solace worldwide. All of the essays in this volume share deep concerns with commemoration's role in preserving the past, and most explore memory, both implicitly and explicitly, in its evolving relationship to history. The examples here are quite rich and transcend expressive genres and media. Studies of trauma, survival, and musical commemoration in the first section include contrasting multiple examples drawn from "a long tradition in Western music" (Fauser); traces of Holocaust historicity turned "inside out" in performances of Ullmann's melodrama (P. Bohlman); and music composed and performed to recall "the Apocalypse" that marked the 1945 destruction of Hiroshima and Nagasaki by atomic bombs (Manabe). The second group of essays link mediation, memory, and musical reenactment, including music commissioned to invoke and preserve memory of the violent 1994 destruction of a Jewish community center in Argentina (Wohl); the revival of guilty memories of a Palestinian massacre cloaked by amnesia, subsequently awakened by sounds heard in a music-laden film (Figueroa); and the use of musical commemoration "to restore and reclaim" individual and collective memories of persecution shared by African Americans, but erased over the course of time (Mosley). Four final essays gathered under the rubric of "Trauma's Persistence and the Politics of Reenactment" include a pilgrimage punctuated by musical events mounted to commemorate the pathways of refugees from Syria crossing Europe during the 2016 crisis (Agnew); the "overwriting of sound" in efforts to upend historical repetition in Poland, along with an effort to dispel musical monumentality while drawing on many modes of musical style in service of commemoration (A. Bohlman); memorial ceremonies at the centennial of the Armernian genocide incorporating compositions by Armenian composers and others whose works have over time come to be broadly associated with remembrance (Alajaji); and finally, the withholding of commemoration as both a strategy of political protest as well as a result of ongoing natural and human-made disasters among those seeking to recognize the impact of the Rwandan genocide in the DRC (Ndaliko).

Commemoration is at its essence a retrospective act, inevitably looking backward to perpetuate traces of events, communities, and individuals at risk of falling out of memory. Approaches to commemoration tend to correspond to retrospective approaches to memory itself, despite the fact that every memory of the past is in fact recreated in the present.[3] Similarly, a core purpose of the public performance of commemoration is to ensure that a memory will be sustained, rendering performance not just about the past event and the present moment, but intending it to echo into the future.

Although this volume does not, with the exception of Figueroa's discussion of the use of sound to trigger both episodic and semantic memory, explore the technical workings of music and memory, it does suggest some exciting new directions in that domain. Recent experimental studies in psychology suggest that memory plays an important role in shaping the imagination and future thinking, revealing "striking similarities between remembering the past and imagining or simulating the future, including the finding that a common brain network underlies both memory and imagination."[4] We can therefore begin to ask what potential these essays hold for interrogating the impact of musical commemoration on the future of performers and the traditions they enact, as well as on listeners. I would like to contribute two brief examples suggesting how commemorative performances speak both to the past and to the future, the first from a repertory of hymns transmitted by Jews of Syrian descent, and the second drawn from a recently composed "secular choral requiem."

In the Syrian Jewish hymn tradition known as the *pizmonim*, individual names are embedded within sung Hebrew poetic texts, in acrostics, and in dedications preceding the songs.[5] In her essay, Imani Danielle Mosley elucidates how the Say Her Name movement has introduced the speaking of black women's names as antidote to oppression of black women and their historical erasure. In my own work on the Syrian Jewish *pizmonim*, the inclusion of names in texts of Hebrew paraliturgical hymns transmitted over the centuries by Jews originally from Aleppo plays a central, if somewhat different role in commemoration. I have found that the inclusion of names of community members provides a mechanism through which both past individual lives are being commemorated and members of the broader community are recalled as well as carried forward into the future. While women's names are only rarely found in Syrian *pizmon* song texts, men's names are commonly found, and their use can be seen to shift over the years during commemorative performances.[6]

We have already read that commemorations assume different shapes over time, standing in relationship to processes such as "overwriting" as discussed by A. Bohlman in her essay. A close look at a single repertory, however, can also reveal how the future listener reinterprets the music performed, effectively overwriting it from the perspective of his or her own experience.

Apart from the relationship of this practice to centuries-old traditions using transformations of words, names, and numbers to link Jewish mysticism with everyday praxis, the presence of names included within song texts link a particular hymn to the individual and family who commissioned the song. For some years, and certainly during the lives of its dedicatee, a song is heard as belonging to the individual to whom it is dedicated; thus a song dedicated to Joseph will be informally referred to as "Joe's *pizmon*," or whatever the name of the person for whom it was composed. A hymn can become more deeply commemorative after the death of the dedicatee, recalling for listeners the deceased individual's life and for some, the occasion for which it was initially composed. But in the future, as years move on, it also is possible for other unrelated individuals to "sing themselves into the song." On some occasions, a man who shares the name, such as Joseph, found in the text will sing the song, and thereby establish a new relationship of the song to himself. This practice is so common that certain verses in songs of some antiquity are reserved for individuals who share a name found within it; after their death, the verse will pass to another person with the same name. Commemorating individuals in songs therefore moves from a textual practice to a performative practice over time. It also becomes a social mechanism through which personal names are both recalled and ritually extended to a subsequent generation, ensuring the presence and performance of the name well into the future.[7]

For a second example, I wish to recall an evening in February 2019 when I attended the East Coast premiere of a secular choral requiem by Los Angeles–based composer Dale Trumbore.[8] The work, titled *How to Go On*, drawn from a poem by Barbara Crooker, commemorates the death of a loved one by asking a profound question about the future: "How can we go on, knowing the end of the story?" Thus this requiem, and its performance, commemorate the most devastating personal losses, evoking memories while simultaneously asking how the moment of performance prepares one for the future.[9] Recognizing that every story will at some point come to an end, Trumbore's composition "answers this question in eight movements that explore our relationship to life and loss, ranging from doubt and introspection to ultimate acceptance of our own mortality."

One might want to argue that commemorative performance of all sorts seeks to imagine the end of remembrance and to construct a future that is reconciled to endings. Indeed, we find this theme woven as a subtle thread throughout much of the fabric of this volume. In her essay, Wohl suggests that when performed in the aftermath of violence, an anthem "demands the attention of the listener, commands belief, and provides a new constellation of possibilities for a better future." Likewise, in describing the sound worlds evoked in concerts commemorating the Armenian genocide, Alajaji writes, "What emerges in these concerts is a 'geography of political possibility.'" Philip Bohlman suggests that "new processes of history form around, and intersect with, the performance of commemoration," transforming themselves to constitute "revival moments." Agnew's reference to "prosthetic memory" opens a path toward the future by suggesting that commemoration potentially contributes to "a new form of public history that generalizes empathy and contributes to a more capacious public sphere" and, through repetition, renders the "original event productive for the future."

In closing, it is sure that performers will continue to remember events through musical performance and that music scholars will continue to write about this ubiquitous phenomenon, themselves contributing to ongoing processes of commemoration.

Notes

1. Jamil Smith, "At the Nipsey Hussle Memorial Service, Tears and Smiles in Equal Measure," *Rolling Stone*, April 12, 2019, https://www.rollingstone.com/music/music-news/nipsey-hussle-memorial-service-821475/

2. Liben Eabisa, "In Ethiopia Candlelight Vigil Held for Slain Eritrean American Artist Nipsey Hussle; April 7, 2019, http://www.tadias.com/04/07/2019/in-ethiopia-candelight-vigil-held-for-slain-eritrean-american-artist-nipsey-hussle/

3. See Kay Kaufman Shelemay, *Let Jasmine Rain Down: Song and Remembrance among Syrian Jews* (Chicago: University of Chicago Press, 1998), 8, for a discussion of the importance of the context of the moment of retrieval for understanding memory, drawing on Daniel L. Schacter, *Searching for Memory: The Brain, the*

Mind, and the Past (Cambridge, MA: Harvard University Press, 1996), 105.

4. Daniel L. Schacter, Donna Rose Addis, Demis Hassabis, Victoria C. Martin, R. Nathan Spreng, and Karl K. Szpunar, "The Future of Memory: Remembering, Imagining, and the Brain," *Neuron Review* 76.4 (2012): 677.

5. Shelemay, *Let Jasmine Rain Down.*

6. See Kay Kaufman Shelemay, "The Power of Silent Voices Women in the Syrian Musical Tradition," in *Music and the Play of Power in the Middle East, North Africa and Central Asia,* ed. Laudan Nooshin (Burlington, VT: Ashgate, 2009), 269–88, for several examples of veiled references to women and the use of women's names in *pizmon* texts.

7. Shelemay, *Let Jasmine Rain Down,* 45–48.

8. Information about the performance and the texts performed is drawn from Mary Galstian's program notes for the concert. The performance by the Harvard-Radcliffe Collegium Musicum also included commemorative choral works by Claudio Monterverdi (*Sestina: Lagrime d'amante al sepolcro dell'amata,* 1614) and Ildebrando Pizzetti (*Messa di Requiem,* 1922). Monterverdi's collection of six madrigals "traces its main character, Glauco, through a series of intense, fantasy-laden moments at the grave of his beloved, Corinna. In Glauco's universe, the death of his love consumes the attention of the heavens and the earth—nymphs come out of the trees, and the muses are beckoned for their tears." In a 1949 interview, Pizzetti "found meaning in setting the text in a style that harkened back to the flowing, contrapuntal melodies of the Renaissance."

9. P. Bohlman recognizes in his essay that "the task of commemoration is profoundly linked to death."

Bibliography

Adelson, Leslie. "Touching Tales of Turks, Germans, and Jews: Cultural Alterity, Historical Narrative, and Literary Riddles for the 1990s." *New German Critique* 80, "Special Issue on the Holocaust" (Spring–Summer 2000): 93–124.

Adorno, Theodor W. "Cultural Criticism and Society." In *Prisms*. Cambridge, MA: MIT Press, 1981.

African American Policy Forum. "#SAYHERNAME: An Evening of Arts and Action." *African American Policy Forum*, March 28, 2017. https://livestream.com/accounts/5045103/events/6767114/videos/152886258/

African American Policy Forum. "Statement: Say Her Name | The Mothers Behind the Movement." *The African American Policy Forum*, December 3, 2018. http://aapf.org/2018/2018/12/statement-say-her-name-the-mothers-behind-the-movement

Agnew, Vanessa. "History's Affective Turn: Historical Reenactment and Its Work in the Present." *Rethinking History* 11, no. 3 (2007): 299–312.

Agnew, Vanessa. "What Is Reenactment?" *Criticism* 46, no. 3 (2004): 327–39.

Akçam, Taner. *A Shameful Act: The Armenian Genocide and the Question of Turkish Responsibility*. New York: Henry Holt and Company, 2006.

Alajaji, Sylvia Angelique. *Music and the Armenian Diaspora: Searching for Home in Exile*. Bloomington: Indiana University Press, 2015.

Al-Hout, Bayan Nuwayhed. *Sabra and Shatila: September 1982*. Ann Arbor, MI: Pluto Press, 2004.

Allen, James. *Without Sanctuary: Lynching Photography in America*. Santa Fe, NM: Twin Palms, 2000.

Althusser, Louis. *On the Reproduction of Capitalism: Ideology and Ideological State Apparatuses*. Translated by G. M. Goshgarian. New York: Verso, 2014.

Anderson, Ben. *Encountering Affect: Capacities, Apparatuses, Conditions*. London: Routledge, 2014.

Anderson, Benedict. *Imagined Communities: Reflection on the Origin and Spread of Nationalism*. Rev. ed. New York: Verso, 2006.

Andermahr, Sonya, ed. *Decolonizing Trauma Studies: Trauma and Postcolonialism*. Special issue of *Humanities*. Basel: MDPI, 2016.

Andraschke, Peter. "Bohuslav Martinů: Musik gegen Krieg und Zerstörung." In

Glasba in Družba v 20. Stoletju / Music and Society in the 20th Century. Ljubljana, Slovenske Konjice, 12.–15. V. 1998, edited by Primož Kuret, 128–39. Ljubljana: Festival Ljubljana, 1999.

Applegate, Celia, and Pamela Potter. "Germans as the People of Music: Genealogy of an Identity." In *Music and German National Identity,* edited by Celia Applegate and Pamela Potter, 1–35. Chicago: University of Chicago Press, 2002.

Arendt, Hannah. *The Origins of Totalitarianism.* New York: Harvest, 1966.

Arns, Inke. "History Will Repeat Itself: Strategies of Reenactment in Contemporary (Media) Art and Performance." In *History Will Repeat Itself,* edited by Inke Arns and Gabriele Horn, 37–63. Frankfurt am Main: Revolver Press, 2007.

Aslanian, Sebouh D. "From 'Autonomous' to 'Interactive' Histories: World History's Challenge to Armenian Studies." In *An Armenian Mediterranean: Words and Worlds in Motion,* edited by Kathryn Babayan and Michael Pifer, 81–125. London: Palgrave Macmillan, 2018.

Aslanian, Sebouh D. "The Marble of Armenian History: Or Armenian History as World History." *Études arméniennes contemporaines* 4 (2014): 129–42.

Assmann, Aleida. *Cultural Memory and Western Civilization: Functions, Media, Archives.* Cambridge: Cambridge University Press, 2011.

Bakalian, Anny. *Armenian-Americans: From Being to Feeling Armenian.* New Brunswick, NJ: Transaction Publishers, 1993.

Bakhtin, Mikhail. 1984. *Rabelais and His World.* Translated by Hélène Iswolsky. Bloomington: Indiana University Press.

Baldwin, James. "Of the Sorrow Songs: The Cross of Redemption." *Views of Black American Music* 2 (1984–85): 7–12.

Bamji, Andrew. *Faces from the Front: Harold Gillies, the Queen's Hospital, Sidcup and the Origins of Modern Plastic Surgery.* London: Helion and Company, 2017.

Barnaby, Andrew. "The Psychoanalytic Origins of Literary Trauma Studies." In *Trauma and Literature,* edited by J. Roger Kurtz, 21–35. Philadelphia: Drexel University Press, 2016.

Bartoszewski, Władysław. *Dni walczącej stolicy.* Warsaw: Wydawnictwa ALFA, 1989.

Béhague, Gerard, and Irma Ruiz. "Argentina." *Grove Music Online.* January 20, 2001.

Benjamin, Walter. *Gesammelte Schriften.* With Theodor W. Adorno and Gershom Scholem, edited by Rolf Tiedemann and Hermann Schweppenhäuser. Frankfurt am Main: Suhrkamp, 1974.

Benjamin, Walter. "Toys and Play." In *Selected Writings,* translated by Rodney Livingstone, vol. 2, edited by Michael W. Jennings, Howard Eiland, and Gary Smith. Cambridge: Belknap Press, 2005.

Bennet, Rachel E. "Staging Auschwitz, Making Witnesses: Performances between History, Memory, and Myth." In *History, Memory, Performance,* edited by David M. Dean, Yana Meerzon, and Kathryn Prince, 153–68. New York: Palgrave Macmillan, 2015.

Berliner, David. "The Abuses of Memory: Reflections on the Memory Boom in Anthropology." *Anthropological Quarterly* 78, no. 1 (2005): 197–211.

Best, Nicholas. *The Greatest Day in History: How, on the Eleventh Hour on the Eleventh*

Day of the Eleventh Month, the First World War Finally Came to an End. New York: Public Affairs, 2008.

Binyon, Laurence. *Selected Poems.* New York: Macmillan, 1922.

Birdsall, Carolyn. *Nazi Soundscapes: Sound, Technology, and Urban Space in Germany, 1933–45.* Amsterdam: Amsterdam University Press, 2012.

Biskupski, M. B. B. *Independence Day: Myth, Symbol, and the Creation of Modern Poland.* Oxford: Oxford University Press, 2012.

Black, Amanda M., and Andrea F. Bohlman. "Resounding the Campus: Pedagogy, Race, and the Environment." *Journal of Music History Pedagogy* 8, no. 1 (2017): 6–27.

Bohlman, Andrea F., and Philip V. Bohlman. "Uncovering Hanns Eisler's *Hollywood Liederbuch.*" *Danish Yearbook of Musicology* 35 (2017): 13–29.

Bohlman, Philip V. "Auf der Bima / Auf der Bühne—Zur Emanzipation der jüdischen Popularmusik un die Jahrhundertwende in Wien." In *Vergleichend-systematische Musikwissenschaft: Beiträge zu Methode und Problematik der systematischen, ethnologischen und historischen Musikwissenschaft,* edited by Elisabeth. T. Hilscher and Theophil Antonicek, 417–49. Tutzing: Hans Schneider, 1994.

Bohlman, Philip V. "'Das Lied ist aus': The Final Resting Place along Music's Endless Journey." In *Music and Displacement: Diasporas, Mobilities, and Dislocations in Europe and Beyond,* edited by Erik Levi and Florian Scheding, 15–30. Lanham, MD: Scarecrow Press, 2010.

Bohlman, Philip V. "Dynamic Diasporas: 'The Song of Zion' in South Asia." In *Sounding Cities: Auditory Transformations in Berlin, Chicago, and Kolkata,* edited by Sebastian Klotz, Philip V. Bohlman, and Lars-Christian Koch, 155–78. Berlin: Lit Verlag, 2018.

Bohlman, Philip V. "How to Get Out of Here: Sounding Silence in the Jewish Cabaretesque." "The Sound Issue," edited by Johnathan M. Hess and Laura S. Lieber, special issue, *AJS Perspectives,* Spring–Summer 2016, 20–21.

Bohlman, Philip V. "Jüdische Lebenswelten zwischen Utopie und Heterotopie, jüdische Musik zwischen Schtetl und Ghetto." *Lied und populäre Kultur/Song and Popular Culture: Jahrbuch des Deutschen Volksliedarchiv* 47 (2002): 25–54.

Bohlman, Philip V. *The Music of European Nationalism: Cultural Identity and Modern History.* Denver, CO: ABC-CLIO, 2004.

Bohlman, Philip V., and Brian Currid. "Suturing History, Healing Europe: German National Temporality in Wolokalamsk Highway." *Musical Quarterly* 85, no. 4 (2001): 681–717.

Booker, Bryan D. *African Americans in the United States Army in World War II.* Jefferson, NC: McFarland, 2008,

Bor, Josef. *Theresienstadt Requiem.* Translated by Gerald Turner. Göttingen: Wallstein, 2010.

Born, Georgina. "Introduction: Music, Sound, and the Transformations of Public and Private Experience." In *Music, Sound and Space: Transformations of Public and Private Experience,* edited by Georgina Born, 1–70. Cambridge: Cambridge University Press, 2013.

Bowan, Kate. "R. G. Collingwood, Historical Reenactment and the Early Music Revival." In *Historical Reenactment: From Realism to the Affective Turn,* edited by Ian McCalman and Paul Pickering, 134–58. London: Palgrave Macmillan, 2010.

Boyle, Deirdre. "Shattering Silence: Traumatic Memory and Re-enactment in Rithy Panh's *S-21: The Khmer Rouge Killing Machine*." *Framework* 50, nos. 1–2 (2009): 95–106.

Boym, Svetlana. *The Future of Nostalgia*. New York: Basic Books, 2001.

Brandstetter, Gabriele. *Poetics of Dance*. Translated by Elena Polzer with Mark Franko. New York: Oxford University Press, 2015.

Brauer, Juliane. "How Can Music Be Torturous? Music in Nazi Concentration and Extermination Camps." *Music & Politics* 10, no. 1 (2016): 1.

Bridgewater, Pamela. "Ain't I a Slave: Slavery, Reproductive Abuse, and Reparations." *UCLA Women's Law Journal* 14, no. 1 (2005): 89–162.

Brison, Susan. "Trauma Narratives and the Remaking of the Self." In *Acts of Memory: Cultural Recall of the Present*, edited by Mieke Bal, Jonathan Crewe, and Leo Spitzer, 39–54. Hanover, NH: University Press of New England, 1999.

Brodsky, Seth. *From 1989, or European Music and the Modern Unconscious*. Berkeley: University of California Press, 2017.

Broussard, Patricia. "Black Women's Post-slavery Silence Syndrome: A Twenty-First Century Remnant of Slavery, Jim Crow, and Systemic Racism—Who Will Tell Her Stories." *Journal of Gender, Race and Justice* 16, no. 2 (2013): 373–422.

Brown, Antonio. "Performing 'Truth': Black Speech Acts." *African American Review* 36, no. 2 (2002): 213–25.

Brown Maurice J. E., and Kenneth L. Hamilton. "Barcarolle." *Grove Music Online*. January 20, 2001.

Bruhn, Siglind. *Musical Ekphrasis: Composers Responding to Poetry and Painting*. Hillsdale, NY: Pendragon, 2000.

Bubaris, Nikos. "Sound in Museums—Museums in Sound." *Museum Management and Curatorship* 29, no. 4 (2014): 391–402.

Buch, Esteban. *Beethoven's Ninth: A Political History*. Translated by Richard Miller. Chicago: University of Chicago Press, 2003.

Buch, Esteban. "La Grande Guerre des musiciens: Composer pendant la guerre, composer avec la guerre." In *La Grande Guerre: Une histoire culturelle*, edited by Philippe Poirrier, 133–54. Dijon: Editions Universitaires de Dijon, 2015.

Buch, Esteban. "Silences de la Grande Guerre." In *Entendre la Grande Guerre: Sons, musiques et silence en 14–18*, edited by Florence Grétreau, 128–33. Paris: Gallimard, 2014.

Buch, Esteban. "Vincent' d'Indy et la Première Guerre mondiale: *Sinfonia Brevis de bello gallico*." In *Vincent d'Indy et son temps*, edited by Manuela Schwartz, 21–36. Sprimont: Mardaga, 2006.

Buckler, Julie, and Emily D. Johnson. "Introduction." In *Rites of Place*, edited by Buckler and Johnson, 14–23.

Buckler, Julie, and Emily D. Johnson, eds. *Rites of Place: Public Commemoration in Russia and Eastern Europe*. Evanston, IL: Northwestern University Press, 2013.

Butler, Judith. *Bodies That Matter*. New York: Routledge, 2011.

Butler, Judith. *Notes toward a Performative Theory of Assembly*. Cambridge, MA: Harvard University Press, 2015.

Bylander, Cindy. "Reponses to Adversity: The Polish Composers Union and Musical Life in the 1970s and 1980s." *Musical Quarterly* 45, no. 4 (2012): 485–90.

Cai, Jindong, and Sheila Melvin. *Beethoven in China: How the Great Composer Became an Icon in the People's Republic.* Hong Kong: Penguin, 2015.

Calico, Joy H. *Arnold Schoenberg's A Survivor from Warsaw in Postwar Europe.* Berkeley: University of California Press, 2014.

Campo-Bowen, Christopher. "'We Shall Remain Faithful': The Village Mode in Czech Opera, 1866–1928." PhD dissertation, University of North Carolina at Chapel Hill, 2018.

Carr, Julian S. "Unveiling of Confederate Monument at University. June 2, 1913." Julian Shakespeare Carr Papers #141, Southern Historical Collection, Wilson Library, University of North Carolina at Chapel Hill.

Caruth, Cathy. *Unclaimed Experience: Trauma, Narrative, History.* Baltimore: Johns Hopkins University Press, 1996.

Casey, Valerie. "The Museum Effect: Gazing from Object to Performance in the Contemporary Cultural-History Museum." Paper presented at the "Archives and Museum Informatics, Europe: Cultural Institutions and Digital Technology" conference, Paris, France, September 8–12, 2003. http://www.archimuse.com/publishing/ichim03/095C.pdf

Cerutti, Gabriela. "La historia de la memoria." *Puentes,* March 2001, 14–25.

Cizmic, Maria. *Performing Pain: Music and Trauma in Eastern Europe.* New York: Oxford University Press, 2012.

Clarke, Joseph. *Commemorating the Dead in Revolutionary France: Revolution and Remembrance, 1789–1799.* Cambridge: Cambridge University Press, 2007.

Clove, Joshua. *1989: Bob Dylan Didn't Have This to Sing About.* Berkeley: University of California Press, 2009.

Connor, Steven. "Choralities." *Twentieth-Century Music* 13, no. 1 (2016): 3–23.

Coombes, Annie E. "The Art of Memory." *Third Text* 52 (2000): 45–52.

Cowgill, Rachel. "Canonizing Remembrance: Music for Armistice Day at the BBC, 1922–7." *First World War Studies* 2, no. 1 (2011): 75–107.

Cowgill, Rachel. "Elgar's War Requiem." In *Edward Elgar and His World,* edited by Byron Adams, 317–62. Princeton, NJ: Princeton University Press, 2007.

Cox, Karen L. *Dixie's Daughters: The United Daughters of the Confederacy and the Preservation of Confederate Culture.* Gainesville: University Press of Florida, 2003.

Craps, Stef. *Postcolonial Witnessing: Trauma Out of Bounds.* London: Palgrave Macmillan, 2012.

Crowley, David. *Warsaw.* London: Reaktion, 2003.

Dabrowski, Patrice M. *Commemorations and the Shaping of Modern Poland.* Bloomington: Indiana University Press, 2004.

Daniel, Ralph T., Elwyn A. Wienandt, and Laurie J. Sampsel. "Anthem." *Grove Music Online.* October 16, 2003.

Daskalov, Roumen Dontchev, Diana Mishkova, Tchavdar Marinov, and Alexander Vezenkov, eds. *Entangled Histories of the Balkans.* Vol. 4: *Concepts, Approaches, and (Self-)Representations.* Leiden: Brill, 2017.

Daughtry, J. Martin. *Listening to War: Sound, Music, Trauma, and Survival in Wartime Iraq.* New York: Oxford University Press, 2015.

De Boeck, Filip. "Beyond the Grave: History, Memory and Death in Postcolonial Congo/Zaïre." In *Memory and the Postcolony,* edited by Richard Werbner, 21–57. London: Zed Books, 1998.

Deconto, Jesse James, and Alan Blinder. "'Silent Sam' Confederate Statue Is Toppled at University of North Carolina." *New York Times*, August 21, 2018.

DeGruy, Joy. *Post-traumatic Slave Syndrome: American's Legacy of Enduring Injury and Healing*. Portland, OR: Uptone Press, 2005.

Der Führer schenkt den Juden eine Stadt. Nazi propaganda film, shot in the concentration at Terezín/Theresienstadt. 1944; Los Angeles: Seventh Art Releasing, 2010. DVD.

Diehl, Chad R. *Resurrecting Nagasaki: Reconstruction and the Formation of Atomic Narratives*. Ithaca, NY: Cornell University Press, 2018.

Dillon, Stephen. "Possessed by Death: The Neoliberal-Carceral State, Black Feminism, and the Afterlife of Slavery." *Radical History Review* 112 (Winter 2012): 113–26.

Döge, Klaus. "Das entsetzliche Grauen zum Ausdruck gebracht: Anmerkungen zu Martinůs *Memorial to Lidice*." In *Bohuslav Martinů*, edited by Ulrich Tadday, 78–91. Musik-Konzepte: Sonderband 11. Munich: Edition Text+Kritik, 2009.

Dorf, Samuel N. *Performing Antiquity: Ancient Greek Music and Dance from Paris to Delphi, 1890–1930*. New York: Oxford University Press, 2019.

Douglass, Frederick. *Narrative of the Life of Frederick Douglass, an American Slave: Written by Himself*. Cambridge, MA: Harvard University Press, 2009.

Dower, John W. *Embracing Defeat: Japan in the Wake of World War II*. New York: Norton, 1999.

Eabisa, Liben. "In Ethiopia Candlelight Vigil Held for Slain Eritrean American Artist Nipsey Hussle." *Tadias Magazine*. April 7, 2019. http://www.tadias.com/04/07/2019/in-ethiopia-candelight-vigil-held-for-slain-eritrean-american-artist-nipsey-hussle/

Eisler, Hanns. *Lieder für eine Singstimme und Klavier*. Edited by Stephanie Eisler and Manfred Grabs. Leipzig: Deutscher Verlag für Musik, 1976.

Elgar, Edward. *The Spirit of England: Three Poems by Laurence Binyon, Set to Music for Tenor or Soprano, Chorus, and Orchestra*. London: Novello, 1917.

Endō Masao. "Kawasaki Masaru." *New Composer* 9 (July 2008): 50–55.

Eng, David L., and David Kazanjian. "Introduction: Mourning Remains." In *Loss: The Politics of Mourning*, edited by David L. Eng and David Kazanjian, 1–28. Berkeley: University of California Press, 2003.

Ermarth, Elizabeth Deeds. *Sequel to History: Postmodernism and the Crisis of Representational Time*. Princeton, NJ: Princeton University Press, 1992.

Ertan, Deniz, and William Brooks. "Modalities of Memorial: The Double Trauma of 1918 and its Aftermaths." Paper presented at the "Music, Nationalism and Transnationalism, Europe-Americas, 1918–1945: Diplomacy, Policy, Aesthetics" conference, Royal Northern College, Manchester, November 23, 2016.

Esquith, Stephen L. "Re-enacting Mass Violence." *Polity* 35, no. 4 (2003): 513–34.

Fast, Susan, and Kip Pegley, eds. *Music, Politics and Violence*. Middletown, CT: Wesleyan University Press, 2012.

Faulk, Karen Ann. *In the Wake of Neoliberalism: Citizenship and Human Rights in Argentina*. Stanford, CA: Stanford University Press, 2012.

Fauser, Annegret. *Musical Encounters at the 1889 Paris World's Fair*. Rochester, NY: University of Rochester Press, 2005.

Fauser, Annegret. *Sounds of War: Music in the United States during World War II.* New York: Oxford University Press, 2013.

Feierstein, Ricardo. *Historia de los Judíos argentinos.* Buenos Aires: Editorial Galerna, 2006.

Fénelon, Fania. *The Musicians of Auschwitz.* Translated by Judith Landry. London: Sphere, 1976.

Fischer-Lichte, Erika. *The Routledge Introduction to Theatre and Performance Studies.* Edited by Ramona Thomasius and Minou Arjomand and translated by Minou Arjomand. New York: Routledge, 2014.

Fogg, Mieczysław, with Zbigniew K. Rogowski. *Od palanta do belcanta: Wspomnienia.* Warsaw: Iskry, 1970.

Foster, Susan Leigh. "Introduction." In *Choreographing History,* edited by Susan Leigh Foster, 3–21. Bloomington: Indiana University Press, 1995.

Frank, Priscilla. "Staged Photographs Reenact Real, Hostile Encounters with NYPD." *Huffington Post,* August 3, 2015, https://www.huffpost.com/entry/staged-photographs-reenact-hostile-encounters-with-nypd_n_55bbea21e4b0b23e3ce2e68c

Franko, Mark. "Epilogue to an Epilogue: Historicizing the Re- in Danced Reenactment." In *The Oxford Handbook of Dance and Reenactment,* edited by Mark Franko, 487–503. New York: Oxford University Press, 2018.

Freud, Sigmund. "Mourning and Melancholia." In *On the History of the Psycho-Analytic Movement, Papers on Metapsychology and Other Works,* edited and translated by James Strachey, vol. 14 of *The Standard Edition of the Complete Psychological Works of Sigmund Freud.* London: Hogarth Press, 1957.

Fujiyama Ichirō, Satō Hachirō, and Koseki Yūji. "Nagasaki no kane." In *Fujiyama ichirō zenkyoku-shū: Nagasaki no kane,* Nippon Columbia, COCP-40431, 2018. First released as single on Columbia Records, 1949.

Fukuyama, Francis. "The End of History?" *National Interest* 16 (Summer 1989): 3–18.

Galstian, Mary. *Program Notes, How to Go On. A Secular Choral Requem by Dale Trumbore. East Coast Premiere. Also Featuring Works by Monteverdi and Pizzetti.* Harvard-Radcliffe Collegium Musicum, February 15, 2019.

Garabed, C. K. "Mincing Words." *Armenian Weekly,* August 8, 2009. https://armenianweekly.com/2009/08/08/ck-garabed-mincing-words/

Giesbrecht, Sabine. *Musik und Propaganda: Der Erste Weltkrieg im Spiegel deutscher Bildpostkarten, Beiträge zur Medienästhetik der Musik.* Vol. 14. Osnabrück: Electronic Publishing Osnabrück, 2014.

Gilbert, Shirli. "Buried Monuments: Yiddish Songs and Holocaust Memory." *History Workshop Journal* 66, no. 1 (2008): 107–28.

Gilbert, Shirli. *Music in the Holocaust: Confronting Life in the Nazi Ghettos and Camps.* Oxford: Oxford University Press, 2005.

Gilroy, Paul. "Diaspora." *Paragraph* 3, no. 17 (2010): 207–12.

Giroux, Henry. "Public Pedagogy as Cultural Politics." In *Without Guarantees: In Honor of Stuart Hall,* edited by Paul Gilroy, Lawrence Grossberg, and Angela McRobbie, 134–47. London: Verso, 2000.

Göçek, Fatma Müge. *Denial of Violence: Ottoman Past, Turkish Present, and Collective*

Violence against the Armenians, 1789–2009. Oxford: Oxford University Press, 2015.

Goebel, Stefan. "Re-membered and Re-mobilized: The 'Sleeping Dead' in Interwar Germany and Britain." *Journal of Contemporary History* 39, no. 4 (2004): 473–85.

Goehr, Lydia. "How to Do More with Words. Two Views of (Musical) Ekphrasis." *British Journal of Aesthetics* 50, no. 4 (2010): 389–410.

Gorbman, Claudia. *Unheard Melodies: Narrative Film Music*. Bloomington: Indiana University Press, 1987.

Gordillo, Gastón. "Resonance and the Egyptian Revolution." *Space and Politics* (blog), 2011. Accessed April 17, 2018. http://spaceandpolitics.blogspot.com/2011/02/resonance-and-egyptian-revolution.html

Gordillo, Gastón. "The Void: Invisible Ruins on the Edges of Empire." In *Imperial Debris: On Ruins and Ruination*, edited by Ann Laura Stoler, 227–51. Durham, NC: Duke University Press, 2013.

Green, Jordan. "Neo-Confederates Found Guilty of Vandalizing Statue Honoring Enslaved People Who Built UNC." *Indy Week*, September 6, 2019. https://indyweek.com/news/orange/neo-confederates-found-guilty-of-vandalizing-statue-honoring

Green, Joseph. *Der Purimshpiler*. Available as video. 1937; Teaneck, NJ: Ergo Films, 2002. DVD.

Gregg, Melissa, and Gregory J. Seigworth, eds. *The Affect Theory Reader*. Durham, NC: Duke University Press, 2010.

Grimley, Daniel M. "'Music in the Midst of Desolation': Structures of Mourning in Elgar's *The Spirit of England*." In *Elgar Studies*, edited by J. P. E. Harper-Scott and Julian Rushton, 220–37. Cambridge: Cambridge University Press, 2007.

Grossberg, Lawrence. "Cultural Studies: What's in a Name? (One More Time)." In *Bringing it All Back Home: Essays on Cultural Studies*, 245–71. Durham, NC: Duke University Press, 1997.

Grossman, David. *Sus eḥad nikhnas le-bar* [*A Horse Walks into a Bar*]. Tel Aviv: Ha-Kibuts ha-me'uḥad, 2014.

Gruber, Ruth Ellen. *Virtually Jewish: Reinventing Jewish Culture in Europe*. Berkeley: University of California Press, 2002.

Hall, Stuart. "Cultural Identity and Diaspora." In *Identity: Community, Culture, Difference*, edited by Jonathan Rutherford, 222–37. London: Lawrence & Wishart, 1990.

Hanheide, Stefan. *Pace: Musik zwischen Krieg und Frieden—Vierzig Werkporträts*. Kassel: Bärenreiter, 2007.

Hayashi Hikaru. *Genbaku shōkei* [*Little Landscapes of Hiroshima*], for mixed chorus. Lyrics by Hara Tamiki. Tokyo: Zenon Music Company, 1982.

Hayashi Hikaru. *Genbaku shōkei: Hayashi Hikaru gasshō sakuhin-shū*. Fontec FOCD 3294, 1996, compact disc.

Heckner, Elke. "Screening the Armenian Genocide: Atom Egoyan's *Ararat* between Erasure and Suture." *Shofar* 28, no. 4, "Holocaust and Genocide Cinema" (2010): 133–45.

Hellouin, Frédéric. *Gossec et la musique française à la fin du XVIIIe siècle*. Paris: Librarie A. Charles, 1903.

Henderson, Marius, and Julia Lange, eds. *Entangled Memories: Remembering the Holocaust in a Global Age.* Heidelberg: Universitätsverlag Winter, 2017.

Herrmann, Bernard. *For the Fallen.* New York: Broude Brothers, 1955.

Hersey, John. "Hiroshima." *New Yorker,* August 31, 1946. http://www.newyorker.com/magazine/1946/08/31/hiroshima

Herzl, Theodor. "Im Speisewagen." In *Gesammelte zionistische Werke,* 5: 421–35. Berlin: Jüdischer Verlag, 1935.

Hiroshima Heiwa Shiryō-kan (Hiroshima Peace Museum). *Hiroshima genbaku sensai shi.* Hiroshima: Hiroshima Peace Museum, 1971.

Hiroshima to Ongaku Iinkai (Hiroshima Music Committee), ed. *Hiroshima to ongaku.* Tokyo: Chōbunsha, 2006.

Hirsch, Marianne. *Family Frames: Photography, Narrative, and Postmemory.* Cambridge, MA: Harvard University Press, 1997.

Hirsch, Marianne. *The Generation of Postmemory: Writing and Visual Culture after the Holocaust.* New York: Columbia University Press, 2012.

Hirsch, Marianne, and Leo Spitzer. *Ghosts of Home: The Afterlife of Czernowitz in Jewish Memory.* Berkeley: University of California Press, 2010.

Hochberg, Gil. "Soldiers as Filmmakers: On the Prospect of 'Shooting War' and the Question of Ethical Spectatorship." *Screen* 54, no. 1 (2013): 44–61.

Hoeckner, Berthold, and Howard C. Nusbaum. "Music and Memory in Film and Other Multimedia: The Casablanca Effect." In *The Psychology of Music in Multimedia,* edited by Siu-Lan Tan, Annabel J. Cohen, Scott D. Lipscomb, and Roger A. Kendall, 235–63. New York: Oxford University Press, 2013.

Hoffman, Eva. *After Such Knowledge: Memory, History, and the Legacy of the Holocaust.* New York: Public Affairs, 2004.

Howe, Blake. "Paul Wittgenstein and the Performance of Disability." *Journal of Musicology* 27, no. 2 (2010): 135–180.

Howe, Blake, Stephanie Jensen-Moulton, Neil Lerner, and Joseph Straus. "Introduction: Disability Studies in Music, Music in Disability Studies." In *The Oxford Handbook of Music and Disability Studies,* edited by Blake Howe, Stephanie Jensen-Moulton, Neil Lerner, and Joseph Straus, 1–12. New York: Oxford University Press, 2015.

Huyssen, Andreas. *Present Pasts: Urban Palimpsests and the Politics of Memory.* Stanford, CA: Stanford University Press, 2003.

Inoue, Masamichi S. *Okinawa and the U.S. Military: Identity Making in the Age of Globalization.* New York: Columbia University Press, 2007.

Janion, Maria. "Słowo i symbol w miesiącach przełomu." In *Kongres Kultury Polskiej, 11–13 grudnia 1981,* edited by Władysław Masiulanis, 37–44. Warsaw: Oficyna Wydawnictwa Volumen Instytut Kultury, 2000.

Jardin, Etienne, ed. *Music and War in Europe from French Revolution to WWI.* Turnhout: Brepols, 2016.

Jinks, Rebecca. *Representing Genocide: The Holocaust as Paradigm?* London: Bloomsbury, 2016.

Kaes, Anton. *Shell Shock Cinema: Weimar Culture and the Wounds of War.* Princeton, NJ: Princeton University Press, 2011.

Kaltenecker, Martin. "'What Scenes!—What Sounds!' Some Remarks on Soundscapes in War Times." In *Music and War in Europe from French Revolution to WWI*, edited by Étienne Jardin, 3–27. Turnhout: Brepols, 2016.

Kaplan, Danny. *The Men We Loved: Male Friendship and Nationalism in Israeli Culture*. New York: Berghahn Books, 2006.

Kaplan, Sara Clarke. "Souls at the Crossroads, Africans on the Water: The Politics of Diasporic Melancholia." *Callaloo* 30, no. 2 (2007): 511–26.

Karavanta, Mina. "The Injunctions of the Spectre of Slavery: Affective Memory and the Counterwriting of Community." *Feminist Review* 104 (2013): 42–60.

Kasbarian, Sossie. "The Myth and Reality of 'Return': Diaspora in the 'Homeland.'" *Diaspora* 18, no. 3 (2009): 358–81.

Kasbarian, Sossie. "The Politics of Memory and Commemoration: Armenian Diasporic Reflections on 2015." *Nationalities Papers* 46, no. 1 (2018): 123–43.

Kassabian, Anahid. "The Sound of a New Film Form." In *Popular Music and Film*, edited by Ian Inglis, 91–101. London: Wallflower Press, 2003.

Katz, Elihu. "Media Events: The Sense of Occasion." *Studies in Visual Anthropology* 6 (1980): 84–89.

Kazanjian, David. "Diasporic *Flânerie*: From *Ruinenlust* to Armenia's Walkscapes." In *An Armenian Mediterranean: Words and Worlds in Motion*, edited by Kathryn Babayan and Michael Pifer, 221–46. London: Palgrave Macmillan, 2018.

Kazanjian, David, and Anahid Kassabian. "Mass Mediating Diaspora: Iranian Exile Culture in Los Angeles." *Diaspora* 5, no. 2 (1996): 313–31.

Kazanjian, David, and Anahid Kassabian. "Naming the Armenian Genocide: The Quest for 'Truth' and a Search for Possibilities." *New Formations* 8 (1989): 81–98.

Kennedy, David M. *Freedom from Fear: The American People in Depression and War, 1929–1945*. New York: Oxford University Press, 2005.

Kernodle, Tammie. "Having Her Say: The Blues as the Black Woman's Lament." In *Women's Voices Across Musical Worlds*, edited by Jane A. Bernstein, 213–31. Boston: Northeastern University Press, 2003.

Kerr, George H. *Okinawa: The History of an Island People*. North Clarendon, VT: Tuttle Publishing, 2011.

Kesner, Ladislav. "The Role of Cognitive Competence in the Art Museum Experience." *Museum Management and Curatorship* 21 (2006): 4–19.

Keyes, Beth. "'The Absurd Disordering of Notes': Dysfunctional Memory in the Post-traumatic Music of Ivor Gurney." In *The Oxford Handbook of Music and Disability Studies*, edited by Blake Howe, Stephanie Jensen-Moulton, Neil Lerner, and Joseph Straus, 447–75. New York: Oxford University Press, 2015.

Kibreah, Bertie. "Ensnare the Thief in the House of Wind: Negotiating Routes of Bāul-ness in Bangladesh." In *Resounding Transcendence: Transitions in Music, Religion, and Ritual*, edited by Jeffers Engelhardt and Philip V. Bohlman, 29–42. New York: Oxford University Press, 2016.

Kino Fumio. *Genshiya no utagoe: Hibaku sakkyokuka no shuki*. Nagasaki: Nagasaki Kokusai Bunka Kyōkai, 1956.

Kirshenblatt-Gimblett, Barbara. *Destination Culture: Tourism, Museums, and Heritage*. Berkeley: University of California Press, 1998.

Klauk, Stephanie. "Italienische Schlachtenmusiken zu Napoleon Bonaparte: Die Schlacht von Marengo." In *Music and War in Europe*, edited by Jardin, 89–104.

Klein, Hans-Günter, ed. *Viktor Ullmann—Materialien.* Hamburg: Von Bockel Verlag, 1992.

Komor, Sophia, and Susanne Rohr, eds. *The Holocaust, Art and Taboo: Transatlantic Exchanges on the Ethics and Aesthetics of Representation.* Heidelberg: Winter, 2010.

Körner, Theodor. "Gebet während der Schlacht." In *Leyer und Schwerdt.* Berlin: Nicolaische Buchhandlung, 1814.

Kraemer, Joseph A. "*Waltz with Bashir* (2008): Trauma and Representation in the Animated Documentary." *Journal of Film and Video* 67, nos. 3–4 (2015): 57–68.

Kramer, Jonathan D. *Postmodern Music, Postmodern Listening.* New York: Bloomsbury, 2016.

Kregor, Jonathan. "Disavowing the Instrumental Battle Piece." *Journal of Musicological Research* 34, no. 3 (2015): 204–23.

Król, Eugeniusz Cesary. "Perzeptionen des Aufstands in Polen." In *Der Warschauer Aufstand 1944: Ereignis und Wahrnehmung in Polen und in Deutschland,* edited by Hans-Jürgen Bömelburg, Eugeniusz C. Król, and Michael Thomae, 171–91. Paderborn: Ferdinand Schöningh, 2011.

Kroustallis, Vassilis. "Failure to Think, Failure to Move: Handicapped Reasoning in *Waltz with Bashir.*" *Jewish Film & New Media* 2, no. 2 (2014): 132–52.

Kurtz, J. Roger. "Introduction." In *Trauma and Literature,* edited by J. Roger Kurtz, 1–18. Philadelphia: Drexel University Press, 2016.

Kubik, Jan, and Michael Bernhard. "Introduction." In *Twenty Years After Communism: The Politics of Memory and Commemoration,* edited by Kubik and Bernhard, 1–6.

Kubik, Jan, and Michael Bernhard. "A Theory of the Politics of Memory." In *Twenty Years After Communism: The Politics of Memory and Commemoration,* edited by Kubik and Bernhard, 7–36.

Kubik, Jan, and Michael Bernhard, eds. *Twenty Years After Communism: The Politics of Memory and Commemoration.* New York: Oxford University Press, 2014.

LaCapra, Dominick. *Experience in Transit: Experience, Identity, Critical Theory.* Ithaca, NY: Cornell University Press, 2004.

Landesman, Ohad, and Roy Bendor. "Animated Recollection and Spectatorial Experience in *Waltz with Bashir.*" *Animation* 6, no. 3 (2011): 353–70.

Landsberg, Alison. *Prosthetic Memory: The Transformation of American Remembrance in the Age of Mass Culture.* New York: Columbia University Press, 2004.

Lang, Cady. "How This Vine Star Is Using the Mannequin Challenge to Spotlight Black Lives Matter." *Time Magazine,* November 10, 2016. https://time.com/4566455/black-lives-matter-mannequin-challenge/

Lanzmann, Claude, dir. *Shoah.* 1985; New York: Criterion Collection, 2013.

Lapedis, Hilary. "Popping the Question: The Function and Effect of Popular Music in Cinema." *Popular Music* 18, no. 3 (1999): 367–79.

Lasker-Wallfisch, Anita. *Inherit the Truth, 1939–1945: The Documented Experiences of a Survivor of Auschwitz and Belsen.* London: Giles de la Mare, 1996.

Levi, Primo. *If This Is a Man / The Truce.* London: Penguin, 1979.

Lichau, Karsten. "'Noise' or 'Silence?': Listening to Sacred Sound in 20th-Century Europe." In *Exploring the Senses: South Asian and European Perspectives on Rituals and Performativity*, edited by Axel Michaels and Christoph Wulf, 145–63. London: Taylor and Francis, 2013.

Lifton, Robert Jay. *Death in Life: Survivors of Hiroshima*. Chapel Hill: University of North Carolina Press, 1991.

Long, Michael. *Beautiful Monsters: Imagining the Classic in Musical Media*. Berkeley: University of California Press, 2008.

Lowenthal, David. *The Past Is a Foreign Country*. Cambridge: Cambridge University Press, 1985.

Manabe, Noriko. "Songs of Japanese Schoolchildren during World War II." In *The Oxford Handbook of Children's Musical Cultures*, edited by Patricia Sheehan Campbell and Trevor Wiggins, 96–113. New York: Oxford University Press, 2012.

Manabe, Noriko. "Western Music in Japan: The Evolution of Styles in Children's Songs, Hip-Hop, and Other Genres." PhD dissertation, City University of New York, 2009.

Mardiganian, Aurora. *Ravished Armenia: The Story of Aurora Mardiganian, the Christian Girl, Who Survived the Great Massacres*. Interpreted by H. L. Gates. New York: International Copyright Bureau, 1919.

Mark, James. *The Unfinished Revolution: Making Sense of the Communist Past in Central-Eastern Europe*. New Haven: Yale University Press, 2010.

"M'Arthur Points Hiroshima Lesson: Says in Message to Peace Fete in Bombed City World Must Reform or Perish." *New York Times*, August 6, 1947, 13.

Mathew, Nicholas. *Political Beethoven*. Cambridge: Cambridge University Press, 2013.

Mathias, Alyssa. "'They Were Sent to Their Deaths from Here:' Sounds of Plurality and Solidarity in Istanbul at the 100th Anniversary of the Armenian Genocide." *Ethnomusicology Review*, May 4, 2015. https://www.ethnomusicologyreview.ucla.edu/content/they-were-sent-their-deaths-here

Mbembe, Achille. *Critique of Black Reason*. Durham, NC: Duke University Press, 2017.

Mbembe, Achille. "Necropolitics." *Public Culture* 15 (2003): 11–40.

McCalman, Ian, and Paul Pickering. "From Realism to the Affective Turn: An Agenda." In *Historical Reenactment: From Realism to the Affective Turn*, edited by Ian McCalman and Paul Pickering, 1–17. London: Palgrave Macmillan, 2010.

Meinhart, Michelle. "Memory and Private Mourning in an English Country House: Lady Alda Hoare's Musical Shrine to a Lost Son." *Journal of Musicological Research* 33 (2014): 39–95.

Memoria AMIA. Buenos Aires: AMIA Comunidad Judía, 2017.

Mendelsohn, Daniel. *The Lost: A Search for Six of Six Million*. New York: Harper Perennial, 2013.

Meng, Michael. *Shattered Spaces: Encountering Jewish Ruins in Postwar German and Poland*. Cambridge, MA: Harvard University Press, 2011.

Migdal, Ulrike. *Und die Musik spielt dazu: Chansons und Satiren aus dem KZ Theresienstadt*. Munich: Piper, 1986.

Milewski, Barbara. "Hidden in Plain View: The Music of Holocaust Survival in Poland's First Post-war Feature Film." In *Music, Collective Memory, Trauma, and Nostalgia in European Cinema after the Second World War*, edited by Michael Baumgartner and Ewelina Boczkowska, 111–37. New York: Routledge, 2020.

Miyamoto, Yuki. *Beyond the Mushroom Cloud: Commemoration, Religion, and Responsibility after Hiroshima.* New York: Fordham University Press, 2011.

Mondolo, Ana María. "El libro 'El himno nacional argentino' de Carlos Vega." *Revista del Instituto de Investigación Musicológica "Carlos Vega"* 26, no. 26 (2012): 271–95.

MONUSCO, DDR/RR. "La reduction des violences communautaires au Nord Kivu." *Bulletin de la RVC,* no. 1, July 1, 2017.

Morag, Raya. *Waltzing with Bashir: Perpetrator Trauma and Cinema.* New York: I.B. Taurus, 2013.

Mosse, George L. *Fallen Soldiers: Reshaping the Memory of World Wars.* New York: Oxford University Press, 1990.

Mulder, Etty. "Orpheus on His Way to the Gas Chambers." http://www.ettymulder.nl/m/images/noodzaak.pdf

Naficy, Hamid. *The Making of Exile Cultures: Iranian Television in Los Angeles.* Minneapolis: University of Minnesota Press, 1993.

Nagai Takashi. *Nagasaki no kane.* 1949; Tokyo: Sanpauro, 1995.

Naliwajek-Mazurek, Katarzyna. "Music and Torture in Nazi Sites of Persecution and Genocide in Occupied Poland, 1939–1945." *World of Music,* n.s. 2, no. 1 (2013): 31–50.

Ndaliko, Chérie Rivers. "In the Presence of Absence: Commemoration and Disavowal in Congo." *Critical Inquiry,* 44, no. 4 (2018): 766–80.

Ndaliko, Chérie Rivers. *Necessary Noise: Music, Film, and Charitable Imperialism in the East of Congo.* Oxford: Oxford University Press, 2016.

New Budapest Orpheum Society. *As Dreams Fall Apart: The Golden Age of Jewish Stage and Film Music, 1925–1955.* Recorded March 2014. Cedille Records, CDR 900000 151, 2014, compact disc.

New Budapest Orpheum Society. *Dancing on the Edge of a Volcano: Jewish Cabaret, Popular and Political Songs 1900–1945.* Recorded March 2002. Cedille Records, CDR 90000 065, 2002, compact disc.

New Budapest Orpheum Society. *Jewish Cabaret in Exile.* Recorded April 2008. Cedille Records, CDR 90000 110, 2008, compact disc.

New Budapest Orpheum Society. *Moments musicaux et modernes: Jewish Modernism in Popular and Political Music.* Accompanying compact disc for Philip V. Bohlman, ed. *Jewish Musical Modernism, Old and New.* Chicago: University of Chicago Press, 2008.

Newland, Marti. "Sounding 'Black': An Ethnography of Racialized Vocality at Fisk University." PhD dissertation, Columbia University, 2014.

Nichanian, Marc. "Catastrophic Mourning." In *Loss: The Politics of Mourning,* edited by David L. Eng and David Kazanjian, 99–124. Berkeley: University of California Press, 2003.

Nichols, Bill. "Documentary Reenactment and the Fantasmatic Subject." *Critical Inquiry* 35, no. 1 (2008): 72–89.

Nichols, Bill. "Irony, Cruelty, Evil (and a Wink) in *The Act of Killing.*" *Film Quarterly* 67, no. 2 (2013): 25–29.

Niewiadomski, Teodor. "Kopiec miał być powstańczym pomnikiem." *Stolica* 47 (1984): 23.

Niżyńska, Joanna. *The Kingdom of Insignificance: Miron Białoszewski and the Quotid-*

ian, the Queer, and the Traumatic. Evanston, IL: Northwestern University Press, 2013.

Notahara Yumi. "Ōki Masao to eiga *Hiroshima no zu*: Kōkyōkyoku dai 5 ban 'Hiroshima' e no kiseki." *Hiroshima Daigaku daigakuin kyōikugaku kenkyūka, Ongaku bunka kyōikugaku kenkyū kiyō* 15 (March 22, 2013): 61–68.

Notahara Yumi. *"Hiroshima" ga narihibiku toki.* Tokyo: Shunjū-sha, 2015.

Notahara Yumi. "Ongaku ni okeru 'Hiroshima'—Taiken no katari to kioku no keishō o megutte." *Kyōto Zōkei Geijutsu Daigaku kiyō* 22 (November 2018): 118–24.

Ochoa Gautier, Ana María. "Silence." In *Keywords in Sound,* edited by David Novak and Matt Sakakeeny, 184–92. Durham, NC: Duke University Press, 2015.

O'Connell, John Morgan. *Commemorating Gallipoli through Music: Remembering and Forgetting.* Lanham, MD: Lexington Books, 2018.

Ōki Masao. *Grand Cantata: Ningen o kaese.* Tokyo: Kawai Gakufu, 1962.

Ōki Masao et al. *Cantata: Take Back the Human I.* Toshiba 26847111, 1961, LP.

Ost, David. *The Defeat of Solidarity: Anger and Politics in Postcommunist Europe.* Ithaca, NY: Cornell University Press, 2005.

Paczkowski, Andrzej. *Revolution and Counterrevolution in Poland, 1980–1989: Solidarity, Martial Law, and the End of Communism in Europe.* Translated by Christina Manetti. Rochester: University of Rochester Press, 2015.

Panossian, Razmik. "Between Ambivalence and Intrusion: Politics and Identity in Armenian-Diaspora Relations." *Diaspora* 7, no. 2 (1998): 149–96.

Pattie, Susan. "New Homeland for an Old Diaspora." In *Homelands and Diasporas: Holy Lands and Other Places,* edited by André Levy and Alex Weingrod, 49–67. Stanford, CA: Stanford University Press, 2005.

Pautz, Michelle C. "*Argo* and *Zero Dark Thirty*: Film, Government, and Audiences." *PS: Political Science & Politics* 48, no. 1 (2015): 120–28.

Peaslee, Robert Moses. "'It's Fine as Long as You Draw, but Don't Film': *Waltz with Bashir* and the Postmodern Function of Animated Documentary." *Visual Communication Quarterly* 18, no. 4 (2011): 223–35.

Peschel, Lisa, ed. *Performing Captivity, Performing Escape: Cabarets and Plays from the Terezín/Theresienstadt Ghetto.* Kolkata: Seagull, 2014.

Pollack, Howard. *Marc Blitzstein: His Life, His Work, His World.* New York: Oxford University Press, 2012.

Poore, Carol. *Disability in Twentieth-Century German Culture.* Ann Arbor: University of Michigan Press, 2007.

Quinault, Roland. "The Cult of the Centenary, c.1784–1914." *Historical Research* 71, no. 176 (1998): 303–23.

Rajk, Lásló. "The Betrayed Citizen: on the Design of the Exhibition." In *The Citizen Betrayed: In Memory of the Victims of the Hungarian Holocaust.* Budapest: Hungarian National Museum, 2006.

Rastegar, Kamran. *Surviving Images: Cinema, War, and Cultural Memory in the Middle East.* New York: Oxford University Press, 2015.

Redmond, Shana L. *Anthem: Social Movements and the Sound of Solidarity in the African Diaspora.* New York: New York University Press, 2014.

Rehding, Alexander. *Music and Monumentality: Commemoration and Wonderment in Nineteenth-Century Germany.* New York: Oxford University Press, 2009.

Rehding, Alexander. "'Ode to Freedom': Bernstein's Ninth at the Berlin Wall." *Beethoven Forum* 12, no. 1 (2005): 36–49.

Rein, Raanan. *Argentina, Israel, and the Jews: Perón, the Eichmann Capture and After.* Translated by Martha Grenzeback. Bethesda: University of Maryland Press, 2003.

Resnais, Alain, dir. *Nuit et brouillard.* Music by Hanns Eisler. Production by Anatole Dauman. 1955; New York: Criterion Collection, 2003.

Reynolds, Bryan, ed. *Performance Studies: Key Words, Concepts and Theories.* New York: Palgrave, 2014.

Rice, Tom. "Listening." In *Keywords in Sound,* edited by David Novak and Matt Sakakeeny, 99–111. Durham, NC: Duke University Press, 2015.

Richter, Petra. "A Music-Political Confession: Anmerkungen zu Martinů's *Memorial to Lidice.*" *Czech Music* 3 (2008): 34–43.

Rigney, Ann. "Burns 1859: Embodied Communities and Transnational Federation." In *Commemorating Writers in Nineteenth-Century Europe: Nation-Building and Centenary Fever,* edited by Joep Leerssen and Ann Rigney, 40–64. Houndsmill, Basingstoke: Palgrave Macmillan, 2014.

Rilke, Rainer Maria. *Die Weise von Liebe und Tod des Cornets Christoph Rilke.* Leipzig: Insel, 1912.

Rogers, Jillian. "Ties That Bind: Mourning, and the Develoment of Intimacy and Alternative Kinship Networks in World War I–Era France." In *Music and War in Europe,* edited by Jardin, 415–43.

Romney, Jonathan, and Adrian Wootton. *Celluloid Jukebox: Popular Music and the Movies since the 50s.* London: British Film Institute, 1995.

Rosenfeld, Morris. *Lieder des Ghetto.* Translated by Berthold Feiwel. 6th ed. Berlin: Hermann Seemann, 1902.

Rothberg, Michael. *Multidirectional Memory: Remembering the Holocaust in the Age of Decolonization.* Stanford, CA: Stanford University Press, 2009.

Rothstein, Robert A. *Two Words to the Wise: Reflections on Polish Language, Literature, and Folklore.* Bloomington, IN: Slavica Publishers, 2008.

Santner, Eric. "History beyond the Pleasure Principle: Some Thoughts about the Representation of Trauma." In *Probing the Limits of Representation: Nazism and the "Final Solution",* edited by Saul Friedländer, 143–54. Cambridge, MA: Harvard University Press, 1992.

Šarić, Ljiljana, Karen Gammelgaard, and Kjetil Rå Hauge, eds. *Transforming National Holidays: Identity Discourse in the West and South Slavic Countries, 1985–2010.* Amsterdam: John Benjamins, 2012.

Saroyan, William. "The Armenian and the Armenian." In *Inhale and Exhale.* New York: Random House, 1936.

Scandura, Jani. "Sweat: A Memory of Waste." *M/C Journal* 13, no. 4 (2010): 2.

Schacter, Daniel L. *Searching for Memory: The Brain, the Mind, and the Past.* Cambridge, MA: Harvard University Press, 1996.

Schacter, Daniel L., Donna Rose Addis, Demis Hassabis, Victoria C. Martin, R. Nathan Spreng, and Karl K. Szpunar. "The Future of Memory: Remembering, Imagining, and the Brain." *Neuron Review* 76 (2012): 677–94.

Schneider, Rebecca. *Performing Remains: Art and War in Times of Theatrical Reenactment.* New York: Routledge, 2011.

Schoenberg, Arnold. *Brettl-Lieder.* Los Angeles: Belmont Music Publishers, 1970.

Schulin, Karin. *Musikalische Schlachtengemälde in der Zeit von 1756 bis 1815.* Vol. 3 of *Eichstätter Abhandlungen zur Musikwissenschaft.* Tutzing: Schneider, 1986.

Schultz, Anna. "Performing Translation in Jewish India: Kirtan of the Bene Israel." In *That Thing Called Music: Essays in Honor of Bruno Nettl,* edited by Victoria Lindsay Levine and Philip V. Bohlman, 56–72. Lanham, MD: Rowman and Littlefield, 2015.

Schwartz, Arturo. "Shalechet." http://new.menashekadishman.com/articles/shalechet-by-arturo-schwartz/#more

Scott, David. *Omens of Adversity: Tragedy, Time, Memory, Justice.* Durham, NC: Duke University Press, 2014.

Seroussi, Edwin. "'Hatikvah:' Conceptions, Receptions and Reflections." *Yuval Online* 9 (2015). http://www.jewish-music.huji.ac.il/content/hatikvah-conceptions-receptions-and-reflections

Shallcross, Bożena, and Ryszard Nycz, eds. *The Effect of Palimpsest: Culture, Literature, History.* Frankfurt am Main: Peter Lang, 2011.

Shelemay, Kay Kaufman. *Let Jasmine Rain Down: Song and Remembrance among Syrian Jews.* Chicago: University of Chicago Press, 1998.

Shelemay, Kay Kaufman. "The Power of Silent Voices: Women in the Syrian Musical Tradition." In *Music and the Play of Power in the Middle East, North Africa and Central Asia,* edited by Laudan Nooshin, 269–88. Burlington, VT: Ashgate, 2009.

Shibata Shingo, Yazawa Hiroshi, and Kinoshita Sonki, eds. *Hankaku nihon no ongaku: Nō moa Hiroshima ongaku dokuhon.* Tokyo: Chōbunsha, 1982.

Shibata, Yuko. *Producing Hiroshima and Nagasaki: Literature, Film, and Transnational Politics.* Honolulu: University of Hawai'i Press, 2018.

Shigezono Yoshio. *Hitori no kyōshi-zō: Shigezono Yoshio no ashiato to uta.* Tokyo: Shigezono Gakkyū Henshū-shitsu, 1981.

Shklar, Judith N. *The Faces of Injustice.* New Haven: Yale University Press, 1990.

Sklaroff, Lauren Rebecca. "Constructing G.I. Joe Louis: Cultural Solutions to the 'Negro Problem' during World War II." *Journal of American History* 89, no. 3 (2002): 958–83.

"Slavery and the Making of the University." Accessed September 16, 2019. https://exhibits.lib.unc.edu/exhibits/show/slavery

Smiley, Jaleesa. "Breaking the Silence: The Voices of Black Women and the Path towards Liberation." American Cultural Studies Capstone Research Papers 3. Western Washington University, 2015.

Smith, Jamil. "At the Nipsey Hussle Memorial Service, Tears and Smiles in Equal Measure." *Rolling Stone,* April 12, 2019. https://www.rollingstone.com/music/music-news/nipsey-hussle-memorial-service-821475/

"The Soldiers Monument Unveiled." *Alumni Review* 1, no. 6 (1913): 184–85. https://archive.org/details/alumnireviewseriv1i6chap/page/184

Sprigge, Martha. "Dresden's Musical Ruins." *Journal of the Royal Musical Association* 144, no. 1 (2019): 83–121.

Stam, Robert, and Ella Shohat. "Critical Ethnic Studies, Identity Politics, and the Right-Left Convergence." In *Critical Ethnic Studies: A Reader,* edited by Nada Elia, David M. Hernández, Jodi Kim, Shana L. Redmond, Dylan Rodríguez, and Sarita Echavez See, 416–34. Durham, NC: Duke University Press, 2016.

Stav, Shira. "Nakba and Holocaust: Mechanisms of Comparison and Denial in the Israeli Literary Imagination." *Jewish Social Studies* 18, no. 3 (2012): 85–98.

Stilwell, Robynn J. "The Fantastical Gap between Diegetic and Nondiegetic." In *Beyond the Soundtrack: Representing Music in Cinema,* edited by Daniel Ira Goldmark, Lawrence Kramer, and Richard Leppert, 184–202. Berkeley: University of California Press, 2007.

Stocker, Michael. "Exhibit Sound Design." *Museum International* 47, no. 1 (1995): 25–28.

Stoler, Ann Laura. "Introduction. 'The Rot Remains': From Ruin to Ruination." In *Imperial Debris: On Ruins and Ruination,* edited by Ann Laura Stoler, 1–35. Durham, NC: Duke University Press, 2013.

Straus, Joseph N. *Extraordinary Measures: Disability in Music.* New York: Oxford University Press, 2011.

Striff, Erin, ed. *Performance Studies.* New York: Palgrave Macmillan, 2003.

Sturkey, William. "Carr Was Indeed Much More Than Silent Sam." *Herald Sun,* October 31, 2017. https://www.heraldsun.com/opinion/article181567401.html

Szpilman, Władysław. *The Pianist: The Extraordinary True Story of One Man's Survival in Warsaw, 1939–1945.* Translated by Anthea Bell. New York: Picador, 1999.

Tandeciarz, Silvia. "Citizens of Memory: Reconfiguring the Past in Postdictatorship Argentina." *PMLA* 122, no. 1 (2007): 151–69.

Tansi, Sony Labou. *Life and a Half.* Edited by Dominic Thomas. Translated by Alsion Dundy. Bloomington: Indiana University Press, 2011.

Taruskin, Richard. "The Modern Sound of Early Music." In *Text and Act.* New York: Oxford University Press, 1995.

Tate, Trudy, and Kate Kennedy, eds. *The Silent Morning: Culture and Memory after the Armistice.* Manchester: Manchester University Press, 2013.

Tausig, Benjamin. "Sound and Movement: Vernaculars of Sonic Dissent." *Social Text* 36, no. 3 (2018): 25–45.

Taylor, Diana. *Disappearing Acts: Spectacles of Gender and Nationalism in Argentina's Dirty War.* Durham, NC: Duke University Press, 1997.

Threadcraft, Shatema. "North American Necropolitics and Gender: On #BlackLivesMatter and Black Femicide." *South Atlantic Quarterly* 116, no. 3 (2017): 553–80.

Tōge Sankichi. *Genbaku shishū.* 1951; Tokyo: Iwanami Shoten, 2016.

Tölölyan, Khachig, and Taline Papazian. "Armenian Diasporas and Armenia: Issues of Identity and Mobilization: An Interview with Khachig Tölölyan." *Études arméniennes contemporaines* 3 (2014): 83–101.

Treat, John W. *Writing Ground Zero: Japanese Literature and the Atomic Bomb.* Chicago: University of Chicago Press, 1995.

Trevisan, Carine. "Le bruit de la guerre." In *La Grande Guerre des musiciens,* edited by Stéphane Audoin-Rouzeau, Esteban Buch, Myriam Chimènes, and Georgie Durosoir, 5–15. Lyon: Symétrie, 2009.

Trouillot, Michel-Rolph. *Silencing the Past: Power and the Production of History.* Boston: Beacon Press, 1995.

Turino, Thomas. *Music as Social Life: The Politics of Participation.* Chicago: University of Chicago Press, 2008.

Ubuki Satoru. *Heiwa kinen shikiten no ayumi.* Hiroshima: Hiroshima Heiwa Bunka Sentā, 1992.

Ullmann, Viktor. *Die Weise von Liebe und Tod des Cornets Christoph Rilke.* Mainz: Schott, 1995.

University of Leeds. "Performing the Jewish Archive." Accessed July 8, 2018, http://ptja.leeds.ac.uk/

Vega, Carlos. *El himno nacional Argentina.* Buenos Aires: Eudeba, 1962.

Vinitzky-Seroussi, Vered, and Chana Teeger. "Unpacking the Unspoken: Silence in Collective Memory and Forgetting." *Social Forces* 88, no. 3 (2010): 1103–22.

Vishniac, Roman. *Children of a Vanished World.* Edited by Mara Vischniac Kohn and Miriam Hartman Flacks. Berkeley: University of California Press, 1999.

Von Eschen, Penny. *Satchmo Blows Up the World: Jazz Ambassadors Play the Cold War.* Cambridge, MA: Harvard University Press, 2004.

Wappenstein, Susana. "The Nation's Bodies: Justice and Belonging in the Aftermath of the AMIA Bombing." In *Landscapes of Memory and Impunity: The Aftermath of the AMIA Bombing in Jewish Argentina,* edited by Annette Levine and Natasha Zaretsky, 8–43. Boston: Brill, 2015.

Ward, Myah, and Charlie McGee. "Silent Sam Toppled in Protest the Night before Classes Begin." *Daily Tar Heel,* August 20, 2018. https://www.dailytarheel.com/article/2018/08/silent-sam-down

Wells, Ida B. "Southern Horrors." In *On Lynchings.* Mineola, NY: Dover Publications, 2014.

Williams, Paul. *Memorial Museums: The Global Rush to Commemorate Atrocities.* New York: Berg, 2007.

Wilson, Jennifer. "Composer Continues to Honor Victims of Hiroshima." *Colorado Springs Gazette,* April 16, 2007. http://gazette.com/composer-continues-to-honor-victims-of-hiroshima/article/21283

Winter, Jay. "Thinking about Silence." In *Aftermath: Legacies and Memories of War in Europe, 1918—1945—1989,* edited by Nicholas Martin, Tim Houghton, and Pierre Purseigle, 183–98. New York: Routledge, 2014.

Wood, Amy Louise. *Lynching and Spectacle: Witnessing Racial Violence in America, 1890–1940.* Chapel Hill: University of North Carolina Press, 2009.

Wright, Melissa. "Necropolitics, Narcopolitics, and Femicide: Gendered Violence on the Mexico-U.S. Border." *Signs* 36, no. 3 (2011): 707–31.

Yamada Kōsaku and Nagai Takashi. "Nanten no hana" (Flowers of Nandin). Tokyo: Hakubi-sha, 1950.

Yoneyama, Lisa. *Hiroshima Traces: Time, Space, and the Dialectics of Memory.* Berkeley: University of California Press, 1999.

Yosef, Raz. *The Politics of Loss and Trauma in Contemporary Israeli Cinema.* New York: Routledge, 2011.

Young, James E. *The Texture of Memory: Holocaust Memorials and Meaning.* New Haven: Yale University Press, 1993.

Zubrzycki, Geneviève. "History and the National Sensorium: Making Sense of Polish Mythology." *Qualitative Sociology* 34 (2011): 21–57.

Zwigenberg, Ran. *Hiroshima: The Origins of Global Memory Culture.* New York: Cambridge University Press, 2014.

Contributors

Vanessa Agnew is Professor of English at the University of Duisburg-Essen and Senior Researcher in the Research School of Humanities & the Arts at the Australian National University. She was educated at the University of Queensland (BMus), New York University (MA), University of Wales (PhD), and Open University (BSc), and was tenured in German studies at the University of Michigan in 2008. Her *Enlightenment Orpheus: The Power of Music in Other Worlds* (Oxford University Press, 2008) won the Oscar Kenshur Prize for Eighteenth-Century Studies and the American Musicological Society's Lewis Lockwood Award. She coedited *Settler and Creole Reenactment* (Palgrave, 2010), special issues of *Rethinking History* 11 (2007) and *Criticism* 46 (2004), and the book series *Historical Reenactment* (Palgrave) and *Music in Society and Culture* (Boydell and Brewer). Coedited books include *The Routledge Handbook of Reenactment Studies: Key Terms in the Field* (Routledge, 2020) and *Refugee Routes* (Transcript, 2020). Her children's book on refugee flight, *It's Not That Bad,* is appearing with Sefa-Verlag.

Sylvia Angelique Alajaji is an Associate Professor of Music at Franklin & Marshall College, where she also teaches in the International Studies program. She is the author of *Music and the Armenian Diaspora: Searching for Home in Exile,* a multisited work that examines the construction of diasporic Armenian subjectivity in the years since the Armenian genocide. Her published work centers on the relationship between music and exilic identity, focusing primarily on Armenian diasporic communities in Lebanon and the United States, and on the intersections of music, popular culture, and politics in the West Bank. Her research is based on extensive fieldwork conducted throughout the Middle East and United

States. She received her PhD in musicology from the University of Rochester's Eastman School of Music. In the spring of 2021, she will serve as the Dumanian Visiting Professor of Armenian Studies at the University of Chicago.

Andrea F. Bohlman is Associate Professor of Music at the University of North Carolina at Chapel Hill, where she studies the political stakes of music making and sound in the twentieth and twenty-first centuries. Her monograph *Musical Solidarities: Political Action and Music in Late Twentieth-Century Poland* (Oxford University Press, 2020) grows out of a decade of research on the work of sound and music in the opposition to state socialism in Poland. She has received prizes and fellowships from the American Council of Learned Societies, the American Musicological Society, the Max Planck Institute for the History of Science, and the National Endowment for the Humanities. She coedited a special issue of *Twentieth-Century Music* with Peter McMurray devoted to tape and tape recording. In 2017, she received the Alfred Einstein Award of the American Musicological Society for her article "Solidarity, Song, and the Sound Document" (*Journal of Musicology*, 2016).

Philip V. Bohlman is the Ludwig Rosenberger Distinguished Service Professor in Jewish History in the Department of Music at the University of Chicago, where he also serves as the Artistic Director of the New Budapest Orpheum Society (NBOS), the ensemble-in-residence of the Humanities Division. He is also Honorarprofessor at the Hochschule für Musik, Theater und Medien Hannover. With the NBOS he has recorded four CDs, the most recent of which, *As Dreams Fall Apart: The Golden Age of Jewish Stage and Film Music 1925–1955* (Cedille Records, 2014), was nominated for a Grammy Award. Together with Christine Wilkie Bohlman, he has received the Donald Tovey Memorial Prize from Oxford University, and with the NBOS he has received the Noah Greenberg Award from the American Musicological Society, both for research and for performance of music from the Shoah. His recent publications include *Wie sängen wir Seinen Gesang auf dem Boden der Fremden!* (LIT Verlag, 2019).

Annegret Fauser is Cary C. Boshamer Distinguished Professor of Music at the University of North Carolina at Chapel Hill. Her research focuses on music of the nineteenth and twentieth centuries, and in particularly that of France and the United States. She is author of *Der Orchestergesang in Frankreich zwischen 1870 und 1920* (1994), *Musical Encounters at the 1889*

Paris World's Fair (2005), *Sounds of War: Music in the United States during World War II* (2013)—for which she received both the Music in American Culture Award of the AMS and an ASCAP Deems Taylor Award—*The Politics of Musical Identity: Selected Writings* (2015), and *Aaron Copland's Appalachian Spring* (2017), honored in 2018 with the ASCAP Foundation's Virgil Thomson Award for Outstanding Music Criticism. She was awarded the 2011 Edward J. Dent Medal of the Royal Musical Association, and from 2011 to 2013 served as the Editor-in-Chief of the *Journal of the American Musicological Society.*

Michael A. Figueroa is Assistant Professor of Music and Associate Director of the Carolina Center for Jewish Studies at the University of North Carolina at Chapel Hill. He is an ethnomusicologist whose research and teaching explore the intersections of music, politics, and religion in Southwest Asia and North Africa and its diasporic communities in the Americas. A specialist in the Israeli-Palestinian conflict, his first monograph will present a musical history of Jerusalem within Zionist thought. His next project will focus on twenty-first-century Arab American musical performance and racial formation. His other interests include intersections of music and non-musical media (poetry, film, and theater), music technology, and global popular music, and his writing has previously appeared in *AJS Perspectives, Ethnomusicology Forum, Ethnomusicology Review, Journal of Music History Pedagogy,* and *Musica Judaica.*

Noriko Manabe is Associate Professor of Music Studies at Temple University. Her research involves music and social movements, popular music, musical analysis, and the music industry in Japan and the Americas. Her monograph *The Revolution Will Not Be Televised: Protest Music after Fukushima* (Oxford University Press) won the John Whitney Hall Book Prize from the Association for Asian Studies, the Book Prize from the British Forum for Ethnomusicology, and Honorable Mention for the Alan Merriam Prize from the Society for Ethnomusicology; an article based on one chapter won the Richard Waterman Prize. She is coeditor of the *Oxford Handbook of Protest Music* (with Eric Drott) and *Nuclear Music* (with Jessica Schwartz), both under contract with Oxford University Press, and series editor for 33-1/3 Japan (Bloomsbury). She has won fellowships from the National Endowment for the Humanities, the Japan Foundation, Kluge, and Social Science Research Council/Japan Society for the Promotion of Science and serves on several editorial boards, including the *Journal of the American Musicological Society* and *Music and Politics.*

Imani Danielle Mosley is Assistant Professor of Musicology at the University of Florida. In 2019, Dr. Mosley received her PhD from Duke University, where her work examined the reception of Benjamin Britten's postwar operas. Her current research addresses digital sonic mapping, acoustics, and ritual in the English churches and cathedrals central to Britten's sacred music. In addition to her work on Britten, she also specializes in contemporary opera, reception history, and masculinities studies. Her contribution to the digital humanities focuses on sonic mapping, data analysis, and digital and computational musicology. Mosley is also an active performer, playing new music written for bassoon and baroque bassoon in various early-music ensembles. She is also a working dramaturg and librettist and collaborated with composer Frances Pollock on the opera *Stinney: An American Execution*, which had its premiere at the Prototype Festival in New York in 2019.

Chérie Rivers Ndaliko is an interdisciplinary and socially engaged scholar of culture and sustainable development in Africa. Building on theories and practices from the humanities, public health, and media and journalism, she works collaboratively with civil society and community organizations, international NGOs, branches of the United Nations, and government bodies to advance interdisciplinary approaches to global problem-solving. Since 2010 she has also served as Director of Research and Education at Yole!Africa in Goma, Democratic Republic of the Congo. Ndaliko is author of *Necessary Noise: Music, Film, and Charitable Imperialism in the East of Congo* (Oxford University Press, 2016; recipient of the 2017 Alan Merriam Award and the 2018 Kwabena Nketia Award), and a coedited volume, *The Art of Emergency: Aesthetics and Aid in African Crises* (Oxford University Press, 2019). She holds a PhD from Harvard University in African Studies and is currently an Associate Professor at the University of North Carolina at Chapel Hill.

Kay Kaufman Shelemay is the G. Gordon Watts Professor of Music and Professor of African and African American Studies at Harvard University. An ethnomusicologist specializing in musics of Africa, the Middle East, and the urban United States, she has published many books, editions, and articles and is currently completing a monograph on musicians from the African Horn who have migrated to the United States. A past president of the Society for Ethnomusicology as well as a longtime congressional appointee to and former Chair of the Board of the American Folklife Center at the Library of Congress, Shelemay is a fellow of the American Academy of Arts and Sciences, the American Academy for Jewish Research, the Ethiopian Academy of Sciences, and the American Philosophical Society. She has been awarded many fellowships and prizes, including the 2010 Jaap Kunst Prize of the Society for Ethnomusicology, and was the Phi Beta Kappa / Frank M. Updike Memorial Scholar for 2010–11.

Lillian M. Wohl is a member of the Área de Investigaciones en Artes del Espectáculo y Judeidad in the Instituto de Artes del Espectáculo at the Universidad de Buenos Aires. While exploring the performance of racial, ethnic, and religious difference in modern Jewish and Latin American musical social worlds, she considers how the cultures of memory and shifting notions of temporality—that is, pasts, presents, and futures—are expressed in music. She specializes in the Southern Cone and has conducted ethnographic research in Argentina, Uruguay, Chile, as well as the United States. From 2017 to 2019, she was Postdoctoral Fellow in Musicology and Assistant Director of Jewish Music Research with the Lowell Milken Fund for American Jewish Music at UCLA. She was Visiting Assistant Professor of Jewish Musicology and Ethnomusicology at the Debbie Friedman School of Sacred Music at Hebrew Union College–Jewish Institute of Religion, New York City (2014–17), and completed a PhD in ethnomusicology at the University of Chicago in 2015. She is currently working on her first monograph, which addresses Jewish belonging and the politics of memory in musical performance in Buenos Aires since the 1990s.

Index